POLITICAL AND COMIC CHARACTERS
OF SHAKESPEARE

POLITICAL
AND COMIC CHARACTERS
OF SHAKESPEARE

JOHN PALMER

LONDON
MACMILLAN & CO LTD
NEW YORK · ST MARTIN'S PRESS
1965

This book is copyright in all countries which
are signatories to the Berne Convention

First Edition 'Political Characters of Shakespeare', 1945
First Edition 'Comic Characters of Shakespeare', 1946
Combined Volume 1962 Reprinted 1964, 1965

MACMILLAN AND COMPANY LIMITED
St Martin's Street London WC 2
also Bombay Calcutta Madras Melbourne

THE MACMILLAN COMPANY OF CANADA LIMITED
70 Bond Street Toronto 2

ST MARTIN'S PRESS INC
175 Fifth Avenue New York 10 NY

PRINTED IN GREAT BRITAIN

CONTENTS

Political Characters

Comic Characters

v

INTRODUCTION

THERE is no reason to believe that Shakespeare had any great respect for men in public life. The evidence is all the other way:

> Get thee glass eyes,
> And, like a scurvy politician, seem
> To see the things thou dost not.

But the Elizabethans expected to find upon the stage kings, princes and generals. The dramatist must therefore fill his scene with political figures. His audience must behold these great ones sitting in council, leading their men into battle, climbing to power or declining to impotence. Shakespeare, taking from Holinshed or Plutarch a story or situation which enabled him to fulfil these expectations, found himself willy-nilly writing a political play. But his characters interested him first and foremost as men; it is an accident that they should be men prominent in public affairs or hoping to be so. It is, indeed, a strange paradox that Shakespeare who, above all other dramatists, was preoccupied with the private mind and heart of the individual, should have written a group of plays unmatched in any literature for their political content.

Shakespeare, since he is forced to take the political field, broadens it to include all human activities in which private passion or personal conviction is brought into relation with public life. For Shakespeare there arises a political issue in the larger sense whenever an individual is required to adjust himself to the practical necessities of his position in a kingdom or commonwealth, to shape a policy or control its application. Brutus, the republican philosopher, is asked to accept the absolute rule of Caesar; Richard II, wayward and introspective, is compelled to measure his frail genius against the cold efficiency of Bolingbroke; Henry V is summoned to show posterity a successful man of action conforming instinctively with the genius of his countrymen and emerging triumphantly as master of the event; Richard III is called upon to exhibit an unbridled intelligence in the attainment and exercise of power; Coriolanus presents the aristocrat in a vain effort to come to terms with the common man. Grouped around these principal figures of the political scene is a crowd of courtiers, prelates and councillors; of loyalists and rebels; of zealous partisans or detached observers; of men who follow their principles or seize their opportunities. Almost every kind of man to be met with in public life, great or mean, wise or foolish, wicked or virtuous, simple or subtle, calculating or generous, is to be found in these plays. Some are sketched with a few apparently negligent strokes; others are drawn with elaborate care. All can be recognised as political characters who have their counterparts in every generation.

A preliminary distinction is necessary. Hamlet, Prince of Denmark, the expectancy and rose of the fair state, is in some respects a political character. His uncle has usurped the throne of Denmark and it is part of Hamlet's task to recover it. That is a political problem. Macbeth, to secure and retain the crown of Scotland, resorts to assassination. That is a political enterprise. But no one would describe either 'Hamlet' or 'Macbeth' as political plays. The spectator's interest in Hamlet and Macbeth is directed, not towards their political activities, but to the psychological effect of those activities upon themselves.

Hamlet, like Richard II, is placed in a situation refractory to his temperament. Both, for very similar reasons, prove unequal to their task. But in 'Hamlet' we are absorbed by a drama of the spirit; in 'Richard II' by a contest between a king unfitted to rule and a politician born to succeed. Macbeth, like Richard III, commits murder to attain his ends. But in 'Macbeth' we are interested in what takes place in the mind of the criminal; in 'Richard III' with his conduct as a public man. The political activities of Hamlet and Macbeth are incidental; the political activities of the two Richards form the substance and texture of the plays in which they appear. It is true that, Shakespeare being Shakespeare, his political characters interest us also as private persons and have an interior life of their own, but they are essentially political characters.

Though Shakespeare had no particular admiration for success in public life, it is not to be inferred that he slighted it. Scores of critics have noted, many with regret, his seemingly contemptuous treatment of the mighty Caesar. Others have found in his portrait of Henry V more than traces of a satirical intention. There is, however, neither contempt nor satire in the dramatist's handling of these highly successful politicians. Certain qualities are necessary to success in public affairs and certain psychological consequences attend the exercise of power. Those qualities and consequences are noted by Shakespeare. Presenting a great dictator or the best of kings, he gives us the historical facts as he found them and depicts, with the entire sympathy of a creative dramatist, a human character with whom those facts can be squared. The astonishing veracity of Shakespeare's political characters is due, indeed, to the small interest which he took in politics as compared with the great interest which he took in human nature. His main concern was not so much with the politics as with the men who made them. He was immune from political bias and his political characters are therefore true for all time. From the extraordinary fact that a production of 'Coriolanus' in Paris recently provoked a political riot and led to the dismissal of a cabinet minister it might be inferred, as indeed it was by several distinguished French critics, that Shakespeare had written a deliberate satire upon democratic institutions. Nothing could be wider of the mark. Shakespeare presented in 1609, without malice or favour, a Roman aristocrat who despised the electorate. Shakespeare was not primarily interested in the merits of aristocracy or democracy as a form of government. He was interested in Coriolanus as an individual who happened to be confronted with a political situation which arises in every period of history and remains with us to-day.

But if Shakespeare had no political bias, he had a natural predilection for certain human qualities and a marked interest in certain types of men. It has indeed been persuasively maintained that he had more sympathy with those who failed in public life, or even in the conduct of their private affairs, than with those who succeeded. The men after his own heart, it is argued, were Brutus, whose every act was a political blunder; Richard II, ineffectual in all he undertook; Hamlet, who, being commanded to destroy King Claudius, fell to speculating whether he ought not rather to destroy himself. Here, again, we must beware of attributing to Shakespeare anything in the nature of a prejudice. It so happens that many of the qualities which make for success in life are more commonplace and less engaging than those which restrain or embarrass men in the pursuit of fortune. The qualities that make for public eminence are certainly less likely to involve their owners in situations which touch the heart or quicken the imagination. Of the materially successful person it is usually enough to know that he succeeded and, if we should be tempted to look farther into the matter, we are likely to discover that his success was due rather to an absence of some of the finer qualities of mind and spirit that belong to humanity at large than to the presence of anything of poignant interest to the dramatic poet. The remarkable thing about Shakespeare is not that he interests us so vividly in the men who failed in public life, but that he has given us so many just and lifelike descriptions of the men who succeeded. We shall find, as we study his political characters in detail, that no distorting preference for one man over another mars the equity of his presentation. If our sympathies lie with Brutus or with Richard II, it is because they were in fact more likeable and more interesting persons than Octavius Caesar or Henry Bolingbroke, and not because Shakespeare deliberately set out to enlist our sympathy on their behalf.

The problems and situations that have confronted public men for the last two thousand years have changed but little. Nor have the various types of public men who deal successfully or unsuccessfully with these problems and situations greatly altered. The political characters of Shakespeare may not be immediately recognisable in the public men of to-day. They have changed their names, and their environment has been superficially transformed. But in their essential qualities, dispositions and conduct they remain the same. The expedients to which they resort, the devices by which they recommend themselves to public favour, the motives by which they are governed, the principles which they profess, even the language which they use to glorify or extenuate their behaviour, can be matched from history at any period or in any place and never more aptly than from our own contemporary records. A politician can find no better handbook to success than the political plays of Shakespeare. Here he can study the flaws of character and errors in policy or practice which may ruin his career. Here, too, he can examine and assess the qualities and habits of mind to be emulated. He will find no better instruction anywhere upon his personal deportment and manner of speech; upon the gentle art of making friends and removing enemies;

upon the adjustment of means to ends and of private conscience
to public necessity. It is not proposed in these studies to emphasise
the extreme relevance of the public activities presented in Shakespeare's political plays to those of the contemporary scene. That relevance is merely an incidental consequence of the fidelity to truth
with which the dramatist depicted his political characters. They are
true to-day because they were true when he created them. The
analogies will not therefore be pressed and it will be for the reader,
as he considers Shakespeare's political characters and situations in detail, to appreciate their bearing upon modern events.

There is one political character which constantly recurs in Shakespeare's historical plays and as constantly illustrates how the poet,
exercising his imagination in the portrayal of political persons, contrives to epitomise, once for all, what is permanent and essential in
their reaction to public events and thus to present a mirror for all
times and occasions. This political character is collective. It is the
crowd which turns from Brutus to Antony, the plebeians who listen
to Menenius Agrippa, the citizens who assemble to buckle fortune
on the back of Richard of Gloucester, the rebels who follow Cade,
the yeomen soldiers at Agincourt to whom a little touch of Harry in
the night brings comfort and inspiration—in a word, the people of
ancient Rome or Plantagenet England, or of any time or land, whose
collective person is a vociferous or silent protagonist in the play of
political forces and events. Shakespeare's portrayal of this character
is true, complete and relevant to any political situation. The dramatist, here as in so many instances, has forestalled the modern
psychologists. It needed no Gustave Le Bon or Sigmund Freud to
instruct Shakespeare in mass psychology, and there are very few propositions or principles laid down in modern text-books on the subject, or practised by modern political leaders, which cannot be illustrated with instances from his plays. No one has contrasted more
vividly the personal conduct of honest Tom, worthy Dick and sensible Harry, as separate individuals, with their collective behaviour
as a mob or as a regimented community. Shakespeare had no experts
in psychology to explain this difference, but he had observed it for
himself in the people who filled the London streets of Tudor England
and he had noted it in the chronicles which supplied him with his

material. The mind of a poet, upon the evidence of things seen and
absorbed into the imagination, jumps instinctively ahead of scientific
discovery and his creations are proof against any subsequent re-
search. Einstein may supersede Newton and it may be found that a
straight line is not necessarily the shortest distance between two
points. But Shakespeare's Hamlet could be prompted by motives
buried deep in the unconscious, though his creator had never heard
of the Œdipus complex.

It is impossible to divorce a political character from the colleagues
with whom he is associated or from the opponents with whom he is
confronted. Brutus must be studied simultaneously with Antony,
Cassius and Caesar; Henry of Monmouth with Harry Hotspur, his
Grace of Canterbury, John Bates and Michael Williams. Each character will accordingly be presented in the company of those who
helped or hindered him in his designs and be shown against his own
political background—Brutus with his confederates and opponents in
the tragedy of 'Julius Caesar'; Richard II with those who played their
parts in the sad story of his deposition and death; Henry V with the
companions of his unregenerate days and with those who sat beside
him in the council chamber or fought beside him at Agincourt;
Richard III with the distinguished ruffians who abetted him in his
designs and the victims, deserving and undeserving, of his ambition;
Coriolanus with those who hailed him as a saviour of society or
hated him as an enemy of the people.

Sooner or later it will be necessary to decide how far Shakespeare,
who impartially presented such a variety of political characters and
described without prejudice such a diversity of political situations,
had any profound political convictions of his own. He wrote for all
time, but he was a citizen of Tudor England. Was Shakespeare, so
far as he was at all interested in politics for their own sake, liberal,
conservative or utopian? Was he content with the absolute rule of
the New Monarchy or instinctively a rebel? These are questions
which need scrupulous examination, not of a passage here and there
in a particular play, but of the whole field.

The reader is warned in advance that this book will abound in
citations from Shakespeare's text. Those who have them by heart
already will be well content to find them again. To those who

are less familiar with the script they will supply the necessary evidence.

John Keats, in a letter to Reynolds written on April 17th, 1817, begs his friend: 'Whenever you write, say a word or two on some passage in Shakespeare that may have come rather new to you, which must be continually happening, notwithstanding that we have read the play some forty times'; and he goes on to transcribe for his friend some lines from 'The Tempest', which, he says, had 'never struck me so forcibly as at present'.

The author of these studies hopes to do for the reader here and there what Reynolds was asked to do for Keats: to say a word or two on some passage in Shakespeare which may have come rather new to him and may possibly surprise the less devout.

The introduction to *Comic Characters of Shakespeare* will be found on page 339.

I

MARCUS BRUTUS

BRUTUS has precisely the qualities which in every age have rendered the conscientious liberal ineffectual in public life. His convictions required him to take the lead in a political conspiracy which, for its success, called for great agility of mind, a deft and callous adjustment of means to ends, acceptance of the brutal consequences which attend an act of violence, and insight into the motives of men less scrupulous and disinterested than himself. In all these respects he was deficient. Brutus, plotting the assassination of Caesar, did violence to his character, entered into association with men whom he did not understand and involved himself in events which he was unable to control. He committed himself to a course of action which could only be justified by principles which had ceased to be valid for the society in which he lived and which entangled him in unforeseen consequences with which he was unable to cope.

Shakespeare presents the essential features of this character in less than one hundred and seventy lines of an exposition so vivid and fluent that its compact efficiency may easily be overlooked. Every line delivered by Brutus in his opening scene with Cassius reveals a distinct aspect of his quality.

Look through it carefully, ticking off the points one by one.

(1) *The recluse*

Caesar with his train has departed to celebrate the feast of Lupercal. Cassius and Brutus are left alone upon the stage:

> CASSIUS: Will you go see the order of the course?
> BRUTUS: I am not gamesome: I do lack some part
> Of that quick spirit that is in Antony.
> Let me not hinder, Cassius, your desires;
> I'll leave you.

(2) *The man divided against himself*

Cassius complains that recently he has not had of Brutus that gentleness and show of love which he has a right to expect. Brutus replies:

> Vexed I am
> Of late with passions of some difference,
> Conceptions only proper to myself;

and he hopes that his friends will not be grieved:

> Nor construe any further my neglect,
> Than that poor Brutus, with himself at war,
> Forgets the shows of love to other men.

(3) *The recoil from action*

Cassius begins with infinite caution to hint at the part which Brutus is expected to play in the conspiracy. Brutus shrinks instinctively from this covert solicitation:

> Into what dangers would you lead me, Cassius,
> That you would have me seek into myself
> For that which is not in me?

(4) *The man who gives himself away*

An instant later, however, this man, who recoils from the necessity to act and denies his fitness for a deed that has begun to take shape in his mind, by a slip of the tongue betrays his secret. On hearing a flourish and shout from the Capitol he exclaims:

> I do fear the people
> Choose Caesar for their king.

Cassius pounces on the unguarded word:

> Ay, do you *fear* it?
> Then must I think you would not have it so.

Brutus can make no further effort to conceal his thoughts. He would not have Caesar crowned. He loves honour more than he fears death. He is ready to undertake any enterprise, 'if it be aught toward the general good'.

(5) *The republican*

Cassius now plays on the hereditary devotion of Brutus to the republican idea. Other men were born as free as Caesar; Cassius and Brutus, Roman for Roman, are as good as Caesar:

> The fault, dear Brutus, is not in our stars,
> But in ourselves, that we are underlings.

Brutus and Caesar: what should be in that 'Caesar'?
Why should that name be sounded more than yours?
Write them together, yours is as fair a name;
Sound them, it doth become the mouth as well;
Weigh them, it is as heavy; conjure with 'em,
'Brutus' will start a spirit as soon as 'Caesar'.
Now, in the names of all the gods at once,
Upon what meat doth this our Caesar feed,
That he is grown so great? Age, thou art shamed!
Rome, thou hast lost the breed of noble bloods!
When went there by an age, since the great flood,
But it was fam'd with more than with one man?

O, you and I have heard our fathers say,
There was a Brutus once that would have brook'd
Th' eternal devil to keep his state in Rome
As easily as a king!

(6) *The reluctant conspirator*

Brutus, as he listens to Cassius, has one ear alert for noises from the Capitol. He interrupts his companion only to surmise that the applauses coming from that quarter are for 'some new honours that are heaped on Caesar' and, when Cassius concludes, he is moved to declare himself yet more openly:

What you would work me to, I have some aim:
How I have thought of this and of these times,
I shall recount hereafter; for this present,
I would not, so with love I might entreat you,
Be any further moved. What you have said
I will consider; what you have to say
I will with patience hear, and find a time
Both meet to hear and answer such high things.
Till then, my noble friend, chew upon this:
Brutus had rather be a villager
Than to repute himself a son of Rome
Under these hard conditions as this time
Is like to lay upon us.

Here, then, in one brief scene, is an epitome of Brutus in six chapters. He is not gamesome and would leave Cassius to attend the festival alone. He had avoided the company of his friends to brood upon conceptions only proper to himself. He is vexed with passions of some difference and is with himself at war. He shrinks from the dangers into which he may be led if he should look too deeply into his convictions and admit the necessity to act upon them. He, nevertheless, betrays involuntarily the secret that vexes him and is successfully brought to a full and frank confession by the skilful prompting of his future confederate. The instinctive reluctance of the political philosopher is not yet, however, overcome and he would not for this present be any further moved. He promises to consider what Cassius has said and concludes with a merely general assurance that Brutus would rather be a villager than accept the situation.

The character of Brutus is thus defined, the quality of Cassius suggested and the argument of the tragedy announced. The dramatist already has his play in full career.

It is not the purpose of these studies to show that Shakespeare as a dramatic craftsman knew his business, but it may be parenthetically claimed that he has certainly made good use of the 170 lines of the scene under analysis and it should not be forgotten, in appreciating this remarkable performance, that Cassius has also found time to deliver the celebrated bravura passages in which he describes Caesar's leap into the Tiber and the fever which he had in Spain.

Caesar and his train return from the Capitol. Brutus, at the suggestion of Cassius, plucks Casca by the sleeve as the procession passes and Casca remains behind to tell them 'after his sour fashion' what happened at the festival.

Brutus, like Hamlet, has the artist's craving for detail in the portrayal of persons and events. Hamlet, on first hearing of the ghost which had appeared at Elsinore, must picture the incident for himself. Precisely how long did the apparition stay? His beard was grizzled, no? Was the face pale or red? So Brutus entreats Casca: Tell us the manner of it. What was the second noise for? Was the crown offered three times to Caesar? These questions follow his own vivid description of Caesar and his train as they enter. Brutus, we realise, has the eye and disposition of a poet:

> The angry spot doth glow on Caesar's brow,
> And all the rest look like a chidden train:
> Calpurnia's cheek is pale; and Cicero

> Looks with such ferret and such fiery eyes
> As we have seen him in the Capitol,
> Being cross'd in conference by some senators.

It is the function of Cassius throughout the tragedy, not only to present in himself a political type, but to act as a foil to Brutus, whose character stands out the more vividly for the contrast. The audience has already begun to appreciate the very different qualities of the two men. But Shakespeare, lest the point should have been missed, drives it home with a final stroke. Casca and Brutus have in turn quitted the stage. Cassius is left alone. Listen, now, to the practical man of affairs, who sees political facts as they are:

> Well, Brutus, thou art noble; yet, I see,
> Thy honourable metal may be wrought
> From that it is disposed: therefore 'tis meet
> That noble minds keep ever with their likes;
> For who so firm that cannot be seduc'd?
> Caesar doth bear me hard; but he loves Brutus:
> If I were Brutus now and he were Cassius,
> He should not humour me.

Cassius frankly admits that if, like Brutus, he had stood in favour with Caesar he would never have allowed himself to be 'seduced' into rebellion. He is the familiar type of politician who plumes himself on being a 'realist' and stoutly affects to base his political conduct on the meanest of motives. The implication that Brutus would do well to avoid politics altogether—for it is meet that noble minds keep ever with their likes—is equally characteristic. It expresses just that blend of admiration and contempt felt by the practical man of affairs for the man of principle.

Cassius, having paid this tribute to his own good sense, declares his intention of resorting to an expedient which shows him to be a political tactician of resource:

> I will this night,
> In several hands, in at his windows throw,
> As if they came from several citizens,
> Writings all tending to the great opinion
> That Rome holds of his name; wherein obscurely
> Caesar's ambition shall be glancèd at.

From Cassius, flaunting his realism by daylight in the streets of Rome, the dramatist jumps forward to Brutus at odds with his idealism by starlight in his orchard. It is surely no accident that the first words uttered by these two men as soon as they find themselves alone should so neatly present the contrast between them. Cassius has just declared that his cause is personal: Caesar bears him hard. He knows precisely what he means to do and why. He has no misgiving concerning his purpose or qualms of conscience concerning the means. Listen now to Brutus:

> It must be by his death: and, for my part,
> I know no personal cause to spurn at him,
> But for the general. He would be crown'd:
> How that might change his nature, there's the question:
> It is the bright day that brings forth the adder;
> And that craves wary walking. Crown him?—that!
> And then, I grant, we put a sting in him,
> That at his will he may do danger with.
> The abuse of greatness is when it disjoins
> Remorse from power; and, to speak truth of Caesar,
> I have not known when his affections sway'd
> More than his reason. But 'tis a common proof,
> That lowliness is young ambition's ladder,
> Whereto the climber-upward turns his face;
> But when he once attains the upmost round,
> He then unto the ladder turns his back,
> Looks in the clouds, scorning the base degrees
> By which he did ascend. So Caesar may.
> Then, lest he may, prevent.

Compare the candid simplicity with which Cassius sees and admits the truth about himself with the confused thinking of Brutus and its sharp divorce from political reality. Cassius has decided that Caesar must be unseated because Caesar dislikes him and because Caesar is the absolute master of Rome. To Cassius it is a matter of indifference whether Caesar be called king, consul or imperator. For Cassius the word 'king' is no more than a bogey with which to frighten a republican philosopher. And how well he has succeeded! For here is Brutus dwelling in soliloquy, not on any abuse of power which

Caesar has committed, not upon any present evils of dictatorship, but upon something which may happen to Caesar and to Rome if Caesar be crowned. Caesar is not himself to be feared, but Caesar with a diadem upon his head may become a public menace; Caesar must die lest, being made king, he should change his nature. The reflective idealist, living in imagination, is more impressed by the idea or symbol of power than by the thing itself.

It too often happens that, when Shakespeare's genius is strikingly manifest in a phrase or passage, his critics are puzzled and even moved to suggest that something has gone wrong with the text. This soliloquy of Brutus, in which the dramatist exhibits a salient and abiding characteristic of the doctrinaire in politics, has been condemned by many commentators. Coleridge found the speech to be 'singular' and confessed frankly that he did not understand it. How could Brutus, he asks, say that he had no cause to spurn at Caesar in his past conduct as a man? Had Caesar not crossed the Rubicon? Had he not entered Rome as a conqueror? Had he not placed his Gauls in the senate? Coleridge is even more disconcerted by the suggestion that Brutus would have had no objection to Caesar provided he remained as good a ruler as he had hitherto shown himself to be. This brilliant critic not only finds the speech 'discordant', but accounts for his inability to 'see into Shakespeare's motive' by quoting just those historical facts which give to the soliloquy its true significance. Brutus cannot see persons or events as they are. That is the essence of his character. Caesar has done all the things of which Coleridge reminds us. He is already a full-blown tyrant. But Brutus takes no account of these realities. He is obsessed by a pedantic horror of kingship, by the republican traditions of his family and by the hypothetical evils which may follow upon the violation of a preconceived theory of government.[1]

Brutus, having delivered his first soliloquy, continues to show how unfitted he is for political leadership. Note how easily he is moved by

[1] Coleridge, unlike critics of a lesser breed, though puzzled by the speech, is reluctant to censure the dramatist. In confessing that he has failed to understand Shakespeare's drift and finds it 'discordant', he interjects with a fine humility: 'This, I mean, is what I say to myself with my present quantum of insight, only modified by my experience in how many instances I have ripened into a perception of beauties where I had descried faults.'

the letters thrown in at his window. That this can be the trick of a seducer never enters his head. He is too honest a soul to suspect knavery in other men. And, in reading these letters, he again betrays his obsession with the historic symbols of sovereignty at a time when a practical politician would be thinking of present abuses:

> My ancestors did from the streets of Rome
> The Tarquin drive, when he was call'd a king.

His mind is set upon abstractions. His conscience, moreover, is troubled and his will perplexed. Shakespeare has already shown him to be a man divided against himself. This, being an essential theme of the play, needs further emphasis:

> Between the acting of a dreadful thing
> And the first motion, all the interim is
> Like a phantasma, or a hideous dream:
> The Genius and the mortal instruments
> Are then in council; and the state of man,
> Like to a little kingdom, suffers then
> The nature of an insurrection.

From this hideous dream, he is harshly awakened to the sordid realities of political enterprise by the arrival of Cassius and his confederates, their hats plucked about their ears, their faces buried in their cloaks. His recoil is immediate:

> O conspiracy!
> Sham'st thou to show thy dangerous brow by night,
> When evils are most free? O! then by day
> Where wilt thou find a cavern dark enough
> To mask thy monstrous visage?

A fastidious contempt of the shameful means necessary to achieve his ends is the constant mark of a political idealist. Brutus carries it to extremes. Later on, we shall find him in one breath demanding money of Cassius to pay his troops and, in the next breath, expressing a passionate disapproval of the methods by which the money has been raised. Meanwhile, he rails against the common precautions incident to conspiracy and protests vehemently against a suggestion that the confederates should confirm their resolution with an oath:

> Unto bad causes swear
> Such creatures as men doubt; but do not stain
> The even virtue of our enterprise,
> Nor th' insuppressive mettle of our spirits,
> To think that or our cause or our performance
> Did need an oath.

These are straws, but they all blow one way. Brutus, with every word he utters, discloses some fresh aspect of his ineffectual, sublime approach to the business in hand.

What follows is more than a straw. Brutus takes his first political decision and it is a blunder which is to bring his enterprise to ruin. His motives are high and his verdict is morally right, but it is nevertheless fatal to success. Decius Brutus demands: 'Shall no man else be touch'd but only Caesar?' Cassius takes up the point:

> Decius, well urged: I think it is not meet,
> Mark Antony, so well beloved of Caesar,
> Should outlive Caesar: we shall find of him
> A shrewd contriver; and you know, his means,
> If he improve them, may well stretch so far
> As to annoy us all; which to prevent,
> Let Antony and Caesar fall together.

Brutus rejects the advice of Cassius. Antony, he contends, is but a limb of Caesar, who can do no more harm than Caesar's arm when Caesar's head is off. In urging this view upon his friends, Brutus further displays his horror at the means to be used against Caesar and seeks to disguise from himself the very nature of his deed. He wishes, characteristically, that Caesar might die without being killed, the bloodless victim in a stately sacrifice:

> We all stand up against the spirit of Caesar;
> And in the spirit of men there is no blood:
> O, that we then could come by Caesar's spirit,
> And not dismember Caesar! But, alas,
> Caesar must bleed for it! And, gentle friends,
> Let's kill him boldly, but not wrathfully;
> Let's carve him as a dish fit for the gods,
> Not hew him as a carcass fit for hounds.

Brutus then dismisses the conspirators. He is again alone and

Shakespeare now has a moment in which to show us that this pedantic and ineffectual conspirator is, in private life, both sensitive and accessible—as responsive to humane, as he is obtuse to political, values. He calls his servant:

> Boy! Lucius! Fast asleep? It is no matter;
> Enjoy the honey-heavy dew of slumber:
> Thou hast no figures nor no fantasies,
> Which busy care draws in the brains of men;
> Therefore thou sleep'st so sound.

This charming touch, disclosing the 'gentle' Brutus, is followed by the famous scene between Brutus and his wife. Portia reproaches her husband:

> You've ungently, Brutus,
> Stole from my bed; and yesternight, at supper,
> You suddenly arose, and walk'd about,
> Musing and sighing.

Incidentally she reveals the intensity of the inner conflict to which Brutus has already confessed:

> It will not let you eat, nor talk, nor sleep,
> And could it work so much upon your shape
> As it hath much prevail'd on your condition,
> I should not know you.

She begs to be made acquainted with his secret. He has some sick offence within his mind and by the right and virtue of her place she claims his confidence:

> Is it excepted I should know no secrets
> That appertain to you? Am I yourself
> But, as it were, in sort or limitation,
> To keep with you at meals, comfort your bed,
> And talk to you sometimes? Dwell I but in the suburbs
> Of your good pleasure? If it be no more,
> Portia is Brutus' harlot, not his wife.

Brutus is prompt to acknowledge an appeal to his sensibilities as a private person. It requires no Shakespeare to discover that an ineffectual politician can be happy and enlightened in his domestic relationships, but the point is worth noting. The gentle Brutus is

never more likeable than when he answers Portia in the orchard at
daybreak:

> O ye gods,
> Render me worthy of this noble wife!
> [*Knocking within.*
> Hark, hark! one knocks. Portia, go in awhile;
> And by and by thy bosom shall partake
> The secrets of my heart.
> All my engagements I'll construe to thee,
> All the charàctery of my sad brows.

The spectator who has followed with attention so far Shakespeare's unfolding of the character of Brutus may at this point be
tempted to ask why, if Brutus be so plainly unfitted for conspiracy,
so shrewd a man as Cassius should have been anxious to secure him
for a leader. The answer comes pat upon the knocking heard while
Brutus and his wife are together. Caius Ligarius has called to be
initiated into the plot. 'What's to do?' he asks. Brutus says he will
explain the matter as they go. And Caius Ligarius exclaims:

> Set on your foot,
> And with a heart new-fired I follow you,
> To do I know not what; but it sufficeth
> That Brutus leads me on.

In addition to a family tradition which goes back to Tarquin, Brutus
has a stainless reputation. All Rome knows him to be honourable,
disinterested, without ambition. Men are ready to follow him with
confidence. His bare word is enough. He lends an air of respectability to the confederacy and, for this reason alone, he is essential to
the enterprise.

Brutus has revealed the inward stress to which his mind and conscience are submitted. He is now to be shown as the professed, self-
conscious stoic in action. A hint of this outward and somewhat artificial stoicism has already been dropped in his farewell remarks to the
conspirators as they leave him alone in the orchard:

> Good gentlemen, look fresh and merrily;
> Let not our looks put on our purposes,
> But bear it as our Roman actors do,
> With untir'd spirits and formal constancy.

That Brutus should liken himself at this critical moment to an actor is a revealing touch and, lest its significance should be lost, Shakespeare is presently to show that the formal constancy which Brutus professes and which he urges upon his friends has by no means obliterated the inner compunction with which he goes into action.

The swiftly moving scenes which precede and follow the killing of Caesar need the closest attention if their full significance as a further revelation of the character of Brutus is to be appreciated. For the key to his conduct at this point of the tragedy is to be sought precisely in the heartbreaking contrast here shown between his formal constancy as an assassin, largely assumed, and the kindly, fastidious nature of the man himself.

Shakespeare makes us sensitive to this aspect of the tragedy at the conclusion of a brief scene in which the conspirators call upon Caesar to conduct him to the Capitol. Caesar thanks them for their pains and courtesy and invites them into his house. This closing incident is covered in four lines:

> CAESAR: Good friends, go in and taste some wine with me;
> And we, like friends, will straightway go together.
> BRUTUS (*aside*): That every like is not the same, O Caesar,
> The heart of Brutus yearns to think upon!

It is the last glimpse we get into the heart of Brutus before Caesar is killed. Shakespeare, at this penultimate moment, warns us not to be deceived by the front of brass which his hero is about to assume after the high Roman fashion. The dramatic measure in these four lines is pressed down and running over. Shakespeare has already shown Brutus flinching from the more seamy aspects of conspiracy, which muffles its face even by night from honest men and proclaims its dark fealty with an oath. The noble Brutus has now to face a last indignity which it is small wonder that he yearns to think upon. He is to take wine with his intended victim in a sacrament of good fellowship; they are to go together like friends to the place of butchery. The incident is not only intensely dramatic in itself but enables us to see behind the stoic mask which Brutus has assumed.

It is impossible to resist recalling now and then conspicuous instances in which Shakespeare's more illustrious critics have found in the finest strokes of his genius occasion to deplore his lack of art.

Coleridge, as we have seen, found the first soliloquy of Brutus 'discordant'. Voltaire found the incident at present under consideration to be 'low, vulgar and barbarous'. Voltaire saw 'Julius Caesar' acted in London. 'These are no Romans who are talking,' he writes; 'they are peasants of a past age conspiring in a wine-shop; and Caesar, who invites them to drink a bottle with him, does not in the least resemble Julius Caesar. The absurdity is outlandish.' Voltaire was, nevertheless, genuinely moved by the play. It was a 'monstrous spectacle', but he felt obliged to confess that 'from time to time sublime points glitter and shine forth like diamonds scattered in the mire.' Nor did he, in this particular instance, disdain the sincerest form of flattery. He imitated Shakespeare's play in a version of its first three acts which he falsely described as a translation and wrote an original tragedy on the same theme, 'La Mort de César', in which he made up for what he considered to be a lack of dramatic interest in the authentic history of the conspiracy by accepting the fable that Brutus was Caesar's son. The point to be noted here, however, is one which will receive further illustration as we proceed, namely, that Shakespeare is never more likely to incur rebuke from his critics than when giving of his best. This incident of Caesar taking wine with the conspirators was certainly not in Voltaire's opinion one of the 'sublime points', and the Frenchman, though he confesses to being moved by the play as a whole, begs his readers to 'pity rather than blame a people for ignorance of what constitutes good taste.'

Brutus, shrinking inwardly, plays his part in the assassination apparently without a qualm. Watch him closely through the scene. It is a model performance of the stoic in action. Popilius Lena, not one of the conspirators, coming up to Casca, wishes that their enterprise may thrive. He leaves the startled Casca, goes up to Caesar and talks with him apart. Casca fears that the whole plot is discovered and that Popilius may be warning Caesar against them. Cassius is mightily disturbed and shows it. 'Brutus, what shall be done?' he exclaims. Brutus, apparently unshaken, urges his confederate to give proof of the virtue which he has himself assumed:

> Cassius, be *constant*:
> Popilius Lena speaks not of our purposes:
> For, look, he smiles, and Caesar doth not change.

It is Brutus who takes control of the proceedings. Metellus Cimber advances to make his petition to Caesar. Brutus realises that the moment has come:

> He is address'd: press near and second him;

and it is Brutus who strikes the final blow. In the confused scene that follows the assassination it is again Brutus who reassures the spectators:

> People and senators, be not affrighted;
> Fly not; stand still: ambition's debt is paid;

and it is Brutus who insists that he and his confederates are alone responsible:

> and let no man abide this deed
> But we, the doers.

It is Brutus, again, who takes the lead, such as it is, in the self-conscious posturing of the assassins over Caesar's body. These men have no policy or plan. They have killed Caesar, but have no idea what to do next beyond going forth into the streets of Rome and crying 'Liberty'. But they are deeply impressed with their own performance and carried away upon a tide of heroic self-importance which calls for some form of symbolic expression. They are seized with a kind of sublime hysteria and Brutus, for all his stoicism, catches the infection:

> Fates, we will know your pleasures:
> That we shall die, we know; 'tis but the time
> And drawing days out, that men stand upon.

Cassius takes the cue:

> Why, he that cuts off twenty years of life
> Cuts off so many years of fearing death;

and Brutus, easing his conscience for the killing of his friend, and carrying to dreadful extremes the sacrificial mood in which he struck the fatal blow, argues that Caesar himself should be grateful for the deed and suggests a blood rite in consummation:

> Grant that, and then is death a benefit:
> So are we Caesar's friends, that have abridged

> His time of fearing death. Stoop, Romans, stoop,
> And let us bathe our hands in Caesar's blood
> Up to the elbows, and besmear our swords:
> Then walk we forth, even to the market-place;
> And waving our red weapons o'er our heads,
> Let's all cry, 'Peace, freedom and liberty!'

Brutus, in the scene of the assassination, has shown physical courage and presence of mind. These virtues do not, however, qualify a man for success in public life. He needs also ability to appreciate political realities and a knowledge of men. Brutus, in the first decisions taken by the conspirators, shows himself constitutionally deficient in both these attributes. He persists in his mistaken estimate of Antony and caps the blunder of sparing his life with the yet more fatal blunder of giving him permission to speak in Caesar's funeral. Antony, he maintains, is a wise and valiant Roman; Antony will be their friend. Cassius is not convinced:

> I wish we may: but yet have I a mind
> That fears him much; and my misgiving still
> Falls shrewdly to the purpose.

Note well the contrast between the behaviour of Brutus and Cassius when Antony comes upon the scene. Brutus, assuring Antony that for him their swords have leaden points, dwells on the purity of their motives and the humanity of their cause:

> Yet see you but our hands
> And this the bleeding business they have done:
> Our hearts you see not; they are pitiful;
> And pity to the general wrong of Rome—
> As fire drives out fire, so pity pity—
> Hath done this deed on Caesar.

Cassius, on the other hand, callously strips the assassination of all moral significance. He assures Antony:

> Your voice shall be as strong as any man's
> In the disposing of new dignities.

The tyrant is dead; we are now to share the spoils and Antony will be consulted in their distribution. This is practical politics. Cassius goes straight to the point and in one stroke of dreadful, unconscious irony completely destroys the high pretensions of his colleague.

Shakespeare has so far used Cassius for his principal foil in revealing the character of Brutus. Cassius is the political realist who, seeing no place for himself in Caesar's Rome and aware that Caesar bears him hard, has decided that Caesar must be slain. Such a man, in every word he utters, presents just the contrast which is needed to throw into relief the moral and intellectual qualities of his friend. But the time has now come to present another aspect of Brutus which, equally with his unpractical idealism, foredooms him to failure as a public man, and Shakespeare employs for this purpose a politician of a very different type. The lean and hungry Cassius gives place to the gamesome Antony; the man who thinks too much to the sanguine opportunist who hardly thinks at all but responds to the mood of the moment. Brutus, the man of sentiment, is now to be contrasted with Antony, the man of passion, and we are soon to realise that passion in politics can be as effective as sentiment is unavailing. Antony uses his private grief to inflame the emotions of the crowd. He is that most effectively mischievous of orators who can blend an emotion sincerely felt with a nicely calculated appeal to the feelings of his audience. Giving free rein to a personal passion he at the same time plays upon the passion of the mob. His blood may be at fever heat, but he keeps a cool head. Above all, he understands the common man and can put himself into immediate sympathy with those about him. He has no political convictions, no programme either of reaction or reform. He intends to save himself and to avenge his friend. He is the politician to whom politics will never be more than a game and who of his own choice would never have concerned himself seriously with public affairs. He is the political amateur who in time of peace excels in sport and revels long o' nights, and who, in time of war, goes into battle as into a stadium.

Antony first appears as an athlete who is to run in the Lupercalia. It is true that during the festival he offers Caesar a kingly crown, but this is merely a personal gesture. He is just the sort of man Caesar would choose for an act which is merely designed to test the feeling of the crowd—a man who, if the act miscarries, may be rebuked as a headstrong, ingenuous and over-zealous admirer. That Antony had

never taken any special interest in politics or shown any political
sense is indicated in the first significant words which are put into his
mouth. Caesar, returning from the games, declares his suspicion of
Cassius. Antony replies:

> Fear him not, Caesar; he's not dangerous;
> He is a noble Roman and well given.

This careless reveller, who has yet to discover his power for mischief,
commits in two lines three major blunders which a trained politician
would have avoided: he tactlessly suggests that Caesar is liable to
fear, a possibility which Caesar at once repudiates; he expresses a
heedless opinion that Cassius is not dangerous; and he bases this
opinion on the ground that Cassius is a member of the aristocracy. It
seldom occurs to members of the ruling class that one of themselves
may lead a revolution, though that is how most revolutions begin.

Antony is, nevertheless, a formidable opponent, as Cassius vainly
insists. It is true that he has not yet taken any serious interest in
politics and that he is deficient in political judgment. It is true, as
Brutus points out, that 'he is given to sports, to wildness and much
company'. But he is a man whose passion, once it is aroused, whose
ready tongue and coarse humanity, whose genius in adapting himself to the moods of men, mark him out as a most dangerous enemy.
It is characteristic of Brutus that he picks on the very quality in
Antony which renders him so formidable as proof that he is not to be
feared. Brutus, the recluse, despises Antony as one who is given to
'much company'. But it is just because Antony is a sociable person
that he can so effectively adapt himself to all occasions.

Shakespeare from the outset strongly underlines the sincerity of
Antony's grief for Caesar. Antony, it is true, flees to his house
amazed on hearing of Caesar's death and takes the obvious precau-
tion of sending his servant to the Capitol with a conciliatory message addressed to the conspirators before he himself ventures to
appear. To this Brutus replies with a safe-conduct:

> Thy master is a wise and valiant Roman;
> I never thought him worse.
> Tell him, so please him come unto this place,
> He shall be satisfied; and, by my honour,
> Depart untouch'd.

But Antony, when he appears, throws caution to the winds. He ignores the welcome accorded him by Brutus. He has eyes only for the fallen Caesar:

> O mighty Caesar! dost thou lie so low?
> Are all thy conquests, glories, triumphs, spoils,
> Shrunk to this little measure?—

and he turns recklessly upon the assassins:

> I know not, gentlemen, what you intend,
> Who else must be let blood, who else is rank:
> If I myself, there is no hour so fit
> As Caesar's death's hour, nor no instrument
> Of half that worth as those your swords, made rich
> With the most noble blood of all this world.
> I do beseech ye, if you bear me hard,
> Now, whilst your purpled hands do reek and smoke,
> Fulfil your pleasure. Live a thousand years,
> I shall not find myself so apt to die.

Note, however, the sudden twist that follows:

> No place will please me so, no mean of death,
> As here by Caesar, and by you cut off,
> *The choice and master spirits of this age.*

That last line provides the key to Antony's conduct in the scenes that follow—grief for Caesar, an outward respect for the assassins, which imposes on Brutus, and a bitter, secret irony, which is clearly appreciated by Cassius.

Antony comes to terms with the conspirators. One by one he takes them by the hand, declaring that he doubts not of their wisdom. Suddenly, however, his grief for Caesar again breaks out:

> That I did love thee, Caesar, O, 'tis true:
> If then thy spirit look upon us now,
> Shall it not grieve thee dearer than thy death,
> To see thy Antony making his peace,
> Shaking the bloody fingers of thy foes,
> *Most noble!* in the presence of thy corse?

The interjection of the words 'most noble' is another superb stroke of character. In the full tide of his sorrow Antony has become aware of the effect of his words on the men who have killed Caesar. He accordingly, with the same outward deference which described them as the choice and master spirits of this age and which will prompt him in his coming oration to insist that they are all, all honourable men, slips in here a tribute to their nobility. He continues, however, to express his grief and admiration for the dead man, declaring that it would become him better to weep his eyes out than to close in terms of friendship with Caesar's murderers. His passion mounts and finds relief in the desperate punning to which Shakespeare's characters so often resort when their feelings become too much for them:

> O world! thou wast the forest to this hart;
> And this, indeed, O world! the heart of thee.
> How like a deer, strucken by many princes,
> Dost thou here lie!

This is too much for Cassius. He interrupts the speaker and there follows a passage in which Antony, Brutus and Cassius, each in a few brief lines, once again declare their several characters:

CASSIUS: Mark Antony,—
ANTONY: Pardon me, Caius Cassius:
      The enemies of Caesar shall say this;
      Then, in a friend, it is cold modesty.
CASSIUS: I blame you not for praising Caesar so;
      But what compact mean you to have with us?
      Will you be prick'd in number of our friends,
      Or shall we on, and not depend on you?
ANTONY: Therefore I took your hands, but was, indeed,
      Sway'd from the point, by looking down on Caesar.
      Friends am I with you all, and love you all,
      Upon this hope, that you shall give me reasons
      Why and wherein Caesar was dangerous.
BRUTUS: Or else were this a savage spectacle:
      Our reasons are so full of good regard
      That were you, Antony, the son of Caesar,
      You should be satisfied.

At the risk of a most damnable iteration, it is impossible to refrain from again remarking how the dramatist, without diminishing the speed of his action or diverting for an instant the interest of his audience, continues to unfold his characters in every word they utter with a consistency which a musician might be tempted to describe as fugal. Antony answers Cassius with a characteristic blend of disarming sincerity and ready dissimulation; Cassius confines himself to the practical issue, demanding to know, once for all, whether Antony means to throw in his lot with the conspirators or no; and Brutus— well, Brutus is ready to give 'reasons'.

The question whether Antony shall or shall not be allowed to speak in Caesar's funeral is then decided. All that Antony asks is permission to produce Caesar's body to the market-place and pay a tribute to his friend. Cassius opposes the request. He takes Brutus aside and urgently pleads with him:

> You know not what you do; do not consent
> That Antony speak in his funeral:
> Know you how much the people may be mov'd
> By that which he will utter?

Cassius knows how dangerous a man like Antony can be. He foresees how easily the crowd may be stirred by an orator who speaks from the heart and can so readily make himself at home with his company. He places no faith in Antony's pretence of being satisfied with 'reasons' and fully appreciates the mockery that underlies Antony's essay in conciliation.

Brutus, on the other hand, is completely deceived in the man and his purpose. Antony has asked for 'reasons'; he shall have his 'reasons' and be satisfied. The republican philosopher persists in believing that, not only Antony himself, but the people to whom an account is to be rendered, will be decisively influenced by rational argument and he finally overrides the objections of Cassius in a speech which, for its simple vanity and ingenuous trust in human nature, is a masterpiece of self-revelation. Antony, he argues, can do us no harm. I shall first address the crowd myself and convince them that our cause is just. Antony shall then speak from the same pulpit in praise of Caesar. A tribute to Caesar from a friend, Brutus maintains, cannot possibly corrupt an audience which has previously been addressed by *me*:

BRUTUS: I will myself unto the pulpit first,
And show the reason for our Caesar's death:
What Antony shall speak, I will protest
He speaks by leave and by permission.
And that we are contented Caesar shall
Have all true rites and lawful ceremonies.
It shall advantage more than do us wrong.
CASSIUS: I know not what may fall; I like it not.
BRUTUS: Mark Antony, here, take you Caesar's body.
You shall not in your funeral speech blame us,
But speak all good you can devise of Caesar,
And say you do't by our permission;
Else shall you not have any hand at all
About his funeral; and you shall speak
In the same pulpit whereto I am going,
After my speech is ended.

The political errors of Brutus are firmly rooted in a certain nobility of mind. He trusts Antony not to abuse his privilege. He believes that the crowd will appreciate a gesture of chivalry to the fallen.

Antony is left alone at the conclusion of this scene. It is always an exciting moment when for the first time a character of Shakespeare has the stage to himself. Cassius, left alone, exposed the main motive of his conduct in half-a-dozen lines. He was out of favour with Caesar and had nothing to hope from Caesar's government. Brutus, left alone, revealed the agony of mind suffered by a man of high principle and gentle disposition called upon to take the lead in an act of violence. Antony, left alone, puts beyond all doubt the sincerity of his grief for Caesar and, in the short scene that follows, gives a foretaste of the ability with which he will exploit any opportunity that offers for revenge:

O, pardon me, thou bleeding piece of earth,
That I am meek and gentle with these butchers!
Thou art the ruins of the noblest man
That ever lived in the tide of times.

His apostrophe to the dead Caesar is interrupted by the entry of a servant of Octavius. Antony at once reveals the man of quick decision who will be guided by events. His first impulse, on being informed that Octavius is coming to Rome still ignorant of Caesar's death, is to warn him to stay away:

> Post back with speed, and tell him what hath chanced:
> Here is a mourning Rome, a dangerous Rome,
> No Rome of safety for Octavius yet;
> Hie hence, and tell him so.

But instantly he changes his mind. He is to address the people in the forum. He will test their response and possibly win them over. It will be better to await the issue, see what happens and advise Octavius accordingly. He calls back the messenger:

> Yet, stay awhile;
> Thou shalt not back till I have borne this corse
> Into the market-place: there shall I try,
> In my oration, how the people take
> The cruel issue of these bloody men;
> According to the which thou shalt discourse
> To young Octavius of the state of things.

The abrupt change of plan is a master-stroke. We see the mind of this fearless, quickwitted and passionate man working at full pressure and the stage is now set for the contrasted orations of Brutus and Antony in the forum.

These two orations cannot be too closely studied. There is a complete political character in each of them. Brutus speaks from the pathetic conviction that he has only to state a case honestly and clearly to the people; the people will be convinced and thereafter remain steadfast in their opinion. It is the fallacy of a liberal-minded politician, who assumes that men in the mass are governed by reason and who ignores the conscious self-interest or, what is even more potent, the irrational impulse of the crowd. It is the tragic error of a civilised man, who believes that it is only necessary to prove, for example, that war is unprofitable or a policy intellectually absurd in order to bring everlasting peace to the nations and Utopia to the individual. Brutus gives to this conviction a form which is marvellously appropriate. He makes no appeal to the emotions of his audience. His speech consists of a series of terse, antithetical sentences, convey-

ing precisely the idea he has in mind. It is Euclidean in its logic,
Tacitean in its tidiness and brevity. It requires from those who listen
a close, consecutive attention. Brutus might be addressing an academy
of science, a congress of philosophers, an audience of literary exquisites, capable of appreciating an exposition in which every sentence contributes to the formal symmetry of the rhetorical design:

Romans, countrymen, and lovers! hear me for my cause, and be silent,
that you may hear: believe me for mine honour, and have respect to mine
honour, that you may believe: censure me in your wisdom, and awake
your senses, that you may the better judge. If there be any in this assembly,
any dear friend of Caesar's, to him I say, that Brutus' love to Caesar was no
less than his. If then that friend demand why Brutus rose against Caesar,
this is my answer: Not that I loved Caesar less, but that I loved Rome
more. Had you rather Caesar were living, and die all slaves, than that
Caesar were dead, to live all free men? As Caesar loved me, I weep for
him; as he was fortunate, I rejoice at it; as he was valiant, I honour him:
but, as he was ambitious, I slew him. There is tears for his love; joy for his
fortune; honour for his valour; and death for his ambition. Who is here so
base that would be a bondman? If any, speak; for him I have offended.
Who is here so rude that would not be a Roman? If any, speak; for him I
have offended. Who is here so vile that will not love his country? If any,
speak; for him I have offended.

It is much to the credit of the Roman citizens that they listened
attentively to this remarkable exercise in dialectic and showed considerable enthusiasm upon its conclusion. The dramatist here shows
extraordinary subtlety in his handling of the crowd. These citizens,
invited to follow a rational argument, are not yet the impassioned
mob which Antony, by appealing to their emotions, will shortly
make of them. The individuals composing it still retain their several
identities. They are impressed by Brutus, even though they do not
understand him. The noble Brutus is a public figure and he is doing
them the honour to render an account of his action and speak to
them as reasonable human beings. They are accordingly ready to
applaud and accept him as their leader. 'Let him be Caesar', cries one,
thereby showing that he approves the speaker, though he has not
understood a single word of the argument. 'Caesar's better parts shall
be crowned in Brutus,' cries another rather more intelligent member

of the crowd. Another suggests that he should be brought in triumph to his house; yet another that he should be given a statue with his ancestors.

The reception accorded to Brutus by the crowd, while showing the dramatist's profound insight into the individual and collective psychology of man as a political animal, also serves to emphasise yet again the political ineptitude of Brutus. His speech has had more success than it deserved. The citizens are with him. But the readiness with which they acclaim him, without having in the least understood his argument, should have warned him against allowing them to fall under the spell of Antony. Brutus has made a speech in which he has carefully explained that he killed Caesar because Caesar was a despot. He bases his trust in the people on the assumption that they share his desire for freedom. The crowd responds with a suggestion that he shall be accorded the honours of a dictator. The cry of 'Let him be Caesar' is as prompt and devastating a non-sequitur to the argument of Brutus as the couplet in which Cassius promised Antony a voice in the disposal of new dignities. But Brutus is blind and deaf to these exposures. Having secured the allegiance of the Roman citizens, he uses it to urge that they shall now listen to Antony:

> Good countrymen, let me depart alone,
> And, for my sake, stay here with Antony:
> Do grace to Caesar's corpse, and grace his speech
> Tending to Caesar's glories; which Mark Antony,
> By our permission, is allow'd to make.

Brutus spoke to the mind in prose. Antony speaks to the emotions in verse. Brutus was brief, cold, honest and plain. Antony is spacious, warm, indirect and full of colour. Antony's reasons are no reasons, but arguments addressed to the sentiment and self-interest of his listeners.

Note, first of all, the skill with which he at once adapts himself to the temper of his audience. He climbs into the pulpit to a chorus of exclamation from the citizens. They are ready to listen to the noble Antony, but "twere best', says one, 'he speak no harm of Brutus here.' 'This Caesar', says another, 'was a tyrant.' And yet another declares: 'We are blest that Rome is rid of him.'

This being the temper of the crowd, Antony disclaims any intention of praising Caesar and, knowing the partiality of simple men for sententious generalities, begins with the seemingly profound, but essentially shallow, observation:

> The evil that men do lives after them;
> The good is oft interrèd with their bones;
> So let it be with Caesar.

This is just the sort of thing to elicit a nodding of muddled heads in confirmation of its wistful cynicism and it has the added advantage of insinuating that Caesar, despite his evil courses, had good qualities which, in the sad nature of things, must be forgotten. Antony, having thus arrested the attention of his audience, continues:

> The noble Brutus
> Hath told you Caesar was ambitious:
> If it were so, it was a grievous fault,
> And grievously hath Caesar answer'd it.

The supple skill with which Antony in these opening lines follows the mood of his audience deserves attention. Brutus is noble and Brutus has charged Caesar with ambition. Antony ventures to suggest with an 'if' that the charge may not be true. But the citizens are not yet ready to accept this suggestion and the speaker, trimming his sails to the wind, adds quickly that Caesar, if ambitious, has paid the last penalty for a grievous fault. The orator, conscious of the chill disapproval excited by his audacity in throwing doubt upon Caesar's ambition, then hastens to remind his listeners that he speaks as a friend of the conspirators:

> Here, under leave of Brutus and the rest,—
> For Brutus is an honourable man;
> So are they all, all honourable men—
> Come I to speak in Caesar's funeral.

With the accidental felicity of the born orator, he has now lighted upon the celebrated refrain which is to give unity and design to his whole speech. Eight times in the course of his oration he uses the word 'honourable' and each time the sarcasm, at first concealed, becomes more open. He does not at first—like so many actors who have played the part—anywhere underline his ironical intention. The mere iteration of the word, supported by facts and arguments intended to suggest that the term may not be altogether appropriate, plays upon the nerves of the citizens who, *themselves*, begin to feel its irrelevance, till at last upon Antony's supreme stroke:

> I fear I wrong the *honourable* men
> Whose daggers have stabb'd Caesar,

one of them cries out in savage repudiation: 'Honourable men! They were traitors.'

We may now consider with what tricks and devices Antony gradually produces this change of temper in the crowd.

Caesar, he says in effect, may have been ambitious, but he was my friend and to me he was 'faithful and just'. Caesar brought many captives home to Rome and their ransoms were paid into the general coffers. Was this ambition? When that the poor have cried, Caesar hath wept; ambition should be made of sterner stuff. Caesar on the Lupercal was offered a kingly crown which three times he refused. Was this ambition? Such arguments, interspersed with the increasingly mischievous:

> But Brutus says he was ambitious;
> And Brutus is an honourable man;

brings the citizens to a frame of mind which emboldens Antony, at exactly the right moment, to remind them of a time when Caesar was dear to them:

> You all did love him once, not without cause;
> What cause withholds you then to mourn for him?

He is growing more sure of his audience. He has begun to grip their hearts. He can now abandon specious argument and let himself go in a burst of emotion which is genuine but, at the same time, most adroitly used:

> O judgment! thou art fled to brutish beasts,
> And men have lost their reason;

adding swiftly, lest his hearers should be disconcerted by an outbreak hardly flattering to their good sense:

> My heart is in the coffin there with Caesar,
> And I must pause till it come back to me.

The pause is filled with exclamations from the crowd. First
Citizen makes a remark which is full of delicious irony. 'Methinks',
he cries, 'there is much *reason* in his sayings.' Brutus had relied upon
'reasons', real reasons, reasons of principle, urged in good faith and
logically delivered. Antony's reasons were of a different order.
Caesar had brought revenue to the state, wept for the miseries of the
poor and refused the crown. These were reasons addressed to the
plain man. They did not prove Antony's case; but they were none
the worse for that and First Citizen was convinced. First Citizen's
use of the word 'reason' to describe what was in reality an appeal to
his pocket and his emotions is one of those apparently negligent
strokes of genius which fill the plays of Shakespeare with echoes and
overtones which are perceived only upon a close scrutiny of the
text.

Other members of the crowd supply a chorus which reveals to
Antony, as he mourns Caesar and covertly observes them, that the
time has come to discard all restraint. 'Caesar has had great wrong,'
says one. 'Caesar would not take the crown and therefore was not
ambitious,' says another. A third is touched to the quick by Antony's
grief for Caesar: 'Poor soul! his eyes are red as fire with weeping.'
A fourth declares: 'There's not a nobler man in Rome than Antony.'
The orator can now abandon all restraint:

> But yesterday the word of Caesar might
> Have stood against the world; now lies he there,
> And none so poor to do him reverence.
> O masters! if I were dispos'd to stir
> Your hearts and minds to mutiny and rage,
> I should do Brutus wrong, and Cassius wrong,
> Who, you all know, are honourable men:
> I will not do them wrong; I rather choose
> To wrong the dead, to wrong myself, and you,
> Than I will wrong such honourable men.

Now, too, the time has come for Antony to play the card which he
has been holding in reserve:

> But here's a parchment, with the seal of Caesar;
> I found it in his closet, 'tis his will:
> Let but the commons hear this testament—
> Which, pardon me, I do not mean to read—
> And they would go and kiss dead Caesar's wounds,
> And dip their napkins in his sacred blood,
> Yea, beg a hair of him for memory.

The citizens naturally ask that the will be read. Antony continues:

> Have patience, gentle friends, I must not read it;
> It is not meet you know how Caesar lov'd you.
> You are not wood, you are not stones, but men;
> And, being men, hearing the will of Caesar,
> It will inflame you, it will make you mad;
> 'Tis good you know not that you are his heirs;
> For, if you should, O! what would come of it?

Antony asks leave of his listeners to come down from the pulpit.
Let them make a ring about Caesar's body. If he must read the will,
he will show them first the man who made it. He has now so complete a control over his audience that he can afford a gesture of impatience and, as they come crowding about him, he protests: 'Nay,
press not so upon me: stand far off.' And he can now indulge his
grief for Caesar without disguise, give it form and colour. With the
cold, measured accents of Brutus still in our ears, we are swept forward upon the tide of an oration in which sincere passion is shaped
by an imagination working at full pressure. Antony was not present
at the death of Caesar, but he reconstructs the whole scene both for
himself and his audience, thereby easing his heart and whipping his
hearers to a frenzy:

> You all do know this mantle: I remember
> The first time ever Caesar put it on;
> 'Twas on a summer's evening, in his tent,
> That day he overcame the Nervii:
> Look! in this place ran Cassius' dagger through:
> See what a rent the envious Casca made:

> Through this the well-belovèd Brutus stabb'd;
> And, as he pluck'd his cursèd steel away,
> Mark how the blood of Caesar follow'd it,
> As rushing out of doors, to be resolved
> If Brutus so unkindly knock'd or no;
> For Brutus, as you know, was Caesar's angel:
> Judge, O you gods, how dearly Caesar lov'd him!
> This was the most unkindest cut of all;
> For when the noble Caesar saw him stab,
> Ingratitude, more strong than traitors' arms,
> Quite vanquish'd him: then burst his mighty heart;
> And, in his mantle muffling up his face,
> Even at the base of Pompey's statua,
> Which all the while ran blood, great Caesar fell.

He plucks away the mantle from Caesar's body:

> Kind souls, what! weep you when you but behold
> Our Caesar's vesture wounded? Look you here,
> Here is himself, marr'd, as you see, with traitors.

The citizens of Rome are by this time an impassioned mob, incapable of anything but ejaculation: O piteous spectacle . . . O noble Caesar . . . O woeful day . . . O traitors, villains . . . O most bloody sight . . . Revenge . . . Burn . . . Fire . . . Kill . . . Slay . . . Let not a traitor live!

But Antony has not yet done with them. His purpose is achieved, but he will permit himself the luxury of a bitter sneer at the men who killed Caesar. He can now not only mock their reasons openly but suggest that their real motive for the crime was self-interest:

> Good friends, sweet friends, let me not stir you up
> To such a sudden flood of mutiny.
> They that have done this deed are honourable:
> *What private griefs they have, alas! I know not,*
> *That made them do it:* they are wise and honourable,
> And will, no doubt, with reasons answer you.

Finally, with an insolent change of front characteristic of the political orator in full spate, he frankly incites to violence the crowd which, a moment ago, he had affected to restrain. In this incitement,

after the manner of all orators, he modestly disclaims any gift of
speech at a moment when he is showing himself to be a master of the
art, pays a sarcastic tribute to the pallid eloquence of Brutus and contrives to depreciate the magnanimity of his enemies in allowing him
to speak in praise of Caesar:

> I am no orator, as Brutus is;
> But, as you know me all, a plain blunt man,
> That love my friend; and that they know full well
> That gave me public leave to speak of him:
> For I have neither wit, nor words, nor worth,
> Action, nor utterance, nor the power of speech,
> To stir men's blood: I only speak right on;
> I tell you that which you yourselves do know;
> Show you sweet Caesar's wounds, poor, poor dumb mouths,
> And bid them speak for me: but were I Brutus,
> And Brutus Antony, there were an Antony
> Would ruffle up your spirits, and put a tongue
> In every wound of Caesar, that should move
> The stones of Rome to rise and mutiny.

There remains a further touch, perhaps the most subtle stroke of
political veracity in this whole astonishing performance. The crowd
makes to stampede from the scene. It will burn the house of Brutus,
seek out all the conspirators. Antony calls them back.

They have forgotten the will.

Shakespeare shows here a perfect understanding of men in the
mass. Antony had counted on the will to secure the support of the
shrewd citizens of Rome. It would enable him to appeal to their
self-interest. Had not Caesar left 'to every several man, seventy-five
drachmas'; and to the people at large his walks, his private arbours
and his orchards? But a crowd is less moved by material profit than
by a passion collectively shared. It is easier to persuade a mass of men
—as is fully appreciated by the modern experts in propaganda—to
sacrifice itself collectively than to act upon a cool assessment of
advantages. A crowd easily loses all sense of profit and loss. It is
moved by motives which may be high or low, genial or barbarous,
compassionate or cruel, but it is above or below reason, and in its
bestial savagery or gross good humour, equally altruistic. The com-

mon sense of each is lost in the emotion of all. It is easier to persuade a crowd to commit suicide than to accept a legacy.

It has been superficially maintained that Shakespeare, in making his Roman citizens forget the will, was merely demonstrating that a crowd is so fickle in its attention and feather-headed in its responses that it cannot keep anything in mind for more than a moment; that it is blown like a straw before the wind and is incapable of any act which requires an effort of memory or concentration. But the dramatist, in this episode, probes deeper than that. Shakespeare was fully alive to the essential difference between a mob and the persons of whom it is composed. Antony calls his Romans back to hear the will because he knows that, though as a mob they are ready to burn down the house of Brutus in a fit of passion, the time will come when as individuals they will again become amenable to argument. Each of them has for the moment lost all sense of his own interest or capacity of reason, but each of them will recover his faculties when he goes home and begins to think things over. He will, in short, begin to wonder whether he has not perhaps behaved like a fool. He will then need something tangible to fall back upon and Caesar's testament will then be remembered.

So Antony, with the reading of Caesar's will, rounds off his performance. The crowd rushes off to burn and slay:

> Now let it work. Mischief, thou art afoot,
> Take thou what course thou wilt!

This mighty scene concludes with the entrance of a messenger who announces that Octavius has arrived in Rome and is at Caesar's house; Cassius and Brutus, before the rage of the people, have rid like madmen through the gates of Rome. 'Fortune is merry,' cries Antony, gamesome to the last, 'and in this mood will grant us anything.'

Antony's conversion of the citizens into a collective monster throws us back to a scene which forms, as it were, a prelude to the play. This Roman crowd was the first character to appear upon the stage. Shakespeare, setting out to show us Brutus killing Caesar for the people, shows us first the people for whom Caesar was killed. It is in holiday mood, having come into the streets to see Caesar and rejoice in his triumph. Though every man is infected with the spirit of festival, no one has yet lost his identity. The cobbler who speaks for these commoners is no reed to be shaken by an orator, but a saucy fellow who can speak, and speak wittily, for himself:

FLAVIUS: Why dost thou lead these men about the streets?
SECOND COMMONER: Truly, sir, to wear out their shoes, to get myself into
    more work.

The tribunes, Flavius and Marcellus, chide them for having so soon forgotten Pompey, their late master. Pompey was once their darling:

> Many a time and oft
> Have you climb'd up to walls and battlements,
> To towers and windows, yea, to chimney-tops,
> Your infants in your arms, and there have sat
> The live-long day, with patient expectation,
> To see great Pompey pass the streets of Rome.

The tribune, though, like Antony, he appeals to their emotions, speaks to them as men. Note that household touch—*your infants in your arms*. It gives almost a domestic flavour to the scene. These are 'certain commoners', they are not yet a mob, but a group of men, each of whom is accessible to reproach:

> And do you now put on your best attire?
> And do you now cull out a holiday?
> And do you now strew flowers in his way,
> That comes in triumph over Pompey's blood?

Not only do the tribunes succeed in their appeal; they are quite humanly impressed by its success:

> See, whe'r their basest metal be not mov'd;
> They vanish tongue-tied in their guiltiness.

Contrast this kindly company of men with the mob which Antony lets loose upon the city after his oration. Antony's citizens are fused into a horde. It has neither pity nor reason. It is not even angry in any rational sense, but filled with the mere primitive rage to destroy. It has humour, but it is the gross humour of the savage. It has no purpose of any kind.

Shakespeare underlines the contrast in a special incident.

The mob sets out to kill the conspirators, but the first person it meets is a harmless old man who has ventured timidly into the streets against his better judgment. It questions him facetiously, playing like a cruel cat with a defenceless mouse till it wearies of the game. Then it makes an end of the business:

THIRD CITIZEN: Your name, sir, truly.
CINNA: Truly, my name is Cinna.
FIRST CITIZEN: Tear him to pieces; he's a conspirator.
CINNA: I am Cinna the poet, I am Cinna the poet.
FOURTH CITIZEN: Tear him for his bad verses, tear him for his bad verses.
CINNA: I am not Cinna the conspirator.
FOURTH CITIZEN: It is no matter, his name's Cinna.
THIRD CITIZEN: Tear him, tear him!

The voices are those of First, Third and Fourth Citizen, but it has ceased to matter a jot who speaks. These creatures have lost all sense of personal identity.

And so the curtain falls upon Act III of the tragedy of 'Julius Caesar'.

Up to this point the action of the play has been simple and continuous. From the scene in which Cassius persuades Brutus to lead the conspiracy to the moment of Caesar's funeral there has been no pause or intermission. Many critics have complained that from this point onward the play loses cohesion and interest. Caesar, who stood at the centre of the argument, is now dead and nothing remains, they say, but an epilogue in which to pass judgment on the assassination and depict its consequences.

This view of the play would seem to miss the essential argument of the tragedy. It assumes that Caesar's death marks the end of one episode and the beginning of another, which is the direct reverse of what Shakespeare intended and achieved. Caesar, far from representing a hiatus in the action, is the link which binds the first and second parts together, and his character is depicted, first to last, so that it may effectively fulfil this function. He is exhibited from the outset as a man who will be mightier in death than in life. The mortal Caesar displays his infirmities so that we may be the more impressed with his immortal genius. Brutus exclaimed in his orchard: 'O, that we then could come by Caesar's spirit and not dismember Caesar', but this is precisely what the assassins failed to do. They dismembered Caesar and Caesar is dead. But Caesar's spirit is very much alive and is to play a decisive part in the future conduct of the play.

A short analysis of the character of Caesar, as unfolded by the dramatist, will accordingly serve as a bridge to carry us over from the first three to the last two acts of the play.

In making this analysis it is essential to grasp a fundamental difference between Shakespeare's method and that of most other dramatists. It is, indeed, more than a difference of method, for it stands at the heart of his genius. The ordinary way of presenting a dramatic hero upon the stage is to build him up feature by feature. He is seen performing actions, and is heard to utter speeches, which reveal his essential traits, and the author is careful to ensure that these traits are consistent. The character is shown to be brave or cowardly, generous or mean, kindly or cruel, simple or sophisticated, and he is allowed to act or speak only in accordance with his primary qualities. Such dramatic characters are easily grasped. They have both simplicity and coherence, being the result of deliberate selection and logical arrangement. Every piece of information about them afforded by the dramatist is in keeping. We are never puzzled by their conduct; nor are we moved to protest that this sort of person would not behave in that sort of way.

Shakespeare frequently goes to the opposite extreme. He has his characters alive and fully-formed in his mind. He takes for granted their primary qualities, which emerge, as it were, by accident. These characters are more than a sum of the traits which they exhibit. They do not come alive, feature by feature. They spring upon the stage in full career. They are not constructed; they enter upon the scene, men and women, rounded and complete in the imagination of the author, who assumes that his audience will recognise them for what they are as soon as they appear. They walk in upon us, each of them 'in his habit as he lived'. Shakespeare can thus exhibit them, if he chooses, behaving as men and women do, at odds with themselves, betraying inconsistencies and contradictions which no other dramatist has

dared to permit in an equal degree. Taking the reality of Hamlet or
Falstaff for granted, he can allow them to act out of character without destroying our belief in them but, on the contrary, increasing our
sense of their human veracity. Hamlet, irresolute in action, courteous
by nature and humane in disposition, surprises but in no way discon-
certs us when he leads an attack upon a pirate ship, is gross with
Ophelia or brutal in his references to the dead Polonius. Falstaff, a
trained soldier of courage and resource, who at Shrewsbury leads his
men into the thick of the battle where they are 'peppered', can yet
find discretion the better part of valour and be exposed to ridicule as
the man who ran away at Gadshill. Commentators on Shakespeare
are puzzled by such inconsistencies and some critics have egregiously
discovered them to be faults. But in no respect is Shakespeare's genius
more manifest than in allowing his characters to act in ways which,
at first sight and to the strictly logical mind, seem at variance with
their essential qualities. It is worth noting that such apparent contradictions become more frequent as Shakespeare grows creatively
more absolute. They are less notable in his political than in his comic
characters and in his tragic characters they become master-strokes of
delineation.

The political character of Caesar as presented by Shakespeare,
which has been condemned by many as a slight, negligent and impertinent libel upon a great man, may with advantage be considered
in the light of this tendency to take essential qualities for granted and
to dwell upon traits in seeming contradiction with them. Caesar's
greatness is assumed throughout the play. It fills the mind of the
dramatist and is communicated to his audience in phrases that fall
from his pen whenever Caesar is mentioned, even by his enemies.
This Caesar has got the start of the majestic world. He bestrides
it like a colossus. His fall is heralded by a 'strange impatience
of the heavens' and by portentous things which shake the minds
of the stoutest of the Romans. Cassius, meeting Casca in the
storm, names to him a man 'most like this dreadful night, prodigious
grown and fearful'. Caesar is about to die and 'all the sway of earth
shakes like a thing infirm'.

The essential greatness of Caesar being thus assumed, Shakespeare
is free to exhibit in him human weaknesses apparently inconsistent

with it. There are many advantages in this method of presentation. It gives reality to Caesar, the man; it suggests that Caesar's spirit is mightier than his person, a suggestion which is essential to the unity of the play; it enables the dramatist to present him in flesh and blood without reducing in stature the men who murder him; finally, it permits the audience to sympathise with Brutus just sufficiently to give poignancy to the disaster which overtakes him.

This last point is of major dramatic importance. The play could not easily have risen to the level of tragedy if Caesar had been portrayed consistently in full majesty. The conspiracy must then have inevitably impressed the audience as no more than a stupid plot contrived by a group of self-seeking politicians under the leadership of a misguided political crank. Such, in effect, it was, but the skilful dramatist, if he is to retain the sympathetic attention of his audience, will not obtrude the fact, but allow it to become fully apparent only at the close.

The infirmities of Caesar are not inventions of the dramatist. They are in part historical and in part derived from Plutarch's delight in the foibles of great men and his tendency to find such foibles more pronounced in his Roman heroes than in the heroes of his native Greece. They are, moreover, infirmities which in a greater or less degree are inseparable from political success and the exercise of power. Caesar, like other men of destiny, is superstitious. Caesar, like other exalted personages, refers to himself in the third person. Caesar, like other men whose position requires them to assume superhuman qualities, claims to be impervious to fear or argument and determined to enforce his will, even though he knows himself to be in the wrong. These are traits common to all dictators.

Caesar's entry into the play at once establishes the key of this imperial symphony. He comes upon the stage, a great crowd following. He calls Calpurnia to his side. 'Peace, ho! Caesar speaks.' The crowd is hushed to silence and awaits the oracle:

> CAESAR: Calpurnia!
> CALPURNIA: Here, my lord.
> CAESAR: Stand you directly in Antonius' way,
> When he doth run his course. Antonius!
> ANTONY: Caesar, my lord?

CAESAR: Forget not, in your speed, Antonius,
　　　　To touch Calpurnia; for our elders say,
　　　　The barren, touchèd in this holy chase,
　　　　Shake off their sterile curse.
　　　　　　ANTONY: I shall remember:
　　When Caesar says 'Do this,' it is perform'd.

All Rome is bent to hear this Caesar. O lame and impotent conclusion! The first words that fall from his lips show faith in an old wives' tale. Caesar is himself half ashamed of his credulity. The belief that Calpurnia's infertility can be cured by the touch of a runner in the feast of Lupercal he attributes, not to himself, but to 'our elders'. There may be something in it, but Caesar does not commit himself.

The procession moves on, but the crowd is hushed a second time. A soothsayer has cried to Caesar.

CAESAR:　　　　　　　　　　　Ha! Who calls?
　CASCA: Bid every noise be still: peace yet again!
CAESAR: Who is it in the press that calls on me?
　　　　I hear a tongue, shriller than all the music,
　　　　Cry 'Caesar!' Speak; Caesar is turn'd to hear.
SOOTHSAYER: Beware the ides of March.
CAESAR:　　　　　　　　　　　What man is that?
BRUTUS: A soothsayer bids you beware the ides of March.
CAESAR: Set him before me; let me see his face.
　CASCA: Fellow, come from the throng; look upon Caesar
CAESAR: What say'st thou to me now? Speak once again.
SOOTHSAYER: Beware the ides of March.
CAESAR: He is a dreamer; let us leave him: pass.

This first brief scene prefigures all the traits whereby Shakespeare is to present the mighty Caesar in flesh and blood. They will be deepened and enlivened as the play proceeds, but very little of substance will be added. Here, announced from the start, is a superstition cautious of revealing itself; an acquired habit, which has become second nature, of regarding himself as already a legendary person; a repudiation in himself of foibles which expose him to ridicule or, indeed, of any qualities which render him merely human. He dismisses the soothsayer as a dreamer, but nevertheless remembers his warning. He collaborates, as it were, in his own deification. *Peace, ho!*

*Caesar speaks. . . . When Caesar says 'Do this', it is performed. . . . Bid
every noise be still: peace yet again.* To such a chorus which endues with
solemnity his least word or whim, Caesar, as though he were re-
ferring to some remote Olympian figure, himself supplies the grave
antiphony: *'Caesar is turned to hear'*: and he bids the soothsayer *'Look
upon Caesar'*, as though inviting an inspection of his divinity. He is
living up to that legend of himself which every successful political
figure is sooner or later driven to create.

But Shakespeare is careful not to leave us under the impression
that this prodigious person, who has come to regard himself as a
public institution, has entirely lost his humanity. Shakespeare, in fact,
seems positively to delight in contrasting the man with his façade.
What could be more shrewd, timely or alert than Caesar's famous
description of Cassius? Caesar, however, even as he gives this signal
proof of a genial and lively perception, must instantly remember that
he is Caesar. Cassius is a man to be feared, but Caesar, being Caesar,
can fear nothing:

> Let me have men about me that are fat;
> Sleek-headed men and such as sleep o' nights:
> Yond Cassius has a lean and hungry look;
> He thinks too much: such men are dangerous.

> Would he were fatter! But I fear him not:
> Yet if my name were liable to fear,
> I do not know the man I should avoid
> So soon as that spare Cassius. He reads much;
> He is a great observer, and he looks
> Quite through the deeds of men; he loves no plays,
> As thou dost, Antony; he hears no music;
> Seldom he smiles, and smiles in such a sort
> As if he mock'd himself, and scorn'd his spirit
> That could be moved to smile at any thing.
> Such men as he be never at heart's ease
> Whiles they behold a greater than themselves,
> And therefore are they very dangerous.
> I rather tell thee what is to be fear'd
> Than what I fear; for always I am Caesar.

The domestic scene in which Calpurnia tries to dissuade Caesar from going to the Capitol, presents this same mischievous contrast of the natural man with the public figure. Caesar has had a bad night. Nor heaven nor earth has been at peace. Calpurnia has thrice cried out in her sleep. Caesar is thoroughly and humanly upset. He sends a servant off to the priests, ordering them to do present sacrifice and report on their success. Calpurnia enters:

> CALPURNIA: What mean you, Caesar? think you to walk forth?
> You shall not stir out of your house to-day.
> CAESAR: Caesar shall forth; the things that threaten'd me
> Ne'er look'd but on my back; when they shall see
> The face of Caesar, they are vanishèd.

Caesar, in the first person, is troubled, but Caesar in the third person cannot admit it. Calpurnia, however, sticks to her guns. She has had bad dreams and heard fearful accounts of horrid sights seen by the watch. Caesar, again protesting his immunity from fear, argues himself into a stolid defiance of omens in which he partially believes:

> CAESAR: What can be avoided
> Whose end is purpos'd by the mighty gods?
> Yet Caesar shall go forth; for these predictions
> Are to the world in general as to Caesar.
> CALPURNIA: When beggars die, there are no comets seen;
> The heavens themselves blaze forth the death of
> princes.
> CAESAR: Cowards die many times before their deaths;
> The valiant never taste of death but once.
> Of all the wonders that I yet have heard,
> It seems to me most strange that men should fear;
> Seeing that death, a necessary end,
> Will come when it will come.

The servant comes to report the result of his errand to the priests. Caesar's adjurations, addressed to himself, grow more eloquent as the portents become more fearful. He lashes himself into an ecstasy of divine assurance:

> CAESAR: What say the augurers?
> SERVANT: They would not have you to stir forth to-day.
> Plucking the entrails of an offering forth,
> They could not find a heart within the beast.

CAESAR: The gods do this in shame of cowardice:
Caesar should be a beast without a heart,
If he should stay at home to-day for fear.
No, Caesar shall not: danger knows full well
That Caesar is more dangerous than he:
We are two lions litter'd in one day,
And I the elder and more terrible:
And Caesar shall go forth.

But mark what follows:

CALPURNIA: Alas! my lord,
Your wisdom is consumed in confidence.
Do not go forth to-day: call it my fear
That keeps you in the house, and not your own.
We'll send Mark Antony to the senate-house;
And he shall say you are not well to-day:
Let me, upon my knee, prevail in this.
CAESAR: Mark Antony shall say I am not well;
And, for thy humour, I will stay at home.

There is no prettier stroke of character in the play. Caesar has declared himself immovable. But Calpurnia, knowing her lord, offers
him a way out and the natural man grasps it with an eagerness which
shows how empty were the protestations of the demigod. 'Call it *my*
fear that keeps you in the house', suggests the tactful wife, and Caesar
complies immediately.

From the entry of Decius, who comes to bring Caesar to the
senate-house, to the moment when Caesar invites the conspirators to
take wine with him, Shakespeare continues to contrast the human
with the legendary figure.

Decius, in his colloquy with Caesar, presents an attitude typical of
the public servant who is accustomed to deal with persons in high
office. He knows Caesar to be great, but refuses to be impressed. He
is the junior minister or high official who seeks compensation for
accepting the supremacy of an abler man by indulging a humorous
perspicacity at his expense and airing an intimate acquaintance with
his foibles. He is the courtier, inwardly proud of his access to august
circles, who nevertheless affects a smiling disparagement of the
privilege. He is the man who lives for a ribbon, but professes amuse-

ment at having to wear it. He will inform you that His Excellency is peevish this morning, having eaten or drunk unwisely the night before; that His Worship grows every day more difficult to manage and is every day more easily misled. He is the man to whom the absurdities of public life are very tolerable, provided they can be successfully exploited and at the same time afford him opportunities for the exercise of a small wit at the expense of a great man. He is the universal valet to whom no one is ever a hero. He sounds an echo, through the ages, of pleasantry exchanged in antechambers, lobbies, corridors or other purlieus where little people attend their masters. He is that familiar creature of the alcove who is always ready to claim that he can drop the right word into the right ear at the right moment.

It was Cassius, discussing ways and means with Brutus in his orchard, who first raised the question: What if Caesar should decide not to attend the meeting of the senate?

> For he is superstitious grown of late,
> Quite from the main opinion he held once
> Of fantasy, of dreams, and ceremonies:
> It may be, these apparent prodigies,
> The unaccustom'd terror of this night,
> And the persuasion of his augurers,
> May hold him from the Capitol to-day.

Decius jumps at the occasion. This is just his line of country:

> Never fear that: if he be so resolved,
> I can o'ersway him; for he loves to hear
> That unicorns may be betray'd with trees,
> And bears with glasses, elephants with holes,
> Lions with toils, and men with flatterers;
>
> Let me work;
> For I can give his humour the true bent,
> And I will bring him to the Capitol.

He catches Caesar in one of his majestic attitudes:

> DECIUS: Caesar, all hail! good morrow, worthy Caesar:
> I come to fetch you to the senate-house.

> CAESAR: And you are come in very happy time,
> To bear my greeting to the senators,
> And tell them that I will not come to-day:
> Cannot, is false, and that I dare not, falser:
> I will not come to-day: tell them so, Decius.
> CALPURNIA: Say he is sick.
> CAESAR: Shall Caesar send a lie?
> Have I in conquest stretch'd mine arm so far,
> To be afeard to tell greybeards the truth?
> Decius, go tell them Caesar will not come.

Decius is outwardly respectful but inwardly amused. With deference he suggests that Caesar's message may be found ridiculous:

> Most mighty Caesar, let me know some cause,
> Lest I be laugh'd at when I tell them so.

Caesar condescends to explain. Calpurnia has dreamed that his statue spouted blood and that many lusty Romans came smiling and bathed their hands in it. Decius, not in the least deceived by Caesar's pretence that he is staying at home to please his wife, sets out to show that the dream is not a bad but a good omen:

> This dream is all amiss interpreted;
> It was a vision fair and fortunate:
> Your statue spouting blood in many pipes,
> In which so many smiling Romans bathed,
> Signifies that from you great Rome shall suck
> Reviving blood, and that great men shall press
> For tinctures, stains, relics, and cognizance.
> This by Calpurnia's dream is signified.

Caesar accepts this interpretation and Decius presses his advantage. He speaks now to the small Caesar whom he claims to know so well. He can address this Caesar in a spirit of mockery which he hardly troubles to conceal—promise him a bauble, declare openly that people may laugh at him or throw doubt upon his courage:

> The senate have concluded
> To give this day a crown to mighty Caesar.
> If you shall send them word you will not come,
> Their minds may change. Besides, it were a mock
> Apt to be render'd, for some one to say

'Break up the senate till another time,
When Caesar's wife shall meet with better dreams.'
If Caesar hide himself, shall not they whisper
'Lo, Caesar is afraid'?

Decius has successfully performed his mission and Caesar makes ready to accompany him. At this moment Brutus enters with the conspirators. The short passage in which Caesar greets them brings him suddenly to life again. He has a word for everyone and it is the right word. This is the real Caesar, courteous and accessible, who has it in him to win hearts and to command respect:

> Caius Ligarius,
> Caesar was ne'er so much your enemy
> As that same ague which has made you lean.

> See! Antony, that revels long o'nights,
> Is notwithstanding up. Good morrow, Antony.

> Bid them prepare within:
> I am to blame to be thus waited for.
> Now, Cinna; now, Metellus; what, Trebonius!
> I have an hour's talk in store for you;
> Remember that you call on me to-day:
> Be near me, that I may remember you.

The scene concludes with Caesar's invitation to take wine with him.

Henceforth Caesar, the man, is lost in Caesar's effigy. To Artemidorus, who intercepts him on his way to the senate-house and entreats him to read first a scroll that touches him nearly, he grandly replies: 'What touches us ourself shall be last served.' To Metellus Cimber, who petitions on his knees that his banished brother may be recalled, he yet more grandly answers:

> I must prevent thee, Cimber.
> These couchings and these lowly courtesies
> Might fire the blood of ordinary men,
> And turn pre-ordinance and first decree
> Into the law of children. Be not fond,
> To think that Caesar bears such rebel blood
> That will be thaw'd from the true quality
> With that which melteth fools; I mean, sweet words,
> Low crookèd court'sies and base spaniel-fawning.

Brutus and Casca join in Cimber's petition and Caesar pays his last egregious tribute to Caesar:

> But I am constant as the northern star,
> Of whose true-fix'd and resting quality
> There is no fellow in the firmament.
> The skies are painted with unnumber'd sparks,
> They are all fire and every one doth shine,
> But there's but one in all doth hold his place:
> So, in the world; 'tis furnish'd well with men,
> And men are flesh and blood, and apprehensive;
> Yet in the number I do know but one
> That unassailable holds on his rank,
> Unshaked of motion.

Caesar's most famous observation in this scene has, however, yet to be heard. It has a curious history. But for a celebrated gibe at Shakespeare for writing it, the line would have been lost to posterity. A contemporary critic, in declaring it to be nonsense, preserved the true reading of the text.

Here a longer parenthesis than usual is justified. Ben Jonson, for he, of course, was the critic who performed this service for us, let slip his censure at the end of a famous paragraph in the 'Discoveries':

'Many times he (Shakespeare) fell into those things could not escape laughter: as when, in the person of Caesar, one speaking to him, "Caesar, thou dost me wrong": he replied, "Caesar did never wrong but with just cause", and such like, which were ridiculous.'

Jonson was not quoting from an imperfect memory at random. He was obviously citing an instance well known to his readers and at which he had frequently mocked in conversation with his friends.

And so we come to the heart of this small mystery. The words quoted by Jonson are nowhere to be found in any printed text of the play. The corresponding passage in the folio text, in which Caesar finally rejects the appeal of Metellus Cimber for the recall of his brother, contains neither Cimber's protest, 'Caesar, thou dost me wrong,' nor Caesar's reply, 'Caesar did never wrong but with just cause.' The folio text gives to Caesar at the conclusion of the speech in which he rejects Cimber's appeal a comparatively tame remark which, in the circumstances, is dramatically irrelevant:

> Know, Caesar doth not wrong, nor without cause
> Will he be satisfied.

There can be no reasonable doubt of the true reading. Jonson's version is dramatic, significant and in character. The folio version is insipid, superfluous and out of character not only with Shakespeare's presentation of Caesar as a whole but with the particular scene which is taking place. Caesar has just insisted that nothing will move him from his purpose. Was he likely to conclude upon a non-sequitur which suggests that he might be satisfied if cause were shown?

Jonson has been accused by some critics of deliberately misreporting his friend in order to hold him up to ridicule or of carelessly misquoting the words from memory. Others, like Gifford, accept Jonson's words as correct but defend them half-heartedly. Gifford trounces the folio reading in which, he says, there is no congruity, the poetry being as 'mean as the sense', but he says of Jonson's version: 'The fact seems to be that this verse, which closely borders on absurdity without being absolutely absurd, escaped the poet in the heat of composition and, being unluckily one of those quaint slips which are readily remembered, became a jocular and familiar phrase of the day.'

But what are we to say of the devoted editors of the first folio who, because this quaint slip had become a jocular and familiar phrase of the day, piously amended it so that posterity might not poke fun at their master? Had it not been for Jonson's faithful record of what he actually heard in the theatre, the folio rendering would have stood without a rival and one of the most natural and telling lines of the tragedy would have been lost forever—as who knows how many have not been lost in other plays.

Caesar did never wrong but with just cause—it is Shakespeare's finishing touch to the portrait of a dictator. It is the last, if it be not also the first, assumption of the man who lives for power that the wrong he does is right. So simple and constant a trait of the man who esteems himself a leader needs no elucidation. Shakespeare's line is not one of those quaint slips of disorderly genius with which he is so often credited. Still less is it in any way absurd, except to minds grown mad with method.

Ave et vale Caesar! We take farewell of his human infirmities and of the false grandeur into which he was betrayed. Henceforth we have to do with that other Caesar, mourned by Antony:

> Thou art the ruins of the noblest man
> That ever livèd in the tide of times;

who still lives in the spirit and who will determine the further progress of the tragedy. The last two acts of the play depict the inexorable fulfilment of Antony's prophetic oration over his body in the senate-house:

> Domestic fury and fierce civil strife
> Shall cumber all the parts of Italy;
> Blood and destruction shall be so in use,
> And dreadful objects so familiar,
> That mothers shall but smile when they behold
> Their infants quarter'd with the hands of war;
> All pity choked with custom of fell deeds:
> And Caesar's spirit, ranging for revenge,
> With Atè by his side come hot from hell,
> Shall in these confines with a monarch's voice
> Cry 'Havoc', and let slip the dogs of war.

Antony here announces the dominant theme of the play and exhibits Caesar as a link between the two sections.

It is a diminished world into which Shakespeare takes us after the death of Caesar. He sweeps aside the curtain and there before us, in Rome which has lost her master, sits a group of ruffians dictating who shall live, who shall be spared, how Caesar's testament shall be dishonoured and the people defrauded:

> ANTONY: These many, then, shall die; their names are prick'd.
> OCTAVIUS: Your brother, too, must die; consent you, Lepidus?
> LEPIDUS: I do consent.
> OCTAVIUS: Prick him down, Antony.
> LEPIDUS: Upon condition Publius shall not live,
>   Who is your sister's son, Mark Antony.
> ANTONY: He shall not live; look, with a spot I damn him.

The final touch to this engaging miniature—it is all done in just over a dozen lines—is Antony's exuberant description of his partner Lepidus as a mere tool, to be discarded as soon as he ceases to be of service:

> And though we lay these honours on this man,
> To ease ourselves of divers slanderous loads,
> He shall but bear them as the ass bears gold,
> To groan and sweat under the business,
> Either led or driven, as we point the way;
> And having brought our treasure where we will,
> Then take we down his load, and turn him off,
> Like to the empty ass, to shake his ears,
> And graze in commons.

It is the epitome of a diplomatic scene to be constantly re-enacted in the councils of Europe. It is startlingly abrupt, amazingly concise; and yet in no way hustles the spectator. We have more than once, in the analysis of certain episodes of the play, been struck with the astonishing amount of character and incident packed into a little room. It is, indeed, the peculiar quality of Shakespeare's style in this tragedy—and all his great plays have their own peculiar quality of style—to convey throughout a sense of spaciousness and leisure, of a smooth simplicity and classic ease, of calm sequence and tranquil performance and yet, at the same time, to exhibit a tenseness and brevity of utterance nowhere else surpassed by its author. We noted at the start of the play how the contrasted characters of Brutus and Cassius, the theme of the play and the initial stages of the action were all conveyed in a single scene, in which Cassius could yet find time for the delivery of two elaborate set speeches to give it colour and deliberation. The two opening scenes of the second part of the play show the same economy of speech relieved by the same unhurried pauses for broader and more opulent effects. In the first short scene of Act IV we have a complete and startling presentment of Rome which has lost her Caesar and, lest the spectator should be stunned with this sudden impact, we have also Antony's vivid and leisurely description of Lepidus as a 'slight, unmeritable man, meet to be sent on errands'.

In the second scene of the Act we are as swiftly immersed in the

famous quarrel between Brutus and Cassius. Shakespeare handles this
episode with the same blend of compactness and freedom. Scarcely
have we recovered from the abrupt entrance of Cassius:

> Most noble brother, you have done me wrong!

when we find ourselves carried at ease upon the full tide of his contention with Brutus in impetuous but majestic verse that destroys all
sense of hurry or undue compression. Shakespeare, in the first scene of
Act IV, shows us the miserable consequences of Caesar's death so far
as it affects one party in the state. In the second scene of the Act he
shows us its consequences for the other party. Cassius and Brutus,
who combined to kill Caesar and to set the Romans free, are discovered after the event to be mutually angry and suspicious. They
are men distracted. Their nerves are on edge. These conspirators,
whose slaying of Caesar was to be a binding sacrament, exchange
retorts which, stripped of their moral implications and nobility of
phrase, reduce them to the level of two children wrangling for pre-
cedence:

> CASSIUS: I am a soldier, I,
> Older in practice, abler than yourself,
> To make conditions.
> BRUTUS: Go to; you are not, Cassius.
> CASSIUS: I am.
> BRUTUS: I say you are not.

Again:

> CASSIUS: When Caesar lived, he durst not thus have moved me.
> BRUTUS: Peace, peace! you durst not so have tempted him.
> CASSIUS: I durst not!
> BRUTUS: No.
> CASSIUS: What, durst not tempt him?
> BRUTUS: For your life you durst not.

To such a level have these noble Romans been reduced. We recall
the words of Antony in the market-place: *Then you and I and all of us
fell down.* The death of Caesar has so far debased the grandeur that
was Rome that her destiny is now to be decided in a contest between
Antony, a merciless adventurer, already false to one of his colleagues,

and Brutus, who before our eyes loses control of his mind and temper. With Antony is Octavius, who trusts nobody:

> And some that smile have in their hearts, I fear,
> Millions of mischiefs;

while with Brutus is Cassius, who dissolves in weak tears and resorts to the pitiful expedient of offering his friend and partner his naked breast and a dagger.

The scene of the quarrel is nevertheless, in its human substance, a noble one. That it is childishly conducted only makes it the more poignant.

The dispute opens with an abrupt statement of the issue. Brutus has condemned one of his adherents for taking bribes. Cassius has written a letter asking that the offence be overlooked. Brutus takes up the challenge:

> BRUTUS: You wrong'd yourself to write in such a case.
> CASSIUS: In such a time as this it is not meet
>   That every nice offence should bear his comment.
> BRUTUS: Let me tell you, Cassius, you yourself
>   Are much condemn'd to have an itching palm.

An itching palm?' cries Cassius and the quarrel is in full spate Brutus alternately raises it to the level of a contest of principle:

> Remember March, the ides of March remember:
> Did not great Julius bleed for justice' sake?
> What villain touch'd his body, that did stab,
> And not for justice? What! shall one of us,
> That struck the foremost man of all this world,
> But for supporting robbers, shall we now
> Contaminate our fingers with base bribes,
> And sell the mighty space of our large honours
> For so much trash as may be graspèd thus?
> I'd rather be a dog, and bay the moon,
> Than such a Roman;

and lowers it to the level of a slanging match:

> Go show your slaves how choleric you are,
> And make your bondmen tremble. Must I budge?

> Must I observe you? must I stand and crouch
> Under your testy humour? By the gods,
> You shall digest the venom of your spleen,
> Though it do split you; for, from this day forth,
> I'll use you for my mirth, yea, for my laughter,
> When you are waspish.

Brutus, as so often before, but with a dramatic irony more penetrating than on any previous occasion, reveals himself as a moralist who shrinks from the sordid expedients of political life but who is nevertheless driven to claim the advantages derived from them. He lectures Cassius for raising money and delivers a speech expressing high distaste for the methods by which such money is obtained. He then hotly complains that Cassius has refused to send him part of the proceeds, coupling this complaint with a statement that he could never descend so low as to collect it for himself:

> I did send to you
> For certain sums of gold, which you denied me;
> For I can raise no money by vile means:
> By heaven, I had rather coin my heart,
> And drop my blood for drachmas, than to wring
> From the hard hands of peasants their vile trash
> By any indirection.

The political philosopher's indictment of extortion is accompanied by a pressing request to go shares.

Brutus is still the political moralist who recoils from the realities of political leadership. He is likewise, here as always, the gentle Brutus. He maintains his attitude of conscious rectitude to the last; but, once tempers are cooled, his natural generosity of mind and his genuine personal affection for Cassius disarms him completely:

> Be angry when you will, it shall have scope;
> Do what you will, dishonour shall be humour.
> O Cassius! you are yokèd with a lamb
> That carries anger as the flint bears fire,
> Who, much enforcèd, shows a hasty spark,
> And straight is cold again.

The quarrel ends on both sides in a reconciliation of two friends, the dearer for having fallen out:

CASSIUS: Has Cassius liv'd
                  To be but mirth and laughter to his Brutus,
                  When grief and blood ill-temper'd vexeth him?
BRUTUS: When I spoke that, I was ill-temper'd too.
CASSIUS: Do you confess so much? Give me your hand.
BRUTUS: And my heart too.
CASSIUS: O Brutus!
BRUTUS: What's the matter?
CASSIUS: Have you not love enough to bear with me,
                  When that rash humour which my mother gave me
                  Makes me forgetful?
BRUTUS: Yes, Cassius; and, from henceforth,
                  When you are over-earnest with your Brutus,
                  He'll think your mother chides, and leave you so.

This confession of ill-temper, wrung from the heart of Brutus, is so startling, on the lips of such a man, that Cassius, in the full tide of his emotion, is struck with an almost incredulous wonder: 'Do *you* confess so much?'

The behaviour of Cassius in this scene needs to be more closely considered. So far, he has figured as the lean and hungry Cassius who thinks too much, the man who killed Caesar because he lacked advancement, the wary realist who urged that Antony also should be slain. This man is now presented as a man of warm feeling:

> For Cassius is aweary of the world;
> Hated by one he loves; braved by his brother;
> Check'd like a bondman; all his faults observed,
> Set in a note-book, learn'd, and conn'd by rote,
> To cast into my teeth. O, I could weep
> My spirit from mine eyes!

There is here a moving contrast, but it is not a contradiction. In the first three Acts Cassius, who plotted Caesar's death from simple envy, is exhibited as a foil to Brutus, who was induced to lead the conspiracy by an appeal to principle. In their quarrel Brutus still strikes and maintains the moral attitude and Cassius is still the practical man of affairs. But now Shakespeare, with a dramatic propriety which was not possible before, can come nearer the heart of his creature. The envy that drove Cassius to kill Caesar was that of a sensitive man, easily moved, conscious of his abilities and snubbed by authority. Such a man is by nature impulsive as well as wary, quick in feeling and temper as well as shrewd, as liable to fall into extremes of hope and despair in time of action as to show courage and resource in time of council and preparation. It will be recalled that in the scene immediately preceding Caesar's assassination, when the conspirators fear that Popilius has discovered their enterprise and may betray them to Caesar, it was Cassius, the man of affairs, whose presence of mind was shaken and not Brutus, the man of ideas. It was Cassius who exclaimed 'Brutus, what shall be done?' It was Cassius who cried out that he was ready to slay himself if they should be 'prevented'. These early glimpses of the human side of Cassius— his emotional instability, his nervous reaction to events, an intensity of feeling bordering on hysteria—prepare us for the man who, de- spite his political foresight and resolution, is easily stirred to anger, despondency, affection, doubt or assurance.

This scene between Brutus and Cassius has been almost universally admired. Rymer, who likened it to 'two drunken Hectors huffing and swaggering for a two-penny reckoning', stands almost alone. Dryden compares Shakespeare's treatment of the quarrel between Brutus and Cassius with the handling by Euripides of the quarrel between Menelaus and Agamemnon and finds it incomparably better done. Shakespeare's contemporary audience received it with so much applause that it is specially mentioned in the commendatory verses by Digges printed in the first folio and with a modern audience it has never been known to miss its mark. Dr. Johnson, who finds the tragedy on the whole 'somewhat cold and unaffecting' and was 'never strongly agitated in perusing it', nevertheless declares that 'the contention and reconcilement of Brutus and Cassius is universally celebrated' and includes it among the particular passages which 'de- serve regard'. Coleridge, giving no reason for his outburst, once startled an audience assembled to hear him lecture by exclaiming: 'I know no part of Shakespeare that more impresses on me the belief of his genius being superhuman than this scene between Brutus and Cassius', while in our own time Professor Bradley, though he finds the episode dramatically unnecessary and contends that its removal would not affect the sequence of events, not only pays a special tribute to this 'famous and wonderful scene', but is driven to consider why it has such power.

We are faced with a strange paradox in the treatment of this scene by Shakespeare's editors and critics. Most of them confess that they are deeply moved and impressed by it. Yet some declare it to be superfluous; some dismiss it, along with the rest of the second part of the play, as an anti-climax to the first part; some find it inconsistent with the characters as previously presented.

Bradley discusses its effect in general terms:

'In this section of a tragedy Shakespeare often appeals to an emotion different from any of those excited by the first half of the play and so provides novelty and generally relief. As a rule this emotion is pathetic; and the pathos is not terrible or lacerating, but, even if painful, is accompanied by a sense of beauty and by an outflow of admiration and affection which come with inexpressible sweetness after the tension of the crisis.'

This is an admirable description of the feeling evoked by the scene and it accounts for the charm which it invariably exercises on the spectator. Bradley's explanation, however, consigns the episode to a secondary place in the tragedy and thus associates him with those who regard the second part of the play as a decline from the first. For him the episode comes as a release from tension and a pathetic interlude.

Is this really its place and function? Does such a reading explain why even the most careless spectator is caught and held? And does it account for that abrupt exclamation of Coleridge, which could only be justified if the scene were a climax such as Shakespeare alone could achieve?

Why is it that audiences, from generation to generation, have left the theatre with this particular passage so vivid in their minds? Why does this episode of the two men quarrelling like children in the tent of Brutus stand out so brightly from the compact scenes of suspense which precede the assassination, the dramatic climax of Caesar's death, the splendour and excitement of Antony's oration. Can the profound effect of this incident on the mind be explained if, with Bradley, we regard it as dramatically irrelevant?

Must we not, on the contrary, accept it as profoundly essential

c

to the progress of the tragedy? More than that. Shakespeare, in his political plays, presents political situations and characters, but his supreme interest is always in the private person. The essential business of his political plays is to show how the private person comes to terms with his political duties, offices or ambitions, and the dramatic climax is always to be found when the protagonists come before us stripped of their public pretensions. So far we have had to do with Brutus and Cassius as noble Romans committed to a political enterprise. It is true that we have had notable glimpses of their private minds. But we are to know them more intimately yet and nothing could be more telling than the device which Shakespeare has adopted for this further revelation. In order to enforce its intimacy he clears the stage. Cassius begins to utter his grievances in company, but Brutus interrupts him: •

> Before the eyes of both our armies here,
> Which should perceive nothing but love from us,
> Let us not wrangle: bid them move away;
> Then in my tent, Cassius, enlarge your griefs.

The two leaders thus put off their public characters. Brutus, the stoic moralist and man of preconceived ideas, is to unmask. We are to see him deeply moved by the simplest of human feelings. He is to quarrel with his friend and make it up under the stress of an emotion which compels him in the end even to overlook the cause of his displeasure and bury all unkindness in a cup of wine. Cassius, the political leader who drove Brutus to the killing of Caesar and would have killed Antony as well, is to be revealed in a mood which levels him with the least sophisticated of men, to appear simply as one who loves his friend, acknowledges his rash humour and cannot drink too much of Brutus' love. The effect of this abrupt descent from the political to the human plane of experience is poignant in the extreme. It accounts for the admiration expressed by such a critic as Coleridge and for the misprision excited in the handful of critics who resent what they regard as a lapse from the high dignity of the tragic argument. Incidentally it secures for Brutus and Cassius, despite the pitiful ruin of their enterprise and the yet more pitiful collapse of their integrity of mind and purpose, a sympathy which illumines all the concluding scenes of the tragedy. It introduces, at exactly the right moment, that outflow of admiration and affection in which Bradley finds a pathos and a sense of beauty not hitherto awakened. Could there be a more supreme tribute to the scene, not as a dramatic irrelevance, but as an essential climax?

The element of pathos is heightened to a supreme level of tenderness by the passage in which Brutus, towards the end of the quarrel, announces the death of Portia:

CASSIUS: I did not think you could have been so angry.
BRUTUS: O Cassius! I am sick of many griefs.
CASSIUS: Of your philosophy you make no use,
        If you give place to accidental evils.
BRUTUS: No man bears sorrow better. Portia is dead.
CASSIUS: Ha! Portia!
BRUTUS: She is dead.
CASSIUS: How 'scaped I killing when I cross'd you so?
        O insupportable and touching loss!

The effect upon us of this whole episode is prolonged and enhanced by the fact that it is Cassius and not Brutus who remains the more affected by it at the close. It lingers in his mind long after Brutus has affected to regard it as a chapter closed. Brutus turns abruptly to business, but Cassius murmurs apart: 'Portia, art thou gone?' Brutus calls him to order: 'No more, I pray you'; and when Brutus bids Cassius good-night, it is Cassius whose heart is still full and flowing:

           O my dear brother!
This was an ill beginning of the night:
Never come such division 'tween our souls!
Let it not, Brutus.

We come now to another of those incidents in which Shakespeare, working at full pressure, has puzzled many of his critics to such bad purpose that they have thrown suspicion on the text of his play or attributed what Shakespeare intended to sheer carelessness or even to a lapse of memory. Upon the termination of the quarrel Titinius and Messala come to the tent and a brief council of war is held. Messala brings messages from Rome, including an announcement that Portia has killed herself. Brutus receives these

tidings as though they were new to him and, in his public character
as a stoic, affects to be quite unmoved:

> BRUTUS: Why, farewell, Portia. We must die, Messala:
> With meditating that she must die once,
> I have the patience to endure it now.
>
> MESSALA: Even so great men great losses should endure.
>
> CASSIUS: I have as much of this in art as you,
> But yet my nature could not bear it so.
>
> BRUTUS: Well, to our work alive. What do you think
> Of marching to Philippi presently?

This evasion of Brutus, true to his assumed character as a public
man, is equally true to his natural disposition. The death of Portia is
for the gentle Brutus a wound so great that he could not speak of it
even to Cassius till Cassius was his friend again. Naturally he shrinks
from any reference to the matter at a public meeting. To brush aside
the grievous tidings comes as naturally to the bereaved husband as to
the general who must cut a heroic figure among his captains. The
whole incident is perfectly in character. Remember how Brutus in
his orchard exhorted his fellow conspirators to 'bear it as our Roman
actors do'. Now again he plays a comedy in the high Roman fashion
to the admiration of Messala and to the indignation of commentators
who complain that his conduct is unworthy. Is it not monstrous that
the noble Brutus, to put it bluntly, should tell a lie in order to increase his reputation as a philosopher?

This particular lie, however, is a revelation of essential truth.
Brutus may be playing a part, but it is one which springs from the
fundamental lie in his character, the lie that impels him to substitute
a public figure for the natural man, that requires him to kill Caesar in
order to live up to assumed principles, that drives him to play the
statesman when he has no mind or quality for the vocation, that
prompts him to offer reasons to a mob with which he has no common ground of temper or understanding—the lie that sooner or later
is imposed on any idealist who enters public life and must use means
which he despises to achieve ends which have no true bearing on the
political realities about him.

Shakespeare, having given us a glimpse of the man Brutus might

so happily have been, now resumes his inexorable exposure of the
public person whose faults and virtues alike unfit him for political
leadership. In the council of war at Sardis, Brutus overrides Cassius
and decides to meet the enemy at Philippi. He has already made
every possible mistake as a politician; now he blunders as a general.
Cassius accepts his decision, but is unconvinced. Octavius hears of it
with cold satisfaction:

> Now, Antony, our hopes are answerèd:
> You said the enemy would not come down,
> But keep the hills and upper regions;
> It proves not so; their battles are at hand;

and Cassius, as the armies make ready to fight, reminds his friend,
Messala, that he yielded to Brutus in this matter against his better
judgment:

> Be thou my witness that against my will,
> As Pompey was, am I compell'd to set
> Upon one battle all our liberties.

Brutus characteristically supports his decision with a general observation upon human life:

> There is a tide in the affairs of men,
> Which, taken at the flood, leads on to fortune;
> Omitted, all the voyage of their life
> Is bound in shallows and in miseries.
> On such a full sea are we now afloat;
> And we must take the current when it serves,
> Or lose our ventures.

The determining motive behind this blunder of Brutus and its easy
acceptance by Cassius lies in the state of mind in which they take the
field. Antony, with his quick insight, understands at once why they
are seeking battle:

> Tut! I am in their bosoms, and I know
> Wherefore they do it: they could be content
> To visit other places; and come down

> With fearful bravery, thinking by this face
> To fasten in our thoughts that they have courage;
> But 'tis not so.

Brutus and Cassius are weary and desperate men and they desire a
swift conclusion. They feel in their bones that their cause is already
lost and, in their last conversation together, these generals, who are
staking everything on a fight where the military chances are even,
discuss the moral propriety of suicide! Each of them gropes in a
shattered world where it is no longer possible to hold fast to the
principles which they have hitherto professed. Cassius, who formerly
held with Epicurus that omens were not to be trusted, recounts how
two mighty eagles had accompanied his soldiers to Philippi:

> This morning are they fled away and gone;
> And in their stead do ravens, crows, and kites,
> Fly o'er our heads, and downward look on us,
> As we were sickly prey.

Brutus, whose philosophy prompts him to condemn suicide as
'cowardly and vile', is moved to assure Cassius that he 'bears too
great a mind' to be taken alive. Their minds are dark with foreboding
and perplexed in the extreme. Nothing is clear and certain:

> But it sufficeth that the day will end,
> And then the end is known.

Time and fate are in the ascendent. The words 'day' and 'end' recur
almost compulsively:

> But this same day
> Must end that work the ides of March begun.

We have yet to bring on to the stage the character that dominates
all these later scenes. Caesar is never for a moment absent or forgotten. He lurks in all that Brutus and Cassius say or do. Even in the
heat of their quarrel they remember Caesar constantly. Cassius offering his heart to Brutus exclaims: 'Strike as thou didst at Caesar.'
Brutus when Cassius cries: 'When Caesar lived, he durst not thus
have moved me,' retorts that Cassius 'durst not so have tempted him'.
These references betray the 'something settled, on which imagination sits on brood', and they prepare us for the scene in which the
spirit that haunts them both comes before Brutus as a monstrous

apparition. It is a visible ghost that visits Brutus in his tent, but note how indefinite and subjective it is, taking shape as though it were an emanation from the distracted conscience of the sufferer:

BRUTUS: Art thou any thing?
 Art thou some god, some angel, or some devil,
 That mak'st my blood cold and my hair to stare?
 Speak to me what thou art.
GHOST: Thy evil spirit, Brutus.
BRUTUS: Why com'st thou?
 GHOST: To tell thee thou shalt see me at Philippi.
BRUTUS: Well; then I shall see thee again?
 GHOST: Ay, at Philippi.
BRUTUS: Why, I will see thee at Philippi, then. (*Exit* GHOST.)
 Now I have taken heart, thou vanishest.

This Caesar, who intrudes into the quarrel between Brutus and Cassius and visits Brutus in his tent, stands likewise in the forefront of the parley between the rival commanders and is thereafter ubiquitous. Antony, taunting Brutus and Cassius, calls back to life the dead Caesar; Octavius draws his sword to avenge Caesar's three-and-thirty wounds. Cassius bids Pindarus slay him with the sword that 'ran through Caesar's bowels', and dying he gasps out:

     Caesar, thou art revenged,
  Even with the sword that kill'd thee.

Brutus, over the bodies of Cassius and Titinius, declares:

  O Julius Caesar, thou art mighty yet!
  Thy spirit walks abroad, and turns our swords
  In our own proper entrails.

It is Caesar who beckons to self-slaughter the man who held it 'cowardly and vile, for fear of what might fall, so to prevent the time of life'. Brutus calls Volumnius to his side:

BRUTUS: Come hither, good Volumnius; list a word.
VOLUMNIUS: What says my lord?
BRUTUS: Why, this, Volumnius:
 The ghost of Caesar hath appear'd to me
 Two several times by night: at Sardis once
 And, this last night, here in Philippi fields:
 I know my hour is come.

VOLUMNIUS: Not so, my lord.
  BRUTUS: Nay, I am sure it is, Volumnius.
          Thou seest the world, Volumnius, how it goes;
          Our enemies have beat us to the pit:
          It is more worthy to leap in ourselves,
          Than tarry till they push us.

And the last words of Brutus declare the theme of the tragedy in a final cadence:

               Caesar, now be still:
     I kill'd not thee with half so good a will.

The battle at Philippi is all clamour and confusion. Brutus, as a leader, is again at fault:

     O Cassius! Brutus gave the word too early;
     Who, having some advantage on Octavius,
     Took it too eagerly: his soldiers fell to spoil,
     Whilst we by Antony are all enclosed;

and Cassius, mistaking the glad reception of Titinius by his friends for capture by his enemies, kills himself before the fight is lost. Distraction in the field presents visibly the distraction in the minds of the conspirators.

Notwithstanding all this, the impression left on the spectator by the last gestures of these unhappy men is one of compassion and high dignity. There is here no common butchery. These souls are nobly hunted. The incidents throughout the second part of the play would be but mean and pitiful, if it were not for the touches whereby Shakespeare constantly lifts his heroes to the level of his theme. The quarrel between Brutus and Cassius is redeemed for tragedy by the death of Portia. The scene in which Caesar's ghost comes before Brutus, the conspirator, as his evil spirit is preceded by a scene in which we are reminded most touchingly of the essential qualities of Brutus, the man. Observe the exquisite courtesy with which he bids Varro and Claudius lie down in his tent; his tender concern for the boy Lucius, nodding over his instrument; his apology to Lucius for asking him to play and for having accused him of mislaying the book which he had forgetfully slipped into his pocket—the book itself 'turned down where I left reading'. Note especially how these

touches, which endear Brutus to our hearts, continue to mark him as
unfitted for the part he has been called upon to play. In this serene
and lovely interlude between an unseemly brawl and a decisive
battle, Shakespeare offers us a moment of repose, but he sweetens our
emotions without relaxing his stern insistence upon the theme of his
tragedy. For what sort of general is this, who in a few hours' time
must take the field but who calls for music and reads a book by
candlelight?

The heartbreaking futility of the battle scenes is relieved by the
same sure hand with noble and affecting incidents. The mutual farewells of Brutus and Cassius have an elegiac quality:

> And whether we shall meet again I know not.
> Therefore our everlasting farewell take:
> For ever, and for ever, farewell, Cassius!
> If we do meet again, why, we shall smile;
> If not, why then, this parting was well made.

One lovely touch succeeds another. Titinius crowns his dead master,
Cassius, with the garland of victory. Brutus mourns his friend:

> The last of all the Romans, fare thee well!
> It is impossible that ever Rome
> Should breed thy fellow. Friends, I owe more tears
> To this dead man than you shall see me pay.
> I shall find time, Cassius, I shall find time.

These passages, which in their fall and substance lie somewhere
between epic and elegy, bring us to the half-dozen lines in which
Brutus accepts his fate with a tired and wistful resignation, from
which, however, there emerges, in sudden splendour, a proud assurance that he wins more glory in defeat than his enemies in victory.
The weariness is of the man who has failed in his political purpose;
the assurance is of the man who can still be happy in the loyalty of
his friends, sure of his moral triumph after expiation, able to perceive in a bright flash of self-knowledge, attained through defeat and
suffering, that nothing remains but to pay the forfeit and abide the
charity of ages yet unborn:

> My heart doth joy that yet, in all my life,
> I found no man but he was true to me.

> I shall have glory by this losing day,
> More than Octavius and Mark Antony
> By this vile conquest shall attain unto.
> So fare you well at once; for Brutus' tongue
> Hath almost ended his life's history:
> Night hangs upon mine eyes; my bones would rest,
> That have but labour'd to attain this hour.

It is Antony, with his instinctive grasp of human values, who pronounces the final verdict:

> This was the noblest Roman of them all;
> All the conspirators save only he
> Did that they did in envy of great Caesar;
> He only, in a general honest thought
> And common good to all, made one of them.
> His life was gentle, and the elements
> So mix'd in him that Nature might stand up
> And say to all the world, 'This was a man!'

The political character of Brutus is presented by Shakespeare in perpetual contrast with other persons of the play. Cassius, Antony, Caesar and the Roman crowd are in turn his foils! The commentator is accordingly drawn beyond the limits of a single portrait and finds at the close that, in handling Brutus, he has been driven to deal as faithfully with all the rest.

He finds also that he has quoted or examined virtually every passage of note in the tragedy and he is tempted to wonder how and why this has happened.

The reason lies perhaps in the texture and style of the composition. There is something almost symphonic in its movement and structure. The themes are stated and developed. Each episode looks back to its origin and forward to an offshoot or repetition in another key. The sequences are in themselves musical, in their alternation of compact and rhythmic phrases with flowing passages in the lyric mood. It possibly drives the comparison too hard to find in this tragedy the three parts of a symphonic movement—statement, development and recapitulation. Yet a case could be made. In Acts I and II the Brutus-Cassius subject is prominently stated; the Antony-Caesar subject is subsidiary. In Act III this material is developed in the assassination of

Caesar and in Antony's oration, the poet adopting the familiar musical device of giving in the development section unexpected prominence to his secondary subject. In Acts IV and V there is a recapitulation of the earlier material in the light of all that has gone before, or, as the musician would say, heard in a different key. Brutus in his tent recalls Brutus in his orchard. There is a symmetry between the two passages. Brutus quarrelling with Cassius in Act IV and haunted to distraction by Caesar's spirit recalls Brutus listening to Cassius in Act I with one ear turned to the Capitol where Caesar, as he fears may be crowned.

The musical analogy, though it may easily be pressed too far in discussing the general structure of the play, is felt consciously by any musically minded listener who hears the initial themes of the tragedy—Brutus, the conspirator; gentle Brutus; Brutus at war with himself; politic Cassius; the gamesome Antony; mighty Caesar. They run through the play, growing in volume and complexity, retaining their identity in an endless variety of moods and forms. There is scarcely a line in this play which does not create echoes in the mind of something past or arouse anticipation of something which is yet to come. Thus the critic, who lingers upon a single phrase, soon finds himself committed to a close study of the composition as a whole.

That a tragedy by Shakespeare should in its form and rhythm play upon the mind in much the same way as a musical symphony only confirms the opinion expressed in some fashion or other by every critic who looks beyond a merely rational foundation for music, poetry and the plastic arts: namely, that genius sees and grasps by intuition a reality which lies behind the phenomena which furnish its raw material.

No adequate psychological explanation of the effect upon the mind of great music has yet been offered which does not postulate this direct access of the composer to reality, and the poet shares it with the musician in so far as his poetry reaches beyond the limits of plain speaking and common observation. When Coleridge suddenly cries out at a point in the tragedy that Shakespeare is superhuman, he obviously feels and means much more than that the dramatist has effectively presented a given dramatic situation, that his characters are true to life, that the words are apt and the action finely conducted. The emotion which moves Coleridge to such an exclamation (which, significantly, he does not justify on any purely literary or dramatic grounds) is in quality similar to that aroused in those who, listening to great music, become abruptly aware of something that transcends experience, something which could never have been expressed by merely taking thought; that here is a beauty which has grown from hidden roots. And Coleridge would never have been so deeply moved by that single incident in the tragedy if he had not, consciously or unconsciously, been aware of echoes and overtones in the notes struck by the poet in that place; of their relation to all that preceded them; of the vital process which had brought him to just that plane of feeling at just that particular moment. He is, in fact, responding as a listener responds to a musical figure or modulation in which the genius of the composer announces itself with an almost intolerable splendour.

II

RICHARD OF GLOUCESTER

THERE have been brief Augustan interludes in the history of the world when it might have seemed a libel upon our civilisation to present Richard Crookback as a political character. The bloody dog is dead. Such was his epitaph. Richard achieved political eminence by killing—or, as we have recently learned to say, by liquidating—those who stood in his way. He secured the support of his principal confederates by involving them in his own sinister performances and promising them a share of the loot. He obtained the consent of his subjects by a carefully rehearsed and grotesque parody of a popular election. On coming to power he destroyed the man who had helped him half way to the crown and drove into rebellion the man who had put it on his head. To include such a person in a gallery of political portraits seems a little hard upon a deserving section of the community remarkable not so long ago for nothing worse than what Dr. Johnson described as a 'strong, natural, sterling insignificance.' Few to-day, however, would fail to recognise in Richard a typical and recurrent example of the political leader.

The ordinary playgoer, whose reactions in such cases are infallible, has never doubted the political veracity of Shakespeare's Richard. What is strange—and yet not strange at all—is that the ordinary playgoer has not only believed but delighted in him:

> Off with his head! Now, by Saint Paul I swear,
> I will not dine until I see the same.

This is after the unregenerate heart of a public which covertly admires a man who comes straight to the point without fear, scruple or procrastination. These are high politics with the gloves off, the foils unbated and the mask removed. Richard is not a good man. But when was a good man popular? He is not a merciful man. But when was mercy esteemed in public life? And though he is neither good nor merciful, he is every endearing thing else. He is brave, witty, resourceful, gay, swift, disarmingly candid with himself, engagingly sly with his enemies. Above all, he has no conscience to trouble him

—not till he sleeps. It is uncommonly refreshing for those who feel the restraint of conscience some fourteen hours a day to see a man upon the stage entirely free of it. On this subject of conscience, we are disposed to sympathise with Second Murderer:

It makes a man a coward: a man cannot steal, but it accuseth him; he cannot swear, but it checks him; he cannot lie with his neighbour's wife, but it detects him: 'tis a blushing shamefast spirit that mutinies in a man's bosom; it fills one full of obstacles: it made me once restore a purse of gold that I found; it beggars any man that keeps it; it is turned out of all towns and cities for a dangerous thing; and every man that means to live well endeavours to trust to himself and live without it.

Richard, turning his conscience out of doors, promises his audience a moral holiday and the promise is kept to such good purpose that those who are most refreshed with his heathen villainies leave the theatre thanking God most fervently for their Christian virtues.

Shakespeare's Richard makes his first appearance in Act V of the Second Part of 'Henry VI.' His pregnant utterance proclaims the man to be:

Priests pray for enemies, but princes kill;

and the play ends with a stirring account of his impetuous valour at the first battle of St. Albans.

Shakespeare, whatever he may have left to his collaborators,[1] took

---

[1] Readers familiar with the controversies which have arisen over the authorship of the Second and Third Parts of 'Henry VI' may object that to build up the character of Shakespeare's Richard from his first appearance in these earlier plays is to ignore the fact that some of the incidents and speeches quoted are from scenes ascribed to another author or authors.

Shakespeare, in writing the Second and Third Parts of 'Henry VI', worked from the text of two plays first published in 1595 and 1597. Some of the text he retained unaltered and some of it he amended; while, here and there, he interpolated single lines or whole passages entirely new.

It is impossible to decide from external evidence who wrote the original plays. The author might have been Shakespeare or somebody writing in collaboration with Shakespeare or with somebody else.

There is, however, clear evidence that Shakespeare revised the original texts very carefully. We may assume that he liked what he kept; that he liked even more what he embellished; that what he interpolated he regarded as an improvement on the original.

This book is not a study of Shakespeare's sources. The reader is merely asked to assume that the passages and incidents cited in the present chapter were regarded by Shakespeare himself as agreeable to his conception of the character.

Richard for his own in the Second and Third Parts of 'Henry VI.' He
has an eye upon him from the start. Richard, though the youngest
of the sons of York, invariably takes the lead of his brothers in word
and deed. In the Third Part of 'Henry VI' he is all for action, whether
it be on the battlefield:

> Sound drums and trumpets, and the king will fly;

or in the Parliament at Westminster:

> Arm'd as we are, let's stay within this house;

and he talks like none of the others:

> See how the morning opes her golden gates,
> And takes her farewell of the glorious sun!
> How well resembles it the prime of youth,
> Trimm'd like a younker prancing to his love!

Note his first abrupt, sensational entry into the Third Part of
'Henry VI':

> Speak thou for me and tell them what I did.
> *(throwing down the Duke of Somerset's head.)*

Richard of Gloucester is presented as a born leader from the first.
In the presence of the great Warwick it is he who prevails in counsel;
in the presence of his father, the Duke of York, it is he who inspires
confidence and courage:

> YORK: The army of the queen mean to besiege us.
> MORTIMER: She shall not need; we'll meet her in the field.
> YORK: What, with five thousand men?
> RICHARD: Ay, with five hundred, father, for a need.

Richard in all his wicked glory is clearly foreshadowed in a remarkable scene at Sandal Castle ('III Hen. VI', Act I, Scene II)
in which the faction of the white rose discusses whether the Duke
of York shall claim the crown. Henry VI is still alive. York has
sworn to let Henry reign in peace and he is concerned about his
oath. Richard breaks in with impetuous irony:

> RICHARD: No; God forbid your Grace should be forsworn.
> YORK: I shall be, if I claim by open war.
> RICHARD: I'll prove the contrary, if you'll hear me speak.
> YORK: Thou canst not, son; it is impossible.

Mark what follows:

> RICHARD: An oath is of no moment, being not took
> Before a true and lawful magistrate,
> That hath authority o'er him that swears:
> Henry had none, but did usurp the place;
> Then, seeing 'twas he that made you to depose,
> Your oath, my lord, is vain and frivolous.
> Therefore, to arms!

This is already the virtuoso whose performances are shortly to hold men fascinated as by the convolutions of a serpent, round on round.

Richard's speech at Sandal concludes with a hint that already the diadem glitters for him more brightly than for other men:

> And, father, do but think
> How sweet a thing it is to wear a crown,
> Within whose circuit is Elysium,
> And all that poets feign of bliss and joy.
> Why do we linger thus? I cannot rest
> Until the white rose that I wear be dyed
> Even in the lukewarm blood of Henry's heart.

We find here to our astonishment that Richard has a virtue. In his prime he will order the killing of his brother, mock at his mother's tenderness or drown her reproaches with drum and trumpet. But Richard at the start fights and schemes not for himself but for his father. After Mortimer's Cross he cannot rest till he knows how York has fared:

> I cannot joy, until I be resolved
> Where our right valiant father is become.

Love for his father is the sole token of humanity shown by Shakespeare's Richard in the whole course of his career. On what did it rest? Not upon admiration for York's valour—all these bloody men are equally brave. Not on respect for York's ability or strength of purpose, for young Richard is ever ready to prompt his father with advice or push him forward when he tires or falters. Yet there is no mistaking the note of hero-worship:

> Methinks, 'tis prize enough to be his son.

Oddly enough it is fierce Margaret who drops the clue. When York was captured at Mortimer's Cross she mocked him thus:

> Where are your mess of sons to back you now?
> The wanton Edward, and the lusty George?
> And where's that valiant crook-back prodigy,
> Dicky your boy, that with his grumbling voice
> Was wont to cheer his dad in mutinies?

Dicky was his father's boy. When York is slain, Richard must have the story in full:

> Say how he died, for I will hear it all;

and, having listened to the end, he cries out in anguish:

> To weep is to make less the depth of grief;
> Tears then for babes; blows and revenge for me!

Immediate action is his sole comfort:

> Shall we go throw away our coats of steel,
> And wrap our bodies in black mourning gowns,
> Numbering our Ave-Maries with our beads?
> Or shall we on the helmets of our foes
> Tell our devotion with revengeful arms?

Not till Richard has lost his father does he begin to invoke his bodily deformity as a thing which sets him apart from his fellows. There is nobody now to love and praise him; he is no longer the 'valiant crook-back prodigy' whose grumbling voice is dear to the creature he most admired. Henceforth he is a man apart:

> I have no brother, I am like no brother;
> And this word 'love', which greybeards call divine,
> Be resident in men like one another,
> And not in me. *I am myself alone.*

First he pursues at white heat his vendetta with Clifford whom he holds responsible for his father's death:

> Nay, Warwick, single out some other chase;
> For I myself will hunt this wolf to death.

He wounds Clifford, marking him for the grave; and, when Clifford is later found dead on the field, wishes his victim alive again that he may prolong his vengeance with mockery:

> What! not an oath? nay, then the world goes hard
> When Clifford cannot spare his friends an oath.
> I know by that he's dead; and, by my soul,
> If this right hand would buy two hours' life,
> That I in all despite might rail at him,
> This hand should chop it off.

Richard, when next we see him, is talking aside with Clarence as they watch their brother Edward, now King of England, wooing Elizabeth to be his queen. Outwardly he is merry, but there is an edge to his wit. Then, with an appalling abruptness he breaks into his first soliloquy. It is a *coup de théâtre*. Richard has fought heart and soul to make his father king. But here in his father's place is his brother. Edward is a handsome and lusty blockhead, wooing a sweet widow for his pleasure, though he is in policy pledged to seek a French alliance. It is easy to imagine with what bitterness of spirit brilliant, clear-sighted Richard sees this 'very very pajock' playing fast and loose with his fortune. The effect upon him of the scene as it proceeds is hinted at just sufficiently to prepare us for the blazing outburst which follows:

> Would he were wasted, marrow, bones, and all,
> That from his loins no hopeful branch may spring,
> To cross me from the golden time I look for!

It is the first indication that Richard has any ambition for himself. He has as yet no plans. He dwells, in fact, upon the almost insurmountable obstacles in his way. Edward still reigns and, even though Edward should die without an heir, there are still Clarence and captive Henry and Henry's son, young Edward, to dispute the succession. As yet he can do no more than flatter himself with impossibilities:

> Why, then, I do but dream on sovereignty;
> Like one that stands upon a promontory,
> And spies a far-off shore where he would tread.

But his desire is fixed and, to fix it more firmly, he insists, as he will insist again and again, that for him there is no alternative:

> Well, say there is no kingdom then for Richard;
> What other pleasure can the world afford?
> I'll make my heaven in a lady's lap,
> And deck my body in gay ornaments,
> And witch sweet ladies with my words and looks.
> O miserable thought! and more unlikely
> Than to accomplish twenty golden crowns!
> Why, love forswore me in my mother's womb:
> And, for I should not deal in her soft laws,
> She did corrupt frail nature with some bribe,
> To shrink mine arm up like a wither'd shrub;
> To make an envious mountain on my back,
> Where sits deformity to mock my body;
> To shape my legs of an unequal size;
> To disproportion me in every part.

Richard's perpetual insistence on his physical deformity is to be a major theme of the play that bears his name. So let us be clear about it from the start. He speaks of it here, and he will speak of it even more exuberantly hereafter, not in grief or envy of other men, but with a kind of inverted pride. He positively revels in the physical blemishes which only throw into more prominent relief the brilliant, imperious qualities of his mind. Already he describes his bodily defects with a quite unmistakable relish, using them as a spur to his ambition:

> Then, since this earth affords no joy to me,
> But to command, to check, to o'erbear such
> As are of better person than myself,
> I'll make my heaven to dream upon the crown.

He accepts the envious mountain on his back as a gift of God and, by St. Paul! he means to live up to it:

> Then, since the heavens have shaped my body so,
> Let hell make crook'd my mind to answer it.

He extorts a profit from every misbegotten circumstance of his birth and turns it to advantage:

> For I have often heard my mother say
> I came into the world with my legs forward:
> Had I not reason, think ye, to make haste
> And seek their ruin that usurp'd our right?

> The midwife wonder'd and the women cried
> 'O, Jesus bless us, he is born with teeth!'
> And so I was; which plainly signified
> That I should snarl and bite and play the dog.

This early soliloquy points us forward to another fundamental trait in Richard. He cannot yet see his way clear to the throne. But the very impossibility of the enterprise is a challenge. He will be an artist in villainy; his wicked deeds are not means to an end but ends in themselves. He promises himself more pleasure in winning than in possessing the crown. It will be his joy to 'check' and to 'o'erbear' his rivals and, having achieved his self-appointed purpose, he will, like an artist whose work is finished, lose interest in the result. It is the game rather than the goal that matters. Already he hugs himself in anticipation:

> I'll drown more sailors than the mermaid shall;
> I'll slay more gazers than the basilisk;
> I'll play the orator as well as Nestor,
> Deceive more slily than Ulysses could,
> And, like a Sinon, take another Troy.
> I can add colours to the chameleon,
> Change shapes with Proteus for advantages,
> And set the murd'rous Machiavel to school.

And with what amazing skill he follows his growing fortunes! To gain his ends he must first of all establish Edward firmly on the throne. The house of Lancaster must be eliminated and the house of York predominant. Clarence, simple, plain Clarence, condemns his brother's impolitic marriage with Elizabeth and, when his advice is rejected, conspires with Warwick for the restoration of King Henry. Richard also disapproves of the marriage, but Edward's folly exactly suits his purpose. With gentle irony, characteristically expressed in terms of holy writ, he commends the match:

> No, God forbid that I should wish them sever'd
> Whom God hath join'd together.

Clarence deserts his brother; Richard remains loyal, but leaves no doubt as to his motive:

> My thoughts aim at a further matter; I
> Stay not for love of Edward, but the crown.

The defection of Clarence and Warwick to the cause of Lancaster provides him with further occasion to display his energy and resource. Edward is captured by the Lancastrians and King Henry is restored to the throne. Richard rescues his brother and urges him to reclaim at once the crown he has lost:

RICHARD: Why, brother, wherefore stand you on nice points?
K. EDWARD: When we grow stronger, then we'll make our claim;
             Till then, 'tis wisdom to conceal our meaning.
HASTINGS: Away with scrupulous wit! now arms must rule.
RICHARD: And fearless minds climb soonest unto crowns.
             Brother, we will proclaim you out of hand.

Richard championed his father for love; he champions his brother because he can do nothing for himself till the house of York is securely seated. All will then be clear for his further progress.

The cause of Lancaster was lost irreparably at Tewkesbury. Henry's son, Prince Edward, was there captured and done to death. King Henry alone remained, a prisoner in the Tower. Once again Richard shows—and never more swiftly and ruthlessly—the stuff of which he is made. Without a word to his brother, now on the throne of England, he gallops from the field of battle to London. 'Where's Richard?' Edward asks. 'To London all in post,' answers Clarence. Edward's comment is naïve but pregnant:

> He's sudden, if a thing comes in his head.

Richard was leaving nothing to chance. Clarence was too weak and Edward too sentimental for the 'serious matter' which he had in mind. King Henry must die. Richard sets out to commit his first deliberate murder for the crown. He acts instantly and alone.

Henry knows at once why Richard has come. He has taken the measure of this sinister playboy:

> What scene of death hath Roscius now to act?

The wise and gentle king sees what is still hidden from the politic ruffians whom Richard will one by one remove from his path. He begins to prophesy, but Richard cuts him short:

> I'll hear no more: die, prophet, in thy speech: (*Stabs him.*)
> For this, amongst the rest, was I ordain'd.

Richard will never be more flagrantly himself than in this, the first of his self-regarding butcheries. In an assumed sardonic wonderment he watches the blood drop downwards from his sword and caps his observation with a simile appalling in its quaint blend of humanity and heartlessness:

> What! will the aspiring blood of Lancaster
> Sink in the ground? I thought it would have mounted.
> See how my sword weeps for the poor king's death!

The play ends with a pleasant family reunion. The three brothers kiss in all confidence and the besotted Edward esteems himself a happy man:

> And now what rests but that we spend the time
> With stately triumphs, mirthful comic shows?

What rested was something very different, namely the tragedy of 'Richard III'. But before we follow this engaging monster into the play that bears his name let us pause for a moment to consider the political background from which he has emerged.

Who and what are these politicians with whom Richard has grown to a precocious maturity? They have been too readily dismissed as figments of the full-blooded Elizabethan stage when they might be more appropriately considered as recurrent political types. This was once a paradox, but the time gives it proof.

York, Suffolk, Warwick, Beaufort and the rest are sadly familiar. These men despise learning. York sets out to dethrone Henry:

> Whose bookish rule hath pull'd fair England down.

They have a supreme contempt for the people. Salisbury, bringing a message from the commons, who fear for the safety of good King Henry, is mocked by Suffolk:

> But all the honour Salisbury hath won
> Is that he was the lord ambassador,
> Sent from a sort of tinkers to the king.

All means are laudable provided their ends are served. Suffolk, plotting the death of Duke Humphrey, puts the thing in a nutshell:

> And do not stand on quillets how to slay him:
> Be it by gins, by snares, by subtlety,
> Sleeping or waking, 'tis no matter how,
> So he be dead; for that is good deceit
> Which mates him first that first intends deceit.

These notable persons kill their competitor, mourn him in public and give him a magnificent funeral. Queen Margaret, who was a party to Humphrey's death, grows rhetorical with sorrow at his loss:

> I would be blind with weeping, sick with groans,
> Look pale as primrose with blood-drinking sighs,
> And all to have the noble duke alive;

and this same queen and her lords, who crown York in mockery before they kill him at Wakefield, justify their procedure with an accepted principle:

> It is war's prize to take all vantages.

None of these men sins from weakness or acknowledges a slip from virtue. They have their own perverted code. Richard's political expedients are those of his time and class. He is distinguished from his contemporaries only by his mental audacity.

For these men any ruse is justified which enables them to take advantage of simple honesty. Richard is resorting to an approved political expedient when he induces the citizens of York to admit his brother upon an assurance that Edward comes only to claim his dukedom:

> But when the fox hath once got in his nose
> He'll soon find means to make the body follow.

Not one of them is true to his pledged word or will not change his party or betray his friends as passion or opportunity may require. Advantage is the only criterion. King Louis, who has promised to support Henry, assumes as a matter of course that Edward's victory annuls his obligation:

> But if your title to the crown be weak,
> As may appear by Edward's good success,
> Then 'tis but reason that I be released
> From giving aid which late I promisèd.

This same Louis, having deserted Henry for Edward, promptly deserts Edward for Henry when he hears that Edward cannot marry his daughter, and Queen Margaret, who curses Warwick for having made Edward king, promptly blesses him when he undertakes to put her husband back on the throne:

> Warwick, these words have turn'd my hate to love;
> And I forgive and quite forget old faults.

Note, too, that these political ruffians, with superb assurance, invoke patriotism and God for all occasions. Says Hastings:

> Let us be back'd with God and with the seas
> Which he has given for fence impregnable,
> And with their helps only defend ourselves;
> In them and in ourselves our safety lies;

on which Clarence, feeling that such noble sentiments should be suitably rewarded, exclaims:

> For this one speech Lord Hastings well deserves
> To have the heir of the Lord Hungerford.

Most significant feature of the time and of its monstrous galaxy of political talent is the corruption of its youth. Henry, the only wise man in this flashily brilliant company, exclaims with sorrow that in such an epoch there is no child but is born untimely or can too quickly die:

> O, pity, God, this miserable age!
> What stratagems, how fell, how butcherly,
> Erroneous, mutinous, and unnatural,
> This deadly quarrel daily doth beget!
> O boy! thy father gave thee life too soon,
> And hath bereft thee of thy life too late.

One of the most poignant episodes in the Third Part of 'Henry VI' is that in which Henry, at the bidding of Margaret, bestows knighthood on his son:

KING HENRY: Edward Plantagenet, arise a knight;
      And learn this lesson, draw thy sword in right.
  PRINCE: My gracious father, by your kingly leave,
      I'll draw it as apparent to the crown,
      And in that quarrel use it to the death.
  CLIFFORD: Why, that is spoken like a toward prince.

This Edward was a brave and comely youth, but to draw his sword in right was for him an empty phrase. He has learned the lesson of his lost generation. He will fight only to secure his inheritance and, for snubbing his father's piety, he is heartily commended by the fierce lords who have nothing but contempt for Henry's moral preoccupations. Henry upholds a principle which is out of fashion:

Thrice is he arm'd that hath his quarrel just,
And he but naked, though locked up in steel,
Whose conscience with injustice is corrupted.

Such is the political background from which Richard of Gloucester emerges to play his part in his own tragedy. Shakespeare's 'Richard III' is a self-contained work of art. It is unnecessary to read the Second and Third Parts of 'Henry VI' to understand it to the full. But it is interesting to note that Shakespeare's fancy was busy on this character long before he took him for a hero and that Richard's essential qualities were all manifest in the earlier plays.

Significantly, as though the scene had been deliberately cleared for his entrance into a house swept and garnished, Shakespeare's Richard enters his own play with a soliloquy.

And what a soliloquy! Richard comes instantly to life in lines which in their fall and management, declare an active mind and a nimble spirit, a man who picks his epithets and savours them on the tongue, who gives rein to a fancy moving freely at its pleasure and yet so admirably controlled that it can adventure fearlessly through a full period of over thirty lines without losing its way; while, across this play of intellect zestfully aware of itself, runs a vein of mockery which, with a precise and amusing exaggeration, flouts the easy

rhetoric as it marches to a conclusion. All those preliminary adjec-
tives have, as it were, an elfin smile in their delivery—*glorious, victor-
ious, dreadful, delightful*:

> Now is the winter of our discontent
> Made glorious summer by this sun of York;
> And all the clouds that lour'd upon our house
> In the deep bosom of the ocean buried.
> Now are our brows bound with victorious wreaths;
> Our bruisèd arms hung up for monuments;
> Our stern alarums changed to merry meetings;
> Our dreadful marches to delightful measures.
> Grim-visaged war hath smooth'd his wrinkled front;
> And now, instead of mounting barbèd steeds
> To fright the souls of fearful adversaries,
> He capers nimbly in a lady's chamber
> To the lascivious pleasing of a lute.

Follows the antithesis, in which Richard gathers up all his previous
history, declares his quality and announces the theme of the tragedy:

> But I, that am not shaped for sportive tricks,
> Nor made to court an amorous looking-glass;
> I, that am rudely stamp'd, and want love's majesty
> To strut before a wanton ambling nymph;
> I, that am curtail'd of this fair proportion,
> Cheated of feature by dissembling nature,
> Deform'd, unfinish'd, sent before my time
> Into this breathing world, scarce half made up,
> And that so lamely and unfashionable
> That dogs bark at me as I halt by them;
> Why, I, in this weak piping time of peace,
> Have no delight to pass away the time,
> Unless to spy my shadow in the sun
> And descant on mine own deformity:
> And therefore, since I cannot prove a lover,
> To entertain these fair well-spoken days,
> I am determinèd to prove a villain.

Richard goes straight into action. Clarence is first on the list of
those who stand in his way and Clarence is already under detention.

Richard, who has traduced his brother to the King and contrived his arrest, meets his victim with an elaborately innocent concern:

> Brother, good day: what means this armèd guard
> That waits upon your grace?

Clarence comments lightly on the misunderstanding under which he has been committed to the Tower. With goblin solemnity Richard shakes his head. The Queen and her relatives, now mighty gossips in this monarchy, are, he suggests, responsible:

> We are not safe, Clarence, we are not safe.

Brackenbury, attending Clarence to the Tower, grows uneasy as the brothers become critical of the Queen's party. Richard retorts:

> We speak no treason, man: we say the king
> Is wise and virtuous, and his noble queen
> Well struck in years, fair, and not jealous;
> We say that Shore's wife hath a pretty foot,
> A cherry lip, a bonny eye, a passing pleasing tongue;
> That the queen's kindred are made gentlefolks:
> How say you, sir? can you deny all this?

The lilting audacity of this rejoinder is pure Richard. It has the familiar but elusive quality which gives to so many of his speeches the oily tang of a smooth olive eaten in the sun. Clarence passes to his doom and Richard looks after him with a whimsical, affectionate, derision:

> Simple, plain Clarence! I do love thee so,
> That I will shortly send thy soul to heaven,
> If heaven will take the present at our hands.

The fleering humility before God of that last line is another touch which we shall find often repeated but never stale.

Thus Clarence pays the debt of his kind. He has played the game and inevitably pays his forfeit—cruel to his enemies, false to his friends, unequal in force or cunning to his brilliant brother. He excites our compassion without moving our hearts. Shakespeare invests his murder with a sentimental poignancy without impairing our fearful pleasure in the impish wickedness that contrived it. It is the honest thought of the spectator who watches Richard at his wicked work: 'If I were cast for a villain, that is the sort of villain I should like to be.' Shakespeare, indeed, feels so secure in our allegiance to Richard that he can allow his victim a touch of beauty at the close, as in the famous dream:

> Methought I saw a thousand fearful wrecks;
> A thousand men that fishes gnaw'd upon;
> Wedges of gold, great anchors, heaps of pearl,
> Inestimable stones, unvalued jewels,
> All scatter'd in the bottom of the sea:
> Some lay in dead men's skulls; and in those holes
> Where eyes did once inhabit, there were crept,
> As 'twere in scorn of eyes, reflecting gems,
> Which woo'd the slimy bottom of the deep,
> And mock'd the dead bones that lay scatter'd by;—

reminding us, however, that this dreamer was the man who, with his brothers, had killed Prince Edward and broken faith with all his confederates in turn:

> Then came wandering by
> A shadow like an angel, with bright hair
> Dabbled in blood; and he squeak'd out aloud,
> 'Clarence is come; false, fleeting, perjur'd Clarence,
> That stabb'd me in the field by Tewkesbury'.

If Richard be the flower of his age, the murderers of Clarence are weeds of the soil from which it sprang. In their gross humour, twinges of conscience, alternate pride and misgiving in face of their own brutality, self-justification in that they act upon orders received and are convinced that their victim richly deserves his death, they run true to the society that bred them:

FIRST MURDERER: How dost thou feel thyself now?
SECOND MURDERER: 'Faith, some certain dregs of conscience are yet within me.

FIRST MURDERER: What we will do, we do upon command.
SECOND MURDERER: And he that hath commanded is the king.

FIRST MURDERER: How canst thou urge God's dreadful law to us,
When thou hast broke it in so dear degree?

FIRST MURDERER: Relent! 'tis cowardly and womanish.

Consider now the second important episode of the tragedy:

Enter the Corpse of KING HENRY THE SIXTH, *borne in an open coffin,*
GENTLEMEN *bearing Halberds to guard it*; LADY ANNE *as Mourner.*

Richard has already announced that he intends to marry Lady
Anne:

What though I kill'd her husband and his father?
The readiest way to make the wench amends
Is to become her husband and her father.

He maintains that marriage with Anne is necessary to his plans.
But Shakespeare significantly allows this motive to fall into the background. Richard's wooing may be dictated by political necessity,
but its prime purpose for the dramatist is to show Richard's insolent
virtuosity in persuasion, his delight in the exercise of his mind and
will, his pride in attempting the impossible and his triumph in its
achievement. The reasons which Richard gives for the attempt are
secondary. Here was a challenge to his wit which, apart from any
question of expediency, was irresistible. For him it was more matter
for a May morning.

The critics are divided upon the merits of this famous scene.
Some wish that Shakespeare had never written it, or declare that he
could never have done so. Others are of opinion that only Shakespeare could have succeeded or even attempted such an astonishing
performance. Even the romantic critics are at loggerheads. On the
one side we have Coleridge declaring bluntly that Shakespeare
'certainly did not write the scenes in which Lady Anne yielded to the
usurper's solicitations'. On the other side we have Lamb, with this
scene in mind, analysing with exquisite discrimination the 'lofty
genius, the man of vast capacity, the profound, the witty, the
accomplished Richard' and blaming Cooke, the actor, for lacking
the 'fine address which was necessary to have betrayed the heart of
Lady Anne.' Lamb had no doubt that here was Shakespeare's genius
working at full pressure. In the very scenes which Coleridge rejected
Lamb finds a supreme test for the actor and the key with which to
unlock the heart of the tragedy. Strip Richard of the virtuosity with
which he woos the Lady Anne and he becomes no more than 'a very
wicked man, who kills little children in their beds'.

Richard of Gloucester would be worth no man's powder and shot as a political character if, with Coleridge, we regarded him as no more than a sublime warning of the 'dreadful consequences of placing the moral in subordination to the intellectual being'. Such an approach carries us back to Dr. Johnson who, on closing the book, found 'some parts trifling, others shocking and some improbable'. Shakespeare's portrayal of Richard stands or falls by this scene. Admittedly it is outrageous that a murderer should woo the woman he has bereaved over the body of his victim. Obviously it is difficult to credit the frailty that falls under the spell of a villainy which does not even trouble to conceal itself. But no one sees this more clearly or puts it more forcibly than Richard himself:

> Was ever woman in this humour woo'd?
> Was ever woman in this humour won?

All that has ever been urged against the success or likelihood of the enterprise is put into Richard's own mouth:

> What! I, that kill'd her husband, and his father,
> To take her in her heart's extremest hate;
> With curses in her mouth, tears in her eyes,
> The bleeding witness of her hatred by;
> Having God, her conscience, and these bars against me,
> And nothing I to back my suit at all,
> But the plain devil and dissembling looks,
> And yet to win her, all the world to nothing!

He forestalls the critics who maintain that Anne's surrender is unnatural:

> Hath she forgot already that brave prince,
> Edward, her lord, whom I, some three months since,
> Stabb'd in my angry mood at Tewkesbury?
> A sweeter and a lovelier gentleman,
> Fram'd in the prodigality of nature,
> Young, valiant, wise, and, no doubt, right royal,
> The spacious world cannot again afford:
> And will she yet debase her eyes on me,
> That cropp'd the golden prime of this sweet prince,
> And made her widow to a woeful bed?

Richard's wooing brilliantly displays every facet of his wicked genius. He mocks the Christian virtues, to which he nevertheless in the same breath appeals:

> Lady, you know no rules of charity,
> Which renders good for bad, blessings for curses.

He flouts the pious faith of his victim and presses his suit in the full flush of his derision:

> ANNE: O, he was gentle, mild, and virtuous!
> RICHARD: The fitter for the King of Heaven, that hath him.
> ANNE: He is in heaven, where thou shalt never come.
> RICHARD: Let him thank me, that holp to send him thither;
> For he was fitter for that place than earth.
> ANNE: And thou unfit for any place but hell.
> RICHARD: Yes, one place else, if you will hear me name it.
> ANNE: Some dungeon.
> RICHARD: Your bed-chamber.

He means not only to win this woman but to win her by being most himself. He will fascinate her by the readiness of his wit, overwhelm her with his wicked audacity, beat down her defences by a blend of insolent assurance and humble submission—all the more effective as it expresses a boundless contempt. She spits at him:

> Never came poison from so sweet a place.

She wishes him dead and he offers his sword:

> Nay, do not pause; for I did kill King Henry,
> But 'twas thy beauty that provokèd me.
> Nay, now dispatch; 'twas I that stabb'd young Edward;
> But 'twas thy heavenly face that set me on.

The eternal bully speaks to the everlasting trollop—and knows that he will prevail. When he throws himself at Anne's feet and protests that he has never sued thus to a living soul, his flattery is meant to impress, but not to deceive, a woman already impotent to resist him. Richard's humility and the lady's scorn are at this stage equally fictitious. She is already won. The whole conduct of the scene and our readiness to accept it are in fact determined by motives which are suggested rather than expressed in the dialogue. Impudently professing that he committed his crimes for love, Richard is asking her in effect to admire his magnificent impertinence. He neither expects nor cares to be believed. What, in any case, is belief? Men and women believe what they wish to believe. He has overcome, not the intelligence, but the will of his victim and her final surrender is upon a note of helpless bewilderment:

> ANNE: I would I knew thy heart.
> RICHARD: 'Tis figured in my tongue.
> ANNE: I fear me both are false.
> RICHARD: Then never man was true.
> ANNE: Well, well, put up your sword.
> RICHARD: Say, then, my peace is made.
> ANNE: That shall you know hereafter.
> RICHARD: But shall I live in hope?
> ANNE: All men, I hope, live so.
> RICHARD: Vouchsafe to wear this ring.
> ANNE: To take is not to give. (*She puts on the ring.*)

There is pathos in these last wistful flickers of resistance. Anne is not convinced; she is overpowered.

Richard, who knew in advance that he would prevail, nevertheless expresses amazement at his success. Note, however, the quality of his exultation. He says nothing of the advantages to be derived from his marriage. Nor does he directly dwell upon it as a triumph of his will and person. His delight is more keen and sinister than that of a merely able man who comes off with flying colours from a difficult enterprise. The mainspring of his pleasure is to have proved that his measureless contempt of human nature, with its weak affections and silly scruples, is justified. His success with Lady Anne vindicates his whole philosophy of life.

Richard, in triumph, disposes once for all of the false idea that he is a man soured by his deformity and driven to revenge himself upon the world in envy of men better favoured than himself. We have noted already that, even when he rationalises his villainy, imputing it to heaven who had sent him legs foremost into the world, he zestfully exaggerates his defects. He is almost in love with that hump upon his back. It is his symbol of promise and power:

> This shoulder was ordain'd so thick to heave;
> And heave it shall some weight, or break my back.

Nowhere is this inverted vanity more joyously expressed than in the speech which follows his conquest of Lady Anne:

> I do mistake my person all this while:
> Upon my life, she finds, although I cannot,
> Myself to be a marvellous proper man.
> I'll be at charges for a looking-glass,
> And entertain some score or two of tailors,
> To study fashions to adorn my body:
> Since I am crept in favour with myself,
> I will maintain it with some little cost.

That Richard takes a crookèd pleasure in his crookèd shape does not, of course, imply that his rationalisations are false. He has been cheated of feature by dissembling nature and, in compensation, he will make it his heaven to dream upon the crown. But where a lesser man would have been driven to seek power from a sense of frustration, as has been the case with many political leaders in history, Richard insists repeatedly that it is his very physical inferiority which makes him unique among men. Everything in Richard's world—even his deformity—nourishes his sense of power. There is nothing negative in his character. He never sins, for sin implies a breach of the moral law accepted by the sinner. Richard has his own code. To that he is always faithful and so lives happy as the day is long. Shakespeare, dismissing him from the scene with Lady Anne, sends him forward to fresh conquests, a political Narcissus who takes pleasure in his own reflection:

> Shine out, fair sun, till I have bought a glass,
> That I may see my shadow as I pass.

Shakespeare, having shown us Richard at the top of his form, can do no more than repeat the achievement. 'Richard III' is in this respect a static composition. We found in 'Julius Caesar' the musical likeness of a symphony with fugal passages. The musical counterpart to 'Richard III' would be, not a symphony, but a set of variations of the early classic type. Our interest lies in the composer's ingenious,

D

almost playful, embroidery of a theme which remains essentially the same. Our attention is sustained, not by any development of character, but by an exhibition of the same unchanging qualities in a different context. Having witnessed Richard's courtship of Lady Anne, we sit back to enjoy further displays of his virtuosity. In the hands of a dramatist less infinite in faculty the performance would be tedious and, in one particular instance, Shakespeare himself hardly sustains the burden. The scene in Act IV in which Richard, having disposed of his first wife, sets out to persuade Queen Elizabeth to further his wooing of her daughter is, in substance, a replica of the scene with Lady Anne. It has, as we shall see, a different psychological setting and purpose, but in itself it is a variation which repeats the earlier performance in a more formal and decorative style. It is more ingenious than convincing and it provokes a momentary impatience. We are tempted to exclaim with Polonius: 'This is too long.' We may even condone at this stage the resentment of Dr. Johnson who declared: 'On this dialogue it is not necessary to bestow much criticism; part of it is ridiculous and the whole improbable.' We do not, in fact, immediately perceive its dramatic relevance; we only note that the earlier scene is repeated with an almost perfunctory exactitude. The Queen shrinks with horror from the man who proposes to marry the woman whose brother he has killed and Richard repeats his now familiar solicitations:

> Say that I did all this for love of her.

He again makes a cynical profession of penitence coupled with an appeal to self-interest and to a weak woman's secret admiration of the successful bully:

> If I did take the kingdom from your sons,
> To make amends I'll give it to your daughter.
> If I have kill'd the issue of your womb,
> To quicken your increase I will beget
> Mine issue of your blood upon your daughter.
>
> The loss you have is but a son being king,
> And by that loss your daughter is made queen.
>
> Again shall you be mother to a king,
> And all the ruins of distressful times

> Repair'd with double riches of content.
> What! we have many goodly days to see.

> Prepare her ears to hear a wooer's tale;
> Put in her tender heart the aspiring flame
> Of golden sovereignty.

And the conclusion of the scene is superficially the same:

> Q. ELIZABETH: Shall I be tempted of the devil thus?
> RICHARD: Ay, if the devil tempt thee to do good.
> Q. ELIZABETH: Shall I forget myself to be myself?
> RICHARD: Ay, if yourself's remembrance wrong yourself.
> Q. ELIZABETH: Yet thou didst kill my children.
> RICHARD: But in your daughter's womb I bury them:
> Where in that nest of spicery they shall breed
> Selves of themselves, to your recomforture.

The Queen leaves Richard upon an ambiguous promise to do what he asks and Richard's immediate reaction, as in the earlier scene, is one of contempt for his victim.[1]

Richard's first undertaking, after he has arranged for the elimination of Clarence, is to aggravate the unpopularity of the Queen's party with the high and mighty war-lords of England. He affects the candid, outspoken dislike of a plain gentleman for these upstarts:

> Who are they that complain unto the king,
> That I, forsooth, am stern and love them not?
> By holy Paul, they love his grace but lightly
> That fill his ears with such dissentious rumours.
> Because I cannot flatter and speak fair,
> Smile in men's faces, smooth, deceive, and cog,
> Duck with French nods and apish courtesy,
> I must be held a rancorous enemy.
> Cannot a plain man live and think no harm,
> But thus his simple truth must be abus'd
> By silken, sly, insinuating Jacks?

The simple Queen, not yet schooled in the sorrows that are to make her wise, doing her best to pacify this honest grumbler, tries to

---

[1] For the dramatic significance of this scene, its underlying differences from the earlier incident and unexpected sequel, see p. 104.

persuade him that she is not, as he so convincingly seems to imagine, in any way responsible for setting the King against his brother Clarence. Richard can only profess to be lost in a wicked world:

> I cannot tell; the world is grown so bad,
> That wrens make prey where eagles dare not perch:
> Since every Jack became a gentleman,
> There's many a gentle person made a Jack.

Poor painted Queen! Richard drives her to desperation, incidentally setting by the ears the opposing factions which he means in due course to destroy. Rivers is moved to intervene, but gets in only a word or two:

Q. ELIZABETH: My lord, you do me shameful injury,
　　　　　　　Falsely to draw me in these vile suspects.
RICHARD: You may deny that you were not the cause
　　　　Of my Lord Hastings' late imprisonment.
RIVERS: She may, my lord; for—
RICHARD: She may, Lord Rivers! why, who knows not so?
　　　　She may do more, sir, than denying that:
　　　　She may help you to many fair preferments,
　　　　And then deny her aiding hand therein,
　　　　And lay those honours on your high deserts.
　　　　What may she not? She may, ay, marry, may she,—
RIVERS: What, marry, may she?
RICHARD: What, marry, may she! marry with a king,
　　　　A bachelor, a handsome stripling too:
　　　　I wis your grandam had a worser match.

Note the vernacular quality of Richard's speech. It is one of his favourite tricks. Elizabeth at the close is reduced to his own assumed level of angry simplicity:

> By heaven, I will acquaint his majesty
> Of those gross taunts I often have endured.
> I had rather be a country servant-maid
> Than a great queen, with this condition,
> To be thus taunted, scorn'd and baited at:
> Small joy have I in being England's queen.

This is one of Richard's star performances. And how, as always, he enjoys it!

> I do the wrong, and first begin to brawl.
> The secret mischiefs that I set abroach
> I lay unto the grievous charge of others.

The sequel to this quarrel with the Queen and her relatives is an equally engaging scene of reconciliation. King Edward, on his death-bed, insists that all parties shall join hands. Hastings, who is soon to rejoice in the judicial murder of Rivers and Grey, embraces them both and protests his perfect love. Buckingham, who is to share the relish of his master in the tragi-comedy of Hastings' death, calls on God to punish him for any breach of an undying friendship. Richard enters and is invited to share in this feast of loving souls. He has just had news that his orders for the murder of Clarence have been successfully carried out, but this is what he says:

> If I unwittingly, or in my rage,
> Have aught committed that is hardly borne
> By any in this presence, I desire
> To reconcile me to his friendly peace:
> 'Tis death to me to be at enmity;
> I hate it, and desire all good men's love.

He makes his apologies to the Queen, to Buckingham, Rivers and Dorset. They have frowned on him without just cause, but he bears them no ill-will:

> I do not know that Englishman alive
> With whom my soul is any jot at odds
> More than the infant that is born to-night:
> I thank my God for my humility.

The scene closes with Richard's announcement of the death of Clarence, in which he contrives to throw the guilt upon the Queen's kindred and to suggest with sorrow that worse may follow.

No one will deny that this episode is dramatically effective. Nor will anyone who is at all familiar with the conduct of political persons at the green tables of Europe during the last twenty years challenge its political veracity.

Richard has two principal confederates in his acquisition of power. Each of them is prepared to go so far and no farther. Hastings helps Richard to become Lord Protector, but refuses to be a party to his designs upon the crown. Buckingham helps Richard to become King, but refuses to be a party to the murder of the princes. Both pay the penalty which invariably overtakes the public person who goes into power politics with moral reservations.

Hastings works for Richard in order to get the better of the Queen's faction and he achieves his purpose when Rivers, Vaughan and Grey are executed at Pomfret. Hastings laughs 'to look upon their tragedy', but he is a ruffian with scruples. Catesby is sent by Buckingham to sound him in the 'greater business' of Richard's accession:

> Go, gentle Catesby,
> And, as it were far off, sound thou Lord Hastings,
> How he doth stand affected to our purpose;
> And summon him to-morrow to the Tower,
> To sit about the coronation.
> If thou dost find him tractable to us,
> Encourage him, and show him all our reasons:
> If he be leaden, icy-cold, unwilling,
> Be thou so too; and so break off the talk,
> And give us notice of his inclination.

Richard merrily adds a postscript:

> Commend me to Lord William: tell him, Catesby,
> His ancient knot of dangerous adversaries
> To-morrow are let blood at Pomfret-castle;
> And bid my friend, for joy of this good news,
> Give Mistress Shore one gentle kiss the more.

Shakespeare depicts for us in Hastings the false security of the politician who deceives himself into thinking that there can be a limited liability in crime and who trusts to his good relations with the more extreme members of his party. He has received a message from Stanley urging him to fly. He refuses to do so. Nothing, he maintains, can be decided without his knowledge and nothing can divide him from his princely leader.

Catesby ably discharges his mission. He finds Hastings firmly opposed to crowning Richard and drops the subject. Hastings thereupon goes confidently to his doom. The stage is set for this incident with superb skill. The audience knows what is in store for him and every word he utters has a supreme dramatic irony which can be enjoyed without any prick of compassion. Nothing, in fact, comes between the spectator and his pleasure in yet another exhibition of our hero's virtuosity. Richard comes late to the Council with a pleasant good day to all and a graceful compliment for Hastings himself. Looking round he perceives the Bishop of Ely:

> My lord of Ely, when I was last in Holborn,
> I saw good strawberries in your garden there;
> I do beseech you send for some of them.

Who but Richard would have asked for strawberries at such a time? Hastings is charmed to be thus of the inner circle. Richard withdraws a moment with Buckingham and the doomed man delivers his last happy speech on earth:

> His grace looks cheerfully and smooth this morning:
> There's some conceit or other likes him well,
> When he doth bid good morrow with such spirit.
> I think there's ne'er a man in Christendom
> Can lesser hide his love or hate than he;
> For by his face straight shall you know his heart.

Richard returns with Buckingham and the blow falls:

RICHARD: I pray you all, tell me what they deserve
        That do conspire my death with devilish plots
        Of damnèd witchcraft, and that have prevail'd
        Upon my body with their hellish charms?
HASTINGS: The tender love I bear your grace, my lord,
        Makes me most forward in this noble presence
        To doom th' offenders, whosoe'er they be:
        I say, my lord, they have deservèd death.

Richard strips his sleeve:

RICHARD: Then be your eyes the witness of their evil:
        Look how I am bewitch'd; behold mine arm
        Is like a blasted sapling, wither'd up:
        And this is Edward's wife, that monstrous witch,
        Consorted with that harlot, strumpet Shore,
        That by their witchcraft thus have markèd me.

HASTINGS: If they have done this thing, my gracious lord,—
RICHARD: If! thou protector of this damnèd strumpet,
   Talk'st thou to me of 'ifs'? Thou art a traitor:
   Off with his head! now, by Saint Paul, I swear,
   I will not dine until I see the same.

Too late Hastings marvels at his false confidence and perceives the bitter folly of his triumph:

   O momentary grace of mortal men,
   Which we more hunt for than the grace of God!
   Who builds his hopes in air of your good looks,
   Lives like a drunken sailor on a mast;
   Ready, with every nod, to tumble down
   Into the fatal bowels of the deep.

His only consolation is a melancholy certitude that he will not be Richard's last victim:

   Come, lead me to the block; bear him my head:
   They smile at me that shortly shall be dead.

Richard has now to obtain the approval of the mayor and citizens for the execution of Hastings. He adopts his favourite character of the simple, confiding person who, having no guile in himself, is slow to suspect it in others:

   So dear I loved the man, that I must weep.
   I took him for the plainest harmless creature
   That breath'd upon this earth a Christian;
   Made him my book, wherein my soul recorded
   The history of all her secret thoughts.

Richard, moreover, knows these citizens. He makes a point of reminding his worship that Hastings has been living in sin with another man's wife. So what was one to expect? The mayor shakes his head sadly over the whole disreputable business:

   Now, fair befall you! he deserved his death;
   And your good graces both have well proceeded,
   To warn false traitors from the like attempts.
   I never look'd for better at his hands,
   After he once fell in with Mistress Shore.

The removal of Hastings is quickly followed by the elimination of Buckingham. Buckingham was privy to all Richard's plans. He was the counsellor, instrument and crony of his master. So devout is his admiration of Richard that he becomes infected with his hero's manners and methods. He imitates with zest Richard's radiant hypocrisy and abrupt violence. When Queen Elizabeth sends her son to sanctuary, it is Buckingham who, in the very accents of Richard, argues that it would be no sin to drag him forth. Sanctuary, he maintains, was never designed to keep children away from their lawful guardians:

> You break not sanctuary in seizing him.
> The benefit thereof is always granted
> To those whose dealings have deserved the place
> And those who have the wit to claim the place:
> This prince hath neither claim'd it nor deserv'd it;
> Therefore, in mine opinion, cannot have it:
> Then, taking him from thence that is not there,
> You break no privilege nor charter.

This is an absolute echo of Richard.

It is Richard's pleasure to start Buckingham upon a scent, sardonically stand aside and allow him to take the lead. It is Buckingham who gives Catesby his instructions upon the sounding of Hastings; it is Buckingham who undertakes to cozen the citizens of London into accepting Richard for their King and who, at a hint from Richard, contrives that they shall seem to press upon him a crown which Richard must appear reluctantly to accept. Buckingham delights in the exercise of a pupil's virtuosity:

> Doubt not, my lord; I'll play the orator,
> As if the golden fee for which I plead
> Were for myself.

He will frame his face to all occasions:

> RICHARD: Come, cousin, canst thou quake, and change thy colour,
> Murder thy breath in middle of a word,
> And then begin again, and stop again,
> As if thou wert distraught and mad with terror?

BUCKINGHAM: Tut, I can counterfeit the deep tragedian;
           Speak and look back, and pry on every side,
           Tremble and start at wagging of a straw,
           Intending deep suspicion: ghastly looks
           Are at my service, like enforcèd smiles;
           And both are ready in their offices,
           At any time, to grace my stratagems.

Richard and Buckingham, in the famous scene with the citizens, are two playboys who enjoy together a private jest. 'Zounds, I'll entreat no more,' exclaims Buckingham when Richard persists in refusing to be King, to which Richard in his character of a holy and devout religious man returns: 'O, do not swear, my lord of Buckingham.' These good companions exchange, as it were, a solemn wink over the heads of the people.

Buckingham is brilliant in execution, but he is never the moving spirit. If he seems to take the initiative, the vital impulse comes always from Richard. Buckingham excels in picking up cues from his leader and he has that tiresome habit of the zealous disciple of invariably trying to go one better. Richard, when they are plotting to fool the citizens into acclaiming him King, suggests:

           Bring them to Baynard's Castle;
       Where you shall find me well accompanied
       With reverend fathers and well-learnèd bishops.

Buckingham jumps at the notion, makes it his own and improves upon the comedy to the point of farce:

           And look you get a prayer-book in your hand,
           And stand between two churchmen, good my lord.

Buckingham thinks it a privilege to work with Richard and plumes himself upon the association. Richard, on the other hand, has the natural contempt of an original mind for a reproduction. It irks him to see this sedulous parody of himself in action. He watches his partner with a sour, reserved amusement. Buckingham is ever full of advice and confident of his ability. Richard accepts him with a mocking assumption of humility:

> My other self, my counsel's consistory,
> My oracle, my prophet! My dear cousin,
> I, as a child, will go by thy direction.

The time will come when Buckingham, too, will have to be put in his place and we shall then find Richard treating his former colleague with a harsh contempt for which at first sight there seems no adequate motive. But the reason is not far to seek. Richard admits no equality of mind or will with Buckingham. He is thus provoked into humiliating his competitor in mischief beyond all reason. This is a not uncommon trait in political life.

There are moments when Buckingham seems to be working for Richard from pure love of the sport. But the political labourer is worthy of his hire and Buckingham makes his bargain well in advance:

> BUCKINGHAM: Now, my lord, what shall we do if we perceive
> Lord Hastings will not yield to our complots?
> RICHARD: Chop off his head, man; somewhat we will do:
> And, look, when I am king, claim thou of me
> The earldom of Hereford, and the moveables
> Whereof the king my brother stood possess'd.
> BUCKINGHAM: I'll claim that promise at your grace's hand.

The scene in which Richard sets out to discover whether Buckingham is prepared to connive at the murder of the princes is brilliantly characteristic. There is no obscure hinting at a dreadful purpose. Richard goes straight to the point:

> RICHARD: Ah! Buckingham, now do I play the touch,
> To try if thou be current gold indeed:
> Young Edward lives: think now what I would speak.
> BUCKINGHAM: Say on, my loving lord.
> RICHARD: Why, Buckingham, I say, I would be king.
> BUCKINGHAM: Why, so you are, my thrice renownèd liege.
> RICHARD: Ha! am I king? 'tis so: but Edward lives.
> BUCKINGHAM: True, noble prince.
> RICHARD: O bitter consequence,
> That Edward still should live! 'True, noble prince!'
> Cousin, thou wast not wont to be so dull:
> Shall I be plain? I wish the bastards dead.

Buckingham is staggered and undertakes to consider the matter. But Richard leaves him no time for reflection:

RICHARD: What sayest thou now? speak suddenly; be brief.
BUCKINGHAM: Your grace may do your pleasure.
RICHARD: Tut, tut, thou art all ice, thy kindness freezes:
      Say, have I thy consent that they shall die?
BUCKINGHAM: Give me some breath, some little pause, dear lord,
      Before I positively speak in this:
      I will resolve your grace immediately. (*Exit.*)

Buckingham withdraws to think over Richard's proposal, but Richard's mind was made up at the first sign of hesitation in his confederate. He does not wait for Buckingham's considered reply. He has no use for a man who has a pitiful, small mind of his own:

> I will converse with iron-witted fools
> And unrespective boys; none are for me
> That look into me with considerate eyes:
> High-reaching Buckingham grows circumspect.

He sends at once for Tyrrel to arrange for the murder of the princes and, when Buckingham returns to deliver his decision, Richard will not so much as hear what he has to say. Buckingham has hesitated. That is enough:

BUCKINGHAM: My lord, I have consider'd in my mind
      The late demand which you did sound me in.
RICHARD: Well, let that rest.

Richard turns from his late colleague with studied indifference. Buckingham claims the promised earldom of Hereford. Richard affects to be sunk in meditation:

BUCKINGHAM: My lord!
RICHARD: Ay, what's o'clock?
BUCKINGHAM: I am thus bold to put your grace in mind
      Of what you promis'd me.
RICHARD: But what's o'clock?
BUCKINGHAM: Upon the stroke of ten.
RICHARD: Well, let it strike.

BUCKINGHAM: Why let it strike?
RICHARD: Because that, like a Jack, thou keep'st the stroke
     Betwixt thy begging and my meditation.
     I am not in the giving vein to-day.

Had Buckingham decided to connive at the murder of the princes? The fact that he reminded Richard of the promised earldom would seem to indicate a willingness to come to terms. But Richard gave him no opportunity to disclose himself. He has no use for waverers. Nor does he wish to be under any further obligation to the man who had aspired to be his boon companion in crime:

> The deep-revolving witty Buckingham
> No more shall be the neighbour to my counsel:
> Hath he so long held out with me untired,
> And stops he now for breath?

So much for Buckingham!—as Colley Cibber was one day to say on Shakespeare's behalf. Buckingham was driven into rebellion and executed, not for refusing to connive at the murder of the princes, but because he hesitated to comply immediately with his leader's suggestion. He lost his head the moment he claimed the right to think for himself.

Shakespeare never allows his political heroes to posture in an empty land. There is always the people. *London—A Street—Enter Two Citizens Meeting*. The street may be shifted to Rome. It may be a forum or a battlefield. But always, sooner or later, it comes to re-mind us that there are humble folk tied to the wheel of history.

The citizens who appear in 'Richard III' are typical subjects of the New Monarchy—a post-medieval form of the totalitarian state. We encounter them first discussing the news of King Edward's death. They foresee a struggle for power between their rulers. Woe to that land that's governed by a child! Each party will try to use him for their own power and pleasure:

> For emulation now, who shall be nearest,
> Will touch us all too near, if God prevent not.

> When clouds are seen, wise men put on their cloaks;
> When great leaves fall, then winter is at hand.

> O, full of danger is the Duke of Gloucester!

These citizens are full of foreboding. They read their masters well, but see no remedy.

Enter a Scrivener. He has been instructed to draw up the indictment of Lord Hastings, summarily executed before the charges against him have even been put on paper. It is a shrewd free citizen of England who speaks for all such as have found themselves similarly helpless in other times and places:

> Here's a good world the while! Who is so gross,
> That cannot see this palpable device?
> Yet who so bold but says he sees it not?
> Bad is the world; and all will come to nought,
> When such ill dealing must be seen in thought.

These citizens can be manoeuvred into a semblance of agreement, but they are not deceived:

> BUCKINGHAM: And when mine oratory drew toward end,
> I bade them that did love their country's good
> Cry 'God save Richard, England's royal king!'
> RICHARD: And did they so?
> BUCKINGHAM: No, so God help me, they spake not a word;
> But like dumb statuas or breathing stones,
> Gazed each on other, and look'd deadly pale.
> Which, when I saw, I reprehended them;
> And ask'd the mayor what meant this wilful silence:
> His answer was, the people were not wont
> To be spoke to but by the recorder.

The recorder was pushed forward:

> When he had done, some followers of mine own,
> At lower end of the hall, hurl'd up their caps,
> And some ten voices cried, 'God save King Richard!'
> And thus I took the vantage of those few.
> 'Thanks, gentle citizens and friends,' quoth I;
> 'This general applause and cheerful shout
> Argues your wisdoms and your love to Richard':
> And even here brake off, and came away.

What follows might serve as a model for the political agents of any caucus, ancient or modern. Buckingham brings the citizens to Richard and the scene is set. It is not a burlesque. Political realities with which we are familiar limp in dull or ferocious travesty far behind it. Buckingham has one staunch adherent in the crowd—the mayor with whom he has previously come to terms. The rest merely listen while the principals play their allotted parts. Buckingham extols the morality of his master:

> Ah, ha, my lord, this prince is not an Edward!
> He is not lolling on a lewd day-bed,
> But on his knees at meditation;
> Not dallying with a brace of courtesans,
> But meditating with two deep divines.

The mayor is suitably impressed:

> See, where he stands between two clergymen!—

and Richard professes his reluctance in the customary terms:

> Will you enforce me to a world of cares?
> Call them again. I am not made of stone,
> But penetrable to your kind entreats,
> Albeit against my conscience and my soul.
>   (*Re-enter* BUCKINGHAM *and the rest.*)
> Cousin of Buckingham, and you sage, grave men,
> Since you will buckle fortune on my back,
> To bear her burden, whether I will or no,
> I must have patience to endure the load.

Now for the wicked uncle! The murder of the princes was a necessary act of state. No usurper in that period of history could think himself secure so long as a more legitimate claimant was alive. Richard had decided to kill the sons of his elder brother before he was made King and long before he sounded Buckingham on the subject He approaches this, the worst of his crimes, in the same sardonic spirit as the rest. Shakespeare makes this quite clear in the scene which Hazlitt decried as 'the fantoccini exhibition of the young princes, Edward and York, bandying childish wit with their uncle.' Hazlitt, for once, was insensitive. The scene is in itself excellent stage-craft. What could be more *theatrically* effective than Richard's playful gift of his dagger to York and the boy's pert allusion to his uncle's deformity. What could be more *theatrically* moving than young Edward's instinctive distrust of the Lord Protector, his premonitory recoil from the Tower, his pathetic exhibition of a mind already alert and inquisitive and of a spirit which aspires to fame:

> An if I live until I be a man,
> I'll win our ancient right in France again,
> Or die a soldier, as I lived a king.

Such moving effects as these would furnish forth a complete outfit for the dozen or so dramatic authors of consequence who have followed Shakespeare over a period of three centuries. To Shakespeare they were little more than tricks of his mighty trade, only to be regarded as facile or insignificant when we compare them with his greater achievements.

Even these tricks, moreover, have a deeper purpose than to wring the simple hearts of the groundlings. For they enable Shakespeare to reveal the mind of Richard at work:

> So wise so young, they say, do ne'er live long.

> Short summers lightly have a forward spring.

> Thus, like the formal Vice, Iniquity,
> I moralise two meanings in one word.

Richard savours the dreadful situation with the same colourful pride in obliquity, the same sinister delight in the ambiguous gesture or phrase, with which he contemplates, in so many diverse forms, the prosecution of his grand design:

> My dagger, little cousin? with all my heart.

One cannot help thinking that, if Hazlitt had looked a little more carefully, not only into the technique of the playwright but into the purpose of the dramatist, he would not have dismissed this scene as altogether unworthy of Shakespeare.

Richard's murder of the princes in the Tower is by common consent and unbroken tradition his best title to be considered as one of the master criminals of history. Charles Lamb, as we have seen, explains our delight in Richard, as he explains our delight in the licentious figures of Restoration Comedy, by assuming that we regard such unedifying persons as characters in a fairy tale. We suspend our ethical judgment and take a holiday from holiness in a moral Alsatia. He insinuates that we instinctively condone the crimes of Richard so that we may enjoy his dexterity, the play of his intellect, the flaunting bravery of his wicked spirit. Richard is to be regarded as a bogeyman who takes his place in the popular fancy along with Henry VIII and Bluebeard. All this, of course, is true and could never be more brilliantly stated. There is, however, another ingredient in our pleasure. For Richard is not an ogre in a fairy tale. He is a recognisable type of public person who wins our sympathy by conducting himself with a refreshing candour, and nowhere is his engaging frankness more vividly displayed than in his character of the wicked uncle who kills little children in their beds. Child murder is a political expedient on which countless generations of men in authority have based their privilege and power. Highly civilised peoples, like the Greeks, who exposed their superfluous babies at birth, have honestly admitted the fact. Less civilised peoples, like the English at the beginning of the nineteenth century, consigned them to mines, workshops and slums where they perished in hundreds of thousands to maintain an opulent heritage. All down the ages the successful politician has shown little or no effective reluctance to out-Herod Herod in his slaughter of the innocents. The crime of Richard is the secular crime of the power politician in every age and there is a sense in which every political leader is a wicked uncle who kills little children in their beds.

What we like and admire in Richard is that he knows, as the politicians seldom know, precisely what he is doing. He presents the situation for what it is and makes no bones about it. We relish his exposure of a truth which in various forms and disguises is a matter of common observation.

Shakespeare permits the lesser villains of the piece to denounce the enormity of the crime:

> The tyrannous and bloody act is done;
> The most arch deed of piteous massacre,
> That ever yet this land was guilty of;

and he spares us no pathetic circumstance in Tyrrel's account of it. But for Richard it is no more than an item in his programme:

RICHARD: Kind Tyrrel, am I happy in thy news?
  TYRREL: If to have done the thing you gave in charge
       Beget your happiness, be happy then;
       For it is done.
RICHARD: But didst thou see them dead?
  TYRREL: I did, my lord.
RICHARD: And buried, gentle Tyrrel?

Kind Tyrrel—*gentle* Tyrrel? How often does Richard, in a casual epithet, express the dreadful, sustained irony of his disposition![1]

[1] It is interesting to compare the fearless direct advance of Richard towards the worst of his crimes with the hesitant groping approach of King John towards the murder of Prince Arthur. Richard looks his action straight in the face. John hardly dares to name it. 'Shall I be plain? I wish the bastards dead,' says Richard to Buckingham. King John, opening his mind to Hubert, is oppressed with the moral enormity of his design. He comes near to it, backs away, prologises and hints at something only to be sounded with a midnight bell or to be spoken in a churchyard:

> Or if that thou couldst see me without eyes,
> Hear me without thine ears, and make reply
> Without a tongue, using conceit alone,
> Without eyes, ears and harmful sound of words;
> Then, in despite of broad-eyed watchful day,
> I would into thy bosom pour my thoughts:
> But, ah, I will not! yet I love thee well.

Richard when the deed is done only wants to know that his victims are dead and buried. John throws back upon Hubert the moral responsibility for a crime which he dare not acknowledge:

K. JOHN: How oft the sight of means to do ill deeds
        Makes ill deeds done! Hadst not thou been by,
        A fellow by the hand of nature marked,
        Quoted and signed to do a deed of shame,
        This murder had not come into my mind:
        But taking note of thy abhorred aspect,
        Finding thee fit for bloody villany,
        Apt, liable to be employed in danger,
        I faintly broke with thee of Arthur's death;
        And thou, to be endearèd to a king,
        Made it no conscience to destroy a prince.
HUBERT: My lord—

Richard has now completed his programme and achieved his purpose. He is King of England and his title is assured. There is still work to do, but from this time forth a subtle difference grows increasingly apparent in his mood and conduct. The dreadful inspiration which has carried him to the achievement of his purpose now perceptibly flags. Richard, after the death of the princes, is like an artist who has put the finishing touch to a masterpiece. For this he was ordained and he has fulfilled his destiny. The virtue—an evil virtue—has gone out of him. He will never again be the jocund adventurer in crime. He will continue to exercise his wits after the old fashion, but there will be something almost mechanical in his further performances, as though he were repeating from habit tricks acquired in the exercise of an original talent. This falling-off in Richard's performance is not due to any falling-off in Shakespeare's creative power. It is an essential feature of the tragedy and profoundly characteristic of the man. Coleridge let fall a sentence in one of his lectures which bears directly on the point we have reached. He was contrasting the characters of Richard III and Henry Bolingbroke. 'In Richard III', said Coleridge, 'the pride of intellect *makes use of ambition as its means*; in Bolingbroke the gratification of ambition is the end and talents are the means.'

Richard, in acquiring the crown, was seeking an outlet for the exercise of his genius. When the crown was won, his interest was abated. Seated on the throne, with all obstacles removed, he has reached the first pause in his career since he stabbed King Henry in

> K. JOHN: Hadst thou but shook thy head, or made a pause,
> When I spake darkly what I purposèd,
> Or turned an eye of doubt upon my face
> As bid me tell my tale in express words,
> Deep shame had struck me dumb, made me break off,
> And those thy fears might have wrought fears in me:
> But thou didst understand me by my signs,
> And didst in signs again parley with sin;
> Yea, without stop, didst let thy heart consent,
> And consequently thy rude hand to act
> The deed, which both our tongues held vile to name.
> Out of my sight, and never see me more!

Shakespeare contrasts at all points the man who claims immunity from the common laws of humanity with the man who accepts but transgresses them.

the Tower. He stands back to look at his work and experiences that awful qualm of disillusion which most men feel when they have attained what was to have been the summit of their achievement. In addressing himself to the tasks that await him in the future he finds it necessary to apply the spur. The man whom King Edward described as 'sudden, if a thing comes in his head' has now to goad himself into action and even to argue the necessity:

> Come; I have heard that fearful commenting
> Is leaden servitor to dull delay;
> Delay leads impotent and snail-pac'd beggary:
> Then fiery expedition be my wing,
> Jove's Mercury, and herald for a king!
> Go, muster men: my counsel is my shield;
> We must be brief when traitors brave the field.

This self-apostrophe rings a new note and it is sounded immediately after Richard's reception of the news that the princes have been removed.

The decline in Richard's genius for decisive action has in it no element of remorse. It springs, on the contrary, from a sense that anything he may have to do next must necessarily be something of an anti-climax. The first, fine careless rapture is exhausted. All he can do henceforth is to maintain his position and accept the necessities which it lays upon him. Queen Margaret, who has a way of suddenly illuminating the drift of Shakespeare's tragedy, gives us the key to the changed situation in which Richard finds himself:

> So now prosperity begins to mellow
> And drop into the rotten mouth of death.

We now perceive why the scene in which Richard sets out to persuade Elizabeth to further his suit to her daughter is but a pale reflection of the earlier scene in which he wooed the Lady Anne. The repetition, though it may be found *theatrically* disappointing, is *psychologically* right. Shakespeare at the height of his powers as a craftsman would have avoided the technical error of presenting, late in the play, a formal variation upon an earlier and more brilliant performance. He would have contrived some other means of indicating the loss of power which overtakes the original mind when it is forced to repeat itself. But the scene, though technically at fault, is dramatically of the highest significance. Richard uses again the arts with which he overcame the scruples of Lady Anne. But the relish is no longer there. The scene has an artificial quality. It is full of ingenious argument and antithetical retort. This artificiality is deliberate. The dramatist falls into verbal conceits because they exactly convey a loss of that urgent, homespun quality which was the secret of Richard's energy in the first flush of his enterprise.

Note, too, that Richard for the first time *fails in his purpose.* Elizabeth, seeming to consent, makes him no definite promise:

> ELIZABETH: Shall I go win my daughter to thy will?
> RICHARD: And be a happy mother by the deed.
> ELIZABETH: I go. Write to me very shortly,
> And you shall understand from me her mind.
> RICHARD: Bear her my true love's kiss; and so, farewell.
> (*Exit* Q. ELIZABETH.)
> Relenting fool, and shallow, changing woman!

Richard takes his success for granted and, as in the earlier scene, pours scorn upon his dupe. But this time it is Richard who is deceived. Elizabeth gives her daughter to Richmond, thus uniting the white rose and the red in a dynasty which is to supplant Richard on the throne and to create the legend of his infamy. Note, too, that Richard takes no real pleasure in his imaginary triumph. His scorn of Elizabeth is no more than a perfunctory flash of contempt. There is here none of the wonder and jollity of his comments upon his earlier performance with Lady Anne. The mood of it is bitter. Richard is for the first time ill-natured. His merry diabolism is in eclipse.

This unfortunate episode is followed immediately by the entrance of Ratcliff and Catesby. They bring news. Richmond is riding a puissant navy on the western coast; Buckingham is waiting to welcome him ashore. Richard's reception of these tidings comes as an abrupt and staggering revelation of the change in him:

> RICHARD: Some light-foot friend post to the Duke of Norfolk:
> Ratcliff, thyself, or Catesby; where is he?
> CATESBY: Here, my good lord.
> RICHARD: Catesby, fly to the duke.

CATESBY: I will, my lord, with all convenient haste.
RICHARD: Ratcliff, come hither. Post thou to Salisbury:
    When thou com'st thither,—(*To* CATESBY) Dull, unmindful
     villain,
    Why stayst thou here, and go'st not to the duke?
CATESBY: First, mighty liege, tell me your highness' pleasure,
    What from your grace I shall deliver to him.
RICHARD: O, true, good Catesby: bid him levy straight
    The greatest strength and power he can make,
    And meet me suddenly at Salisbury.
CATESBY: I go.
RATCLIFF: What, may it please you, shall I do at Salisbury?
RICHARD: Why, what wouldst thou do there before I go?
RATCLIFF: Your highness told me I should post before.
RICHARD: My mind is changed.

Where is the nimble intelligence, the clean jump into action, the single-mindedness and self-mastery which we have come to associate with Richard? We sit back in amazement. Is it the same man? He gives an order and fails to complete it, issues instructions and changes his mind, abuses Catesby because he stays to know his errand. Another messenger arrives:

   Out on you, owls! nothing but songs of death?
            (*He strikes him.*)

This momentary loss of self-control bears no proportion to the gravity of the situation. Richard has faced greater odds and never turned a hair. There is some other cause at work.

These lapses, we note, are for a moment only. Immediately after the confused colloquy with Ratcliff and Catesby Richard encounters the ambiguous Stanley and is himself again:

RICHARD: Stanley, what news with you?
STANLEY: None good, my lord, to please you with the hearing;
    Nor none so bad, but may be well reported.
RICHARD: Hoyday, a riddle! neither good nor bad!
    What need'st thou run so many miles about,
    When thou mayst tell thy tale the nearest way?
    Once more, what news?

Stanley tells his news and shuffles uncomfortably under Richard's impetuous, familiar irony. Richmond is on the seas. He comes to claim the crown. Richard draws himself up in astonishment:

> Is the chair empty? is the sword unsway'd?
> Is the king dead? the empire unpossess'd?
> What heir of York is there alive but we?
> And who is England's king but great York's heir?
> Then, tell me, what doth he upon the seas?

He mocks and bluntly denounces Stanley's evasions. He does not trust the man and says as much:

RICHARD: Where be thy tenants and thy followers?
    Are they not now upon the western shore,
    Safe-conducting the rebels from their ships?
STANLEY: No, my good lord, my friends are in the north.
RICHARD: Cold friends to me: what do they in the north,
    When they should serve their sovereign in the west?
STANLEY: They have not been commanded, mighty king;
    Please it your majesty to give me leave,
    I'll muster up my friends, and meet your grace,
    Where and what time your majesty shall please.
RICHARD: Ay, ay, thou wouldst be gone to join with Richmond:
    But I'll not trust thee.
STANLEY: Most mighty sovereign,
    You have no cause to hold my friendship doubtful:
    I never was nor never will be false.
RICHARD: Go then and muster men: but leave behind
    Your son, George Stanley: look your heart be firm,
    Or else his head's assurance is but frail.

Richard in this scene is active, resolute and peremptory, but we remember those earlier symptoms of disorder. We wait for them to reappear and wonder what they may mean. He pitches his tent on Bosworth Field. He is still in full command and all seems well with him:
      Come, noble gentlemen,
> Let us survey the vantage of the ground;
> Call for some men of sound direction;
> Let's want no discipline, make no delay;
> For, lords, to-morrow is a busy day.

> Give me some ink and paper in my tent:
> I'll draw the form and model of our battle,
> Limit each leader to his several charge,
> And part in just proportion our small power.

> Fill me a bowl of wine. Give me a watch.
> Saddle white Surrey for the field to-morrow.
> Look that my staves be sound, and not too heavy

Then comes his own abrupt confession that something is amiss. He calls again to Ratcliff:

> Give me a bowl of wine:
> I have not that alacrity of spirit,
> Nor cheer of mind, that I was wont to have.

Still, however, we await the clue to his condition. What has happened to the essential Richard? Why is he losing his grip? Is it possible that he begins to weary in ill-doing?

This brings us to the fantastically symmetrical scene in which the ghosts of the slain, from Prince Edward, killed at Wakefield, to Buckingham, executed at Salisbury, come in turn to the tents of Richmond and of Richard to bless the one and curse the other.

The formality of this supernatural visitation robs it of any horror or even of mystery. In form and effect it is more like an interlude or ballet than a dramatic incident. These ghosts are presented as belonging to a different world from that in which we have moved hitherto. Richard, in the conscious exercise of his faculties, has denied reality or relevance to the moral force of conscience. But here, as in a morality masque, come mincing the ethical powers. They are ghosts of the virtues which Richard mocked even when craving a blessing from his mother:

> RICHARD: Madam, my mother, I do cry you mercy;
> I did not see your grace: humbly on my knee
> I crave your blessing.
> DUCHESS: God bless thee! and put meekness in thy mind,
> Love, charity, obedience, and true duty!
> RICHARD: Amen; (Aside) and make me die a good old man!
> That is the butt-end of a mother's blessing:
> I marvel that her grace did leave it out.

The virtues which he scorned—love, charity, obedience and true duty—now posture as abstract figures of retribution. It is a homily in fancy dress:

> God and good angels fight on Richmond's side;
> And Richard falls in height of all his pride.

These visitations have no affinity with the apparitions which tormented Macbeth. They are not embodiments of an active remorse. When Macbeth struck at his victims he struck into the quick of his own soul. Conscience was the constant companion of his sentient life. It whispered beside him before, during and after the act. It painted a dagger on the air and filled an empty stool at the banquet. In Richard's conscious life, on the contrary, there is no misgiving. No spectres could haunt his waking hours. Richard's ghosts emerge in sleep from the unconscious depths of his being. Shakespeare, following in imagination the working of a human mind, has again anticipated the modern psychologist.[1] Richard suffers no effective remorse. But when his will and intellect are in abeyance, the unconscious mind takes charge. Here, at last, in this pressure of subliminal forces, is the explanation of his moment of irresolution and loss of self-mastery in the scene with Ratcliff and Catesby. Here, too, is the underlying cause of his startling confession that he has lost his old alacrity of spirit and cheer of mind.

Shakespeare is at special pains to indicate that Richard suffers no moral discomfort in his waking hours. Every act, until he attains the crown and reaction sets in, is enjoyed in performance and relished in retrospect. The first indication that the repressed forces of conscience are at work is given not by any act or speech of Richard but by his wife:

> For never yet one hour in his bed
> Have I enjoy'd the golden dew of sleep,
> But have been wakèd by his timorous dreams.

The clue casually dropped in these lines is taken up and developed in the scene where Richard, again in sleep, is cursed by the symbols of a conscience which in his waking life has found no explicit utterance.

[1] See the chapter on Marcus Brutus for a discussion of Shakespeare's handling of the mass psychology of a crowd (p. 30).

The scene in the tent at Bosworth Field is firmly linked with two earlier scenes in the play in which Richard shows himself obdurate to the moral forces that work for his ruin and defeat. They are the scenes in which Queen Margaret appears as chorus to the tragedy, predicting the downfall of Richard and of Richard's accomplices. Nemesis, she declares, will overtake them all, and Richard, dreadful minister of retribution upon the lesser fry, will finally destroy himself.

The first of these passages occurs very early in the play. Clarence is still alive. Richard's major victims still grace his triumph. Queen Margaret curses Elizabeth. May her son Edward die untimely as did her own! She curses Rivers, Dorset and Hastings who had stood by when her child was slain. Above all, she curses Richard and warns the others, including Buckingham, against him. Hastings is appalled:

> My hair doth stand on end to hear her curses.

Richard listens with indifference. He even grasps the occasion to establish his public character as a Christian gentleman:

> I cannot blame her: by God's holy mother,
> She hath had too much wrong; and I repent
> My part thereof that I have done to her.

Margaret's appalling commination merely pricks him to further business and he hugs his villainy with a zest renewed:

> Clarence, whom I, indeed, have laid in darkness,
> I do beweep to many simple gulls;
> Namely, to Stanley, Hastings, Buckingham;
> And tell them 'tis the queen and her allies
> That stir the king against the duke, my brother.
> Now they believe it; and withal whet me
> To be revenged on Rivers, Vaughan, Grey:
> But then I sigh; and, with a piece of scripture,
> Tell them that God bids us do good for evil:
> And thus I clothe my naked villany
> With old odd ends stol'n forth of holy writ;
> And seem a saint, when most I play the devil.

Margaret's curses may frighten the others, but Richard holds himself immune:

> Our aery buildeth in the cedar's top,
> And dallies with the wind, and scorns the sun.

The second comminatory passage of the tragedy is yet more conclusive. Margaret's curse has been all but completely fulfilled. Rivers and Grey are dead. Hastings has been struck down. The princes are slain. Buckingham is in rebellion. Dorset has fled the country. But Richard is still untouched and on him is turned in full bent the chorus of bereaved women. The scene is long. It is a set piece and, significantly, has the same formal quality which distinguishes the masque of the spectres on Bosworth Field. It prefigures a nemesis on the moral plane—a plane on which Richard, in the prime of his faculties, cannot be reached. It is a choric interlude, in which the diction and gestures of the persons represented are deliberately contrasted with the normal speech of the tragedy—a tentative device which Shakespeare was one day to use with complete assurance in the scenes between Hamlet and his father's ghost and in the enactment before Claudius of the murder of Gonzago. The three women sit upon the ground to recite their litany. Each takes up the thought and phrase of each in a woeful canon that rises to a fearful climax:

> Cancel his bond of life, dear God! I pray,
> That I may live to say, The dog is dead!

Into this scene of studied lamentation marches Richard and his train, with drums and trumpets. His mother upbraids him. Elizabeth clamours for her children. Richard is merely impatient:

> A flourish, trumpets! strike alarum, drums!
> Let not the heavens hear these tell-tale women
> Rail on the Lord's anointed: strike, I say!
>   (*Flourish. Alarums.*)
> Either be patient, and entreat me fair,
> Or with the clamorous report of war
> Thus will I drown your exclamations.

The old sardonic humour twinkles still in Richard's profession of shocked surprise: *Rail on the Lord's anointed!* He refuses with a dry courtesy to accept any reproof from his mother. 'I will be mild and

gentle in my speech,' she promises at last. To which he responds:
'And brief, good mother.'

It is a small point, but worth noting, that the dramatist even
here secures for Richard the sympathy of his audience. We have had
more than enough of the cursing queans. We are in the mood to ask
with the Duchess herself: 'Why should calamity be full of words?'
The Duchess is brief enough, but makes good use of her time. Some
of her epithets are worth retaining. She knows her son pretty well—
wayward, wild, daring, bold, venturous, proud, subtle, sly and
bloody. 'Let me march on and not offend you, Madam,' says
Richard, very sensible and polite. 'You speak too bitterly,' he protests a moment later with an assumption of heavenly patience. And
when the Duchess has pronounced upon him a mother's curse, he
turns from her without a word—to undertake the seduction of
Elizabeth.

Fittingly enough it is Richard's mother, in a last speech to her
son, who explicitly links these comminatory passages with the scene
in Richard's tent on Bosworth Field:

> My prayers on the adverse party fight;
> And there the little souls of Edward's children
> Whisper the spirits of thine enemies
> And promise them success and victory.
> Bloody thou art, bloody will be thy end.

The three scenes are in formal progression, written in the same
distant key, each emphasising the impenitent rejection by Richard
of moral values which belong to another world.

The soliloquy into which Richard starts out of his dream in the
tent on Bosworth Field is an astonishing example of Shakespeare's
psychological intuition. The active, imperious, sardonic Richard,
struggling up into conscious life, calls instantly upon his mind and
will. They respond, uncertainly at first, but pricked into flashes of
wit and resolution which show that the fully-awakened man is still
the Richard we have learned to know. His first cry is one of sheer
defiance. He bursts from the haunted confines of his vision with a
line that only he could have used at such a moment:

> Give me another horse!

He has been visited in sleep by eleven ghosts. All prophesy his over-throw. All bid him despair and die. He wakes up—and calls for another horse!

And he continues:

> Soft! I did but dream.
> O coward conscience, how dost thou afflict me!
> The lights burn blue. It is now dead midnight.
> Cold fearful drops stand on my trembling flesh.
> What do I fear? myself? there's none else by:
> Richard loves Richard; that is, I am I.
> Is there a murderer here? No. Yes, I am:
> Then fly. What, from myself? Great reason why
> Lest I revenge. What! myself upon myself?
> Alack! I love myself.

Conscience has crept upon him in his sleep and afflicted him griev-ously. But conscience is a coward. He wonders to find himself in a sweat. What is it that he fears? Himself? The terse, homely play of his wit upon that theme—absurd, because Richard is Richard and loves himself—is in perfect character. So the argument goes on—no empty catechism, but a dialogue pointed at the heart of the eternal problem of conscience and personality. The reasoning becomes almost playful and concludes upon a whimsical note:

> There is no creature loves me;
> And if I die, no soul will pity me:
> Nay, wherefore should they, since that I myself
> Find in myself no pity to myself?

Richard has been shaken to the soul and he admits his discomfi-ture:

> By the apostle Paul, shadows to-night
> Have struck more terror to the soul of Richard
> Than can the substance of ten thousand soldiers
> Armèd in proof, and led by shallow Richmond;

but the point emphasised by the dramatist is that his mind and will stay firm. He defies augury. The sun neglects to shine upon his army but—
> what is that to me
> More than to Richmond? for the selfsame heaven
> That frowns on me looks sadly upon him.

Come, bustle, bustle—the word he likes best springs to his lips and he passes at once to the business of the day. He settles the order of battle and states for the last time the sinister faith in which he has lived and in which he is about to die:

> Every man unto his charge:
> Let not our babbling dreams affright our souls:
> Conscience is but a word that cowards use,
> Devised at first to keep the strong in awe:
> Our strong arms be our conscience, swords our law.

A moment later he is addressing his soldiers, man to man, in a speech full of blunt confidence in a strong cause:

> Let's whip these stragglers o'er the seas again;
> Lash hence these overweening rags of France;

> If we be conquer'd, let men conquer us,
> And not these bastard Bretons; whom our fathers
> Have in their own land beaten, bobb'd and thump'd.

And so to battle:

> Fight, gentlemen of England! fight, bold yeomen!
> Draw, archers, draw your arrows to the head!
> Spur your proud horses hard, and ride in blood;
> Amaze the welkin with your broken staves!

> A thousand hearts are great within my bosom.

Bosworth Field is the shortest battle in all the plays of Shakespeare. Richard's end, like the man, is violent, audacious and sudden:

Alarums. Enter KING RICHARD.

RICHARD: A horse! a horse! my kingdom for a horse!
CATESBY: Withdraw, my lord. I'll help you to a horse.
RICHARD: Slave, I have set my life upon a cast,
    And I will stand the hazard of the die.
    I think there be six Richmonds in the field;
    Five have I slain to-day, instead of him.
    A horse! a horse! my kingdom for a horse!

Is it an accident that Richard, facing his last fight on earth, echoes in his cry for a horse the words with which he broke from his haunted sleep of the night before? Accident, perhaps, but of the kind in which Shakespeare is prolific and whose profound felicity strikes swiftly at the imagination and is even more fully appreciated upon reflection. It is a flash of spirit in which Richard reveals himself as a man to whom the effort was everything and the result indifferent. Recall the passion with which he saw his kingdom, afar off, as a thing to be achieved:

> How sweet a thing it is to wear a crown;
> Within whose circuit is Elysium
> And all that poets feign of bliss and joy.

But now he is ready to exchange it for a horse—a horse which will enable him to die as he has lived, fighting the pigmies.

Admiration for Richard in his overthrow has been unstinted through the ages.

In our own time two critics as different in mind and temper as John Masefield and Bernard Shaw find themselves strangely linked in celebrating Richard's conduct in defeat. Masefield writes: 'The intellect of Richard . . . is restless, swift and sure of its power. It is sure, too, that the world stays as it is from something stupid in the milky human feelings. Richard is a 'bloody dog' let loose in a sheep-fold . . . but nobler than the sheep he destroys. He is the one great intellect in the play. . . . Richard is certain, as only fine intellect can be, that he will triumph. It is part of his tragedy that it is not intellect that triumphs in this world, but a stupid, though righteous, something incapable of understanding intellect.'

Bernard Shaw wrote to the actor Forbes-Robertson, in 1903: 'No actor has ever done the curious recovery by Richard of his old gaiety of heart in the excitement of the battle. . . . He is again the ecstatic prince of mischief of the "Shine out, fair sun, till I have bought a glass" phase, which makes the first act so rapturous. All Nietzsche is in the lines:

> Conscience is but a word that cowards use,
> Devised at first to keep the strong in awe:
> Our strong arms be our conscience, swords our law.

And after all the pious twaddle of Richmond his charging order is delicious:

> Let us to't pell-mell;
> If not to heaven, then hand in hand to hell.

The offer of his kingdom for a horse is part of the same thing: any means of keeping up the ecstasy of the fight is worth a dozen kingdoms.'

Richard III on Bosworth Field certainly goes to the head of all Nietzscheans.

The romantic critics—all except Coleridge—were not less spell-bound by the triumphant energy of Richard at the close. Hazlitt wrote of Kean's playing of the battle scene: 'He fights at last like one drunk with wounds; and the attitude in which he stands, his hands stretched out, after his sword has been wrested from him, has a preternatural and terrific grandeur, as if his will could not be disarmed and the very phantoms of his despair had power to kill.'

Lamb, more inquisitive in his approach, tries to explain his fascination. With his eyes fixed on Richard, he wrote of Shakespeare's villains in general: 'We think not so much of the crimes which they commit as of the ambition, the aspiring spirit, the intellectual activity which prompts them to overleap those moral fences.'

Coleridge, on the other hand, recoils in perplexity from a character which so deeply moved his great contemporaries. Coleridge could not get away from the fact that Richard was a wicked man and for once this greatest of all Shakespeare's critics was at fault. He did not allow for the fact that Shakespeare has relegated the moral issues of the tragedy to a plane remote from that on which Richard dazzles his admirers. The dramatist in no way obscures the distinction between right and wrong. Richard is a wicked man. But Shakespeare did not want his audience to be continually reminding themselves that his hero was by all human and divine standards unworthy of admiration. He leaves this aspect of the tragedy to a chorus of cursing queans and a masque of apparitions. Having thus disposed of the moral issue, he freely devotes his genius to the portrayal of Richard in all his sinister magnificence, with the result that the spectators are swept into a mood of devil-worship and are even tempted to ignore the plain meaning of the fundamental lesson of the play. Coleridge remained obstinately immune from this diabolic intoxication. Starting from the assumption—correct as far as it goes —that Shakespeare 'here as in all his great parts develops in a tone of sublime morality the dreadful consequences of placing the moral in subordination to the mere intellectual being', he successfully resists the author's mighty spell and even finds it difficult to believe that his beloved poet could have written some of the scenes in which our ecstatic prince of mischief so enchantingly reveals his essential quality. He misjudges the play from an ethical obsession and thus recedes to the level of his famous predecessor, Dr. Johnson, who, reading it with a grudging and somewhat stupefied admiration, concluded with the observation: 'Some parts are trifling, others shocking and some improbable.'

Shakespeare, in persuading us, as it were, to suspend our moral judgment, so that we may enjoy the gesture and flourish of an intellect untrammelled by conscience, plays upon his audience in the theatre the trick of the political leader who, accepting the Macchiavellian view of the prince's function in society, has focused upon himself the admiration of the cities and nations and empires of the world since history began. Richard is the superman who haunts the imagination and fills the sad chronicles of mankind. He belongs to a world in which justice and virtue stand remote, waiting for the hour when those who take the sword shall, if a little tardily, perish by the sword.

E

III

RICHARD OF BORDEAUX

SHAKESPEARE'S 'Richard II' is too often read as the tragedy of a private individual. Attention is focused upon Richard's personality and upon elements in his character which would have been just as interesting if he had never been called upon to play the part of a king. We are fascinated by the unfolding of his brilliant, wayward and unstable disposition, his pathetic lapses from bright insolence to grey despair, the facility with which he dramatises his sorrows and takes a wilfully aesthetic pleasure in his own disgrace. The political implications of the play are correspondingly neglected. And this is only natural. In all simplicity—and in essentials no tragedy was ever simpler—'Richard II' is the story of a sensitive, headstrong, clever, foolish man, graceless in prosperity, in calamity gracious. But this simple story has a setting and the setting is high politics. The fact that Richard is a king not only enhances the pathos of his fall, but sets him in a political environment in which the dramatist is not seldom interested for its own sake.

Men living under Elizabeth would think it strange that anyone should need to insist that 'Richard II' is a political play. To Shakespeare's audience its political significance was immediate and tremendous. It went to the heart of a burning question. Ministers of State wrote letters about it. It was years before the censor of books would allow the most famous of its scenes to be printed. It was played on one occasion as a propaganda piece and became the subject of a state trial. Queen Elizabeth, inspecting the Tower records with William Lambarde at Greenwich, was moved to exclaim: 'I am Richard II, know ye not that?' and to add with displeasure that 'this tragedy was played forty times in streets and houses.'

We are shortly to concentrate on the political aspects of the play which are significant for all times and places. First, however, it seems necessary to ask why 'Richard II' should have struck Shakespeare's contemporaries so forcibly not merely as a political play, but as by far the most topical political play of the period.

The ordinary Englishman who saw Shakespeare's tragedy in 1595 had lived in peace under a strong Government—and, what is even more important, an incontestably legitimate Government—for over a hundred years. But he still remembered the government of the house of Lancaster, which had been neither strong nor legitimate, and the hideous interim of civil war before Henry of Richmond married Elizabeth of York and provided England with a dynasty acceptable to God and man. In the years following 1595 the whole kingdom was on tenterhooks. Who was to succeed Elizabeth Tudor? The Virgin Queen was as coy of her successor as she had been of the suitors who years before, in despite of the gossips and in the teeth of her physician, might have helped her to solve the problem in the way of nature. Many were called but none was chosen. All that the Englishman held most dear had found a satisfying symbol in the Tudor monarch, ruling by divine right, holding a sacred office, to question whose authority was treason, to trouble whose peace was an impiety. But the Tudor monarch was about to die childless. Was England to fall back into the old disorder, horror, fear and mutiny which had followed the usurpation of Bolingbroke?

Shakespeare chose this moment to write a play in which a legitimate king is deposed and the dreadful consequences of a disputed succession to the crown foretold with eloquence and particularity. This play, moreover, which was topical enough in 1595, when Robert Cecil was invited to witness it at Channon Row, became yet more topical when in 1601 Essex had it ostentatiously performed at the Globe theatre on the eve of his rebellion. This was miching mallecho and meant mischief. There was no treason in the play, as Elizabeth and her Privy Council well knew, but there was undoubted treason in this particular performance. Essex had already cast himself for the part of Bolingbroke and had even gone so far as to accept in 1599 the dedication of a prose history on the reign of Henry IV in which he was addressed in effect as heir apparent to the throne. The prose history was suppressed and the gentleman who procured the performance of Shakespeare's play in 1601 was afterwards hanged. Neither Shakespeare nor his company, however, was molested. Shakespeare was no more responsible for the scandal caused in London by his 'Richard II' in 1601 than for the scandal caused in Paris by his 'Coriolanus' in 1935. He had written in each case a political play recognisably true of any period for the kind of situation and the type of public persons presented. Elizabeth disliked the play and very properly, according to her lights, regarded its performance before a select body of conspirators as a hanging matter. But for once the right persons were hanged—not the author, nor even the players, but certain members of the audience, who thus paid the penalty, which some might consider excessive, for confusing a work of art with a political manifesto.

Apart from the special circumstances which gave a topical interest to the play in the last years of Elizabeth, Shakespeare's Richard was bound to make a very strong appeal to his contemporaries on more general grounds. Richard of Bordeaux had towards the end of the sixteenth century become a legendary figure. His deposition had acquired a mystical significance. For over two centuries he had stood to poets and historians, both in England and in France, for a supreme example of that tragical fall of princes which appealed so strongly to the imagination and conscience of the post-mediaeval world. To the legitimists he was a martyr and his enforced abdication a sacrilege. To the Lancastrians his removal was a necessary act of providence. To all alike he was a tragic symbol of the instability of human fortune. Those who took the mystical view of his fall did not hesitate to compare his passion with that of Christ. Even those who, in deference to the house of Lancaster, affected to regard his deposition as a salutary act of state, were deeply affected by this saddest of all stories of the deaths of kings and tended to regard its protagonists as blind agents of a divine purpose rather than conscious masters of the event. Bolingbroke and Richard, in the Tudor imagination, played their parts as in a mystery, Richard accepting his humiliation as a cup that might not pass away and Bolingbroke, unconscious instrument in bringing about a second fall of man, achieving his triumph as a thing pre-ordained. This sacramental approach to the tragedy, which Shakespeare inherited and to which he gave exquisite humanity in the person of Richard, was an essential element in its contemporary appeal.[1]

[1] The blending of the mystical and the realist approach to the tragedy of Richard is finely described by Dr. Dover Wilson in his introduction to the play in the New

To most of Shakespeare's countrymen this contemporary aspect of the play is still alive. The English, in dealing faithfully with their kings for over a thousand years of history, have contrived to retain a mystical respect for the royal office without in any way forgoing their right of judgment on the royal person. The waters of the rough rude sea of English politics have washed the balm from half a dozen anointed kings without in any way detracting from the consecration of their successors. God save the King—but God help him if his subjects should find him troublesome. When the occasion arises—and it has arisen no less than four times since Richard died at Pomfret—the English people can always be trusted to demonstrate that a sincere reverence for monarchy is compatible with a distinctly uncivil treatment of the monarch. Nothing in fact so signally illustrates the force of English sentiment for royalty than its successful survival of so many royal persons who have left their country for their country's good. The emotions aroused in an Elizabethan by the enacted deposition of a king have outlived two revolutions and the importation of two foreign princes.

The central situation in Shakespeare's play thus retains much of its original appeal. But even if this were not the case, the political interest of the play and its relevance to the public life of our own or of any time would be scarcely affected. For Shakespeare's handling of the sacramental aspect of royalty is only one component of his tragedy. His main purpose is to exhibit in Richard the qualities which unfitted him to rule, to show his exquisite futility in dealing with public affairs, to present a playboy politician coping ineffectually with men seriously intent on the business of getting what they want, to contrast the man of imagination who lives unto himself with men of the world who adapt themselves to the event. A play with such a theme is necessarily a political play. 'Richard II', for all its lyrical quality, is concerned with public affairs and with the kind of men who in every generation delude themselves into the belief that they are making history. Over against Richard, whose personal disaster

Cambridge Edition. This introduction, in its handling of the sources of the play, relating them to the finished tragedy and throwing into relief the contemporary ideas and tendencies from which it emerged, is a masterpiece of Shakespearean criticism.

touches the heart of the spectator, Shakespeare has set in juxtaposition a group of politicians and an analysis of political events which
claim the attention no less forcibly.

With these preliminary observations in mind let us consider for a
moment the opening scene of the tragedy.

Henry, surnamed Bolingbroke, Duke of Hereford and son to
John of Gaunt, has publicly accused of high treason no less a person
than Thomas Mowbray, Duke of Norfolk. Richard summons them
to a hearing. The two men decline to be reconciled and the King is
reluctantly obliged to make arrangements for a trial by battle. Such
is the bare outline of this short scene of some two hundred lines. It
serves its dramatic purpose well enough if we see in it no more than
a robustious squabble between two angry noblemen who refuse to
be pacified by their sovereign. The essential ingredients of this short
scene are crystal clear on the surface—a king who is plainly not
master in his own house; two haughty subjects who huff it in the
royal presence, professing a reverence for Majesty which nevertheless stops short of obedience; a suggestion that this Richard, who
is not sufficiently sure of himself to call his troublesome subjects
to order, is quick to see through their assurances of respect; a
promise of exciting and turbulent events shortly to follow. Here,
surely, is matter enough to fill the first two hundred lines of any
play.

But there is more to it than that. Look a little more closely at the
political environment into which the dramatist, with his customary
abrupt felicity, introduces the hero of his tragedy.

Bolingbroke accuses Mowbray of complicity in the murder of the
Duke of Gloucester. He knows perfectly well, however, that Richard
himself is by many held responsible for Gloucester's death. In accus-
ing Mowbray, Bolingbroke is covertly attacking the King's government. He is playing the party game of His Majesty's Opposition,
using the gestures of the period. Mowbray, of course, knows what
Bolingbroke is driving at. So does everybody else. But nobody
would think of admitting it. The real issues are not even mentioned.
Bolingbroke, attacking the King, accuses his opponent of treason to
the King, Mowbray, who is of the King's party and who, if he did not
murder Gloucester himself, was at least an accessory to the crime by

negligence, affects to be defending himself against a merely personal charge. All that full-blooded talk by Bolingbroke about the devotion of a subject's love and by Mowbray about his spotless reputation is no more than the impassioned rhetoric of two rival politicians assuming in public the attitudes required of them by the situation. The other persons present are equally aware of the facts, but they, too, are expected to assume that Bolingbroke and Mowbray really mean what they say. These are two loyal gentlemen and their good faith must in decency be accepted. Each of them is lying and everyone present knows that they are lying, but each, according to the rules of the game, must be believed. The scene thus reveals itself on examination to be a notably accurate presentation of a familiar—and indeed typical—situation in public life, in which the outward professions of the persons concerned bear little or no relation to their real purposes and passions.

Mowbray has the better platform manner. It has a certain dignity:

> A jewel in a ten-times-barr'd-up chest
> Is a bold spirit in a loyal breast.
> Mine honour is my life; both grow in one;
> Take honour from me, and my life is done.

Bolingbroke is less fruitily impassioned, but no less ready to maintain with conviction that his actions are wholly determined by the loftiest motives. He calls on heaven to be the record of his speech. His divine soul is ready to answer in heaven for the truth and justice of his cause.

Shakespeare here presents the normal behaviour of notable persons discussing a political or diplomatic issue in public. The uninstructed onlooker enjoys the quarrel for its own sake. But the spectator who knows that all this high-and-mighty bickering has no more bearing on the facts of the dispute than the mutual recriminations of rival candidates for a parliamentary seat or the notes exchanged between foreign ministers in a time of international crisis, has, in addition to his enjoyment of the superficial cut-and-thrust of the formal encounter, the extra pleasure of understanding what it is all about. He sees through the pretences of the performers to the real subject matter of the performance.

Shakespeare leaves no doubt in the mind of an alert and intelligent spectator as to the facts of the dispute, but he does not rely on the ability of his audience to grasp them at a first performance. He does not, in fact, let us know immediately, if we did not know it before, that Richard was himself implicated in Gloucester's death. He lets *that* cat out of the bag at a later stage. Shakespeare has the fact well in mind, but it was not essential for him to stress it in the opening scene, where our attention is rightly concentrated on the more superficial aspects of the quarrel and on Richard's manifest inability to quash it. The subtler political implications of the incident are unfolded progressively. Shakespeare was too skilful a dramatist to demand the attention of his audience for more than one important thing at a time.

There is another aspect of this first scene which can only be fully appreciated at a later stage. Its main dramatic purpose is to show Richard facing a political situation with which he is unable to cope successfully. Towards the end of the play we are to see Bolingbroke confronted with a situation precisely similar at all points. We shall then see the usurper dealing promptly and effectively with this mediaeval equivalent of a cabinet crisis. He calls his refractory noblemen to order and successfully handles in five minutes an incident such as had cost Richard his throne.

There is yet another level on which this first simple episode of the play may be appreciated. On the political facts, almost every word uttered by Bolingbroke and Mowbray is a wilful misrepresentation. They nevertheless play their parts with complete conviction and everybody present accepts their posturing as the outcome of a genuine passion for truth and justice. This raises a point which crops up repeatedly in Shakespeare's political plays: how far does he deliberately satirise in his politicians the inconsistency of their professions with their performance? Mowbray is presented as a fine figure of a man and we shall shortly be quoting with admiration some of the moving things he has to say as a patriotic English gentleman. Did Shakespeare intend thereby to emphasise only the more effectively that he was a lamentable impostor?

It is on this third level of appreciation that Shakespeare provides us with surprising examples in many plays of his effortless grasp of the realities of political life. Mowbray and Bolingbroke are not presented as consciously fraudulent persons. They play the game according to the rules of their time and class. Mowbray loves his country, is loyal to the King and entirely convinced of his own honesty. Bolingbroke no less sincerely sees himself as a faithful public servant. He is morally sure of himself and prepared to hazard his life in defence of an honourable cause. Both are equally mistaken in themselves; and the facts, as presented by the dramatist, are not in accord with the pretensions of either party. But no satire is intended. The two men are presented without malice. They are political persons and that is how political persons behave.

The spectator's interest in the scene is naturally concentrated on the part played by Richard himself. The King has little to say, but every word is significant. He promises himself a bad quarter of an hour. The appeal is 'boisterous' and the appellants will be difficult to manage:

> High-stomach'd are they both, and full of ire,
> In rage deaf as the sea, hasty as fire.

He accepts the rules of the game and plays it with dignity. To Mowbray, who asks leave to present his case against a kinsman of the King, Richard gravely rejoins:

> Now, by my sceptre's awe I make a vow,
> Such neighbour nearness to our sacred blood
> Should nothing privilege him, nor partialise
> The unstooping firmness of my upright soul:
> He is our subject, Mowbray; so art thou:
> Free speech and fearless I do thee allow.[1]

After listening patiently to the accuser and the accused, he attempts with an assumption of playful good humour to reconcile the parties:

> Forget, forgive; conclude and be agreed;
> Our doctors say this is no month to bleed.

---

[1] Note the political irony of this rejoinder. Mowbray is *defending* the King. Richard graciously gives him permission to do so and assures him that he will not allow himself to be moved by any partiality for his kinsman, Bolingbroke, who is *attacking* him.

He appeals personally to Mowbray:

RICHARD: Rage must be withstood:
           Give me his gage: lions make leopards tame.
MOWBRAY: Yea, but not change his spots:

Neither will consent to a peace and Richard finally accepts the inevitable. He closes the proceedings with a set speech in which the formal decencies of a false situation are solemnly maintained:

> We were not born to sue, but to command:
> Which since we cannot do to make you friends,
> Be ready, as your lives shall answer it,
> At Coventry, upon Saint Lambert's day:
> There shall your swords and lances arbitrate
> The swelling difference of your settled hate:
> Since we cannot atone you, we shall see
> Justice design the victor's chivalry.

Shakespeare makes it very plain that Richard is fully alive to all the political implications of the situation. In his first words to the contending parties he drily dismisses their professions of respect:

BOLINGBROKE: Many years of happy days befal
             My gracious sovereign, my most loving liege!
MOWBRAY: Each day still better other's happiness;
             Until the heavens, envying earth's good hap,
             Add an immortal title to your crown!
RICHARD: We thank you both: yet one but flatters us,
             As well appeareth by the cause you come;
             Namely, to appeal each other of high treason.

The reproof is shrewd and neatly turned. Richard's position requires him to accept the pleadings of the parties. But he is not going to let anyone imagine that he attaches the slightest value to their professions and, in asking Bolingbroke to state his case, he covertly warns his cousin to remember that, in attacking Mowbray, he is sailing dangerously near the wind:

> What doth our cousin lay to Mowbray's charge?
> It must be great that can inherit us
> So much as of a thought of ill in him.

Bolingbroke prefers his charges and concludes with a vigorously complacent picture of himself as appointed by heaven to chastise an injurious villain by whose contriving his uncle Gloucester had sluiced out his innocent soul through streams of blood:

> Which blood, like sacrificing Abel's, cries,
> Even from the tongueless caverns of the earth,
> To me for justice and rough chastisement;
> And, by the glorious worth of my descent,
> This arm shall do it, or this life be spent.

Richard is thereby provoked to a further disclosure of his private mind. Bolingbroke is professing his loyalty, but he is in fact challenging the King's man. In a bitter, penetrating aside Richard exclaims:

> How high a pitch his resolution soars!

He already divines in Bolingbroke an ambition which reaches instinctively beyond its immediate purpose, and, in assuring Mowbray that he may fearlessly answer the charges brought against him, Richard puts the predestined usurper in his place with a crushing exactitude:

> Mowbray, impartial are our eyes and ears:
> Were he my brother, nay, my kingdom's heir,—
> *As he is but my father's brother's son—*
> Now, by my sceptre's awe I make a vow,
> Such neighbour nearness to our sacred blood
> Should nothing privilege him.

This king is already showing qualities of mind that put him in a different class from the noble persons surrounding him. He is contemptuous of the game which he is required to play, but plays it becomingly and with a sidelong smile. He may blunder fatally in his handling of persons and events, but there is never any doubt of his intelligence. It is equally clear from the outset that he has the courage of his fitful genius. He sees through these proud, turbulent and practical men of affairs, and he is not afraid to let them know it.

Mowbray's answer to the charges brought against him by Bolingbroke clearly illuminates the harsh political background against which the tragedy of Richard is to be unfolded. Mowbray has been accused of peculation and murder. He admits to having pocketed a

quarter of the sum which was earmarked to pay the King's soldiers
at Calais, but this, he pleads, was only to recoup himself for expenses
incurred on a previous account. Let that pass. On the accusation of
murder, he seems unnecessarily candid—until we realise that he is
merely stating facts that were common knowledge:

> For Gloucester's death,
> I slew him not; but to mine own disgrace
> Neglected my sworn duty in that case.
> For you, my noble lord of Lancaster,
> The honourable father to my foe,
> Once did I lay an ambush for your life,
> A trespass that doth vex my grievèd soul;
> But ere I last receiv'd the sacrament
> I did confess it, and exactly begg'd
> Your grace's pardon, and I hope I had it.

What could be fairer than that? Mowbray's ingenuous apology
is a fair measure of the accepted political standards of the time.
He was not guilty of Gloucester's murder, he merely did nothing
to prevent it. He had tried to murder Gaunt, but he had apologised
to the party concerned and hoped that the incident was closed.
It is necessary to keep these facts in mind if we are fairly to judge
Richard's less amiable reactions to some of the later speeches and
to the conduct in general of his noble kinsmen.

The second scene of the play, which is devoted to a conversation
between John of Gaunt and the Duchess of Gloucester, has no other
purpose than to underline the political implications of the first. The
widowed Duchess urges Gaunt to exact retribution for her husband's
death. She belongs to that long line of noble dames used by Shakespeare in his political plays to remind the spectator that there are
human, and even moral, considerations which should not be altogether ignored in public life. Gaunt has decided to let the matter rest
and, in defending his decision, explicitly insists that Richard himself
was a party to the crime:

> But since correction lieth in those hands
> Which made the fault that we cannot correct,
> Put we our quarrel to the will of heaven.

> God's is the quarrel; for God's substitute,
> His deputy anointed in His sight,
> Hath caused his death; the which if wrongfully,
> Let heaven revenge; for I may never lift
> An angry arm against His minister.

The Duchess is unconvinced:

> Call it not patience, Gaunt; it is despair:
> In suffering thus thy brother to be slaughter'd,
> Thou showest the naked pathway to thy life,
> Teaching stern murder how to butcher thee:
> That which in mean men we intitle patience
> Is pale cold cowardice in noble breasts.

The political wisdom of the bastard feudalism of fourteenth-century England could not be more lucidly expressed.

The scene between Gaunt and the Duchess, which discloses the political realities of the dispute between Mowbray and Bolingbroke, is followed by the famous scene in which we are invited to enjoy for its own sake the pageantry of the royal lists at Coventry, where these impressive champions, plated in habiliments of war, commit their several causes to heaven and proceed with high solemnity to face the ordeal by battle. It is a gallant show and Shakespeare is too good a dramatist to spoil its effect by insisting unseasonably that it is also, in effect, an amusingly veracious study in the public deportment of men in high places. Richard ceremoniously invites the champions to declare their business. The defendant in armour and the appellant in armour respond according to the protocol. Each professes his truth and nobility of purpose. Each takes a devoted leave of his sovereign. Mowbray still has the better platform manner:

> However God or fortune cast my lot,
> There lives or dies, true to King Richard's throne,
> A loyal, just, and upright gentleman:
> Never did captive with a freer heart
> Cast off his chains of bondage and embrace
> His golden uncontroll'd enfranchisement,
> More than my dancing soul doth celebrate
> This feast of battle with mine adversary.
> Most mighty liege, and my companion peers,

> Take from my mouth the wish of happy years.
> As gentle and as jocund as to jest,
> Go I to fight; truth has a quiet breast.

The more vigilant spectator may detect a subtle difference in Richard's addresses to the two men. Surely there is a touch of irony in his words to Bolingbroke:

> Cousin of Hereford, as thy cause is right,
> So be thy fortune in this royal fight;

and a touch of affectionate approval in his valediction to Mowbray:

> Farewell, my lord; securely I espy
> Virtue with valour couchèd in thine eye.

But these are hints to the wary. The simple onlooker is absorbed by the knightly courtesy of it all and is as eager for the fight as the champions themselves.

Then comes the grand surprise. The charge is sounded. But stay, the King has thrown his warder down! Defendant and appellant are bidden to lay aside their spears and Richard withdraws with his council while the champions disarm. Presently he emerges and announces his decision. The King, to save his peace, banishes them both—Bolingbroke for ten years and Mowbray for life:

> Draw near,
> And list what with our council we have done.
> For that our kingdom's earth should not be soil'd
> With that dear blood which it hath fosterèd;
> And for our eyes do hate the dire aspect
> Of civil wounds plough'd up with neighbours' swords;
> And for we think the eagle-wingèd pride
> Of sky-aspiring and ambitious thoughts,
> With rival-hating envy, set on you
> To wake our peace, which in our country's cradle
> Draws the sweet infant breath of gentle sleep;
>
> .   .   .   .   .   .
>
> Therefore, we banish you our territories.

It is a veritable sensation in court.

It should be noted that the King's decision is no sudden freak of temperament but a considered act of state. Richard is acting with the

approval of his council and Gaunt himself is a consenting party to
the arrangement. When the old man laments that he may not live to
see his banished heir again, Richard pertinently reminds him:

> Thy son is banish'd upon good advice,
> Whereto thy tongue a party-verdict gave.

Richard's interruption of the ordeal by battle at the eleventh hour
has often been cited as evidence of his impulsive disposition. But the
scene has a greater and very different significance if we suppose that
Richard had decided beforehand to quash the proceedings. For him
the whole elaborate to-do, with its heralds and trumpets, solemn
appeals to heaven, ceremonious farewells and heroic attitudes, was
matter for a May morning. He knows that these doughty champions
are inflating themselves to no purpose. The actor playing Richard
should watch them with a twinkle, impishly awaiting the moment
when he will knock the bottom out of all these political high jinks.
There is a merry side to the puerility of Richard, the boy-king who
would never grow up. The whole scene is in the nature of a practical
joke.

We should like to have been present at the cabinet meeting which
found so discreet a remedy for a situation which was as embarrassing
for Gaunt, leader of the King's opposition, as for the King, leader of
his own government. If Mowbray had killed Bolingbroke, Gaunt
would have lost his son. If Bolingbroke had killed Mowbray, the
King would have lost a loyal servant. All the sleeping dogs, which it
is the whole art of politics to let lie, would in either case have been
set barking to the discomfiture of both parties. Shakespeare must
have been sorely tempted to show us the King and his ministers discussing at length the real issues of the dispute. But he chose to concentrate upon his grand surprise of the interrupted combat and to
fix the interest of his public on the gorgeous preliminaries of the
tournament. He preferred to present Mowbray and Bolingbroke to
the simple spectator as *bona fide* champions and to reveal them to the
more judicious as figures of fun only at the eleventh hour.

The dramatist, in the final result, has it both ways—the tournament for what it is worth and, for those who look below the surface,
the political comedy as well. It is the reward of an artist who sees

things as they are that his rounded achievement defies all the categories. It can be enjoyed as a true and faithful presentment of men and things, as an emotional experience and as an act of judgment. The general effect is a combination of all three.

Shakespeare, having sprung his grand surprise on the audience in the lists at Coventry, instinctively refrains from bringing his champions to earth. From silver trumpets to brass tacks would have been too steep a fall. Bolingbroke and Mowbray maintain their heraldic attitudes to the last. Mowbray in particular is permitted to make a dignified and sincerely affecting retirement from public life:

> The language I have learn'd these forty years,
> My native English, now I must forgo:
> And now my tongue's use is to me no more
> Than an unstringèd viol or a harp,
> Or like a cunning instrument cased up,
> Or, being open, put into his hands
> That knows no touch to tune the harmony.
>
> I am too old to fawn upon a nurse,
> Too far in years to be a pupil now:
> What is thy sentence then but speechless death,
> Which robs my tongue from breathing native breath?

He is to the last a faithful subject. He had every right to protest that his sentence was unjust. Richard would undoubtedly have preferred to banish Bolingbroke for life and Mowbray for ten years. But he had been obliged to secure Gaunt's consent to the arrangement and Mowbray had to be sacrificed to the opposition. Mowbray understands and accepts the situation. He cannot explicitly defend himself without exposing the King to further embarrassment. He submits loyally to the decision, though he cannot refrain from suggesting that it was unmerited:

> A heavy sentence, my most sovereign liege,
> And all unlook'd for from your highness' mouth:
> A dearer merit, not so deep a maim
> As to be cast forth in the common air,
> Have I deservèd at your highness' hands.

Bolingbroke presses his case to the end:

> Confess thy treasons ere thou fly the realm;
> Since thou hast far to go, bear not along
> The clogging burthen of a guilty soul.

But Mowbray is not to be pricked, even at this bitter moment, into making things difficult for his master and confines himself to warning Richard against his enemy:

> No, Bolingbroke, if ever I were traitor,
> My name be blotted from the book of life,
> And I from heaven banish'd as from hence!
> But what thou art, God, thou, and I do know;
> And all too soon, I fear, the king shall rue.

One cannot help reflecting that, if Richard, for his time of need, had retained by his side so devoted a servant as Thomas Mowbray, Bolingbroke would less easily have compassed his designs.[1]

Bolingbroke's manner of accepting the King's award is highly characteristic. He persists, as we have just noted, in re-affirming the

---

[1] Shakespeare undoubtedly had this thought in mind. Years later Mowbray's son, in rebellion against Henry IV, recalls the lists at Coventry and the part played in that scene by his father:

> The king that loved him, as the state stood then,
> Was force perforce compell'd to banish him:
> And then that Henry Bolingbroke and he,
> Being mounted and both rousèd in their seats,
> Their neighing coursers daring of the spur,
> Their armèd staves in charge, their beavers down,
> Their eyes of fire sparkling through sights of steel
> And the loud trumpet blowing them together,
> Then, then, when there was nothing could have stay'd
> My father from the breast of Bolingbroke,
> O, when the king did throw his warder down,
> His own life hung upon the staff he threw;
> Then threw he down himself and all their lives
> That by indictment and by dint of sword
> Have since miscarried under Bolingbroke.

This is only one of many references back to 'Richard II' which occur throughout the two succeeding plays. Shakespeare's tetralogy—'Richard II', the First and Second Parts of 'Henry IV' and 'Henry V'—is a sequence not only in history but in theme and motive. In all four plays the dramatist looks forward and backward and carries in his mind all that has gone before and all that is to come. Thus we are able to find in the fourth Act of the third play of the series a passage which reveals what was present in his mind, though not explicitly stated, when he was writing the first Act of the first play.

justice of his cause and receives his sentence with a forced humility in which there lurks an element of sly defiance:

> Your will be done: this must my comfort be,
> That sun that warms you here shall shine on me;
> And those his golden beams to you here lent
> Shall point on me and gild my banishment.

You will look in vain, however, for any suggestion that Bolingbroke yet aims higher than a subject should. Richard is alive to his ambition; Mowbray warns the King that he is dangerous. But Bolingbroke gives no sign of his purpose—and for an excellent reason. He is that most dangerous of all climbing politicians, the man who will go further than his rivals because he never allows himself to know where he is going. Every step in his progress towards the throne is dictated by circumstances and he never permits himself to have a purpose till it is more than half fulfilled. From first to last his friends and enemies alike are always more clearly aware of his intentions than the man himself.

This is especially true of Richard, who divines in Bolingbroke the secret, unsleeping treachery of one who plays instinctively for his own hand. Richard's distrust is covertly conveyed in the present scene by his suddenly requiring both parties to swear upon his royal sword that they will not conspire against him in exile. The admonition, administered to Mowbray as well as to Bolingbroke, is in fact addressed to Bolingbroke alone:

> You never shall, so help you truth and God!
> Embrace each other's love in banishment;
> Nor never look upon each other's face;
> Nor never write, regreet, nor reconcile
> This louring tempest of your home-bred hate:
> Nor never by advisèd purpose meet
> To plot, contrive, or complot any ill
> 'Gainst us, our state, our subjects, or our land.

Bolingbroke swears the oath and Richard appears to be satisfied. He even indulges his essential good nature by remitting four years of Bolingbroke's sentence out of consideration for the sorrowing

Gaunt. Bolingbroke's comment on Richard's mercy is to observe
how fine a thing it is to be an absolute monarch:

> How long a time lies in one little word!
> Four lagging winters and four wanton springs
> End in a word: such is the breath of kings.

Bolingbroke maintains his enigmatic silence even after Richard
has departed. His friends press round him with expressions of con-
dolence, but he is not to be drawn into speech. Gaunt is moved to
protest against his almost inhuman reticence:

> O! to what purpose dost thou hoard thy words,
> That thou return'st no greeting to thy friends?

Bolingbroke's answer is to play for sympathy as an unhappy man
condemned to exile. Gaunt is thereby diverted into uttering words
of comfort, exquisitely moving but addressed, we feel, to the wrong
person:

> All places that the eye of heaven visits
> Are to a wise man ports and happy havens.
> Teach thy necessity to reason thus;
> There is no virtue like necessity.

> Suppose the singing birds musicians,
> The grass whereon thou tread'st the presence strew'd,
> The flowers fair ladies, and thy steps no more
> Than a delightful measure or a dance.

It is difficult to imagine Bolingbroke consoling himself with the
accents of divine philosophy or to picture him as taking any pleasure
in singing-birds. He quits the stage on a political peroration:

> Where'er I wander, boast of this I can,
> Though banish'd, yet a trueborn Englishman.

So for a moment we take leave of Henry, surnamed Bolingbroke,
Duke of Hereford and son to John of Gaunt. During his temporary
absence from the scene let us look a little more closely into his
character and place in the tragedy.

There are two apparently opposite views of Bolingbroke's conduct in this first of the three plays in which he figures. But the opposition is superficial and it disappears as we begin to grasp his funda-

mental qualities. Coleridge, significantly enough, puts forward now one and now the other, without seeming to be in any way aware of their inconsistency.

Critics who keep exclusively to the first view describe Bolingbroke as a long-headed conspirator, consciously bent on obtaining the crown from the outset, concealing a fixed purpose under a show of false humility, deliberately advancing step by step to the achievement of his purpose. Coleridge, when he writes of the 'preconcertedness of Bolingbroke's scheme' and the 'decorous and courtly checking of his anger in subservience to a predetermined plan' appears to favour this interpretation. Hazlitt, too, comes very near it when he describes Bolingbroke as 'seeing his advantage afar-off, but only seizing on it when he has it within his reach, humble, crafty, bold and aspiring, encroaching by regular but slow degrees.'

Critics who whole-heartedly espouse the second view see in Bolingbroke a man who, in the words of Dr. Dover Wilson, 'appears to be borne upward by a power beyond his volition.' According to this reading of the character there is no premeditation in the conduct of Bolingbroke, no indication of a deep design. He takes in Shakespeare's tragedy the part assigned to him in the chronicles which saw in the deposition of Richard something more than a story of successful ambition at the expense of an unsuccessful king. It is a view of Bolingbroke in relation to Richard which comes from Holinshed himself, who wrote: 'In this dejecting of the one and advancing of the other, the providence of God is to be respected and his secret will to be wondered at.'

Shakespeare has created in Bolingbroke a character which fits perfectly into this mystical view of the tragedy, but which can at the same time be enjoyed as faithfully portraying a political opportunist in almost any period or environment. Shakespeare's Bolingbroke, in following his fortune, instinctively adapts himself to the moment. His intentions remain obscure, even to himself, till they are in effect fulfilled. He thus conveys the impression that he is just as much the victim of necessity as master of the event, and Coleridge, who diagnoses premeditation, can without essentially contradicting himself also describe him as 'scarcely daring to look at his own views or to acknowledge them as designs.'

For confirmation of a reading in which instinctive premeditation is reconciled with an equally instinctive yielding to circumstance we have the final word of Bolingbroke himself. It is the word of a dying king. He looks back over the troubled years of his reign and, though pregnantly conscious of the 'indirect crook'd ways, whereby he had achieved the crown, he nevertheless meditates on the blindness with which he once pursued his infant fortune, and he goes on to state explicitly that he had acted throughout undesignedly, as a man thrust on by force of circumstance:

> Though then, God knows, I had no such intent,
> But that necessity so bowed the state
> That I and greatness were compell'd to kiss.[1]

The noblemen who assisted Bolingbroke to win the crown also take this view. More than once, telling the story in retrospect, they comment on the way in which circumstances conspired to smooth his way to the throne, so that at the last he only needed to accept what destiny had thrust into his hands. Worcester, for example, meeting the King years later at Shrewsbury, describes the whole process as it struck the men who had contributed to the event:

> You swore to us,
> And you did swear that oath at Doncaster,
> That you did nothing purpose 'gainst the state;
> Nor claim no further than your new-fall'n right,
> The seat of Gaunt, dukedom of Lancaster:
> To this we swore our aid. But in short space
> It rain'd down fortune, showering on your head;
> And such a flood of greatness fell on you,
> What with our help, what with the absent king,
> What with the injuries of a wanton time,
> The seeming sufferances that you had borne,
> And the contrarious winds that held the king
> So long in his unlucky Irish wars,
> That all in England did repute him dead:
> And from this swarm of fair advantages
> You took occasion to be quickly woo'd
> To grip the general sway into your hand.

[1] See below, p. 210.

This reading of Bolingbroke is consistent with all that we have yet seen of him in the first Act of 'Richard II'. It will become even more explicit as we follow him through the play.

It is Shakespeare's way to concentrate on one thing at a time. The stage is now clear for a firm handling of the political issues which lay behind the King's sentence of exile.[1] The hints already conveyed that Richard divines the character and intentions of Bolingbroke more clearly than Bolingbroke himself now blossom into direct and vivid statement. Richard, King by divine right, has noted in his rival the arts whereby a man may aspire to rule by popular favour. He has observed Bolingbroke's courtship of the common people:

> How he did seem to dive into their hearts
> With humble and familiar courtesy,
> What reverence he did throw away on slaves,
> Wooing poor craftsmen with the craft of smiles
> And patient underbearing of his fortune.
>
> Off goes his bonnet to an oyster-wench;
> A brace of draymen bid God speed him well
> And had the tribute of his supple knee,
> With 'Thanks, my countrymen, my loving friends';
> As were our England in reversion his,
> And he our subjects' next degree in hope.

Unfortunately Richard's perceptions have little relation to his conduct. Bolingbroke is dangerous, but Richard, in the Elizabethan sense, is secure. He anatomises in Bolingbroke the qualities that crave wary walking, but carelessly embarks upon a career which is to cost him his life and crown. The Irish are in rebellion. He will cross the sea in person to suppress them, leaving his kingdom open to invasion and his subjects to foot the bill:

---

[1] The editors who divided Shakespeare's plays into Acts should, as Dr. Johnson has pointed out, have concluded Act I with the banishment of Bolingbroke and started Act II with Richard's subsequent comments on the episode. They chose instead to include in Act I the short scene with Aumerle. This scene in time, temper and subject should obviously be Scene I of Act II and not, as printed in all editions, Scene IV of Act I.

We will ourself in person to this war:
And, for our coffers with too great a court
And liberal largess are grown somewhat light,
We are enforced to farm our royal realm;
The revenue whereof shall furnish us
For our affairs in hand: if that come short,
Our substitutes at home shall have blank charters;
Whereto, when they shall know what men are rich,
They shall subscribe them for large sums of gold,
And send them after to supply our wants.

This is bad enough, but worse is to follow. News is brought that
John of Gaunt is sick. Richard blithely embraces the occasion:

Now put it, God, in the physician's mind
To help him to his grave immediately!
The lining of his coffers shall make coats
To deck our soldiers for these Irish wars.
Come, gentlemen, let's all go visit him:
Pray God we may make haste, and come too late!

Richard's treatment of the dying Gaunt is one of the prime causes
of his downfall. It is also the least amiable episode of his career.
Shakespeare, writing the famous scene in which Gaunt with his
dying breath celebrates the glories of England, tarnished by an unworthy king, seems deliberately bent on setting us against his hero.
Why this exaltation of Gaunt at Richard's expense? No character in
Shakespeare has a finer end. The prologue is rich in promise:

O, but they say the tongues of dying men
Enforce attention like deep harmony.

The setting sun, and music at the close,
As the last taste of sweets, is sweetest last;

and the promise is nobly fulfilled in lines quoted by generations of
Englishmen, that can never be worn threadbare:

This royal throne of kings, this scepter'd isle,
This earth of majesty, this seat of Mars,
This other Eden, demi-paradise,
This fortress built by Nature for herself
Against infection and the hand of war,

This happy breed of men, this little world,
This precious stone set in the silver sea,
Which serves it in the office of a wall,
Or as a moat defensive to a house,
Against the envy of less happier lands,
This blessèd plot, this earth, this realm, this England,
This nurse, this teeming womb of royal kings:

This land of such dear souls, this dear, dear land,
Dear for her reputation through the world,
Is now leased out,—I die pronouncing it,—
Like to a tenement or pelting farm:
England, bound in with the triumphant sea,
Whose rocky shore beats back the envious siege
Of watery Neptune, is now bound in with shame,
With inky blots and rotten parchment bonds:
That England, that was wont to conquer others,
Hath made a shameful conquest of itself.

For this prophet, new-inspired, Richard has neither respect nor mercy. Clearly he is deeply moved by the speech, but that only makes him all the more savage in retort. He rounds on the sick man in a flash of temper:

And thou a lunatic lean-witted fool,
Presuming on an ague's privilege,
Dar'st with thy frozen admonition
Make pale our cheek, chasing the royal blood
With fury from his native residence.
Now, by my seat's right royal majesty,
Wert thou not brother to great Edward's son,
This tongue that runs so roundly in thy head
Should run thy head from thy unreverent shoulders.

It may be urged in extenuation that Richard had small reason to spare the father of Bolingbroke. When York protests:

I do beseech your majesty, impute his words
To wayward sickliness and age in him:
He loves you, on my life, and holds you dear
As Harry, Duke of Hereford, were he here;

Richard retorts with a touch of shrill hysteria:

> Right, you say true: as Hereford's love, so his;
> As theirs, so mine; and all be as it is.

There is, however, neither haste nor temper to excuse his reception of the news, a minute or so later, that Gaunt is dead. His comment is touched with feeling for the common lot of man:

> The ripest fruit first falls, and so doth he;
> His time is spent, our pilgrimage must be.
> So much for that;

but there is no yielding on the personal issue. Gaunt is dead. *So much for that*—and Richard at once announces that he will seize his uncle's plate, coin and revenues.

Critics who insist that Shakespeare has an ethical purpose in his tragedies tend to regard this scene, in which Richard shows us the worst of his character, as a deliberate preparation for the retribution which is to follow. But the world in which Shakespeare's characters move is not a moral gymnasium. It is a world in which men and women reveal their hearts and minds, engage our sympathy and evoke our perpetual wonder at the intricate working of simple or subtle souls. The dramatist, in this present instance, while he uncompromisingly exposes the flaws in Richard's character which lie at the heart of his tragic failure, is not bringing him to judgment, but presenting him with a compassionate understanding of his frailty. Richard does not forfeit our sympathy. We feel that his rash, fierce blaze of riot cannot last and this mitigates our censure. Nor is his conduct altogether unjustified. Richard saw in this Galahad of the sceptred isle a political enemy masquerading as a patriot, a cantankerous nobleman whose son had already made mischief in the land and was to make more. Richard's behaviour, heartless and unseasonable enough in all conscience, is that of a spoiled child of fortune, as he then was, resenting a rebuke peculiarly exasperating in that it was, in the specific instance, deserved but, from such a man, misplaced.

The question still remains: why does Shakespeare weight the scales so heavily against Richard in this scene? Why give to Gaunt, at the very moment when Richard is to behave so badly, the finest speech in the play? Why did Shakespeare permit himself an outburst of lyrical ecstasy whereby he risked putting his hero irretrievably in the shade and thus killing his play dead in the first Act?

The answer is to be found in the mood and structure of the tragedy. Gaunt, in his dying speech, is but one of many voices to which a single tune is given: the voice of Mowbray, mourning his exile from England; the voice of Gaunt, declaring his love of England; the voice of Richard, saluting with his hand the dear earth of England. To all these voices is given in turn the chorus-theme which serves as background to the political figures of the story. In every one of Shakespeare's political plays we feel the constant presence of a country and a people. In 'Richard II' it assumes a lyrical form, flowering through the texture of the verse on all possible occasions. Shakespeare, coming to Gaunt on his deathbed, saw a magnificent opportunity and seized it without misgiving. He was confident, if he gave the matter a conscious thought, that our sympathy with Richard would survive this splendid interlude and he even contrived that it should reveal the character of his hero to better effect than the more cautious approach which common prudence would have dictated to a journeyman playwright.

The political implications of Richard's decision to seize his uncle's property have now to be considered. But here we must pause to make the acquaintance of a new character, the most important person in the play after Richard and Bolingbroke, and one of the most interesting in the whole gallery of Shakespeare's political portraits.

Edmund of Langley, Duke of York, belongs to a type of politician which has made more English history in the bulk than any other. He is a public figure not from choice but by nativity. Shakespeare found him in the chronicles in the shape of a man who loved hunting and good cheer and avoided the council chamber—just the kind of person, in fact, to provide a contrast in temperament with Richard and in ability with Bolingbroke. York has no refinement of understanding and no political ambition. He is a sturdy, honest, well-meaning man, prompt with sensible advice but easily flustered, shrewd enough to see what's coming but not clever or resolute enough to prevent it. He stands for the average gentleman amateur in public life, as true to his friends and as firm in his principles as the times allow. Normally he makes the best of a bad business—which is usually not so bad after all, either for himself or for the nation. Such men are loyal to a government as long as it has legal or traditional status and the means to enforce it. With every appearance of probity and devotion—by no means wholly assumed—they contrive to find themselves in the long run sturdily swimming with the tide. These men of moderate intelligence and average sensibility are normally the backbone of the English political system. Every now and then a member of this class, of more outstanding ability than the rest, will step forward from the ranks when it becomes necessary to direct the allegiance of a party, a government or a people to new fountains of authority. English history has two illustrious examples of the type in James Monk, who served the Commonwealth till it was time to bring King Charles back to Whitehall, and in John Churchill, who served King James till it was time to call King William from The Hague. The politician who saves his country by turning his coat is God's most precious gift to a people which prefers a change of government to a revolution.

Such a person is Shakespeare's Edmund of Langley, Duke of York. He stays with Richard till Richard can no longer usefully be served and he serves Bolingbroke with an equally good conscience as soon as Bolingbroke has successfully assumed the crown. He needs careful watching, for Shakespeare fits him so smoothly into the pattern of the play that his importance is apt to be overlooked. We discover him, upon his first effective appearance, urging Gaunt not to waste breath in admonishing his wilful nephew:

> Direct not him whose way himself will choose.

This very sound advice comes at the conclusion of a speech engagingly appropriate in the mouth of so representative an Englishman. Richard, York contends, is too full of foreign notions. The royal ear is no longer open to wholesome English counsel:

> No; it is stopp'd with other flattering sounds,
> As praises, of whose taste the wise are fond,
> Lascivious metres, to whose venom sound

> The open ear of youth doth always listen,
> Report of fashions in proud Italy,
> Whose manners still our tardy apish nation
> Limps after in base imitation:
> Where doth the world thrust forth a vanity—
> So it be new, there's no respect how vile—
> That is not quickly buzz'd into his ears?
> Then all too late comes counsel to be heard.

But nobody ever listens to York. Gaunt rejects his warning and, when Gaunt is dead and his property attached, Richard pays no attention to his uncle's protests. York wisely insists that, if the King of England, ruling by right of birth and the feudal law, deprives Bolingbroke of his succession to the estates of his father, he will be destroying not only his own title to the crown but everybody's title to anything at all. The barons of England hold their stake in the country by primogeniture:

> Take Hereford's rights away, and take from Time
> His charters and his customary rights,
> Let not to-morrow then ensue to-day;
> Be not thyself; for how art thou a king
> But by fair sequence and succession?

> You pluck a thousand dangers on your head,
> You lose a thousand well-disposèd hearts,
> And prick my tender patience to those thoughts
> Which honour and allegiance cannot think.

York speaks like a true conservative in defence of the traditional rights of property. It cuts him to the heart that his sovereign, apex of the feudal pyramid, should have such small respect for the broad base on which it rests. He might have added that Richard, in seizing the estates of Bolingbroke, was providing his enemy with an excellent pretext for unlawfully returning to England to claim a lawful inheritance.

Richard's answer has the urchin brevity and wilfulness which characterise all his acts of sovereignty:

> Think what you will, we seize into our hands
> His plate, his goods, his money, and his lands,

York departs, shaking his wise old head. If Richard is determined to ruin himself, he can only wash his hands of the business: 'I'll not be by the while.'

York, however, is not permitted to escape into private life. Richard sends off messengers to effect the seizure of Gaunt's property and announces that to-morrow he will sail for Ireland. What follows is almost a stroke of humour in a play that but rarely invites a smile:

> And we create, in absence of ourself,
> Our uncle York lord governor of England;
> For he is just and always loved us well.

York has just scolded Richard roundly, proffered him advice which has been discourteously rejected and retired with ominous allusions to what must come of the 'bad courses' of his nephew. All this has passed clean over Richard's head. York is his uncle and York shall therefore act as his regent. Richard is quick to utter more than his mind on all occasions and, as is common with free speakers, he attaches little or no importance to what anybody else may say. He is in no way disconcerted by his uncle's reproaches and abrupt retirement. *For he is just and always loved us well.*

The argument urged upon Richard by York is picked up immediately by the Lords Willoughby, Ross and Northumberland as soon as Richard leaves the stage. *Our* lives, *our* children and *our* heirs are threatened, exclaims Northumberland. But he knows of eight tall ships, well furnished by the Duke of Brittany, which are waiting to bring over Bolingbroke and his friends. Here, then, is a means of making things secure for themselves and of serving the nation:

> If then we shall shake off our slavish yoke,
> Imp out our drooping country's broken wing,
> Redeem from broking pawn the blemish'd crown,
> Wipe off the dust that hides our sceptre's gilt
> And make high majesty look like itself,
> Away with me in post to Ravenspurgh.

This is the first effective appearance of a character whose fortunes Shakespeare is to follow through three successive plays. Northumberland, the man who helps to put Bolingbroke on the throne and

who afterwards does his best to unseat him, is a man in whom dis-
loyalty is almost a matter of principle. He lives in perpetual discon-
tent with himself, his friends and the world at large. He abandons
every cause as soon as he has persuaded his colleagues to take it up.
He has thoroughly mastered the art of identifying his private interests and temperamental grudges with a zeal for the public welfare
and he performs this act of identification so easily that it needs a wary
eye to take and keep the measure of his suave iniquity. He is the sort
of political leader who starts a rebellion and leaves his partners to
face the consequences. He will take to his bed when his son is fighting
at Shrewsbury and steal across the border into Scotland when his
friends are marching south to meet his enemies. He is Shakespeare's
presentation, valid for any generation, of the malcontent without a
cause, the rebel without a conviction. To-day he speaks boldly for
the Opposition and abstains from voting against the Government.

The report that Bolingbroke has landed at Ravenspurgh comes to
London simultaneously with the news that Northumberland and his
party have absconded. York, Richard being by this time away in
Ireland, receives the news in a fluster. The nobles are fled. The com-
mons are cold. The coffers are empty. Posts must be sent to the
King. Arms must be collected and men mustered.

> If I know
> How or which way to order these affairs,
> Thus thrust disorderly into my hands,
> Never believe me. Both are my kinsmen:
> The one is my sovereign, whom both my oath
> And duty bids defend; the other again
> Is my kinsman, whom the king hath wrong'd,
> Whom conscience and my kindred bids to right.
> Well, somewhat we must do.

York is as distracted in conscience as in counsel. His bewilderment is
admirably conveyed. The very verse is disjointed and breathless as
the old man turns this way and that. Note the touching futility of the
abrupt, disconnected order to his servant:

> Go, fellow, get thee home, provide some carts
> And bring away the armour that is there.

It is a masterly little scene and serves, better than pages of explicit commentary on Richard's fecklessness, to expose the levity with which the King has left his kingdom unprovided.

Meanwhile Northumberland is meeting Bolingbroke at Ravens-purgh. Their first colloquy is a model of political deportment as between masters of the game. Evidently Bolingbroke has not been sparing of his charm and Northumberland, as they come upon the scene in the wilds near Berkeley Castle, repays him in kind:

> I am a stranger here in Gloucestershire:
> These high wild hills and rough uneven ways
> Draw out our miles, and make them wearisome;
> And yet your fair discourse hath been as sugar,
> Making the hard way sweet and delectable;

and Bolingbroke returns:

> Of much less value is my company
> Than your good words.

To them enters Harry Percy, who in years to come will aptly remember this first meeting with Bolingbroke. It is for all present an occasion big with consequence and the use to be made of it by Shakespeare in two histories as yet unwritten affords a remarkable instance of the continuity with which he follows his political characters from play to play. Harry Percy, Bolingbroke and Northumberland, firmly rooted already in his imagination, though they may grow and put forth the shoots proper to their growth, can never change their essential quality.

Northumberland introduces his son:

NORTHUMBERLAND: Have you forgot the Duke of Hereford, boy?
PERCY: No, my good lord; for that is not forgot
Which ne'er I did remember: to my knowledge
I never in my life did look on him.
NORTHUMBERLAND: Then learn to know him now: this is the duke.
PERCY: My gracious lord, I tender you my service,
Such as it is, being tender, raw and young,
Which elder days shall ripen and confirm
To more approvèd service and desert.

> BOLINGBROKE: I thank thee, gentle Percy; and be sure
>   I count myself in nothing else so happy
>   As in a soul remembering my good friends;
>   And as my fortune ripens with thy love,
>   It shall be still thy true love's recompense:
>   My heart this covenant makes, my hand thus seals it.

The Lords Ross and Willoughby are then presented. Percy stands apart and, if the actor knows his business, will seem a trifle impatient of these civilities:

> BOLINGBROKE: Welcome, my lords. I wot your love pursues
>   A banish'd traitor; all my treasury
>   Is yet but unfelt thanks, which, more enrich'd,
>   Shall be your love and labour's recompense.
> ROSS: Your presence makes us rich, most noble lord.
> WILLOUGHBY: And far surmounts our labour to attain it.
> BOLINGBROKE: Evermore thanks, the exchequer of the poor;
>   Which, till my infant fortune comes to years,
>   Stands for my bounty.

The scene is well enough in itself, however carelessly we read. But observe how already it hints at a significance for all concerned which only a distant sequel will in the fullness of time reveal. Harry Hotspur describes this very incident years later in terms which show that, tender, raw and young as he may have been at the time, he has already taken the measure of Bolingbroke's ingratiating ways. Hotspur has a natural dislike of humbug and a keen flair for its presence. Forestalling four years of troubled history, let him speak for himself:

> Why, what a candy deal of courtesy
> This fawning greyhound then did proffer me!
> Look, 'when his infant fortune came to age',
> And 'gentle Harry Percy', and 'kind cousin';
> O, the devil take such cozeners!

Hotspur *almost* remembers the very words of Bolingbroke—almost, but not quite perfectly, as is only natural.[1]

---

[1] The scene in which Hotspur recalls his first meeting with Bolingbroke ('I Hen. IV', Act I, Sc. III) is more extensively quoted in the chapter on Henry of Monmouth. See below, p. 201.

The short scene which follows the meeting between Bolingbroke and the absconded peers provides us with a further example of Shakespeare's sureness of touch in the handling of a political situation.

York has come to meet the rebel lords as the King's regent. Bolingbroke respects his loyalty. He does not attempt to force the issue, but with consummate skill he so conducts the interview that York first finds himself committed to neutrality and subsequently drawn into an ambiguous acceptance of the usurper. Bolingbroke does not ask for his support, but York, before he knows it, is being gently urged in the direction of acting as intermediary in procuring Richard's voluntary abdication.

When Bolingbroke kneels to his uncle, York bluntly challenges his false obeisance:

> YORK: Show me thy humble heart, and not thy knee,
>   Whose duty is deceivable and false.
> BOLINGBROKE: My gracious uncle—
> YORK: Tut, tut!
>   Grace me no grace, nor uncle me no uncle:
>   I am no traitor's uncle; and that word 'grace'
>   In an ungracious mouth is but profane.
>   Why have those banish'd and forbidden legs
>   Dar'd once to touch a dust of England's ground?
>
>   Com'st thou because the anointed king is hence?
>   Why foolish boy, the king is left behind,
>   And in my loyal bosom lies his power.

But Bolingbroke has taken the measure of this honest champion of things as they are—or ought to be. He strikes instantly at the weak joint in his uncle's armour. He was banished as Hereford. He returns to claim his rights as Lancaster:

>   Will you permit that I shall stand condemn'd
>   A wandering vagabond; my rights and royalties
>   Pluck'd from my arms perforce and given away
>   To upstart unthrifts? Wherefore was I born?
>   If that my cousin king be King of England,
>   It must be granted I am Duke of Lancaster.

>   I am a subject,
>   And challenge law: attorneys are denied me,
>   And therefore personally I lay my claim
>   To my inheritance of free descent.

This is too much for a feudal prince who, as Bolingbroke reminds
him, has also a son who looks to inherit his father's lands. York will
not admit that Bolingbroke is in the right, but cannot deny that
he has a grievance. The rebel lords are prompt with assurances that
Lancaster has come only to claim his lawful dues and York throws in
his hand:

>   Well, well, I see the issue of these arms:
>   I cannot mend it, I must needs confess,
>   Because my power is weak and all ill left;
>   But if I could, by Him that gave me life,
>   I would attach you all and make you stoop
>   Unto the sovereign mercy of the king;
>   But since I cannot, be it known to you
>   I do remain as neuter.

Bolingbroke at once presses his advantage:

>   But we must win your grace to go with us
>   To Bristol castle, which they say is held
>   By Bushy, Bagot and their complices,
>   The caterpillars of the commonwealth,
>   Which I have sworn to weed and pluck away.
> YORK: It may be I'll go with you: but yet I'll pause;
>   For I am loath to break our country's laws.

Thus York, the champion of lawful authority, is drawn into the
camp of the usurper and becomes his intermediary with Richard.
He goes to Bristol; he is present at the condemnation to death of the
caterpillars of the commonwealth, thus condoning what is in effect
an act of sovereignty on the part of Bolingbroke; and, before
Richard has set foot in his kingdom, he is sending letters to Richard's
queen on Bolingbroke's behalf.

Shakespeare, having dealt faithfully with the political issues of his
play in the foregoing scenes, now fixes our attention on the absorbing spectacle of a gifted, sensitive and undisciplined character ex-

posed to the high tension of a tragic destiny. Politics, for a while, fall
into the background. The reactions of Bolingbroke, York and
Northumberland are still worth watching; there is always an interest
in observing how public persons demean themselves in the presence
of emotions which exceed their comprehension or experience. But
the mood of the play changes abruptly at this point. Richard enters
upon the coast of Wales; drums and a flourish of trumpets die away
into silence; history pauses and tragedy takes the stage.[1]

Richard himself establishes the change of key:

> I weep for joy
> To stand upon my kingdom once again.
> Dear earth, I do salute thee with my hand,
> Though rebels wound thee with their horses' hoofs:
> As a long-parted mother with her child
> Plays fondly with her tears and smiles in meeting,
> So, weeping, smiling, greet I thee, my earth,
> And do thee favour with my royal hands.
> Feed not thy sovereign's foe, my gentle earth,
> Nor with thy sweets comfort his ravenous sense;
> But let thy spiders, that suck up thy venom,
> And heavy-gaited toads lie in their way,
> Doing annoyance to the treacherous feet
> Which with usurping steps do trample thee:
> Yield stinging nettles to mine enemies;
> And when they from thy bosom pluck a flower,
> Guard it, I pray thee, with a lurking adder
> Whose double tongue may with a mortal touch
> Throw death upon thy sovereign's enemies.

It should be borne in mind that the speaker of these lyric numbers
has just landed on the shores of his kingdom. He is confronted with a
political situation which calls for immediate action. But Richard has
no mind or will to spare for the business in hand. He has started upon

[1] Again the division into Acts is injudicious and illogical. The scene in which
Bushy and Green are condemned to death, which is Act III, Sc. I, of the play, should
quite obviously be Act II, Sc. IV. This scene concludes the political manoeuvres of
Bolingbroke and his confederates and leaves all clear for Richard's return, when
he will take the centre of the stage and focus our attention henceforth on the
tragedy of his fall from power.

that dramatisation of himself as a tragic figure which will be henceforth the dominant theme of the play. Narcissus is already absorbed
in the contemplation of his royal image. From that nothing will turn
him aside. Looking round on his followers, he notes their astonishment that he should be thus wasting the precious hours:

> Mock not my senseless conjuration, lords,

he exclaims and starts off again in full career:

> This earth shall have a feeling and these stones
> Prove armèd soldiers, ere her native king
> Shall falter under foul rebellion's arms.

The Bishop of Carlisle respectfully reminds his sovereign that God
preferably helps those who help themselves:

> The means that heaven yields must be embraced,
> And not neglected; else, if heaven would,
> And we will not, heaven's offer we refuse,
> The proffer'd means of succour and redress.

Aumerle is more explicit:

> He means, my lord, that we are too remiss;
> Whilst Bolingbroke, through our security,
> Grows strong and great in substance and in friends.

But Richard's mind and fancy are otherwise engaged:

> Not all the water in the rough rude sea
> Can wash the balm from an anointed king;
> The breath of worldly men cannot depose
> The deputy elected by the Lord:
> For every man that Bolingbroke hath press'd
> To lift shrewd steel against our golden crown,
> God for his Richard hath in heavenly pay
> A glorious angel.

This is Shakespeare's first direct tribute to the sacramental tradition which for his contemporaries was part of the legend that had
grown round Richard's deposition. Richard, in his reference to a
legion of angels on which he can call for his defence, suggests an
analogy between the passion which he is called upon to suffer, and

from which he makes no real effort to escape, and that of Christ. These references will become more explicit as the tragedy proceeds.

Bad news now comes by every post. Salisbury reports that the Welshmen who were to have supported Richard are dispersed and fled. Scroop enters. His face promises more evil tidings. All is grist to the mill of Richard's self-centred artistry:

> Mine ear is open and my heart prepared:
> The worst is worldly loss thou canst unfold.
> Say, is my kingdom lost? why, 'twas my care;
> And what loss is it to be rid of care?
> Strives Bolingbroke to be as great as we?
> Greater he shall not be; if he serve God,
> We'll serve Him too, and be his fellow so;
> Revolt our subjects? that we cannot mend;
> They break their faith to God as well as us:
> Cry woe, destruction, ruin and decay;
> The worst is death, and death will have his day.

Scroop tells his lamentable tale. Bolingbroke has a mighty following; the whole kingdom is in arms against the crown. Where, then, asks Richard, are the men of my party? Where is Bagot? What is become of Bushy? Where is Green? Have they, too, made peace with Bolingbroke? Mark what follows:

> SCROOP: Peace have they made with him indeed, my lord
> RICHARD: O villains, vipers, damn'd without redemption!
> Dogs, easily won to fawn on any man!
> Snakes, in my heart-blood warm'd, that sting my heart!
> Three Judases, each one thrice worse than Judas!
> Would they make peace? terrible hell make war
> Upon their spotted souls for this offence!

> SCROOP: Sweet love, I see, changing his property,
> Turns to the sourest and most deadly hate.
> Again uncurse their souls; their peace is made
> With heads, and not with hands: those whom you curse
> Have felt the worst of death's destroying wound
> And lie full low, graved in the hollow ground.

Richard's vehement cursing of his friends upon an ambiguous report of their behaviour has often been quoted by critics as an instance of the unstable impetuosity of his character. It is even more significant as revealing in Richard a self-absorption so complete that he cannot properly attend to what is being said. No one could possibly have mistaken the meaning of Scroop's 'Peace have they made with him, indeed, my lord' unless he were wholly self-engrossed, or could have failed to receive the news of the death of his hapless followers without some word of regret. But Richard hasn't a syllable or a thought to spare for Bushy or for Bagot. The announcement of their summary execution by Bolingbroke is just another fillip to his climbing sorrow:

> Let's talk of graves, of worms and epitaphs;
> Make dust our paper and with rainy eyes
> Write sorrow on the bosom of the earth.

He sees himself walking in a long procession of kings born to illustrate the tragical fall of princes, who are set on high but who in the end must live with bread, feel want, taste grief, need friends and refuse to be mocked with solemn reverence:

> For God's sake, let us sit upon the ground
> And tell sad stories of the death of kings:
> How some have been deposed, some slain in war;
> Some haunted by the ghosts they have deposed,
> Some poison'd by their wives, some sleeping kill'd;
> All murder'd: for within the hollow crown
> That rounds the mortal temples of a king
> Keeps Death his court, and there the antic sits,
> Scoffing his state and grinning at his pomp,
> Allowing him a breath, a little scene,
> To monarchize, be fear'd and kill with looks,
> Infusing him with self and vain conceit,
> As if this flesh which walls about our life
> Were brass impregnable; and humour'd thus
> Comes at the last, and with a little pin
> Bores through his castle wall, and farewell king!

The Bishop of Carlisle again ventures a rebuke:

> My lord, wise men ne'er sit and wail their woes
> But presently prevent the ways to wail.

Richard, for a moment, condescends to business. His uncle York has an army. Where is he to be found? Scroop informs him that York has abandoned the field. Richard's cup is now full. There is nothing left to mar the luxury of his grief:

> Beshrew thee, cousin, which didst lead me forth
> Of that sweet way I was in to despair!
> What say you now? what comfort have we now?
> By heaven, I'll hate him everlastingly
> That bids me be of comfort any more.

Richard discharges his army and takes refuge in Flint Castle. Thither marches Bolingbroke with York and Northumberland in attendance. York is still loyal to Richard in spirit. Bolingbroke has as yet no formal right to his allegiance. Nor has Bolingbroke laid claim to it. He still entertains the wilful stillness of the man who waits upon his fortune. But Northumberland knows what Bolingbroke will do before Bolingbroke has confessed it even to himself. York knows it, too. There is a characteristic passage between them in which Bolingbroke contrives to remain graciously neutral:

NORTHUMBERLAND: The news is very fair and good, my lord:
     Richard not far from hence hath hid his head.
   YORK: It would beseem the Lord Northumberland
     To say 'King Richard': alack the heavy day
     When such a sacred king should hide his head!
NORTHUMBERLAND: Your grace mistakes me; only to be brief,
     Left I his title out.
   YORK: The time hath been,
     Would you have been so brief with him, he would
     Have been so brief with you, to shorten you,
     For taking so the head, your whole head's length.
BOLINGBROKE: Mistake not, uncle, further than you should.
   YORK: Take not, good cousin, further than you should,
     Lest you mistake the heavens are o'er our heads.
BOLINGBROKE: I know it, uncle, and oppose not myself
     Against their will.

Bolingbroke's message to Richard is a masterpiece of political statement. He comes in all submission, but with an army which he ostentatiously parades before the walls. He comes with a humble request, but, if the request be not granted, he will enforce it at the point of the sword. Let Richard rage in fire, Bolingbroke will weep his waters on the earth:

> Henry Bolingbroke
> On both his knees doth kiss King Richard's hand
> And sends allegiance and true faith of heart
> To his most royal person; hither come
> Even at his feet to lay my arms and power,
> Provided that my banishment repeal'd
> And lands restored again be freely granted:
> If not, I'll use the advantage of my power
> And lay the summer's dust with showers of blood
> Rain'd from the wounds of slaughter'd Englishmen:
> The which, how far off from the mind of Bolingbroke
> It is such crimson tempest should bedrench
> The fresh green lap of fair King Richard's land,
> My stooping duty tenderly shall show.

This is the cue for Richard to resume the stature of a king. York, looking up to the battlements, comments on his royal appearance and yearns to think on what must follow:

> Yet looks he like a king: behold, his eye,
> As bright as is the eagle's, lightens forth
> Controlling majesty: alack, alack, for woe,
> That any harm should stain so fair a show!

Northumberland stands forth to deliver Bolingbroke's message. Richard checks him with a superb gesture:

> We are amazed; and thus long have we stood
> To watch the fearful bending of thy knee,
> Because we thought ourself thy lawful king:
> And if we be, how dare thy joints forget
> To pay their awful duty to our presence?
> If we be not, show us the hand of God
> That hath dismiss'd us from our stewardship;
>
> And though you think that all, as you have done,
> Have torn their souls by turning them from us,
> And we are barren and bereft of friends;

> Yet know, my master, God omnipotent
> Is mustering in his clouds on our behalf
> Armies of pestilence; and they shall strike
> Your children yet unborn and unbegot,
> That lift your vassal hands against my head
> And threat the glory of my precious crown.

Northumberland delivers his master's message, concluding with a solemn oath:

> His coming hither hath no further scope
> Than for his lineal royalties and to beg
> Enfranchisement immediate on his knees:
> Which on thy royal party granted once,
> His glittering arms he will commend to rust,
> His barbèd steeds to stables, and his heart
> To faithful service of your majesty.
> This swears he, as he is a prince, is just;
> And, as I am a gentleman, I credit him.

To which Richard very civilly replies:

> Northumberland, say thus the king returns:
> His noble cousin is right welcome hither;
> And all the number of his fair demands
> Shall be accomplish'd without contradiction:
> With all the gracious utterance thou hast
> Speak to his gentle hearing kind commends.

But the strain of royally maintaining a false show of courtesy is too great. He turns to Aumerle. Has he not debased himself in speaking the traitor fair? Should he not rather defy his enemy? Aumerle counsels prudence. Fight the intruder with gentle words till time brings friends and forces with which to meet him on a more equal footing. Richard, no longer a king who weighs advice, but a man whose pride has been wounded to the quick, cries out:

> O God! O God! that e'er this tongue of mine,
> That laid the sentence of dread banishment
> On yon proud man, should take it off again
> With words of sooth! O that I were as great
> As is my grief, or lesser than my name!

Northumberland brings back an answer from Bolingbroke, but Richard cannot wait to receive it. He is again the man of sorrows and has thrown his dignity to the winds:

> What must the king do now? must he submit?
> The king shall do it: must he be deposed?
> The king shall be contented: must he lose
> The name of king? o' God's name, let it go:
> I'll give my jewels for a set of beads,
> My gorgeous palace for a hermitage,
> My gay apparel for an almsman's gown,
> My figured goblets for a dish of wood,
> My sceptre for a palmer's walking-staff,
> My subjects for a pair of carvèd saints
> And my large kingdom for a little grave,
> A little little grave, an obscure grave;
> Or I'll be buried in the king's highway,
> Some way of common trade, where subjects' feet
> May hourly trample on their sovereign's head.

He grows more exquisitely fanciful as self-pity entices him from one conceit to another. He scatters himself, as Coleridge expresses it, into a multitude of images and endeavours to shelter himself from that which is around him by a cloud of his own thoughts. He finds Aumerle, his tender-hearted cousin, weeping beside him and brings him into the picture:

> Or shall we play the wanton with our woes,
> And make some pretty match with shedding tears?
> As thus, to drop them still upon one place,
> Till they have fretted us a pair of graves
> Within the earth; and, therein laid,—there lies
> Two kinsmen digg'd their graves with weeping eyes.

One of the most moving touches in Shakespeare's delineation is Richard's bleak perception, now and then, that his fancies are regarded by those about him as foolishly irrelevant. We have heard him exclaim on a former occasion: *Mock not my senseless conjuration, lords!* Now, again, he becomes abruptly aware that he has lost touch with the real world and is playing his part on a stage before spectators who find him fantastic or even ridiculous:

> Well, well, I see
> I talk but idly, and you laugh at me.

These moments, in which Richard sees himself as possibly the only appreciative witness of his tragedy, are the more affecting as they aggravate rather than restrain his excess of feeling. A brief moment of lucidity is in the present instance followed by an outbreak of almost intolerable hysteria:

RICHARD: Most mighty prince, my Lord Northumberland,
What says King Bolingbroke? will his majesty
Give Richard leave to live till Richard die?
You make a leg, and Bolingbroke says ay.
NORTHUMBERLAND: My lord, in the base court he doth attend
To speak with you; may it please you to come
down.
RICHARD: Down, down I come; like glistering Phaëton,
Wanting the manage of unruly jades.
In the base court? Base court, where kings grow
base,
To come at traitors' calls and do them grace.
In the base court? Come down? Down, court!
down, king!
For night-owls shriek where mounting larks should
sing.

Northumberland's comment is drily expressive:

> Sorrow and grief of heart
> Makes him speak fondly, like a frantic man.

King Richard, in the base court, brushes aside Bolingbroke's sustained pretences of respect. He sees himself as the royal martyr, victim of circumstance and the strong hand. Bolingbroke kneels to him:

RICHARD: Up, cousin, up; your heart is up, I know,
Thus high at least, although your knee be low.
BOLINGBROKE: My gracious lord, I come but for mine own.
RICHARD: Your own is yours, and I am yours, and all.
BOLINGBROKE: So far be mine, my most redoubted lord,
As my true service shall deserve your love.

> RICHARD: Well you deserve: they well deserve to have,
> That know the strong'st and surest way to get.
> Uncle, give me your hand: nay, dry your eyes;
> Tears show their love, but want their remedies.
> Cousin, I am too young to be your father,
> Though you are old enough to be my heir.
> What you will have, I'll give, and willing too;
> For do we must what force will have us do.

We come now to the famous scene of abdication in Westminster Hall. It is remembered necessarily as a supreme exhibition of Richard's quality. But the political background is worth attention if only for its faithful rendering of the reactions of public men to the impact and artistry of human emotion expressed in beauty and without reserve. Shakespeare, though his eyes are fixed on Richard, never loses sight of the dramatic contrast between his practical politicians and the suffering, wayward spirit of the fallen King. The scene opens, as so many scenes at this particular point in Shakespeare's plays, with an episode apparently novel but in fact recalling and developing the main initial theme of the tragedy. Bolingbroke is dealing masterfully with precisely the same political situation which confronted Richard at the beginning of the play. Bolingbroke in the first Act charged Mowbray with being privy to the death of Gloucester. Bagot, in the fourth Act, confronts Aumerle with precisely the same charge. Bagot, like Mowbray, denies Aumerle's accusation. Challenges are flung down on either side, but Bolingbroke firmly suppresses the unruly peers:

> Lords appellants,
> Your differences shall all rest under gage
> Till we assign you to your days of trial.

He takes complete control of the situation and incidentally—a revealing touch, this—he adopts the royal 'we' in announcing his decision.

Into this scene, clearly designed to show that Bolingbroke has the political tact and resolution in which Richard has proved so grievously deficient, comes York to announce that an abdication has been arranged:

> Great Duke of Lancaster, I come to thee
> From plume-pluck'd Richard; who with willing soul
> Adopts thee heir, and his high sceptre yields
> To the possession of thy royal hand.
> Ascend his throne, descending now from him;
> And long live Henry, of that name the fourth!

Not by a single word or gesture, though he is already behaving like a king, has Bolingbroke laid any explicit claim to the crown. But now his destiny is plain. His chance has come and he seizes it with the readiness of a patient man who, moving deviously to his journey's end, at last sees the road clear before him:

> In God's name, I'll ascend the regal throne.

But stay; there is a hitch in these well-ordered proceedings. The Bishop of Carlisle bars the way of the usurper. Richard, he protests, is still the King. There is none present noble enough to judge his royal master and, even if Richard were a common thief, he should not be condemned unheard:

> What subject can give sentence on his king?
> And who sits here that is not Richard's subject?
> Thieves are not judged but they are by to hear,
> Although apparent guilt be seen in them;
> And shall the figure of God's majesty,
> His captain, steward, deputy-elect,
> Anointed, crownèd, planted many years,
> Be judg'd by subject and inferior breath,
> And be himself not present?

The Bishop goes on to warn the rebel lords of what must follow the elevation of a traitor:

> Disorder, horror, fear and mutiny
> Shall here inhabit, and this land be call'd
> The field of Golgotha and dead men's skulls.
> O! if you raise this house against this house,
> It will the woefullest division prove
> That ever fell upon this cursèd earth.

Northumberland takes it upon himself to order the instant arrest of the Bishop, but Bolingbroke intervenes. It must not appear that he is

taking the kingdom by force; there must be no doubt that Richard
has in fact voluntarily surrendered his rights. He turns to York:

> Fetch hither Richard, that in common view
> He may surrender; so we shall proceed
> Without suspicion.

Thus is Richard called upon to play the famous scene in which he
unkings himself and he plays it with a vengeance. These men have
summoned him to comply with a formality. He will shame them,
if he can; wring their hearts, if it be possible. In any case, he will
make it a bad quarter of an hour for everyone concerned:

> Alack, why am I sent for to a king,
> Before I have shook off the regal thoughts
> Wherewith I reign'd? I hardly yet have learn'd
> To insinuate, flatter, bow and bend my limbs:
> Give sorrow leave awhile to tutor me
> To this submission. Yet I well remember
> The favours of these men: were they not mine?
> Did they not sometime cry, 'All hail!' to me?
> So Judas did to Christ.

York explains the purpose for which he has been called:

> To do that office of thine own good will
> Which tired majesty did make thee offer,
> The resignation of thy state and crown
> To Henry Bolingbroke.

'Here, cousin, seize the crown', cries Richard and his fancy takes
wings. The crown is a deep well; he and Bolingbroke are two
buckets—his own deep down and full of tears, Bolingbroke's empty
and mounting aloft in the air. Bolingbroke twice interrupts. Somehow Richard must be kept to the point. 'I thought you had been
willing to resign,' he protests. Richard flashes back:

> My crown, I am; but still my griefs are mine:
> You may my glories and my state depose,
> But not my griefs; still am I king of those.

He invites Bolingbroke to meet him in another flight of fancy but Bolingbroke is not to be put off. Bluntly he asks:

> Are you contented to resign the crown?

Richard is contented, but after his own fashion:

> Now mark me, how I will undo myself:
> I give this heavy weight from off my head
> And this unwieldy sceptre from my hand,
> The pride of kingly sway from out my heart;
> With mine own tears I wash away my balm,
> With mine own hands I give away my crown,
> With mine own tongue deny my sacred state,
> With mine own breath release all duteous rites:
> All pomp and majesty I do forswear.
>
> God save King Henry, unking'd Richard says,
> And send him many years of sunshine days!
> What more remains?

Bolingbroke has brought Richard to the point and his work is done. What more remains he leaves to the callously officious Northumberland. Richard's abdication must be justified to the people of England. No one knows that better than Bolingbroke. But this supple, audacious and secret man has the politician's art of allowing others to do the ignoble things necessary for his advancement while he himself remains in the background to reap the profit and show to advantage in gestures of mercy, magnanimity and honest care for the public weal.

A document has been prepared setting forth the misdemeanours of the fallen king. Northumberland suggests that Richard should read the charges:

> That, by confessing them, the souls of men
> May deem that you are worthily depos'd.

Richard replies:

> Must I do so? and must I ravel out
> My weaved-up follies? Gentle Northumberland,
> If thy offences were upon record,

> Would it not shame thee in so fair a troop
> To read a lecture of them? If thou wouldst,
> There shouldst thou find one heinous article,
> Containing the deposing of a king,
> And cracking the strong warrant of an oath,
> Mark'd with a blot, damn'd in the book of heaven.

He looks round upon the assembled lords. They are obviously feeling the strain. They have no liking for scenes and there has never been such a scene as this. They stand about awkwardly, uneasily, a little pitifully. And Richard, for the third time in the play, sees himself as the Christ betrayed:

> Though some of you, with Pilate, wash your hands,
> Showing an outward pity; yet you Pilates
> Have here deliver'd me to my sour cross,
> And water cannot wash away your sin.

Northumberland is inexorable and finally drives Richard to a sudden blaze of human temper, in striking contrast with the mood in which he adorns and cherishes his grief:

NORTHUMBERLAND: My lord, dispatch; read o'er these articles.
RICHARD: Mine eyes are full of tears, I cannot see:
         And yet salt water blinds them not so much
         But they can see a sort of traitors here.

NORTHUMBERLAND: My lord,—
RICHARD: No lord of thine, thou haught insulting man.

Soon, however, his imagination is at work again and inspires him to one of his most striking images:

> O, that I were a mockery king of snow,
> Standing before the sun of Bolingbroke,
> To melt myself away in water-drops!

Finally comes his last command:

> An if my word be sterling yet in England,
> Let it command a mirror hither straight,
> That it may show me what a face I have,
> Since it is bankrupt of his majesty.

For the men about him how unexpectedly frivolous is this request! And yet how appropriate! Narcissus has reached the supreme moment of his tragedy and calls for a looking-glass.

Bolingbroke sends an attendant for the mirror. Northumberland still presses Richard. Let him read the paper while the glass is fetched. This is too much even for Bolingbroke:

> BOLINGBROKE: Urge it no more, my Lord Northumberland.
> NORTHUMBERLAND: The commons will not then be satisfied.
> RICHARD: They shall be satisfied: I'll read enough,
> When I do see the very book indeed
> Where all my sins are writ, and that's myself.

The attendant returns and Richard is allowed his most memorable gesture:

> Was this face the face
> That every day under his household roof
> Did keep ten thousand men? Was this the face
> That, like the sun, did make beholders wink?
> Was this the face that faced so many follies,
> And was at last out-faced by Bolingbroke?
> A brittle glory shineth in this face:
> As brittle as the glory is the face;
> (*Dashes the glass against the ground.*)
> For there it is, crack'd in a hundred shivers.
> Mark, silent king, the moral of this sport,
> How soon my sorrow hath destroy'd my face.

Bolingbroke's comment—

> The shadow of your sorrow hath destroy'd
> The shadow of your face—

is not intended as a sneer, though behind it lurks the contempt of a realist for the imaginative exercises of the artist. He is not insensitive to the scene and, in reaction against the impression it has made upon him, he is prompted to reflect that it has no dynamic relation to the world of action. He suggests that Richard's sorrow is largely of the imagination. The sorrow may be real, but its expression is histrionic—in fact, a shadow. Richard acknowledges the force of this observation but construes it with a difference:

> Say that again.
> The shadow of my sorrow! Ha! let's see:
> 'Tis very true, my grief lies all within;
> And these external manners of laments
> Are merely shadows to the unseen grief
> That swells with silence in the tortured soul.

And now suddenly he is tired of the shadow-show and asks leave to go. 'Whither?' asks Bolingbroke, and Richard, with the petulance of a hurt child, replies: 'Whither you will, so I were from your sights.'

So ends a scene in which Shakespeare's gifts as poet and dramatist are for the first time perfectly united. It goes instantly to the heart, but yields its treasures the more abundantly as it is the more closely studied. It is full of wonders. Not the least is the way in which it combines the sacramental, the aesthetic and the purely human elements in the dramatic character of Richard and the situation in which he finds himself. The speech in which Richard divests himself of crown and sceptre is likened by Walter Pater in his 'Appreciations' to an inverted rite, a rite of degradation, a 'long, agonising ceremony' in which the order of coronation is reversed. The sacramental analogy with Christ's passion has already been noted. The rebel peers who deliver up their lord to his sour cross are thrice stigmatised as Judases in the course of the play. It is Shakespeare's supreme achievement to have retained this mystical aspect of the tragedy and yet in no way to have impaired its humanity. The consecrated king, impiously discrowned, shades away into the poet king, in whom suffering induces a lyric ecstasy; who, in his turn, gives place to the mere human victim of misfortune, subject to everyday infirmities of mind and will, with whom we can live in fellowship. This Richard, who undoes himself with hierophantic solemnity, who humbles, or pities, or exalts himself in imagination, is also the man who turns on Northumberland in a flash of temper and reveals himself, all at once, as a very ordinary creature. Nor do we feel any incongruity or rift in the total performance. The three elements are completely fused. The king, the artist and the man are the person we have come to know as Richard. No play of Shakespeare has a more perfect unity of tone, texture and feeling. Yet no play has drawn upon a greater diversity of thematic material. Shakespeare, deriving from tradition, from recorded facts and from his own mind a bewildering complex of emotions and ideas, has produced a play which is all of a piece.

The scene of Richard's deposition fills, as it should, the whole fourth Act of the tragedy. It is the summit of the play and of Shakespeare's dramatic achievement at the time when it was written.[1] From this summit we descend in the fifth Act to the foregone conclusion of Richard's death and premonitory hints of the expiation which will be required of the usurper in future histories. The descent is well-contrived and there is much to be observed on the way down.

First we are taken to a street in London. Richard, being led to the Tower, is intercepted by his queen.

This is the third appearance of the Queen as a speaking character and her first appearance in a scene with her husband. Shakespeare, happily misled by his authorities, has given her a part in the play for which there is no warrant in history. Richard's first queen, Anne, dearly loved and extravagantly mourned, had been dead seven years. His second queen, Isabella, was only nine years old. Shakespeare, in presenting Richard as a king who failed in his public office, felt the need of showing him also in a more intimate relationship. Here, too, was an opportunity of adding a touch, here and there, to that English background against which the whole tragedy

---

[1] The scene has, of course, a long and curious history. It was omitted from early published editions of the play and not printed till 1608, five years after the death of Elizabeth. There is no reason to believe, however, that it was not acted upon the stage in 1595—indeed, it was almost certainly this scene which made the play so dangerously topical and accounted for its performance no less than forty times in the years immediately following its production.   Another fact about this scene of interest to the literary historian is that it drew from Dr. Johnson perhaps the most unfortunate of his comments upon Shakespeare. Part of it he declares is 'proper', but part 'might have been forborne without much loss'. He concludes with the observation: 'The author, *I suppose*, intended to write a very moving scene.' The eighteenth century has never so unhappily condescended to the genius of the sixteenth than in Johnson's criticism of this particular play. He seems to have had no idea, first to last, what it was all about. He found Richard 'imperious and oppressive' in prosperity, but in his distress 'wise, patient and pious'—a view of the character which makes complete nonsense of the tragedy from start to finish and which drove Dr. Johnson to his final conclusion: 'nor can it be said much to affect the passions or enlarge the understanding.'

is played. The Queen, in her garden at Langley, lies full in the fresh green lap of fair King Richard's land, which, like Prospero's island, is full of noises heard above the brazen clamour of its barons and in the hushed pauses of their plotting. From the scene in which a pride of rebel lords sets forth to meet Bolingbroke we are taken to a scene in which a forsaken wife is grieved and anxious for 'sweet Richard'. From the scene in which Richard comes lamentably down to the court where kings grow base we are taken to where a queen and her ladies devise pastimes. A gardener binds up his dangling apricocks and thinks it a pity that the commonwealth cannot be trimmed and dressed as neatly as his hedges and borders. No one can fail to feel in his heart, though he may not be aware of its peerless cunning, the effect of the speech with which the scene at Langley concludes. The Queen has heard that Richard is deposed. The gardener, who has commented so wisely and gently on the faults which have ruined his master, looks sadly after his mistress:

> Here did she fall a tear; here, in this place,
> I'll set a bank of rue, sour herb of grace:
> Rue, even for ruth, here shortly shall be seen,
> In the remembrance of a weeping queen.

Dynasties change; the masters of England have opened the purple testament of bleeding war, which will not be closed for a hundred years to come; a simple plain man, in compassion for a weeping queen, sets a sweet herb. Only a moment before she has upbraided him as a 'little better thing than earth' for his evil tidings and called down God's curse upon his flowers. He has accepted her rebuke and bears no malice. In this garden at Langley England is wise and kind; there is here a fragrance which will outlive the futilities of history.

Shakespeare thus prepares us for a last meeting between husband and wife and we realise, when the Queen speaks, if we have not already done so, that Richard is a man beloved:

> But soft, but see, or rather do not see,
> My fair rose wither.

>   Thou most beauteous inn,
> Why should hard-favour'd grief be lodged in thee,
> When triumph is become an alehouse guest?

Shakespeare here gives us but a glimpse of that lovely quality in Richard which fascinated the chroniclers and survived a hundred years of Lancastrian detraction. Yet he does not falter in his portrayal of Richard's blemishes of mind and will. Now or never Richard should forget himself and speak from the heart. But no; he is still the absorbed spectator of his own tragedy, in which he is now all set to play the penitent:

> Learn, good soul,
> To think our former state a happy dream;
> From which awak'd, the truth of what we are
> Shows us but this! I am sworn brother, sweet,
> To grim Necessity, and he and I
> Will keep a league till death. Hie thee to France
> And cloister thee in some religious house:
> Our holy lives must win a new world's crown.

The Queen very naturally resents this performance:

> What! is my Richard both in shape and mind
> Transform'd and weaken'd? hath Bolingbroke deposed
> Thine intellect? hath he been in thy heart?
> The lion dying thrusteth forth his paw
> And wounds the earth, if nothing else, with rage
> To be o'erpower'd; and wilt thou, pupil-like,
> Take thy correction mildly, kiss the rod,
> And fawn on rage with base humility,
> Which art a lion and a king of beasts?

But Richard is incorrigible:

> Good sometime queen, prepare thee hence for France:
> Think I am dead and that even here thou tak'st,
> As from my death-bed, thy last living leave.
> In winter's tedious nights sit by the fire
> With good old folks, and let them tell thee tales
> Of woeful ages, long ago betid;
> And ere thou bid good night, to quit their griefs,
> Tell thou the lamentable tale of me,
> And send the hearers weeping to their beds.

At this point Shakespeare brings on to the stage the man of all others most fitted to impersonate the new political order. Northumberland arrives with fresh instructions from Bolingbroke. Richard is to be taken to Pomfret. This is Richard's cue for prophecy. Retribution inevitably attends the success of wicked men. Triumph, the alehouse guest, has no abiding place:

> Northumberland, thou ladder wherewithal
> The mounting Bolingbroke ascends my throne,
> The time shall not be many hours of age
> More than it is, ere foul sin gathering head
> Shall break into corruption: thou shalt think,
> Though he divide the realm and give thee half,
> It is too little, helping him to all;
> And he shall think that thou, which know'st the way
> To plant unrightful kings, wilt know again,
> Being ne'er so little urged, another way
> To pluck him headlong from the usurped throne.
> The love of wicked men converts to fear;
> That fear to hate, and hate turns one or both
> To worthy danger and deservèd death.

Northumberland is not, however, a man to be moved by premonitions. He has come to execute an order. 'My guilt be on my head and there's an end,' he answers curtly, and, when the Queen begs that Richard may go with her to France, he retorts with a shrug for her simplicity: 'That were some love, but little policy.'

We are not to see Richard again till we find him playing his last part in the solitude of his prison at Pomfret. But Shakespeare has much to do in the interval. He has first to show us two celebrated companion portraits, one of Bolingbroke in his triumph and the other of Richard in his fall. It is York who executes the commission. Here is Bolingbroke:

> Then, as I said, the duke, great Bolingbroke,
> Mounted upon a hot and fiery steed,
> Which his aspiring rider seem'd to know,
> With slow but stately pace kept on his course,
> Whilst all tongues cried 'God save thee, Bolingbroke!'
> You would have thought the very windows spake,

So many greedy looks of young and old
Through casements darted their desiring eyes
Upon his visage, and that all the walls
With painted imagery had said at once
'Jesu preserve thee! welcome, Bolingbroke!'
Whilst he, from the one side to the other turning,
Bareheaded, lower than his proud steed's neck,
Bespake them thus: 'I thank you, countrymen':
And thus still doing, thus he pass'd along.

And here is Richard:

As in a theatre, the eyes of men,
After a well-grac'd actor leaves the stage,
Are idly bent on him that enters next,
Thinking his prattle to be tedious;
Even so, or with much more contempt, men's eyes
Did scowl on Richard: no man cried 'God save him!'
No joyful tongue gave him his welcome home;
But dust was thrown upon his sacred head;
Which with such gentle sorrow he shook off,
His face still combating with tears and smiles,
The badges of his grief and patience.

York has accepted the situation and finds God's purpose at work
even in the humiliation of his late master:

That had not God, for some strong purpose, steel'd
The hearts of men, they must perforce have melted,
And barbarism itself have pitied him.
But heaven hath a hand in these events,
To whose high will we bound our calm contents.

Nor has he long to wait for an opportunity to demonstrate his
loyalty to the new dynasty. For Bolingbroke is already threatened
with conspiracy. Richard's friends, headed by the Abbot of Westminster, are plotting a restoration and York's own son, Aumerle, is
involved. His father counsels him to accept the accomplished fact:

Well, bear you well in this new spring of time,
Lest you be cropp'd before you come to prime.

But York, even as he delivers this advice, sees dangling from his son's bosom a seal. He demands to see the writing and presently he is spelling out proof that his son, and a dozen other lords, have sworn to kill Bolingbroke at Oxford. He calls for his boots. The King must be warned. It is bad enough that Richard should have been deposed. And now before anyone has had time to settle down under the new dispensation, here is yet another attempt to upset the established order. Is treason to become the fashion in England?

The scenes in which Aumerle's conspiracy is plotted, discovered, reported to Bolingbroke and suppressed are usually omitted on the stage. It is assumed that the interest of the audience is so strongly absorbed by Richard's personal tragedy that the political results of his abdication can be ignored. This was not Shakespeare's intention. It must again be insisted that 'Richard II' is a political play, with a political theme which had a poignant interest for an Elizabethan audience. Bolingbroke has deposed a king ruling by right of birth and consecration. The consequences were to be written red in the history of England for the next hundred years and to haunt the memories of Englishmen for as long again. The scenes in which Bolingbroke is confronted with civil war as an immediate result of his usurpation are essential to Shakespeare's design. It is, moreover, dramatically interesting to see how Bolingbroke handles this dangerous conspiracy while we still have vividly in mind the conduct of Richard in a similar situation. Bolingbroke thanks York for his intelligence:

> O loyal father of a treacherous son!
> Thou sheer, immaculate and silver fountain,
> From whence this stream through muddy passages
> Hath held his current and defiled himself!

Bolingbroke is fulsome in his acknowledgment of a service rendered and turns the moral situation inside out. York, who deserted Richard, is praised for his loyalty. Aumerle, who has remained true to his allegiance, is abused for treachery. Bolingbroke pardons Aumerle, but suppresses the insurrection with an iron hand.

Shakespeare's presentation of Aumerle's conspiracy has yet another dramatic purpose. It supplies the crowning motive for his instigation

of Exton to the murder of Richard. Characteristically it is an ambiguous instigation:

> Have I no friend will rid me of this living fear?

He looks round and there is Exton to overhear and execute his
thought. He has been moved to the deposition of a king without
explicitly avowing his intention. He is moved to the crowning act of
murder in the same somnambulist fashion and, when the deed is
done, can in a sense, disavow the intention:

> They love not poison that do poison need,
> Nor do I thee: though I did wish him dead,
> I hate the murderer, love him murderèd.

He can even regard the act as though it had been performed not by,
but upon, him:

> Lords, I protest, my soul is full of woe,
> That blood should sprinkle me to make me grow.

Richard, soliloquising in his prison at Pomfret, is like an actor
reviewing the scenes in which he has played and reflecting on their
relation to reality. He is still dramatising his own introverted responses to the tragedy that has befallen him and he discusses how
these histrionic introversions may be prolonged into the solitude in
which he finds himself:

> I have been studying how I may compare
> This prison where I live unto the world.
>
> Thus play I in one person many people
> And none contented: sometimes am I king;
> Then treasons make me wish myself a beggar,
> And so I am: then crushing penury
> Persuades me I was better when a king;
> Then am I king'd again: and by and by
> Think that I am unking'd by Bolingbroke,
> And straight am nothing: but whate'er I be,
> Nor I nor any man that but man is
> With nothing shall be pleased, till he be eased
> With being nothing.

How apt is this annihilating conclusion of a self-centred mind, brooding in a wilful seclusion from its kind! These still-breeding thoughts are doomed to sterility and can bear no fruit! The man who lives in imagination only has no place in the world of experience. Richard is himself aware at last of the cause of his ruin. The friendly music that breaks upon his solitude sets him thinking how different his story might have been if he had kept his ears open to the harmonies and rhythms of the life about him:

> Music do I hear?
> Ha, ha! keep time: how sour sweet music is,
> When time is broke and no proportion kept!
> So is it in the music of men's lives.
> And here have I the daintiness of ear
> To check time broke in a disorder'd string;
> But for the concord of my state and time
> Had not an ear to hear my true time broke.
> I wasted time, and now doth time waste me;

and he concludes upon a note of genuine human feeling:

> This music mads me; let it sound no more;

> Yet blessing on his heart that gives it me!
> For 'tis a sign of love.

It is not without significance that this sign of love has come to Richard from a man whom he did not even remember, a poor groom of the stable who with much ado had obtained leave to visit his royal master. This poor groom had seen Bolingbroke in his coronation, riding on roan Barbary. Richard has here the cue for a last exquisite fancy. But what he has to say is for the first time touched with a wistful charity towards man and beast:

> RICHARD: Rode he on Barbary? Tell me, gentle friend,
>   How went he under him?
> GROOM: So proudly as if he disdain'd the ground.
> RICHARD: So proud that Bolingbroke was on his back!
>   That jade hath eat bread from my royal hand;
>   This hand hath made him proud with clapping him.

> Would he not stumble? would he not fall down,
> Since pride must have a fall, and break the neck
> Of that proud man that did usurp his back?
> Forgiveness, horse! why do I rail on thee,
> Since thou, created to be awed by man,
> Wast born to bear?

For Richard now it is finished. There is a brave blaze of anger at the last. He beats the keeper who comes to him with a poisoned dish. He strikes down two of the men who come to murder him and it is Exton himself who strikes him down. He dies a king, whose sanctity no abdication can compromise before God:

> RICHARD: That hand shall burn in never-quenching fire
>   That staggers thus my person. Exton, thy fierce hand
>   Hath with the king's blood stain'd the king's own land.
>   Mount, mount, my soul! thy seat is up on high,
>   Whilst my gross flesh sinks downward, here to die.

The character of Richard has provoked comparisons which, however, only serve to stamp him as unique among the creations of Shakespeare. His futility as a man of action has led many critics to put him in the same gallery with Henry VI, Marcus Brutus and Hamlet. But to none of these three men does he bear any real resemblance except for the fact that they, too, were men unfitted to play the part imposed on them by circumstance.

Henry was a saint and a scholar, required to assert his authority over a full-blooded, termagant queen and as graceless a set of political ruffians as ever reached high office in the land. He loved books, hated war, sought peace and believed in justice. He grieved not for himself, but for a kingdom in disorder and cruelties committed in his name. His weakness, as the world assesses weakness, was that of the altruist. He was a model of non-resistance and a pattern of humility in a society which believed only in power. Hazlitt once observed how Shakespeare, dealing with men who on a superficial view seem much of the same complexion and who appear in almost identical situations, presents characters wholly distinct. It is possible to go further. These characters, who tend to be hung in the same gallery, are often more remarkable for their essential differences than for any real similarity. Even when appearing to make the same speech to the same occasion, they talk a different language in a different mood and with a wholly different meaning. Turn back to the speech in which Richard rejects the splendours of royalty:

> I'll give my jewels for a set of beads.

Consider the catalogue of precious things which Richard is prepared to discard—his gorgeous palace, his gay apparel, his figured goblets. His subjects he will exchange for a pair of carvèd saints. Every epithet expresses the sophistication of an aesthete whose hermitage is presented as pleasantly to the fancy as the palace for which it is bartered. Consider, too, the flagellant self-pity of the epithets that come last of all—the *little, little* grave, an *obscure* grave. The words themselves and the fall of the lines in which they bloom like flowers in an exotic garden betray their derivation. This is not the utterance of an afflicted heart, seeking peace in surrender and simplicity, but of a man who finds consolation in a wilfully induced luxury of grief. We follow the working of an imagination that wantons in the pleasures of the humble.

Read now the similar, but how different, speech of Henry on the battlefield at Towton. Henry sorrows, not for himself, but for the strife and treachery in which he is entangled. He has so little wish to be king—a part in which Richard postured as readily as in any other—that he feels he is doing well for his family in agreeing that his son shall be disinherited. He sincerely envies a man who can live remote from great affairs and, unlike Richard, who, seeing himself in a bedesman's gown, merely changes his apparel, he shares with all his heart the rustic joys and sorrows of a simple hind. His imagination looks abroad into the world for things outside himself, whereas Richard looks always within himself for his own reflection.

The speech in which Henry's mood is crystallised is of a limpid simplicity. There is hardly an epithet. The picture is seen for itself and needs no touch of the self-conscious artist:

> O God! methinks it were a happy life,
> To be no better than a homely swain.
>
> So many hours must I tend my flock,
> So many hours must I take my rest;

So many hours must I contemplate;
So many hours must I sport myself;
So many days my ewes have been with young;
So many weeks ere the poor fools will ean;
So many years ere I shall shear the fleece.

And to conclude, the shepherd's homely curds,
His cold thin drink out of his leather bottle,
His wonted sleep under a fresh tree's shade,
All which secure and sweetly he enjoys,
Is far beyond a prince's delicates,
His viands sparkling in a golden cup,
His body couchèd in a curious bed.[1]

The comparison with Brutus serves only to mark an equally essential contrast. Brutus failed as a politician because he had fixed principles and a rigid mind. Richard failed because he had no principles
at all and a mind of quicksilver. Brutus misjudged political events
and public persons because he saw them always in the light of his
own convictions. Richard could read the hearts and purposes of the
men about him, but having no convictions, only imaginative reactions to events and persons, was unable to use his insight effectively.
Brutus was shut off from the world by his philosophy, Richard by
his absorption in the play of a self-regarding fancy.

The comparison with Hamlet, more often drawn by the critics,
is more delicately fallacious. Goethe compared Hamlet, on whom a
tragic duty has been imposed, to a beautiful vase in which an acorn
has been planted. The acorn in growing shivers its frail container
into fragments. Yeats compares Richard to a vessel of porcelain,
contrasting him with Henry V, the vessel of clay, which Shakespeare
was to fashion later. Here are two poets, writing respectively of the
two characters, using quite independently the same image.

Hamlet and Richard are admittedly alike in their nervous sensibility, their preoccupation with things imagined rather than things
experienced, their habit of dramatising the issues presented to them,
their constant outpouring of heart and mind in words of incompar-

[1] Hazlitt, comparing these two speeches, writes: 'This (Henry's speech) is a true
and beautiful description of a naturally quiet and contented disposition and not like
the former (Richard's speech) the splenetic effusion of disappointed ambition.'

able felicity, their chameleon changes of mood and temper, their stultification and defeat by grosser spirits. But how superficial are these likenesses compared with the fundamental difference in texture of the two characters! To put them together is to compare a wilful child 'pretending' in a playroom with a grown man searching into the depths of his nature and the ultimate mysteries of human life. Richard is interested only in himself and the figure he cuts in a world of his own contriving. Hamlet's interest is universal. Unlike Richard, who moves always from the general to the particular—the particular being his own destiny and passion—Hamlet moves as inevitably from the particular to the general. The tragedy in which he is immersed is his cue for infinite speculation. His personal wrongs are viewed as an epitome of all the ills that flesh is heir to. His hesitations and misgivings prompt him to analyse the source of all the hesitations and misgivings which distract the human mind. There is no character in all Shakespeare's plays so self-centred as Richard; no character less self-centred than Hamlet, who, in brooding on his own problem, sees it instinctively as the problem of every man; who, in the bitterness of his own suffering, can lose himself in the woes of Hecuba or follow the dust of Alexander till it be found stopping a hole to keep the wind away. No character in all Shakespeare's plays is less capable than Richard of meeting and speaking with men as they are. Hamlet, on the contrary, meets every man for what he is and is instantly on speaking terms with them all—from Osric, the waterfly, to a ghost from the grave. Richard's imagination, governed by his sensibility, turns perpetually inward as inevitably as Hamlet's imagination, governed by his intellect, turns perpetually outward. To Richard nothing has interest or significance but what concerns himself. To Hamlet nothing has interest or significance till it can be related with the scheme of things entire.

If these characters, superficially alike, prove on closer acquaintance to be essentially different, it is equally true that characters superficially different often prove to be in essentials more truly comparable. No two men could seem more unlike in their disposition and fortune than Richard of Bordeaux and Richard of Gloucester. Yet here, surely, are two portraits which might with advantage be hung side by side. The contrast between them serves only to emphasise their fundamental kinship. Both are men of the artist type, the first working in imagination and the second in action. Both are ego-centric, the one concentrating upon a self-created image within the mind which changes its form to reflect sensations and experiences passively received, the other concentrating upon the impact of his mind and will upon the external world of men and events. Each is the child of Narcissus: Richard, the fair rose, who calls for a mirror that he may see the brittle glory of a face that did keep ten thousand men every day under his household roof; Richard Crookback, en-amoured of his own deformity, who calls on the fair sun to shine out that he may see his shadow as he passes from one piece of mischief to another.

Thus, the two Richards present in their contraries the same fundamental truth. The man who is self-centred in imagination and the man who is self-centred in action are equally out of touch with reality, and equally doomed to destruction. The first withdraws from reality to live in a false world of his own creation. The other loses the real world in an effort to fashion it according to his own will and pleasure.

HENRY OF MONMOUTH

THERE is no character more popular in drama or fiction than that of the young scapegrace who suddenly betters expectation and surprises the world with his wisdom, prowess, magnanimity and success. When he is Prince of Wales, who is to become King of England and to excel in what for five hundred years was to be the national English pastime of beating the French, the appeal is irresistible. Henry of Monmouth, as Shakespeare found him in the chronicles, was already cast for this enviable impersonation. He had done all that was necessary to make him the darling of English history—from neglecting his studies, which many English worthies have claimed as a distinction in later life, to assaulting the Lord Chief Justice of England, which puts well into the shade the reminiscences of most public persons who can claim to have redeemed the promise of their greener days. Here was an opportunity not to be missed by a dramatist who must first secure the attention of a mixed audience before he can dare to invite its more judicious members to realise that there is more in his tale perhaps than meets the eye.

Here, too, is a grand occasion for Shakespeare's critics to study the varying levels of intelligence from which his political characters can be approached. He is to handle a subject which lends itself so easily to successful commonplace that to avoid a merely brilliant exercise in platitude seems almost impossible. What can we reasonably expect from this story of the bad boy who becomes a conquering hero but a merely ingenious treatment of a hopelessly conventional theme? That, in fact, is precisely what Shakespeare from the outset promises the simple spectator. He makes no apparent attempt to avoid the obvious. On the contrary, he presents it openly and with a flourish. Here, for all and more than it is worth, is madcap Harry who plays highwayman and fetches the Lord Chief Justice of England a box on the ear, because he is just the high-spirited, devil-may-care young fellow whom most successful Englishmen affect to have been in their salad days; who forgives and praises the man who, without fear or favour, punished him for breaking the King's peace, because, for all his wildness, he is sound at heart and respectful of wise authority; who turns from low jinks to high endeavour; who makes amends for beating up the officers of the Crown in defiance of the civil law by beating up the foreigner with the concurrence of the Church. All this is conveyed with a zest and simplicity so remarkable that for generations Henry of Monmouth has been accepted by most Englishmen, including some of Shakespeare's most famous critics, as the portrait of a stainless Christian warrior and an heroic example of what every happy man would wish to be. Shakespeare, indeed, has handled his conventional theme so successfully that his play has been hailed as a masterpiece by those who appreciate just this aspect of his achievement and nothing more.

All this, however, is no more than a beginning—good as far as it goes, but so far from being the last word on the subject that many of Shakespeare's best critics, from Hazlitt onwards, have indignantly refused to accept Henry of Monmouth as Shakespeare's portrait of a national hero. They not only decline to admire him. They find him positively odious and as near to being a bore as any of Shakespeare's major characters.

This, of course, may mean one or more of many things. It may mean that Shakespeare, while seeming to approve and perpetuate the legend of Henry's greatness, deliberately intended to strip this fine figure of an English soldier of his inordinate pretensions, skilfully combining an appeal to the romantic nationalism of the many with an appeal to the more judicious realism of the few. Or it may mean that Shakespeare fell in all good faith beneath the spell of his hero. Or it may mean that he agreed, for the sake of an effectively popular play, to identify himself with the legend and to present his countrymen with as impressive an image of God's Englishman as the historical facts and his own skill in their manipulation allowed. Or it may mean that he simply took the character as he found it in the chronicles and, setting his imagination to work, brought it upon the stage to think, speak and act as that particular kind of person must of necessity think, speak and act in conformity with his nature. The result of this last procedure would be, in outward seeming, the portrait of a successful man of action, respected and adored by those who

G

respect and adore success in public life. It would equally be the portrait of a man who would arouse hostility or disdain in persons who are convinced that men who succeed in public life are more distinguished by their limitations of mind and heart than by any excess of the finer human qualities. Shakespeare, if this were his procedure, intended neither a transfiguration nor a satire. He took his hero for better or for worse. He says in effect: 'Here is your mirror of all Christian kings. No one can deny that he cuts a very splendid figure. You may like him or not; that is not my affair. I have imagined for you such a man and he is just the sort of man who would behave as this man behaved and achieve what he achieved.'

The mood in which Shakespeare follows the career of Henry of Monmouth through the First and Second Parts of 'Henry IV' and 'Henry V', and the startlingly different effect produced on minds of diverse quality by this royal imp of fame, will be more suitably discussed when the plays have been studied. We are for the moment concerned to discover, not what may be read into these three brilliant histories, but what is actually there.

Note, first of all, that Shakespeare announces well in advance that he means to accept the popular legend. He even runs before history in establishing the tradition of the wild young prince. When Bolingbroke assumed the crown in 1399 Henry was only twelve years old. But Shakespeare, hurrying to state his theme, ignores chronology. In the last Act of 'Richard II' Bolingbroke demands:

> Can no man tell me of my unthrifty son?
> 'Tis full three months since I did see him last:
> If any plague hang over us, 'tis he.
> I would to God, my lords, he might be found:
> Inquire at London, 'mongst the taverns there,
> For there, they say, he daily doth frequent,
> With unrestrainèd loose companions,
> Even such, they say, as stand in narrow lanes,
> And beat our watch and rob our passengers.

Who could guess in 1596 that, among the unrestrainèd loose companions, so casually mentioned by an indignant father, there was shortly to step forward a certain Sir John Falstaff? Shakespeare keeps *that* card up his sleeve to the last possible moment. Bolingbroke, in the first scene of the first play in which Henry of Monmouth comes in person upon the stage, makes no reference to Sir John. He alludes, however, to another character who is also to serve as a touchstone of the Prince's quality. He has just had news of Hotspur's victory at Holmedon and his mind flies straight at the contrast:

> Yea, there thou mak'st me sad and mak'st me sin
> In envy that my Lord Northumberland
> Should be the father to so blest a son,
> A son who is the theme of honour's tongue;
> Amongst a grove, the very straightest plant;
> Who is sweet Fortune's minion and her pride:
> Whilst I, by looking on the praise of him,
> See riot and dishonour stain the brow
> Of my young Harry. O, that it could be proved
> That some night-tripping fairy had exchanged
> In cradle-clothes our children where they lay,
> And call'd mine Percy, his Plantagenet!
> Then would I have his Harry, and he mine.

Falstaff, meanwhile, is waiting behind the curtain. Of the immortal sprite, who was born about three of the clock in the afternoon with a white head and something of a round belly, there will be little or nothing to say in these pages. Our attention will be as strictly as possible confined to Sir John Falstaff, Knight, in so far as he was himself a political character or used by Shakespeare to indicate just how and where his other political characters stand in relation to the world at large. We shall, in fact, be concentrating on a piece of Falstaff so small in proportion to the total generous bulk of the man that it is commonly ignored. It is something of a shock to realise that he was a political character at all or had anything to do with public affairs, and it will be felt by many as something of an outrage to rank him, for any purpose whatever, with such persons as Prince John of Lancaster or the Earl of Worcester. But was not Sir John Falstaff entrusted with a charge of foot at Shrewsbury? Did he not raise forces for the King in Gloucestershire? Did he not attend a parley between the King and envoys of the rebel host? Did he not, if it comes to that, cross swords with Douglas and take prisoner a very valiant gentleman, Coleville of the Dale, who felt it no dishonour to surrender to so excellent a soldier? Falstaff has as much right to be seriously considered as an active public servant of the King's party as any other of the captains at Shrewsbury. Above and beyond all this, he is, from the merely political point of view, essential to Shakespeare's design. He is a point of contact between two worlds. In him the larger life of humanity, at its most genial and exuberant, is brought into touch with the narrow life of the public person at its most calculating and unscrupulous.

Whether Shakespeare deliberately intended to enforce this significant contrast is neither here nor there. The juxtaposition is constant throughout the play and it is sharply and even shockingly apparent in the very first encounter between Falstaff and the Prince.

Consider carefully the startling impact of the first memorably dramatic stroke in Shakespeare's presentation of the two men. The Prince is shown in all his quips and his quiddities. He is Jack Falstaff's mad wag, a sweet wag, sweet Hal, honey lord, the most comparative, rascallest, sweet young prince. He has consented to highway robbery at Gadshill. This may be low life, but it is good fellowship. These are wild oats, but they are wholesome. A young man who begins with cutting purses for the fun of the thing is not improbably a young man who will cut something of a figure on reaching years of discretion. But stay! this is a false start. Henry is left alone and Shakespeare seizes this opportunity to warn us instantly in a soliloquy that Henry's waggery is only skin-deep:

> I know you all, and will awhile uphold
> The unyok'd humour of your idleness:
> Yet herein will I imitate the sun,
> Who doth permit the base contagious clouds
> To smother up his beauty from the world,
> That, when he please again to be himself,
> Being wanted, he may be more wonder'd at,
> By breaking through the foul and ugly mists
> Of vapours that did seem to strangle him.

Henry may mean precisely what he says; in that case he consorts with inferior persons from pure policy; he is misconducting himself in Eastcheap, so that later on, in Westminster, he may startle and impress the world with his good behaviour. Perhaps, however, he is merely trying, with false reasons, to justify his present way of life; in that case he combines an honest liking for vulgar society with a sharp sense of his own superior station. In either event what becomes of the prince of good fellows? Henry, if he means what he says, is a false good fellow who does nothing without premeditation. If, on the contrary, he is merely looking for a reason to be merry with his friends, surely he might have found a better one. To plead that he is permitting their base contagious clouds to smother up his beauty in order that he may shine all the more brightly when they have served his turn is not the sort of excuse which would have suggested itself to a really good companion.

It is a favourite device with Shakespeare in presenting a dramatic character to give us a leading clue to his disposition in a first soliloquy. Here, then, in this first serious speech of Henry of Monmouth, we should expect to find his most constant and essential quality. Nor are we deceived. For, as we follow his career through fifteen acts of the three Histories that lie ahead, we shall find him, at every significant turn in his affairs, exhibiting precisely the trait which is so startlingly thrust upon our notice at his first appearance. Whatever Henry may be doing—whether it be drinking sack with Falstaff or consenting to highway robbery with Poins, threatening to sack a city or exposing his loyal subjects to the hazards of war—he must satisfy himself that he is doing only what is right and proper. We shall discover that all but very few of his speeches in the three plays are speeches of self-justification. His first significant speech is, in fact, the preliminary statement of a leading motive.

Henry undoubtedly enjoys the low life of Eastcheap. The plea that he consorts with low companions merely in order that he may surprise the world later on with a timely reformation is merely his way of finding a good and sufficient reason for doing something he wants to do. That he should pitch on this particular kind of reason is equally characteristic. It is a good, worldly reason, but it is not an attractive or a generous reason.

Henry of Monmouth, when he finds a good excuse to think well of himself, does not easily let it go. Throughout his madcap career he holds fast to the pious assumption that, in amusing himself with Falstaff, he is preparing to stagger society with a well-timed reformation and that he is in the meantime collecting useful information and experience. He assures his dying father:

> If I do feign,
> O, let me in my present wildness die
> And never live to show the incredulous world
> *The noble change that I have purposèd!*

Shakespeare leaves us to decide for ourselves how far Henry really conducts himself according to plan, or how far he is merely creating an alibi for his misdemeanours. Most of us will conclude upon the evidence that the two interpretations are complementary rather than exclusive. Both readings are implicit in the famous scene in which, coming upon the stage for the first time as Henry V, he encounters the Lord Chief Justice who had but lately committed him to prison for contempt of court. Henry confirms the Lord Chief Justice in his office and praises him for enforcing the law. And Henry concludes:

> My father is gone wild into his grave,
> For in his tomb lie my affections;
> And with his spirit sadly I survive,
> To mock the expectation of the world,
> To frustrate prophecies, and to raze out
> Rotten opinion, who hath writ me down
> After my seeming. The tide of blood in me
> Hath proudly flow'd in vanity till now:
> Now doth it turn and ebb back to the sea,
> Where it shall mingle with the state of floods
> And flow henceforth in formal majesty.

The contrition here expressed presupposes that the Eastcheap revels were genuine wild oats. It is to be noted, however, that Henry, even when confessing that the tide of blood in him has proudly flowed in vanity, contrives at the same time to slip in an oblique reference to the fact that he always intended to mock the expectation of the world.

In the First and Second Parts of 'Henry IV' Shakespeare, in three major characters, contrasts the Prince's invincible priggery with just the qualities most fitted to set it off. No one better than Falstaff could throw into relief the moral and mental limitations of a budding statesman. No one better than Hotspur could suggest the abyss in temperament that separates the man who is too impulsive for success—too generous, too lacking in self-control and, above all, too deficient in the arts of deceiving either himself or his friends—from the man who even as a youth grooms himself instinctively for high office and keeps half an eye on the main chance even in his revels. Hotspur and Falstaff are alike incapable of any form of humbug. Practical Falstaff, who dismissed honour as a mere word, and romantic Hotspur, who is ready to pluck bright honour from the pale-faced moon, are congenial in their single-heartedness. These two fare together as companionably as Don Quixote and Sancho Panza. Henry of Monmouth belongs to a different world. For him in the long run honour, like love or good life, is but a means to achieve what he must first persuade himself to regard as a worthy end.

The third person to bring out the essential quality of Henry, the Prince, is his father, Henry, the King. The character of the man who intends to succeed with the approval of his conscience is unfolded beside that of the man who has succeeded in despite of his conscience and is dying of a broken spirit. Henry of Monmouth is the son of his father. Conscience, in Bolingbroke, is sick; in his heir it is merely sensitive. The contrast between them, their essential likeness and unlikeness, is a major theme.

Falstaff, Hotspur and Bolingbroke—all three must fade so that Henry of Monmouth may thrive. Falstaff dies of a heart that is fracted and corroborate, babbling of green fields; Hotspur becomes food for worms at Shrewsbury, the budding honours on his crest cropped to make a garland for the head of a rival who sees in him no more than a valiant rebel and a victim of ambition; Bolingbroke utters a dying wish that the soil of his achievement may go with him into the earth and that his son may quietly reap the benefit of his father's crime.

What, more precisely, is Falstaff's place in the political scheme? First he embodies the genial humanity and free play of mind which the political leader inevitably forgoes when he confines himself within the restricted field of public affairs. Falstaff, simply by being himself, puts King and Prince, soldiers and conspirators, in their proper place. His mere existence is a standing comment on their solemn gestures and policies. Henry of Monmouth, to be a successful king, must repudiate Sir John. And how much the poorer he will be for that repudiation!

Falstaff is also of significance to the political scheme in that he plays an active, if modest, part in the public life of his time, which brings him into touch with the leading men of affairs. In these encounters the men of policy are, for a moment, seen from the point of view of the natural man. Their illusions of dignity and power are exposed to the light of humour and common sense.

Then, again, Falstaff's political activities bring into view the underside of high policy and heroic war. Falstaff not only mocks at honour which cannot set to a leg, but, in abuse of the King's commission, lines his pockets with bribes extorted from unwilling conscripts and leads his rustic army to death or mutilation as part of the day's work. If we are not horrified at what he does, that is only because our censure is disarmed by the exuberant honesty of the culprit. He seeks no excuses for his behaviour. He makes no fine speeches. His cynicism, if it makes his conduct no more acceptable than that of his betters, just as certainly makes it no worse.

Falstaff is obviously no fit company for a hero. Henry, though not insensible to the delectable humours of Eastcheap, knows from the outset that, if he is to be a great king, Falstaff, with all he represents, must be discarded. It was not an easy sacrifice. Henry is a man of lively intelligence who deliberately narrows his outlook so that he may see only the business in hand. He limits his mind to the performance of a political task and forcibly persuades himself that everything he does to that end is his humble duty.

Henry will discard Falstaff when he must, but keep him as long as he may. In the first interview with his father, when the King upbraids him for his loose behaviour, he promises an immediate reformation:

> I shall hereafter, my thrice gracious lord,
> Be more myself.

But in the very next scene we find him back at the Boar's Head; he has procured Falstaff a charge of foot. Conscience and care for his reputation prompt him to cut loose from an 'oily rascal' who is 'known as well as Paul's', but Falstaff has for him a fascination which makes it very difficult for him consistently to preserve the stained-glass attitudes proper to an heir apparent. He returns from Westminster to Eastcheap, not to bid his old friend farewell, but to enlist him as a companion in arms. Falstaff is to go with him to Shrewsbury. Nor is this the last occasion on which he lapses from grace. After Shrewsbury occurs the famous incident in which he strikes the Lord Chief Justice and is committed to prison for contempt of court. The episode is not shown but only reported. Shakespeare, however, gives it considerable prominence. The Lord Chief Justice reminds Falstaff: 'The King hath severed you and Prince Harry,' but the Prince again repairs to the Boar's Head and, in the disguise of a drawer, hears himself dispraised before the wicked.

This second relapse is used by Shakespeare to show Henry's natural predilection for low company—which is incidentally better company than princes are normally allowed to enjoy—at odds with the queasy conscience of a hero by predestination. It is the first scene in which Henry appears in the Second Part of 'Henry IV'. It is a most revealing passage. Nowhere else does Henry more poignantly disclose his deep-seated craving to stand well with himself and with the world. He is alone with Poins, to whom he opens his heart. 'Doth it not show vilely in me to desire small beer?' Poins agrees that it is unbecoming in a prince to remember so weak a composition. The Prince then wonders at his condescension to low life:

What a disgrace is it to me to remember thy name! or to know thy face to-morrow! or to take note how many pair of silk stockings thou hast, viz. these, and those that were thy peach-coloured ones! or to bear the inventory of thy shirts; as, one for superfluity, and one other for use!

Next comes a reference to another leading motive of the play. The King is sick and the Prince is believed by many to be waiting for his father's crown. Rather than rest under such an imputation, he will unbosom himself to a companion whom he despises and cannot refrain from insulting in the act:

PRINCE: Marry, I tell thee, it is not meet that I should be sad, now my father is sick: albeit I could tell to thee,—as to one it pleases me, for fault of a better, to call my friend,—I could be sad, and sad indeed too.
POINS: Very hardly upon such a subject.

PRINCE: By this hand, thou thinkest me as far in the devil's book as thou and Falstaff for obduracy and persistency: let the end try the man. But I tell thee, my heart bleeds inwardly that my father is so sick: and keeping such vile company as thou art hath in reason taken from me all ostentation of sorrow.

POINS: The reason?

PRINCE: What wouldst thou think of me, if I should weep?

POINS: I would think thee a most princely hypocrite.

PRINCE: It would be every man's thought; and thou art a blessèd fellow to think as every man thinks: never a man's thought in the world keeps the road-way better than thine: every man would think me an hypocrite indeed.

The last and greatest of the scenes at the Boar's Head, in which Falstaff must leave unpicked the sweetest morsel of the night, is Henry of Monmouth's carnival or farewell to flesh. The King's messenger knocks at the door. Affairs of state are peremptory. The Prince's conscience will not again suffer any backsliding and he leaves Eastcheap with a *mea culpa,*

> By heaven, Poins, I feel me much to blame,
> So idly to profane the precious time.

And so we come to that last scene of all which has made so painful an impression on so many even of the most whole-hearted admirers of warlike Harry. Certainly he never appears to less advantage than when he turns away his friend:

> I know thee not, old man: fall to thy prayers;
> How ill white hairs become a fool and jester!
> I have long dream'd of such a kind of man,
> So surfeit-swell'd, so old, and so profane;
> But, being awak'd, I do despise my dream.
> Make less thy body hence, and more thy grace;
> Leave gormandizing; know the grave doth gape
> For thee thrice wider than for other men.
> Reply not to me with a fool-born jest:
> Presume not that I am the thing I was;
> For God doth know, so shall the world perceive,
> That I have turn'd away my former self;
> So will I those that kept me company.

This repudiation falls icily upon a victim caught utterly defenceless. Falstaff has ridden post to London, ingenuously confident of his reception:

FALSTAFF: Stand here by me, Master Robert Shallow; I will make the king do you grace: I will leer upon him, as 'a comes by: and do but mark the countenance that he will give me.

PISTOL: God bless thy lungs, good knight.

FALSTAFF: Come here, Pistol; stand behind me. O, if I had had time to have made new liveries, I would have bestowed the thousand pound I borrowed of you. But 'tis no matter; this poor show doth better: this doth infer the zeal I had to see him.

SHALLOW: It doth so.

FALSTAFF: It shows my earnestness of affection,—

SHALLOW: It doth so.

FALSTAFF: My devotion,—

SHALLOW: It doth, it doth, it doth.

FALSTAFF: As it were, to ride day and night; and not to deliberate, not to remember, not to have patience to shift me,—

SHALLOW: It is best, certain.

FALSTAFF: But to stand stained with travel, and sweating with desire to see him; thinking of nothing else, putting all affairs else in oblivion, as if there were nothing else to be done but to see him.

Falstaff was never more lovingly presented. Even self-interest is forgotten upon sight of his royal Hal:

FALSTAFF: God save thee, my sweet boy!

KING: My lord chief-justice, speak to that vain man.

CH. JUSTICE: Have you your wits? know you what 'tis you speak?

FALSTAFF: My king! my Jove! I speak to thee, my heart!

The shock is tremendous. It was nevertheless implicit in the Prince's first soliloquy and it has been foreshadowed time and again. The discarding of Falstaff was, in fact, not only a political but a human necessity. That Falstaff, himself, for all his cynical shrewdness, should never have suspected it only goes to show how wide and deep is the gulf between human nature and political conduct. It should be noted, too, that Shakespeare has led up to this scene, not merely by express suggestions here and there, but by effecting a subtle but quite unmistakable change in tone between the two plays of which it is the climax. The full-blooded gaiety of the First Part of 'Henry IV' gives place in the Second Part to a more realistic handling of character and situation. The humours of the Boar's Head are changed. Falstaff's men in buckram raise laughter without a qualm. Falstaff with Doll Tearsheet on his knee—*I am old, I am old*—raises laughter of a different quality. So, too, do the scenes in Gloucestershire, where Falstaff, in his deliberate exploitation of Justice Shallow, is no longer the sprite of Gadshill. We are made to feel that there can be no possible companionship between a fat old man, living on his wits, and the King of England. Doll herself strikes a premonitory note, preparing us for the moment when Henry of Monmouth, with less affection but with greater dignity, will upbraid Falstaff with his white hairs:

DOLL: Thou whoreson little tidy Bartholomew boar-pig, when wilt thou leave fighting o' days and foining o' nights, and begin to patch up thine old body for heaven?

It remains to glance briefly at the political encounters in which Falstaff actively participates. Note, first, his behaviour as bearer of the King's commission on a public road near Coventry. He has recruited a company for the royal forces, pricking for service good householders and contracted bachelors, who had as lief hear a devil as a drum, but allowing them to buy out their services, so that in the end he is left with a posse of old soldiers, discarded serving-men, ostlers and tattered prodigals, the cankers of a calm world and a long peace. Henry encounters him on the way:

PRINCE: But tell me, Jack, whose fellows are these that come after?
FALSTAFF: Mine, Hal, mine.
PRINCE: I did never see such pitiful rascals.
FALSTAFF: Tut, tut; good enough to toss; food for powder, food for powder; they'll fill a pit as well as better: tush, man, mortal men, mortal men.

Falstaff takes his company to Shrewsbury field and there—but let him tell the brief story in his own words:

I have led my ragamuffins where they are peppered: there's not three of my hundred and fifty left alive; and they are for the town's end, to beg during life.

We shall be haunted with the memory of these pitiful rascals when we stand with King Henry and his band of brothers on the field of Agincourt. Falstaff's account of their passing is a practical soldier's comment on martial enterprise. To the horrors and hazards of war he brings the chill verdict of common sense and the defensive mechanism of humour. His dreadful levity is that of the hardened warrior. He comes to the battlefield without illusions, accepts his fair share of the action, sees things for what they are and delivers judgment. He has fought with his company to the last man but three and arrives upon the scene to find Sir Walter Blunt lying dead on the ground. He will not part with his sword, even to the Prince, but is willing to share with him the bottle of sack which, as an old campaigner, he carries in his pistol-case. As to the fighting, he will do what he must but no more:

Well, if Percy be alive, I'll pierce him. If he do come in my way, so: if he do not, if I come in his willingly, let him make a carbonado of me. I like not such grinning honour as Sir Walter hath: give me life; which if I can save, so; if not, honour comes unlooked for, and there's an end.

It is the application in practice of his final catechism:

FALSTAFF: I would it were bed-time, Hal, and all well.
PRINCE: Why, thou owest God a death. (*Exit.*)
FALSTAFF: 'Tis not due yet; I would be loath to pay him before his day. What need I be so forward with him that calls not on me? Well, 'tis no matter; honour pricks me on. Yea, but how if honour prick me off when I come on? how then? Can honour set to a leg? no: or an arm? no: or take away the grief of a wound? no. Honour hath no skill in surgery, then? no. What is honour? a word. What is in that word, honour? air. A trim reckoning! Who hath it? he that died o' Wednesday. Doth he feel it? no. Doth he hear it? no. It is insensible, then? Yea, to the dead. But will it not live with the living? no. Why? detraction will not suffer it. Therefore I'll have none of it: honour is a mere scutcheon; and so ends my catechism.

The speech is almost too familiar for quotation, but let it be remembered as a necessary qualification of what is shortly to be said so eloquently elsewhere upon the other side.

If Falstaff is necessary to Shakespeare's presentation of total war, he is hardly less important in relation to the public men who determine its issues. Falstaff is present on two occasions when high matters of policy are debated. In the parley which precedes the battle of Shrewsbury, Worcester, in arms against the King, protests his innocence and love of peace. This is too much for Sir John, who slips into the discussion with an irreverent comment. The Prince silences him instantly. One touch of Falstaff and these public persons will begin to look merely silly:

> WORCESTER: Hear me, my liege:
>   For mine own part, I could be well content
>   To entertain the lag-end of my life
>   With quiet hours; for I do protest,
>   I have not sought the day of this dislike.
>   KING: You have not sought it! how comes it, then?
> FALSTAFF: Rebellion lay in his way, and he found it.
>   PRINCE: Peace, chewet, peace!

Henry's rebuke is touchingly conveyed. He is human enough to realise that there is much to be said for the comic approach. His use of the familiar word 'chewet', which to the Elizabethans carried a simultaneous suggestion of a magpie and of minced meat dressed with butter, is very companionable. He is not reproving an impertinence, but deprecating a levity with which he is secretly inclined to sympathise.

Falstaff's honest cynicism at Shrewsbury stands in clear contrast with as pretty a piece of knavery as ever issued from a public conference. The King offers the rebels a peaceful settlement with grace for all, but Worcester takes back to Hotspur a completely false report of the King's message. He fears (a) that the King will not keep his word and (b) that Hotspur may be tempted to accept it in all good faith. He accordingly tells Hotspur that the King has refused to listen to their grievances and is preparing to take the field. Hotspur is thus committed to a battle which need never have been fought if there had been on either side a touch of the honour for which Hotspur died or a grain of the humour in which Falstaff survived.[1]

Falstaff shows to even better advantage in a later episode against a background of politic princes. The King, wishing to separate him

[1] For a further reference to this incident as it bears on the character of Hotspur' see p. 208.

from Henry, has attached him to the staff of Henry's younger brother, Prince John of Lancaster, whose army has been sent to suppress a second insurrection of the northern lords. It is typical of the change of mood between the First and Second Parts of 'Henry IV' that in the first play rebellion concludes with a battle and in the second with an armistice treacherously used by the King's party to arrest and execute the leaders of the opposition. Lancaster offers them fair terms:

> My lord, these griefs shall be with speed redress'd;
> Upon my soul, they shall. If this may please you,
> Discharge your powers unto their several counties,
> As we will ours: and here between the armies
> Let's drink together friendly and embrace,
> That all their eyes may bear those tokens home
> Of our restorèd love and amity.

The rebel lords at once dismiss their forces, but Lancaster delays the demobilisation of the royal army and arrests his enemies, coolly pointing out that, although he had undertaken to redress their grievances, he had not promised to spare their lives. He concludes with a dedication of this coldblooded piece of knavery to the glory of God.

Such is the situation into which Falstaff comes sword in hand. He has had no word of the armistice and he meets Coleville of the Dale with whom he is ready, if necessary, to do battle:

Do ye yield, sir? or shall I sweat for you? If I do sweat, they are the drops of thy lovers, and they weep for thy death: therefore rouse up fear and trembling, and do observance to my mercy.

Lancaster enters and announces that the rebel army is dispersed. He then turns on Falstaff, the only person who has so far conducted himself like a soldier and a gentleman, and rates him for coming late to the field. Falstaff's reply would have raised a smile in any other man:

Do you think me a swallow, an arrow, or a bullet? Have I, in my poor and old motion, the expedition of thought? I have speeded hither with the very extremest inch of possibility; I have foundered nine score and odd posts: and here, travel-tainted as I am, have, in my pure and immaculate valour, taken Sir John Coleville of the dale, a most furious knight and valorous enemy. But what of that? he saw me, and yielded; that I may justly say, with the hook-nosed fellow of Rome, 'I came, saw, and over-came.'

There is more in the same vein; but Lancaster is not amused. He deprives Falstaff of his prisoner, whom he sends to the block with the rest of his captives, and bids farewell to Falstaff himself with the promise:

> I, in my condition,
> Shall better speak of you than you deserve.

Falstaff sends after him a parting shot:

> I would you had but the wit; 'twere better than your dukedom;

and speaks his epitaph in three lines:

> Good faith, this same young sober-blooded boy doth not love me; nor a man cannot make him laugh.[1]

So much for Prince John of Lancaster. He emerges for a moment from the obscurity of formal history to stand beside the greatest re-presentative in comic literature of the inexhaustible humours of flesh and blood.

From Falstaff, who concludes from his catechism that to be pricked on by honour merely to be pricked off is to show more valour than discretion, to Hotspur, for whom it were an easy leap to pluck bright honour from the pale-faced moon, seems as great a distance as could well be imagined in human character. But between these two men, who must die before Henry of Monmouth can assume the status of a hero, there is an essential kinship. The warm blood that runs in the veins of these two darlings of Shakespeare's imagination is of a dif-ferent quality from the cold blood which the Prince 'did inherit of his father.' In Hotspur, as in Falstaff, there is a singleness of mind, a quickness of fancy and a flow of spirit which challenge at every turn the relatively artificial conduct of the men, good, bad or indifferent,

---

[1] This, of course, is the cue for Falstaff's famous speech on the cordial properties of sherris-sack. It has no political implications, but there is a striking reference to the cold blood which Prince Harry 'did naturally inherit of his father', which shows Sir John to be a deep observer of men.

by whom they are surrounded. The contrast between Henry of
Monmouth and Falstaff has been sufficiently emphasised. The contrast between Henry of Monmouth and Henry Percy is no less significant. Who can imagine Hotspur, in whom impulse and action fly
together, seeking to place on any shoulders but his own the responsibility for his actions? Who can imagine him undertaking an heroic
enterprise from policy? Who can imagine him discarding a friend
to follow his fortune?

Hotspur belongs to a small company of characters which Shakespeare has drawn with such felicity that critics have suspected them
to reflect something of his own mind and disposition. These characters differ greatly from one another, but they all—Hotspur, Biron,
Mercutio, Faulconbridge, Enobarbus—are men whose speech fits
them like a glove: who are never so much themselves as when
their tongues run away with them; in whom we recognise a
soundness of heart and a lucidity of spirit against which the chican-
eries of men and circumstances stand out in high relief. They are too
nimble of mind to suffer an impostor, too generously human to be
worldly-wise.

Hotspur jumps into immortality with the famous speech in which
he apologises for having shown a notable lack of respect for a King's
messenger:

> But I remember, when the fight was done,
> When I was dry with rage and extreme toil,
> Breathless and faint, leaning upon my sword,
> Came there a certain lord, neat, trimly dress'd,
> Fresh as a bridegroom; and his chin, new reap'd,
> Show'd like a stubble-land at harvest-home;
> He was perfumèd like a milliner,
> And 'twixt his finger and his thumb he held
> A pouncet-box.
>
> And still he smiled and talk'd;
> And as the soldiers bore dead bodies by,
> He call'd them untaught knaves, unmannerly,
> To bring a slovenly unhandsome corse
> Betwixt the wind and his nobility.
> With many holiday and lady terms

He question'd me; amongst the rest, demanded
My prisoners in your majesty's behalf.
I then, all smarting with my wounds being cold,
To be so pester'd with a popinjay,
Out of my grief and my impatience,
Answer'd neglectingly I know not what,
He should, or he should not; for he made me mad
To see him shine so brisk and smell so sweet
And talk so like a waiting gentlewoman
Of guns and drums and wounds,—God save the mark!—
And telling me the sovereign'st thing on earth
Was parmaceti for an inward bruise;
And that it was great pity, so it was,
This villainous salt-petre should be digg'd
Out of the bowels of the harmless earth,
Which many a good tall fellow had destroy'd
So cowardly; and but for these vile guns,
He would himself have been a soldier.
This bald, unjointed chat of his, my lord,
I answer'd indirectly, as I said;
And I beseech you, let not his report
Come current for an accusation
Betwixt my love and your high majesty.

The whole man is portrayed in this outburst—full-blooded, impetuous, not picking his words or mincing his impressions, easily defiant but confident that a frank apology will be as frankly met and understood, unguarded in his reactions to men and affairs from the engaging simplicity of his faith in fair dealing as between soldiers. He has the robust gaiety of an athletic disposition, as remote from the sinuous duplicity of political life as is the shrewd, irreverent exuberance of Falstaff.

A sovereign quality in Hotspur is his complete indifference to profit or place. The prisoners taken at Holmedon were his by the laws of war and their ransom his perquisite. But he is not unwilling to surrender them. All he asks in return is that the King should redeem his kinsman, the Earl of Mortimer, who is prisoner to Glendower. This the King refuses to do, falsely charging Mortimer with cowardice and treason. The King, of course, has his reasons. Richard had proclaimed Mortimer to be his heir and Mortimer had as good, or a better, title to the crown. Hotspur indignantly protests that Mortimer is a loyal and valiant gentleman, but the King is not to be moved. He is more afraid of Mortimer than of Percy. He declares that Mortimer may starve on the barren mountains and he forbids Hotspur to speak of him again.

This drives Hotspur to a frenzy. His friend, the noble Mortimer, stands attainted with 'base and rotten policy'. The issue is between the chivalry in which Hotspur lives and breathes and this same 'base and rotten policy' which prompts the King to distrust the men who helped to put him on the throne. Hotspur sees in Bolingbroke everything he most abhors—ingratitude, insincerity, avarice, the fear to lose and the determination to retain by fair means or foul what he has acquired with the help of others. Is it for such a man that his father and his uncle 'put down Richard, that sweet lovely rose'— only to be repaid with insult and suspicion?

> Speak of Mortimer!
> 'Zounds! I will speak of him; and let my soul
> Want mercy, if I do not join with him:
> Yea, on his part I'll empty all these veins,
> And shed my dear blood drop by drop i' the dust,
> But I will lift the down-trod Mortimer
> As high i' the air as this unthankful king,
> As this ingrate and canker'd Bolingbroke.

Hotspur's anger is intensely personal, springing from a fierce contempt of everything between men that does not square with his own simple code:

> By heaven, methinks it were an easy leap,
> To pluck bright honour from the pale-fac'd moon,
> Or dive into the bottom of the deep,
> Where fathom-line could never touch the ground,
> And pluck up drownèd honour by the locks;
> So he that doth redeem her thence might wear
> Without corrival all her dignities:
> But out upon this half-fac'd fellowship!

The Earl of Worcester, that same Worcester who not so long ago had broken his staff of office and deserted Richard for Bolingbroke, has already laid his plans, but Hotspur is too lost in his passionate recoil from all that savours of policy to give ear or mind to them. To his uncle and father he is 'fey'. There is no handling such a man till the fit be exhausted:

WORCESTER: He apprehends a world of figures here,
But not the form of what he should attend.
Good cousin, give me audience for a while.

HOTSPUR: I cry you mercy.

WORCESTER: Those same noble Scots
That are your prisoners,—

HOTSPUR: I'll keep them all;
By God, he shall not have a Scot of them;
No, if a Scot would save his soul, he shall not:
I'll keep them, by this hand.

WORCESTER: You start away,
And lend no ear unto my purposes.
Those prisoners you shall keep.

HOTSPUR: Nay, I will; that's flat:
He said he would not ransom Mortimer;
Forbad my tongue to speak of Mortimer;
But I will find him when he lies asleep,
And in his ear I'll holla 'Mortimer!'
Nay,
I'll have a starling shall be taught to speak
Nothing but 'Mortimer', and give it him,
To keep his anger still in motion.

WORCESTER: Hear you, cousin; a word.

HOTSPUR: All studies here I solemnly defy,
Save how to gall and pinch this Bolingbroke:
And that same sword-and-buckler Prince of Wales,
But that I think his father loves him not
And would be glad he met with some mischance,
I'd have him poison'd with a pot of ale.

WORCESTER: Farewell, kinsman: I will talk to you,
When you are better temper'd to attend.

NORTHUMBERLAND: Why, what a wasp-stung and impatient fool
Art thou to break into this woman's mood,
Tying thine ear to no tongue but thine own!

HOTSPUR: Why, look you, I am whipp'd and scourged with
                    rods,
            Nettled and stung with pismires, when I hear
            Of this vile politician, Bolingbroke.
            In Richard's time,—what do ye call the place?—
            A plague upon't—it is in Gloucestershire;—
            'Twas where the madcap duke his uncle kept,
            His uncle York;—where I first bow'd my knee
            Unto this king of smiles, this Bolingbroke,—
            'Sblood!—
            When you and he came back from Ravenspurgh.
NORTHUMBERLAND: At Berkeley castle.
HOTSPUR: You say true:
            Why, what a candy deal of courtesy
            This fawning greyhound then did proffer me!
            Look! 'when his infant fortune came to age,'
            And 'gentle Harry Percy,' and 'kind cousin';
            O, the devil take such cozeners! God forgive me!
            Good uncle, tell your tale; for I have done.
WORCESTER: Nay, if you have not, to't again;
            We'll stay your leisure.
                    HOTSPUR: I have done, i' faith.

That is a long quotation, but it is one of the best scenes Shakespeare ever wrote and cannot be too often read. Each of the three
characters, though one of them has but a single short speech, is clearly
shown. Worcester has imagination enough to understand something
of Hotspur's quality and even to respect it. Only Northumberland,
ignoble from his first appearance in 'Richard II' to his last shameful
exit in the Second Part of 'Henry IV', is insensible. The son whom he
is inciting to rebellion and will betray in the act is, to his politic
mind, an impatient fool.

Hotspur, when next he appears, is deep in conspiracy and contemptuous of any gentleman who in policy hangs back from the
enterprise. Again the temptation to quote at length is irresistible:

(*Enter* HOTSPUR *solus reading a letter.*)

'*But for mine own part, my lord, I could be well contented to be there, in respect of the love I bear your house.*' He could be contented: why is he not,
then? In respect of the love he bears our house: he shows in this he loves

his own barn better than he loves our house. Let me see some more. '*The purpose you undertake is dangerous*';—why, that's certain: 'tis dangerous to take a cold, to sleep, to drink; but I tell you, my lord fool, out of this nettle, danger, we pluck this flower, safety. '*The purpose you undertake is dangerous: the friends you have named uncertain: the time itself unsorted: and your whole plot too light for the counterpoise of so great an opposition.*' Say you so, say you so? I say unto you again, you are a shallow cowardly hind, and you lie. What a lack-brain is this! By the Lord, our plot is a good plot as ever was laid; our friends true and constant: a good plot, good friends, and full of expectation; an excellent plot, very good friends. What a frosty-spirited rogue is this! Why, my lord of York commends the plot and the general course of the action. 'Zounds! an I were now by this rascal, I could brain him with his lady's fan. Is there not my father, my uncle and myself? lord Edmund Mortimer, my lord of York and Owen Glendower? Is there not besides the Douglas? Have I not all their letters to meet me in arms by the ninth of the next month? and are they not some of them set forward already? What a pagan rascal is this! an infidel! Ha! you shall see now in very sincerity of fear and cold heart, will he to the king and lay open all our proceedings. O, I could divide myself and go to buffets, for moving such a dish of skim milk with so honourable an action! Hang him! let him tell the king; we are prepared. I will set forward to-night.

What genial contempt is here for all trimmers, what simple trust in his friends, what buoyant confidence in his undertaking! The frosty-spirited rogue was a wiser man. But who does not feel it better to be wrong with Hotspur than right with the world?

In the famous meeting between the confederate rebels at Bangor, Shakespeare relieves his politics with a domestic interlude, enlarging his portrait of a beloved conspirator to that of a man complete in all his relationships.

We have already had a glimpse of Hotspur with his wife. She knows that he has some enterprise in hand. He is too full of it for concealment. He must mutter even in his sleep of sallies and retires, of palisadoes, frontiers, parapets, cannon and culverin. She wants to know what it all means, but Hotspur will tell her nothing. To her pleading speech of twenty-eight lines he replies by inquiring after his horse. Is it the roan with the crop ear? His wife insists:

LADY PERCY: But hear you, my lord.
HOTSPUR: What sayst thou, my lady?
LADY PERCY: What is it carries you away?
HOTSPUR: Why, my horse, my love, my horse.
LADY PERCY: Out, you mad-headed ape!
        A weasel hath not such a deal of spleen
        As you are toss'd with. In faith,
        I'll know your business, Harry, that I will.
        I fear my brother Mortimer doth stir
        About his title, and hath sent for you
        To line his enterprise: but if you go—
HOTSPUR: So far afoot, I shall be weary, love.
LADY PERCY: Come, come, you paraquito, answer me
        Directly unto this question that I ask:
        In faith, I'll break thy little finger, Harry,
        An if thou wilt not tell me all things true.

HOTSPUR: Constant you are,
        But yet a woman: and for secrecy,
        No lady closer; for I well believe
        Thou wilt not utter what thou dost not know;
        And so far will I trust thee, gentle Kate.
LADY PERCY: How! so far?
HOTSPUR: Not an inch further. But hark you, Kate:
        Whither I go, thither shall you go too;
        To-day will I set forth, to-morrow you.
        Will this content you, Kate?
LADY PERCY: It must of force.

This scene inevitably calls to mind Brutus in his orchard, similarly entreated by Portia. But what a difference between the English and the Roman style! The encounter between Hotspur and his wife is household stuff; the meeting between Brutus and Portia is a marriage of two minds. Hotspur's teasing affection, his cavalier conviction that a wife should know no more of her husband's business than is necessary, his assumption that there is a time for work and a time for play:

                This is no world
   To play with mammets and to tilt with lips:
   We must have bloody noses and crack'd crowns—

comes far short of Brutus (Ye gods, render me worthy of this noble wife!). But who shall decide which of the two pairs is better matched or more likely to endure wind and weather? Harry loves Kate as she is well content to be loved for all her playful pretences of ill-usage. 'O wondrous him, O miracle of men,' she cries after Shrewsbury has been fought and Harry slain:

> and by his light
> Did all the chivalry of England move,
> To do brave acts.

It is not in English Kate to complain with Roman Portia that she dwells but in the suburbs of her lord's affection because he refuses to discuss with her the state of the nation.

It is through Lady Percy that Shakespeare pictures for us the very speech and gait of the man—the stammering utterance which suggests a mind that outruns itself; the distinctive walk of a warrior who spends his days in heavy armour and on horseback:

> He was indeed the glass
> Wherein the noble youth did dress themselves:
> He had no legs that practis'd not his gait;
> And speaking thick, which nature made his blemish,
> Became the accents of the valiant;
> For those that could speak low and tardily
> Would turn their own perfection to abuse,
> To seem like him: so that in speech, in gait,
> In diet, in affections of delight,
> In military rules, humours of blood,
> He was the mark and glass, copy and book,
> That fashion'd others.

Hotspur, at Bangor, shows all his paces. He is impatient with Glendower, whose grandiloquence and wizardry bore him to death:

> Sometimes he angers me
> With telling me of the moldwarp and,
> Of the dreamer Merlin and his prophecies,
> And of a dragon, and a finless fish the ant,
> A clip-wing'd griffin, and a moulten raven,
> A couching lion, and a ramping cat,
> And such a deal of skimble-skamble stuff

As puts me from my faith. I tell you what:
He held me last night at least nine hours
In reckoning out the several devils' names
That were his lackeys: I cried 'hum', and 'well, go to',
But mark'd him not a word. O! he's as tedious
As a tired horse, a railing wife;
Worse than a smoky house: I'd rather live
With cheese and garlic in a windmill, far,
Than feed on cates and have him talk to me
In any summer-house in Christendom.[1]

When the Welshman declares that at his nativity the frame and huge foundation of the earth shaked like a coward, Hotspur retorts: 'Why, so it would have done at the same season, if your mother's cat had kittened.' Hotspur is all for things as they are in nature:

GLENDOWER: I can call spirits from the vasty deep.
HOTSPUR: Why, so can I, or so can any man;
But will they come when you do call for them?
GLENDOWER: Why, I can teach you, cousin, to command
The devil.
HOTSPUR: And I can teach thee, coz, to shame the devil
By telling truth: tell truth and shame the devil.
If thou have power to raise him, bring him hither,
And I'll be sworn I've power to shame him hence.
O, while you live, tell truth and shame the devil!

When the conspirators plot on the map the limits of their power, Hotspur protests:

Methinks my moiety, north from Burton here,
In quantity equals not one of yours:
See how this river comes me cranking in,
And cuts me from the best of all my land
A huge half-moon, a monstrous cantle out.
I'll have the current in this place damm'd up;
And here the smug and silver Trent shall run
In a new channel, fair and evenly;
It shall not wind with such a deep indent,
To rob me of so rich a bottom here.

[1] Observe how in Hotspur's speeches the metre often makes allowance for his stammer.

'Not wind?' exclaims Glendower, 'it shall, it must; you see it doth.'
Note, however, that he concedes the point:

> GLENDOWER: Come, you shall have Trent turn'd.
> HOTSPUR: I do not care: I'll give thrice so much land
> To any well-deserving friend;
> But in the way of bargain, mark you me,
> I'll cavil on the ninth part of a hair.

Protest and surrender are equally in character. Hotspur cares nothing
for acres more or less, but flies into opposition at the mere thought
of being put upon.

We draw to an end of this splendid scene, with Hotspur lying in
his wife's lap and listening, under protest, to a Welsh ballad. Then,
of course, though he has no ear for music, he must have an English
ditty:

> HOTSPUR: Come, Kate, I'll have your song too.
> LADY PERCY: Not mine, in good sooth.
> HOTSPUR: Not yours, in good sooth! Heart! you swear like a
> comfit-maker's wife. Not you, 'in good sooth', and
> 'as true as I live', and 'as God shall mend me,' and
> 'as sure as day'.
> And giv'st such sarcenet surety for thy oaths,
> As if thou never walk'dst further than Finsbury.
> Swear me, Kate, like a lady as thou art,
> A good mouth-filling oath; and leave 'in sooth',
> And such protest of pepper-gingerbread,
> To velvet-guards and Sunday-citizens.
> Come, sing.
> LADY PERCY: I will not sing.

And so to battle—deserted by his father, betrayed by his own
impetuosity and his uncle's trickery. Northumberland sends word
that he is sick. Hotspur breaks out:

> 'Zounds! how has he the leisure to be sick
> In such a justling time?

> Sick now! droop now! this sickness doth infect
> The very life-blood of our enterprise;
> 'Tis catching hither, even to our camp.

But he instantly recovers and is soon arguing that his father's absence
is all to the good:

> It lends a lustre and more great opinion,
> A larger dare to our great enterprise,
> Than if the earl were here; for men must think,
> If we without his help can make a head
> To push against a kingdom, with his help
> We shall o'erturn it topsy-turvy down
> Yet all goes well, yet all our joints are whole.

It is characteristic of Hotspur that he never thinks of *blaming* his
father. It does not occur to him that Northumberland's indisposition
is diplomatic rather than physical and, when Worcester seems to
suggest it—

> It will be thought
> By some, that know not why he is away,
> That wisdom, loyalty, and mere dislike
> Of our proceedings, kept the earl from hence,—

Hotspur promptly rejects the inference.

The King's envoy to the rebels is Sir Walter Blunt, a man as
honest and forthright as Hotspur himself. To him Hotspur states his
grievances. It is a frank, artless assertion of wrongs suffered by himself and his family, infused with a hearty dislike of Bolingbroke and
his devious ways. Hotspur's trust in human nature is touchingly indicated in a reference to the services rendered by his father to Bolingbroke on his return from exile. Northumberland (maintains his dutiful and ingenuous son) was 'in kind heart and pity moved' to help a
'poor, unminded outlaw, sneaking home'. Hotspur unthinkingly
ascribes to his friends and relatives an honesty and a warmth of disposition which is peculiar to himself. His whole case against Bolingbroke is that he is a man who '*seems* to weep over his country's
wrongs', who wears a '*seeming* brow of justice' to gain his own ends,
who breaks faith with his friends and who incidentally has wronged
the Percies root and branch. There are no politics in this indictment:
this is a personal quarrel between gentlemen. Note also that Hotspur,
having unburdened himself of his indignation, is quite ready to come
to terms:

> BLUNT: I would you would accept of grace and love.
> HOTSPUR: And may be so we shall.

Worcester watches the whole scene with misgiving; this is not the way to conduct a public meeting. Hotspur is accordingly manœuvred into the background and it is Worcester himself who meets the King in final parley. The King offers fair terms:

> We love our people well; even those we love
> That are misled upon your cousin's part;
> And, will they take the offer of our grace,
> Both he and they and you, yea, every man
> Shall be my friend again and I'll be his;
> So tell your cousin, and bring me word
> What he will do.

Worcester, as we have noted,[1] dare not take this message back to his nephew. He knows how easily Hotspur may be moved to give even the devil his due. He puts the case of a politician whose security hangs on the good faith of another politician with admirable force and lucidity:

> It is not possible, it cannot be,
> The king should keep his word in loving us;
> He will suspect us still, and find a time
> To punish this offence in other faults.

> Look how we can, or sad or merrily,
> Interpretation will misquote our looks,
> And we shall feed like oxen at a stall,
> The better cherish'd, still the nearer death.

Worcester gives his nephew a false account of his mission and Hotspur, unsuspicious of the 'base and rotten policy' that has brought him to the field, goes confidently to his death.

Henry of Monmouth is meanwhile biding his time. In speech with the King he has already prophesied how it would be:

> Percy is but my factor, good my lord,
> To engross up glorious deeds on my behalf;
> And I will call him to so strict account,
> That he shall render every glory up.

[1] See above, p. 194.

They meet at Shrewsbury and Hotspur's budding honours are cropped to make a garland for the head of Harry, Prince of Wales. It is difficult to believe that Hotspur is dead. We expect him to rise up and stammer forth an indignant protest against his enemy's generous but shallow requiem:

> Ill-weav'd ambition, how much art thou shrunk!
> When that this body did contain a spirit,
> A kingdom for it was too small a bound;
> But now, two paces of the vilest earth
> Is room enough: this earth that bears thee dead,
> Bears not alive so stout a gentleman.

Could any words serve better to fix indelibly the contrast between the two men? There is no real 'ambition' in Hotspur, but from Henry of Monmouth the charge was inevitable. He honours his enemy in all simplicity with a tribute that cheapens his own victory and obscures the spirit of the fallen.

Thus Hotspur lies dead on the field. Prone beside him is Falstaff, who, with great presence of mind, is counterfeiting death to escape the sword of Douglas. Henry of Monmouth looks down upon them both. Falstaff will rise again. He will bear away the dead Hotspur on his back and the stage will be cleared of them both, so that the living Harry may shine supreme in a grey world. As the hero enlarges his stature, the earth shrinks to his measure. Henry of Monmouth, with his propensity for half-truths, tells Hotspur as they make ready to fight:

> Two stars keep not their motion in one sphere;
> Nor can one England brook a double reign.

That Harry of England could not live in the same world with Harry Percy is true, but these two stars were never in one sphere. Harry of England had to destroy Hotspur—and Falstaff too—not because they were rivals but because they were incompatibles.

The Prince's epitaph on Hotspur is, by a happy coincidence, followed by his epitaph on Falstaff. The latter is infinitely more gracious than anything he will say hereafter:

> What, old acquaintance! could not all this flesh
> Keep in a little life? Poor Jack, farewell!

> I could have better spared a better man:
> O, I should have a heavy miss of thee,
> If I were much in love with vanity!
> Death hath not struck so fat a deer to-day,
> Though many dearer, in this bloody fray.
> Embowell'd will I see thee by and by:
> Till then in blood by noble Percy lie.

Falstaff, however, is not so easily slain. He springs to life again in a speech that shows how necessary it will be for him to die in earnest if we are to take seriously the world into which Henry of Monmouth will survive:

FALSTAFF (*rising up*): Embowelled! if thou embowel me to-day, I'll give you leave to powder me and eat me too, to-morrow. 'Sblood, 'twas time to counterfeit, or that hot termagant Scot had paid me scot and lot too. Counterfeit? I lie, I am no counterfeit: to die is to be a counterfeit; for he is still but the counterfeit of a man who hath not the life of a man: but to counterfeit dying, when a man thereby liveth, is to be no counterfeit, but the true and perfect image of life indeed. The better part of valour is discretion; in the which better part, I have saved my life. 'Zounds, I am afraid of this gunpowder Percy, though he be dead: how, if he should counterfeit too and rise? By my faith, I am afraid he would prove the better counterfeit.

There is a third conspicuous figure of the tetralogy who must die before Henry of Monmouth can enjoy his inheritance. Bolingbroke usurped the crown which his son was to wear, as he hoped, with a better grace:

> God knows, my son,
> By what by-paths and indirect crook'd ways
> I met this crown; and I myself know well
> How troublesome it sat upon my head.
> To thee it shall descend with better quiet,
> Better opinion, better confirmation;
> For all the soil of the achievement goes
> With me into the earth.

Bolingbroke, on assuming the crown of England, lamented that blood should sprinkle him to make him grow. Then and there he vowed to make a voyage to the Holy Land to wash off the guilt of

Richard's death. He has grown prematurely old when next we meet him, and he is still talking of the Holy Land:

> Forthwith a power of English shall we levy,
> Whose arms were moulded in their mother's womb
> To chase these pagans in those holy fields
> Over whose acres walk'd those blessèd feet
> Which fourteen hundred years ago were nail'd,
> For our advantage, on the bitter cross.

His conscience is sick. On that theme Shakespeare has expended much eloquence and some of his finest poetry. Bolingbroke is tormented by the insecurity of power attained by violence. He owes too much to the friends who helped him in order to help themselves. He suffers, too, the remorse of a sinner who, like Claudius of Denmark, is unable to repent because he cannot bring himself to surrender the fruits of his sin. He can only hope that God will consider his crime to have been sufficiently expiated in his own person and that he may be able to pass on to his son an unblemished succession. But even this hope seems denied, for riot and dishonour stain the brow of his young Harry and he sees as part of his punishment the inordinate and low desires affected by his heir:

> I know not whether God will have it so,
> For some displeasing service I have done,
> That, in his secret doom, out of my blood
> He'll breed revengement and a scourge for me;
> But thou dost in thy passages of life
> Make me believe that thou art only mark'd
> For the hot vengeance and the rod of heaven
> To punish my mistreadings.

Shakespeare was clearly fascinated by the spectacle of this unhappy man, enticed by circumstance—encouraged, as it might almost seem, by providence—to commit a crime which was to stain with blood the pages of English history for over a century; reaping its first consequences in a reign filled with conspiracy and civil war; defrauded even of the conventional gesture of penitence of which he dreams in every quiet pause between one rebellion and the next; meeting his enemies with a brave face, though he had within himself no peace of mind; driven by lack of confidence in his friends or belief in his title to be arbitrary with everyone who challenged him and to provoke antagonism by the very acts which he hoped would strengthen his position:

> For all my reign hath been but as a scene,
> Acting that argument.

Shakespeare's pleasure in his creatures may be measured by the quality of their utterance. Bolingbroke, as he climbed to power, had none of the eloquence which Shakespeare so lavishly allows him in his sad pre-eminence. The dramatist, who, without emotion, epitomised in the upstart politician the qualities that secured him the crown, reserves his poetry for the King who has become aware of what has happened to his soul. Bolingbroke then achieves a fullness of utterance which shows that his author's imagination is deeply engaged:

> How many thousand of my poorest subjects
> Are at this hour asleep! O sleep, O gentle sleep,
> Nature's soft nurse, how have I frighted thee,
> That thou no more wilt weigh my eyelids down
> And steep my senses in forgetfulness?
> Why rather, sleep, liest thou in smoky cribs,
> Upon uneasy pallets stretching thee,
> And hush'd with buzzing night-flies to thy slumber,
> Than in the perfumed chambers of the great?
>
> Wilt thou upon the high and giddy mast
> Seal up the ship-boy's eyes, and rock his brains
> In cradle of the rude imperious surge,
> And in the visitation of the winds,
> Who take the ruffian billows by the top,
> Curling their monstrous heads, and hanging them
> With deaf'ning clamour in the slippery clouds,
> That, with the hurly, death itself awakes?
> Canst thou, O partial sleep, give thy repose
> To the wet sea-boy in an hour so rude,
> And in the calmest and most stillest night,
> With all appliances and means to boot,
> Deny it to a king? Then happy low, lie down!
> Uneasy lies the head that wears a crown.

This Bolingbroke, who is forever looking back on his career with
an almost ingenuous surprise that he should have aimed so high and
come so far, is tempted to wonder whether any man would have the
courage to live at all if he could see in advance what the future had
in store. O God! (he exclaims) that one might read the book of fate
and see:

> how chances mock,
> And changes fill the cup of alteration
> With divers liquors! O, if this were seen,
> The happiest youth, viewing his progress through,
> What perils past, what crosses to ensue,
> Would shut the book, and sit him down and die.

He remembers that Richard and Northumberland were once
friends, that two years later they were at war, that Northumberland
had toiled for himself like a brother but was now his enemy. 'Are
these things then necessities?' he asks, and answers himself like a
practical man of affairs for whom there is no escape: 'Then let us
meet them like necessities.'

Bolingbroke recurs perpetually to Richard's deposition and to the
crusade whereby he hopes to redeem his fault. For that matter, all the
participants in Richard's tragedy are equally obsessed. Hotspur's reference to the pulling down of that sweet lovely rose has already
been quoted. Worcester, in his parley with the King before Shrewsbury, recalls how, out of regard for Bolingbroke, he had in Richard's
time broken his staff of office and posted to meet the usurper at
Ravenspurgh. Scrope, Archbishop of York, who, as a legitimist,
rebels against Bolingbroke,

> And doth enlarge his rising with the blood
> Of fair King Richard, scraped from Pomfret stones,

speaks for them all:

> They that, when Richard lived, would have him die,
> Are now become enamour'd on his grave.

Westmoreland, in Gaultree Forest, speaks to much the same purpose. He recalls the lists at Coventry and all the rights and wrongs
associated in men's minds with the cause of Lancaster. Here, for a

H

moment, the opposing parties, subdued by these tragic memories, seem on the point of reaching an accommodation, till the cold treachery of Prince John of Lancaster sprinkles with fresh blood the fatal feud.

The two short scenes in which Shakespeare takes leave of Boling-broke in the Jerusalem chamber at Westminster recapitulate, as in a coda, the leading motives of his full career. First, the theme of penitence:

> Now, lords, if God doth give successful end
> To this debate that bleedeth at our doors,
> We will our youth lead on to higher fields
> And draw no swords but what are sanctified.

Next the carking distrust of what may happen to the kingdom after his death:

> The blood weeps from my heart when I do shape
> In forms imaginary the unguided days
> And rotten times that you shall look upon
> When I am sleeping with my ancestors.

News then comes that the rebels are defeated and that 'peace puts forth her olive everywhere.' But not even these fair tidings can cure a mind distraught with years of achieving and retaining power:

> And wherefore should these good news make me sick?
> Will Fortune never come with both hands full,
> But write her fair words still in foulest letters?
> She either gives a stomach and no food;
> Such are the poor, in health; or else a feast
> And takes away the stomach; such are the rich,
> That have abundance and enjoy it not.

And so we come to the last famous scene in which father and son, in their last moments together, are brought to an intimate revelation of themselves. Henry of Monmouth addresses the crown which lies upon his father's pillow:

> O polish'd perturbation! golden care!
> That keep'st the ports of slumber open wide
> To many a watchful night! Sleep with it now!

> Yet not so sound and half so deeply sweet
> As he whose brow with homely biggin bound
> Snores out the watch of night.

He strikes here the attitude of public persons in all times and places who, in assuming power, profess to be taking up a burden which they would gladly avoid and sigh without sincerity for the treasure of the humble.[1] But Shakespeare does not allow us to be quite so easily deceived in Henry as is Henry in himself. The Prince is moved to place on his head the polished perturbation:

> Lo! here it sits,
> Which heaven shall guard; and put the world's whole strength
> Into one giant arm, it shall not force
> This lineal honour from me.

Was Bolingbroke so grievously mistaken after all in supposing that his son was not very reluctant to take up the succession? He was grieved as a father to think that his son was impatient for his decease:

> See, sons, what things you are!
> How quickly nature falls into revolt
> When gold becomes her object!
> For this the foolish over-careful fathers
> Have broke their sleep with thoughts, their brains with care,
> Their bones with industry.

Here Bolingbroke was wrong. But Henry, the King, came very near the truth in attributing to Henry, Prince of Wales, a certain alacrity in assuming his responsibilities as heir apparent. His shrewd reproach (Thy wish was father, Harry, to that thought), though it wrongly presupposed a lack of filial affection (for Henry was a good son, so long as he might do as he pleased), was not so wide of the mark in respect of a young man by no means averse from his inheritance:

> Dost thou so hunger for mine empty chair
> That thou wilt needs invest thee with mine honours
> Before thy hour be ripe? O foolish youth!
> Thou seek'st the greatness that will overwhelm thee.

[1] Compare Richard III in his scene with the citizens. Richard impishly caricatures the attitude. Henry assumes it in all good faith. (See p. 97.)

Henry's love for his dying father comes as near to a genuine affection as he ever showed. It had not kept him from adding to the King's afflictions during life, but it rings true as far as it goes. His protestations of unwillingness to assume the crown, however, though delivered with all the conviction which Henry of Monmouth never lacked in showing himself to the world, are flatly out of key with his declaration of a moment before. We have seen him put the crown on his head. We have noted how in that very act he was transported and how he defied the world to deprive him of his right. But now he declares:

> I spake unto this crown as having sense,
> And thus upbraided it: 'The care on thee depending
> Hath fed upon the body of my father;
> Therefore, thou best of gold art worst of gold.'
>
>   Thus, my most royal liege,
> Accusing it, I put it on my head,
> To try with it, as with an enemy
> That had before my face murder'd my father,
> The quarrel of a true inheritor.
> But if it did infect my blood with joy,
> Or swell my thoughts to any strain of pride;
> If any rebel or vain spirit of mine
> Did with the least affection of a welcome
> Give entertainment to the might of it,
> Let God for ever keep it from my head,
> And make me as the poorest vassal is
> That doth with awe and terror kneel to it!

Prince Henry's account to his father of what he said is not flagrantly unlike what he actually did say. It is the same but not the same. It is, in fact, precisely the gloss we should expect of a young man who at critical moments is never at a loss to present himself to advantage.

Bolingbroke is now to give Henry his 'very latest counsel'. He surveys briefly the griefs and quarrels of his reign and alludes, not without satisfaction, to his successful liquidation of the men who helped him to power. The passage in which he refers to these activities includes an ingenuous admission that the motive behind his

frustrated plans to recover the Holy Sepulchre for Christendom was
not wholly pious in its intention:

> And all my friends, which thou must make thy friends,
> Have but their stings and teeth newly ta'en out;
> By whose fell working I was first advanced,
> And by whose power I well might lodge a fear
> To be again displaced: which to avoid,
> I cut them off; and had a purpose now
> To lead out many to the Holy Land,
> Lest rest and lying still might make them look
> Too near unto my state.

Bolingbroke's profession of remorse and desire for atonement has
been one of the recurrent themes of the play. Shakespeare at this final
moment flicks aside the mask. It is a last revealing glimpse into the
mind of this 'King of Smiles' who dies of a broken heart but who
can only be contrite with reservations. Bolingbroke must be politic
even in penance; his very act of atonement was designed to secure a
firmer grasp on the fruits of his offence.

Having admitted that he purposed to go with his nobles to
Jerusalem in order to prevent them from making trouble for him at
home, Bolingbroke finally commends to his son the expedient of
establishing himself more firmly on the throne by exploiting the
patriotism of his subjects in wars abroad:

> Therefore, my Harry,
> Be it thy course to busy giddy minds
> With foreign quarrels; that action, hence borne out,
> May waste the memory of the former days.

It is the last testament of a man who has achieved power and the
worldly wisdom that comes of its exercise. Bolingbroke bequeaths
to his heroic son a lineal honour to be maintained with foreign conquests, a tender conscience and a firm desire to hold on to the things
of this world without forfeiting his interest in the next. We find the
influence of these bequests constantly at work whenever we look below the glittering surface of the martial epic to which Shakespeare
is now to devote himself.

Shakespeare enters now upon the supreme task for which

his stage is set. He is to show us a hero in action and to embody in the person of a king that militant patriotism which Milton, a generation later, was to see in the likeness of an eagle mewing her mighty youth. The spirit in which he embarked on this enterprise has been indicated in its preparation. Henry of Monmouth's world, which was wide enough to include Falstaff and Hotspur, has been successively narrowed to his royal measure. The generous disorders of Eastcheap and Shrewsbury, where life was ardent, complex and manifold, give place to the comparatively artificial simplicity of an epic performance in which all interest is centred upon a single figure, and this single figure is itself contracted to become a symbol of successful valour and authority. Henry of Monmouth does not cease to be a man, or Shakespeare would have ceased to be interested. But the man dwindles as the hero is enlarged. This, in fact, is the process which gives to the play its significance as a study in character. Henry's heroic speeches are, of their kind, the best ever trumpeted by a martial poet from the battlements of time. But the human interest of the play lies elsewhere. It is to be sought in the constant effort of the shrinking man to come to terms with the swelling monarch.

Shakespeare, in his opening chorus, audibly braces himself for an effort, a not very congenial effort. He is to frame appropriate speech for a more than lifesize pageant of might, dominion, majesty and power. The poet, who so easily found language for exquisite Richard, ardent Hotspur, the fiery and delectable shapes of Falstaff, the heart-sickness of Bolingbroke, now begs for a muse of fire to ascend the brightest heaven of invention. He is to write of something which is both more and less than human and he feels the need of an invocation. This chorus is usually read as an apology for the shortcomings of the unworthy scaffold on which Shakespeare is to stage his imaginary puissance. But it is equally a warning that Henry of Monmouth is now to be presented in a setting of formal grandeur alien to the resources of a poet who writes from nature:

> Then should the warlike Harry, like himself,
> Assume the port of Mars; and at his heels,
> Leash'd in like hounds, should famine, sword, and fire
> Crouch for employment.

This is to be a sculptor's piece, in marble or bronze, rather than a picture whose red and white nature's own sweet and cunning hand laid on.

From the invocation we descend abruptly to practical politics. In a more self-conscious artist than Shakespeare we should suspect deliberate irony. The poet invokes a muse of fire and lo! here is the Archbishop of Canterbury discussing with the Bishop of Ely how to divert the King from an impending confiscation of Church property. But if this be irony, it is the irony of simple truth presented for its own sake. There is no suggestion that these amiable priests are in the least to blame for their very natural alarm at the prospect of having to contribute a thousand pounds by the year to the King's coffers. Nor is there a hint of censure for the ingenious project whereby they agree to divert the King from plundering the Church by demonstrating his legal right to plunder France. It is all in the chronicles and Shakespeare reports it without malice.

To those who have had little direct intercourse with the political mind, lay or clerical, the passage in which the two prelates discuss the pious reformation of the King may not seem to accord very well with the passages in which they wickedly conspire to urge their sovereign to lay claim to certain dukedoms and generally to the crown and seat of France. But Shakespeare had observed that it is just those men in public life who most admire their leader who are usually most assiduous in using him to forward their own small interests and purposes. He had also noticed that a high moral tone is never more customary in public affairs than in the prosecution of designs which are morally indefensible. Shakespeare, moreover, has a very special reason for allowing the Archbishop to sing the praises of a monarch providentially redeemed. He has continually to build up his hero and, throughout the play, he instinctively tends to do this *indirectly*, in comments delivered by friends and followers of the King, rather than *directly*, through the words and actions of the King himself. There is, in fact, a notable contrast between Henry of Monmouth, mirrored as an English king in the admiration of his subjects, and Henry of Monmouth revealed as the very human person with whom Shakespeare is more directly concerned. The fascination of the play for those who look below the surface lies in this contrast.

Apotheosis of the king proceeds hand in hand with disturbingly intimate revelations of the man. They are warp and woof in a tapestry from which a central figure of heraldic simplicity is, on a closer view, discerned as a fallibly human creature.

His Grace of Canterbury disingenuously reveals how entirely Henry has succeeded in his design of impressing the world with his 'noble change':

> The breath no sooner left his father's body,
> But that his wildness, mortified in him,
> Seem'd to die too; yea, at that very moment,
> Consideration like an angel came
> And whipp'd the offending Adam out of him.
>
> Hear him but reason in divinity,
> And, all-admiring, with an inward wish
> You would desire the king were made a prelate:
> Hear him debate of commonwealth affairs,
> You'd say it hath been all in all his study:
> List his discourse of war, and you shall hear
> A fearful battle render'd you in music:
> Turn him to any cause of policy,
> The Gordian knot of it he will unloose,
> Familiar as his garter: that, when he speaks,
> The air, a charter'd libertine, is still,
> And the mute wonder lurketh in men's ears,
> To steal his sweet and honey'd sentences.

There is much more of this and, when Canterbury has done, Ely takes up the theme:

> The strawberry grows underneath the nettle,
> And wholesome berries thrive and ripen best
> Neighbour'd by fruit of baser quality:
> And so the prince obscured his contemplation
> Under the veil of wildness; which, no doubt,
> Grew like the summer grass, fastest by night,
> Unseen, yet crescive in his faculty.

There is nothing wrong with the testimonial, except that the source and the occasion are less edifying than we might wish.

The scene in which Henry demands to know whether he may with right and justice lay claim to the throne of France presents, with an ease that almost wholly conceals the tact with which the thing is done, the splendid effigy of a righteous sovereign simultaneously with the breathing likeness of a man we have come to know. Note the solemnity of the King's appeal to the primate for spiritual leadership:

> And God forbid, my dear and faithful lord,
> That you should fashion, wrest, or bow your reading,
> Or nicely charge your understanding soul
> With opening titles miscreate, whose right
> Suits not in native colours with the truth;
> For God doth know how many now in health
> Shall drop their blood in approbation
> Of what your reverence shall incite us to.
> Therefore take heed how you impawn our person,
> How you awake our sleeping sword of war:
> We charge you, in the name of God, take heed;
> For never two such kingdoms did contend
> Without much fall of blood; whose guiltless drops
> Are every one a woe, a sore complaint
> 'Gainst him whose wrongs give edge unto the swords
> That make such waste in brief mortality.

Now consider the facts. Canterbury as we know, has his brief prepared. To meet a threat to the temporal possessions of the Church he has hit on the device of engaging the King's energies and interests abroad. To this end he has assembled his arguments and we must presume that Henry himself, who on his father's advice is already pledged to the undertaking, is not without an inkling of their purport. But the King does not for that abate one jot of his moral dignity. His adjuration thus serves three dramatic purposes. It presents him as a model of kingly righteousness; it shifts the responsibility for a war of conquest on Holy Church; it expresses his inner need to appease the tender conscience which he has inherited from his father. Incidentally it exposes, with consummate fidelity to fact, the ways, means and gestures of public persons in high office, who first decide what they must do as practical men of affairs and afterwards contrive to secure God's blessing on their endeavours.

The speech in which Canterbury argues with an apparently scrupulous disinterestedness that Henry has a legal right to the throne of France is rarely heard in full upon the stage. Shakespeare allows him a set piece of juridical casuistry so true to life that it brings into the theatre something of the tedium and prolixity which is to be expected from a political platform. Even Henry himself hardly has patience to hear him to the end and interrupts with a blunt question:

> Can I with right and justice make this claim?—

and the Archbishop gives him the answer he needs:

> The sin upon my head, dread sovereign.

There follows a general chorus of encouragement and approbation from the assembled lords, in which Canterbury and Ely bear the palm:

> Stand for your own; unwind your bloody flag.

Henry may now with a quiet conscience 'forage in blood of French nobility'. He is assured that the hearts of his subjects lie already pavilioned in the fields of France, and Canterbury concludes:

> O! let their bodies follow, my dear liege,
> With blood and sword and fire to win your right;
> In aid whereof we of the spiritualty
> Will raise your highness such a mighty sum
> As never did the clergy at one time
> Bring in to any of your ancestors.

In the council of war that follows occurs a passage in which the irony of political fact might well lead us into the error of suspecting once again a satirical intention on the part of the dramatist. Henry points out that, while he is invading France, the Scots will very probably invade England. Canterbury, lest his plan of engaging the King in a war of conquest should miscarry, hastens to reassure his sovereign. We are interested less in the statecraft exhibited by the English primate than in the unconscious assumption by the lords and prelates of the Council who are urging Henry to attack the French that for the Scots to attack the English would be a lawless and wicked act of treachery. The English invading France are lions and eagles; the Scot invading England is a weasel; and the gentlemen who talk of two precisely similar enterprises in such different terms are as sincere in their commendation of the one party as in their moral reprobation of the other.

One other point is worth noting in these public proceedings. Henry is to be presented as a model of efficient royalty. Unlike Richard of Bordeaux, who sailed from England to fight the Irish, leaving all behind him at sixes and sevens, Henry of Monmouth, before he ventures abroad, must be satisfied that all is safe and well-ordered at home. The Archbishop comes to his assistance with a celebrated dissertation on bees:

> Therefore doth heaven divide
> The state of man in divers functions,
> Setting endeavour in continual motion;
> To which is fixèd, as an aim or butt,
> Obedience: for so work the honey-bees,
> Creatures that by a rule in nature teach
> The act of order to a peopled kingdom.
> They have a king and officers of sorts;
> Where some, like magistrates, correct at home,
> Others, like merchants, venture trade abroad,
> Others, like soldiers, armèd in their stings,
> Make boot upon the summer's velvet buds;
> Which pillage they with merry march bring home
> To the tent-royal of their emperor;
> Who, busied in his majesty, surveys
> The singing masons building roofs of gold,
> The civil citizens kneading up the honey,
> The poor mechanic porters crowding in
> Their heavy burdens at his narrow gate,
> The sad-eyed justice, with his surly hum,
> Delivering o'er to executors pale
> The lazy yawning drone.

This archbishop certainly knows his business. The King wishes to make war; the Archbishop assures him that it is right and just for him to do so and offers him a mighty sum as insurance against the risk of losing an even mightier sum if the King should remain at peace. The King is anxious to believe that everything will go well in his absence; the Archbishop comforts his sovereign with an idyllic description of honey-bees in midsummer. He thus fulfils to perfection the traditional function of a good churchman, making it possible for his sovereign to do what he has already decided to do with a quiet mind and with the concurrence of Almighty God.

Henry is now ready to receive the French Ambassador:

> Now are we well resolved; and by God's help,
> And yours, the noble sinews of our power,
> France being ours, we'll bend it to our awe,
> Or break it all to pieces.

The French Ambassador enters and delivers a 'pleasant' message. The Dauphin of France has sent the King of England a tun of treasure. The 'tun' is opened and found to contain tennis balls. Note, incidentally, that Henry's ultimatum to France *has already been presented*. Henry, in his solemn appeal to the Archbishop for an assurance that his claim was just, was not seeking spiritual or legal advice on a step to be taken; he was inviting moral approbation for a *fait accompli*.

The Dauphin's 'pleasant' message provokes Henry to justify once again the irregularities of his youth:

> And we understand him well,
> How he comes o'er us with our wilder days,
> *Not measuring what use we made of them.*

Next he must throw upon the Dauphin, as he has already thrown upon Holy Church, entire responsibility for all the misery and suffering which he is about to inflict on the people of France:

> And tell the pleasant prince this mock of his
> Hath turn'd his balls to gun-stones; and his soul
> Shall stand sore chargèd for the wasteful vengeance
> That shall fly with them; for many a thousand widows
> Shall this his mock mock out of their dear husbands;
> Mock mothers from their sons, mock castles down;
> And some are yet ungotten and unborn
> That shall have cause to curse the Dauphin's scorn.

Finally he commits his cause to heaven:

> But this lies all within the will of God,
> To whom I do appeal; and in whose name
> Tell you the Dauphin I am coming on,
> To venge me as I may and to put forth
> My rightful hand in a well-hallow'd cause.

And so to war—with Chorus to celebrate the simple ardours of preparation:

> Now all the youth of England are on fire,
> And silken dalliance in the wardrobe lies;
> Now thrive the armourers, and honour's thought
> Reigns solely in the breast of every man:
> They sell the pasture now to buy the horse,
> Following the mirror of all Christian kings.

But first a dramatic episode intervenes to remind us of the dynastic insecurity which is Henry's prime motive for undertaking the conquest of France. The Lords Cambridge, Scroop and Grey have conspired to assassinate the King at Southampton. Henry has intercepted their letters and he unmasks them in a scene in which are displayed some of the more important qualifications of a hero for success in public life—a courage, not quite so careless as it seems; a conviction that he is moved by no private passion but thinks only of the nation; a *disinterested* ruthlessness in the performance of an act of state necessary to his own security:

> Touching our person seek we no revenge;
> But we our kingdom's safety must so tender,
> Whose ruin you have sought, that to her laws
> We do deliver you.

Two predominant traits in Henry's characterare again clearly emphasised. He has skilfully contrived a situation in which he can disclaim all personal responsibility for sending these men to death. Prior to their own condemnation they have been tricked into advising the King to show no mercy to a man arrested for speaking treason. Thus Henry has them sentenced in advance out of their own mouths:

> The mercy that was quick in us but late,
> By your own counsel is suppress'd and kill'd:

> You must not dare, for shame, to talk of mercy;
> For your own reasons turn into your bosoms,
> As dogs upon their masters.

And just as Henry could not refrain from delivering to Falstaff a homily that soothed his own constant need for moral reassurance, so now he cannot let slip this better occasion. In the rebuke which he addresses to Scroop, he lifts the episode to a plane in which he may regard himself as God's justiciary and his own stern, impartial conduct of affairs as a special aspect of the divine order of things:

> O, how hast thou with jealousy infected
> The sweetness of affiance! Show men dutiful?
> Why, so didst thou: seem they grave and learned?
> Why, so didst thou: come they of noble family?
> Why, so didst thou: seem they religious?
> Why, so didst thou.
>
> And thus thy fall hath left a kind of blot,
> To mark the full-fraught man and best indued
> With some suspicion. I will weep for thee;
> For this revolt of thine, methinks, is like
> Another fall of man.

Henry always excels in putting his enemies in the wrong. Seldom have conspirators received so eloquent and high-minded a sentence from their sovereign.

Shakespeare has yet another thing to do before he can take us with Henry to France—something that lies very near his heart.

In the epilogue to the Second Part of 'Henry IV' he promised his audience:

> If you be not too much cloyed with fat meat our humble author will continue the story, with Sir John in it.

But Shakespeare's muse of fire, invoked for the portrayal of warlike Harry, could never tolerate the intrusion of Falstaff. Shakespeare has to kill Falstaff for the same reason that he had to kill Mercutio. His play was not large enough to contain him. Falstaff at Agincourt is as unthinkable as Mercutio beside the tomb of the Capulets. Shakespeare could not possibly face the risk of bringing Sir John within

speaking distance of Henry of Monmouth in his glory. One touch
of Falstaff, in daylight, would have effectively destroyed all touch of
Harry in the night. No one knew this better than Henry himself.
Shakespeare did not have to go out of his way to kill Falstaff. Henry
of Monmouth was obliged to kill him in self-defence.

'The King has killed his heart', says Mistress Quickly. 'The King
hath run bad humours on the knight,' says Corporal Nym. 'His
heart is fracted and corroborate,' says Pistol. No character of Shakespeare, not even Hamlet, with his quire of angels, had a finer end.
It would be out of place to quote even a line of the speech in which
the death of Falstaff is described. There is nothing deeper or more
delicate in the whole range of Shakespeare. We may even wonder
how he dared to break the limited perfection of his achievement in
'Henry V' with this sudden stroke of subtle and profound humanity.
Yet how could he forbear taking this last farewell of his creature?
Let the heroic muse be for a moment forgotten and let history retire:

> For Falstaff, he is dead,
> And we must yearn therefore.

Henry of Monmouth, setting out for the conquest of France,
sends envoys in advance with a pedigree in support of his claim to
the French crown. He takes this opportunity yet again to disclaim
any responsibility for the woeful consequences which will follow a
refusal of his demands. Exeter announces that his sovereign is coming, in fierce tempest, like a Jove—

> And bids you, in the bowels of the Lord,
> Deliver up the crown, and to take mercy
> On the poor souls for whom this hungry war
> Opens his vasty jaws; and on your head
> Turning the widows' tears, the orphans' cries,
> The dead men's blood, the pining maidens' groans,
> For husbands, fathers, and betrothèd lovers,
> That shall be swallow'd in this controversy.

Shakespeare is now to dramatise the piteous and terrible subject of
war. Many of his plays are distressed or enlivened with alarums and
excursions and we are shifted from one part of the field to another.
But the fighting in these other histories and tragedies is incidental.

In 'Henry V' war is itself a theme—its glories, humours and passions; its dutiful courage and proud cruelty; its brilliant surface and the horrors that lie beneath. Shakespeare presents this theme of war with an impartial but absorbed interest in all its phases. There is, indeed, no play in which Shakespeare's peculiar blend of moral detachment and imaginative sympathy is seen to better advantage, with the result that 'Henry V' is at once the glorification of a patriot king and an exposure of the wicked futility of his enterprise. Nothing, for example, could be more striking than the contrast between the reasons for which Henry went to war and the spirit in which the English armies follow him. He cynically sets out to busy giddy minds with foreign quarrels, but at Agincourt he is identified with every patriotic Englishman who ever lived. The causes of the war are forgotten in the heroism that war inspires. It begins as a conspiracy against the nation; it continues as a brotherhood in which the nation is glorified. Henry, prompted by a subtle father and fortified by the complicity of a politic priest, invaded France to save his dynasty. But all that is forgotten on the field of Agincourt, where an English king is identified with the valour of simple men whose loyalty consecrates his leadership.

The contrast in mood and purpose between the politicians, for whom war is an instrument of policy, and the people, who fight for King and country, is splendidly maintained in the choruses. Henry, discussing with Canterbury a certified pedigree in support of his territorial claims, gives place to a vivid picture of England committed to a great adventure:

> O England! model to thy inward greatness,
> Like little body with a mighty heart,
> What mightst thou do, that honour would thee do,
> Were all thy children kind and natural!

We behold a fleet majestical, a city on the inconstant billows dancing:

> Play with your fancies, and in them behold
> Upon the hempen tackle ship-boys climbing;
> Hear the shrill whistle which doth order give
> To sounds confused; behold the threaden sails,

> ' Borne with the invisible and creeping wind,
> Draw the huge bottoms through the furrow'd sea,
> Breasting the lofty surge.

We are told to imagine England stripped of her sons, all eager for service and confident in their leaders:

> Follow! follow!
> Grapple your minds to sternage of this navy,
> And leave your England, as dead midnight still,
> Guarded with grandsires, babies and old women,
> Either past or not arriv'd to pith and puissance;
> For who is he, whose chin is but enrich'd
> With one appearing hair, that will not follow
> These cull'd and choice-drawn cavaliers to France?

We are to entertain conjecture of a time,

> When creeping murmur and the poring dark
> Fills the wide vessel of the universe.

> The poor condemnèd English,
> Like sacrifices, by their watchful fires
> Sit patiently, and inly ruminate
> The morning's danger; and their gesture sad,
> Investing lank-lean cheeks and war-worn coats,
> Presenteth them unto the gazing moon
> So many horrid ghosts.

We are to be present, too, at the homecoming of those happy few who fought on Crispin's day:

> But now behold,
> In the quick forge and working-house of thought,
> How London doth pour out her citizens!
> The mayor and all his brethren in best sort,
> Like to the senators of th' antique Rome,
> With the plebeians swarming at their heels,
> Go forth and fetch their conquering Caesar in.

In these glimpses of a people at war we lose, as in the wars of history, all sense of war's origin or purpose. These choruses supply a splendid frame to the picture and an epic quality to the action. Within this frame, and in this mood, the separate episodes of war—heroic, familiar, humorous, tragical, comical, terrible, piteous, shallow or profound—are presented with a scrupulous fidelity. This is war, in whose presence there is no pause for malice or extenuation.

Henry of Monmouth now emerges as the complete soldier. On military deportment he is the Superlative Sergeant-Major:

> In peace there's nothing so becomes a man
> As modest stillness and humility;
> But when the blast of war blows in our ears,
> Then imitate the action of the tiger;
> Stiffen the sinews, summon up the blood,
> Disguise fair nature with hard-favour'd rage;
> Then lend the eye a terrible aspect;
> Let it pry through the portage of the head
> Like the brass cannon.
>
> Now set the teeth and stretch the nostril wide,
> Hold hard the breath, and bend up every spirit
> To his full height.

Rallying a company, he is the Absolute Captain:

> Be copy now to men of grosser blood,
> And teach them how to war. And you, good yeomen,
> Whose limbs were made in England, show us here
> The mettle of your pasture; let us swear
> That you are worth your breeding; which I doubt not;
> For there is none of you so mean and base,
> That hath not noble lustre in your eyes.
> I see you stand like greyhounds in the slips,
> Straining upon the start. The game's afoot:
> Follow your spirit, and upon this charge
> Cry 'God for Harry, England, and Saint George!'

Visiting his men before day breaks on the field of Agincourt, he is the Ubiquitous Commander:

> O now, who will behold
> The royal captain of this ruin'd band
> Walking from watch to watch, from tent to tent,
> Let him cry 'Praise and glory on his head!'

> For forth he goes and visits all his host,
> Bids them good morrow with a modest smile,
> And calls them brothers, friends, and countrymen.
> Upon his royal face there is no note
> How dread an army hath enrounded him;
> Nor doth he dedicate one jot of colour
> Unto the weary and all-watchèd night,
> But freshly looks and over-bears attaint
> With cheerful semblance and sweet majesty;
> That every wretch, pining and pale before,
> Beholding him, plucks comfort from his looks:
> A largess universal, like the sun,
> His liberal eye doth give to every one,
> Thawing cold fear, that mean and gentle all
> Behold, as may unworthiness define,
> A little touch of Harry in the night.

All ranks acknowledge the spell of his leadership—even the raga-muffins, for Ancient Pistol bears his testimony with the rest:

> The king's a bawcock, and a heart of gold,
> A lad of life, an imp of fame;
> Of parents good, of fist most valiant:
> I kiss his dirty shoe, and from heart-string
> I love the lovely bully.

He has the right word and gesture for every occasion, whether it be to commend the care and valour of Welsh Fluellen or to hear with mistful eyes—as who would not?—Exeter's moving tale of the twin deaths of York and Suffolk on the field of battle:

> Tarry, dear cousin Suffolk!
> My soul shall thine keep company to heaven;
> Tarry, sweet soul, for mine, then fly abreast,
> As in this glorious and well-foughten field,
> We kept together in our chivalry.

To the enemy he speaks for his soldiers in accents which convey exactly their habit of mind and turn of phrase. His message to the Constable of France, who comes for ransom before the battle, has just that sober defiance, with a grim twinkle to it, and that modesty, prouder than any insolence, which mark the Englishman of tradition in a tight corner:

> Good God! why should they mock poor fellows thus?
> The man that once did sell the lion's skin
> While the beast lived, was killed with hunting him.

> Let me speak proudly: tell the Constable,
> We are but warriors for the working-day;
> Our gayness and our gilt are all besmirch'd
> With rainy marching in the painful field;
> There's not a piece of feather in our host—
> Good argument, I hope, we will not fly—
> And time hath worn us into slovenry:
> But, by the mass, our hearts are in the trim;
> And my poor soldiers tell me, yet ere night
> They'll be in fresher robes, or they will pluck
> The gay new coats o'er the French soldiers' heads
> And turn them out of service.

Finally, he speaks, as no one before or since, for all who have found grace and splendour in the gallant fellowship of war:

> If we are mark'd to die, we are enow
> To do our country loss; and if to live,
> The fewer men, the greater share of honour.
> God's will! I pray thee, wish not one man more.

> Rather proclaim it, Westmoreland, through my host,
> That he which hath no stomach to this fight,
> Let him depart; his passport shall be made
> And crowns for convoy put into his purse:
> We would not die in that man's company
> That fears his fellowship to die with us.

> We few, we happy few, we band of brothers;
> For he to-day that sheds his blood with me
> Shall be my brother; be he ne'er so vile,
> This day shall gentle his condition:
> And gentlemen in England now a-bed
> Shall think themselves accursed they were not here,
> And hold their manhoods cheap whiles any speaks
> That fought with us upon Saint Crispin's day.

The theme of honour is sounded here on the bugles and for once the perilous word rings true. Some may think that this day gentles not so much the condition of Henry's soldiers as that of Henry himself. We forgive the Prince who denied his companions in Eastcheap for the sake of the King who acknowledges his brethren at Agincourt.

In all this we find a splendidly sustained presentment of the heroic side of war. But Shakespeare exhibits just as vividly the underside. This royal captain, who exclaims when the battle is won, 'O God, thy arm was here!', orders every soldier to kill his prisoners when the French seem about to rally and this order is commended as a just reprisal by honest Gower:

They have burned and carried away all that was in the king's tent; wherefore the king, most worthily, hath caused every soldier to cut his prisoner's throat. O, 'tis a gallant king!

The King's army is presented at Agincourt as a band of brothers, but in its ranks are Pistol and Nym, driven willy-nilly with blows to the breach, and Bardolph who will steal anything and call it purchase. Bardolph is hanged for robbing a church and what this army is likely to do if it gets out of hand is described by Henry himself:

> We may as bootless spend our vain command
> Upon the enragèd soldiers in their spoil
> As send precepts to the leviathan
> To come ashore. Therefore, you men of Harfleur,
> Take pity of your town and of your people,
> Whiles yet my soldiers are in my command;
> Whiles yet the cool and temperate wind of grace
> O'erblows the filthy and contagious clouds
> Of heady murder, spoil, and villainy.
> If not, why, in a moment, look to see
> The blind and bloody soldier with foul hand
> Defile the locks of your shrill-shrieking daughters;
> Your fathers taken by the silver beards,
> And their most reverend heads dash'd to the walls;
> Your naked infants spitted upon pikes,
> Whiles the mad mothers with their howls confus'd
> Do break the clouds, as did the wives of Jewry
> At Herod's bloody-hunting slaughtermen.

Shakespeare, in presenting a hero, clearly indicates the price which humanity must pay for his achievements. What heroic war means for a land invaded and despoiled is described by the Duke of Burgundy as graphically as the triumphant return of Henry to England. From the King on Blackheath, 'giving full trophy, signal and ostent quite from himself to God', we are taken to France where naked, poor and mangled peace still lies at the hazard of a contract between princes:

> Alas! she hath from France too long been chased,
> And all her husbandry doth lie on heaps,
> Corrupting in its own fertility.
> Her vine, the merry cheerer of the heart,
> Unprunèd dies; her hedges even-pleach'd,
> Like prisoners wildly over-grown with hair,
> Put forth disorder'd twigs; her fallow leas
> The darnel, hemlock and rank fumitory
> Doth root upon, while that the coulter rusts
> That should deracinate such savagery;
> The even mead, that erst brought sweetly forth
> The freckled cowslip, burnet and green clover,
> Wanting the scythe, all uncorrected, rank,
> Conceives by idleness, and nothing teems
> But hateful docks, rough thistles, kecksies, burs,
> Losing both beauty and utility:
> And as our vineyards, fallows, meads and hedges,
> Defective in their natures, grow to wildness,
> Even so our houses and ourselves and children
> Have lost, or do not learn for want of time,
> The sciences that should become our country,
> But grow like savages.

Even more audacious than these incursions of the horrors of war into a play which sets out to present Henry of Monmouth as the mirror of all Christian kings are the passages in which the rough, familiar humours of the camp challenge with a frank, inevitable impertinence the fine attitudes of the happy warrior. It is less damaging to the pose of a military hero to suggest that his proceedings spread death, misery and destitution among the innocent, or that circumstances may make it necessary for him to cut the throats of his prisoners or to hang one of his own soldiers for stealing a pyx, than to allow ordinary, decent, sensible men to comment shrewdly and freely upon his performances or even to come within measurable distance of his person. But Shakespeare had no choice in the matter. Warlike Harry, if he were to retain the interest of his creator, must stand the test of direct contact with men of normal stature and disposition. He must breathe the same air as John Bates and Michael Williams, come to terms with Fluellen, even hazard a word with Ancient Pistol. Above all, the heroics of war, if they are to survive at all, must prove sufficiently robust to prevail over the common sense of the natural man who cries out with Falstaff's boy: 'Would I were in an alehouse in London! I would give all my fame for a pot of ale and safety.'

These humours of the camp, far from destroying the heroical aspects of war, give them solidity and a human reference. Fluellen, discussing sapper tactics with Gower; Macmorris, swearing it is no time to discourse, what with the weather and the wars and the King and the dukes and the day, which is hot, and the town, which is 'beseeched'; Jamy, who will do good service or 'lig i' the grund' for it —and 'that is the breff and the long'; Pistol, cudgelled by the valiant Welshman into eating his leek for mocking at 'an ancient tradition, begun upon an honourable respect and worn as a memorable trophy of predeceased valour'—these episodes are as necessary to Shakespeare's picture of total war as Henry's summons to the citadel of Harfleur or his famous speech on the eve of Crispin's day.

But Shakespeare does more than just permit these homely incursions into the heroic field. He deliberately brings them to terms with Henry himself—not merely in comic interludes but as serious and essential items in his presentation of the royal character. There is no more significant or instructive episode in the play than the conversation between Henry and his private soldiers on the eve of Agincourt. In this encounter Shakespeare pauses in his presentation of a hero and shows us the heart of a man. He relinquishes the set task which he has undertaken, as an English patriot, to resume an enterprise which lies nearer his heart. We have been losing Henry, the man, in the successful politician and the royal captain. Now there is a pause in the rhetoric. Henry of Monmouth has come to the supreme moment of his career and Shakespeare at this time of crisis is bent on showing us how this situation affects the mind and conscience of the person concerned.

No two characters could be more cunningly contrived for this business than John Bates and Michael Williams. The episode is apt to be too lightly dismissed. A king, patrolling his camp by night in disguise, meets two humble men-at-arms. They fall into argument. The argument grows to a quarrel and one of the soldiers accepts the king's glove. He will wear it in his cap and take his unknown adversary a box on the ear, if it should ever be challenged. It is a merry incident and the audience waits with pleasurable expectation for the sequel, in which the soldier will realise his mistake and be magnanimously pardoned by a king of good fellows. Here, again, Shakespeare plays his favourite trick of presenting the simple spectator with something entertaining in itself which at the same time fulfils a deeper purpose. For John Bates and Michael Williams give Henry of Monmouth something to think about. Their random thrusts, going straight to the mark, reveal him more clearly and completely than ever before.

The scene is short and every rift is packed with ore:

(*Enter three soldiers,* JOHN BATES, ALEXANDER COURT *and* MICHAEL WILLIAMS.)

COURT: Brother John Bates, is not that the morning which breaks yonder?

BATES: I think it be; but we have no great cause to desire the approach of day.

WILLIAMS: We see yonder the beginning of the day, but I think we shall never see the end of it. Who goes there?

K. HENRY: A friend.

WILLIAMS: Under what captain serve you?

K. HENRY: Under Sir Thomas Erpingham.

WILLIAMS: A good old commander and a most kind gentleman: I pray you, what thinks he of our estate?

K. HENRY: Even as men wrecked upon a sand, that look to be washed off the next tide.

BATES: He hath not told his thought to the king?

K. HENRY: No; nor it is not meet he should. For, though I speak it to you, I think the king is but a man, as I am: the violet smells to him as it doth to me; the element shows to him as it doth to me; all his senses have but human conditions: his ceremonies laid by, in his nakedness he appears but a man; and though his affections are higher mounted than ours, yet, when they stoop, they stoop with the like wing. Therefore when he sees reason of fears, as we do, his fears, out of doubt, be of the same relish as ours are: yet, in reason, no man should possess him with any appearance of fear, lest he, by showing it, should dishearten his army.

It is the first sincerely human utterance we have had from Henry of Monmouth. Even in the moving scenes which preceded the death of his father he spoke as a man who was testing the effect of his words upon himself and fitting them to the occasion. But now for a moment he emerges from the legend to which he consciously or half consciously adapts his behaviour. The King, he insists, is but a man, though he cannot afford to admit so much to the world.

Bates unexpectedly takes him at his word in retorts that are pure soldier—blunt and sceptical, cynical without bitterness, matter-of-fact and yet sturdily devoted:

BATES: He may show what outward courage he will; but I believe, as cold a night as 'tis, he could wish himself in Thames up to the neck; and so I would he were, and I by him, at all adventures, so we were quit here.

K. HENRY: By my troth, I will speak my conscience of the king: I think he would not wish himself anywhere but where he is.

BATES: Then I would he were here alone; so should he be sure to be ransomed, and many poor men's lives saved.

K. HENRY: I dare say you love him not so ill to wish him here alone, howsoever you speak this to feel other men's minds: methinks I could not die anywhere so contented as in the king's company; his cause being just and his quarrel honourable.

WILLIAMS: That's more than we know.

BATES: Ay, or more than we should seek after; for we know enough, if we know we are the king's subjects: if his cause be wrong, our obedience to the king wipes the crime of it out of us.

So the argument is started. Bates all unwittingly has stung Henry to the quick. At every significant moment of his career he has been prompted to justify his conduct and at the same time to evade moral responsibility for his actions. This is the man who, summoning the

French garrison at Harfleur to surrender, declared to the governor
of the city:

> What is it then to me, if impious war,
> Array'd in flames like to the prince of fiends,
> Do, with his smirch'd complexion, all fell feats
> Enlink'd to waste and desolation?
> What is't to me, when you yourselves are cause,
> If your pure maidens fall into the hand
> Of hot and forcing violation?

And now, out of the mouth of John Bates, he finds himself charged
with precisely the burden he has always sought to avoid. Here, too,
is Michael Williams to drive it home:

But if the cause be not good, the king himself hath a heavy reckoning to
make; when all those legs and arms and heads, chopped off in a battle,
shall join together at the latter day and cry all 'We died at such a place';
some swearing, some crying for a surgeon, some upon their wives left poor
behind them, some upon the debts they owe, some upon their children
rawly left. I am afeard there are few die well that die in a battle; for how
can they charitably dispose of any thing, when blood is their argument?
Now, if these men do not die well, it will be a black matter for the king
who led them to it; whom to disobey were against all proportion of subjection.

Driven to the wall, Henry is prompt in his defence. Despite his
lifelong evasions he has been brought to a point where the imminent
death of twenty thousand men is laid to his account. He answers as
best he can. But what a poor, muddled and irrelevant answer it is!
Playing tricks with his conscience, he has become incapable of even
so much as an honest piece of reasoning. The head is attainted with
the heart. Williams has plainly declared that a king who induces his
subjects to fight for him in a bad cause must be held responsible for
the lives of his men. Henry catches at a conclusion in the soldier's
argument which is not really relevant to the main charge. Rebutting
a proposition which neither Bates nor Williams has seriously maintained, he protests that *wicked* soldiers who die in battle must be held
responsible for their private sins and that the king cannot be held
accountable for their damnation. The case is glibly presented—when
was Henry ever at a loss for words?—but it has no bearing on the

simple issue raised by Bates and Williams, namely that a king who leads his soldiers to war without a good and sufficient reason has a heavy reckoning to pay on the day of judgment. Henry's plea is a sheer evasion of the issue:

So, if a son that is by his father sent about merchandise do sinfully miscarry upon the sea, the imputation of his wickedness, by your rule, should be imposed upon his father that sent him: or if a servant, under his master's command transporting a sum of money, be assailed by robbers and die in many irreconciled iniquities, you may call the business of the master the author of the servant's damnation: but this is not so: the king is not bound to answer the particular endings of his soldiers, the father of his son, nor the master of his servant; for they purpose not their death, when they purpose their services.

Henry, having tried to extricate himself by wilfully misrepresenting the charge, next tries to shift the responsibility from himself to the victims of his ambition:

Besides, there is no king, be his cause never so spotless, if it come to the arbitrement of swords, can try it out with all unspotted soldiers: some, peradventure, have on them the guilt of premeditated and contrived murder; some, of beguiling virgins with the broken seals of perjury; some, making the wars their bulwark, that have before gored the gentle bosom of peace with pillage and robbery. Now, if these men have defeated the law and outrun native punishment, though they can outstrip men, they have no wings to fly from God: war is his beadle, war is his vengeance; so that here men are punished for before-breach of the king's laws in now the king's quarrel: where they feared the death, they have borne life away; and where they would be safe, they perish: then if they die unprovided, no more is the king guilty of their damnation than he was before guilty of those impieties for the which they are now visited.

This devastating comment of a royal captain on the quality and composition of his 'band of brothers' is followed by the inevitable homily in which, here as elsewhere, he seeks compensation for the moral discomfort of his position:

Therefore should every soldier in the wars do as every sick man in his bed, wash every mote out of his conscience; and dying so, death is to him advantage; or not dying, the time was blessedly lost wherein such preparation was gained: and in him that escapes, it were not sin to think that, making God so free an offer, He let him outlive that day to see His greatness, and to teach others how they should prepare.

Henry argues that a good general is not responsible for the sins of his wicked soldiers. He has incidentally suggested that war, being God's beadle, is a moral institution. The two soldiers, in simple generosity, forbear to press their contention that kings, good or bad, are responsible for the wars which their subjects are in duty compelled to undertake under their leadership, and they courteously concede the secondary point so warmly urged by their opponent:

WILLIAMS: 'Tis certain, every man that does ill, the ill upon his own head, the king is not to answer it.

BATES: I do not desire he should answer for me; and yet I determine to fight lustily for him.

The argument is now concluded. It is followed by the quarrel between the King and Williams, in which Shakespeare for a moment lightens the mood of his play in order that he may, some thirty lines later on, enhance by contrast the solemnity of the King's famous soliloquy:

K. HENRY: I myself heard the king say he would not be ransomed.

WILLIAMS: Ay, he said so, to make us fight cheerfully; but when our throats are cut, he may be ransomed, and we ne'er the wiser.

K. HENRY: If I live to see it, I will never trust his word after.

WILLIAMS: You pay him then. That's a perilous shot out of an elder-gun, that a poor and a private displeasure can do against a monarch! you may as well go about to turn the sun to ice with fanning in his face with a peacock's feather. You'll never trust his word after! come, 'tis a foolish saying.

K. HENRY: Your reproof is something too round; I should be angry with you, if the time were convenient.

WILLIAMS: Let it be a quarrel between us, if you live.

K. HENRY: I embrace it.

WILLIAMS: How shall I know thee again?

K. HENRY: Give me any gage of thine, and I will wear it in my bonnet, then, if ever thou darest acknowledge it, I will make it my quarrel.

WILLIAMS: Here's my glove: give me another of thine.

K. HENRY: There.

WILLIAMS: This will I also wear in my cap: if ever thou come to me and say, after to-morrow, 'This is my glove', by this hand I will take thee a box on the ear.

K. HENRY: If ever I live to see it, I will challenge it.

WILLIAMS: Thou darest as well be hanged.

The dramatic significance of this passage, amusing in itself, is abruptly disclosed as soon as Henry is left alone. Then we realise that Henry, apparently unaffected by his encounter with the two soldiers and carrying off the situation with a practical joke, is inwardly bruised and shaken:

> Upon the king! let us our lives, our souls,
> Our debts, our careful wives,
> Our children, and our sins lay on the king!
> We must bear all.

The fifty magnificent lines which follow merely embroider the theme. They are often read—or misread—as expressing a great king's sense of the futility of pomp and the loneliness of a pre-eminence which he would gladly discard:

> 'Tis not the balm, the sceptre and the ball,
> The sword, the mace, the crown imperial,
> The intertissued robe of gold and pearl,
> The farcèd title running 'fore the king,
> The throne he sits on, nor the tide of pomp
> That beats upon the high shore of this world,
> No, not all these, thrice-gorgeous ceremony,
> Not all these, laid in bed majestical,
> Can sleep so soundly as the wretched slave,
> Who with a body fill'd and vacant mind
> Gets him to rest, cramm'd with distressful bread;
> Never sees horrid night, the child of hell,
> But, like a lackey, from the rise to set
> Sweats in the eye of Phoebus, and all night
> Sleeps in Elysium; next day after dawn,
> Doth rise and help Hyperion to his horse,
> And follows so the ever-running year,
> With profitable labour, to his grave.

All this is very fine, but essentially no more than a recoil from the moral burden thrust upon him as a ruler. John Bates and Michael Williams have left him face to face with his responsibility. He may try to evade it in specious argument, but there is no escaping the truth that speaks through these blunt, honest and simple men; and, driven to the wall, he bemoans his fate in an access of self-pity and of almost childish petulance against those who seek to lay so heavy a charge upon his conscience:

> O hard condition,
> Twin-born with greatness, subject to the breath
> Of every fool, whose sense no more can feel
> But his own wringing!

From this recoil to a final indictment of idol ceremony is an easy step and from sonorous invective against the proud dream that plays so subtly with a king's repose it is a yet easier step for Henry to see himself as a royal martyr wearing out his life in the service of his people:

> The slave, a member of the country's peace,
> Enjoys it; but in gross brain little wots
> What watch the king keeps to maintain the peace,
> Whose hours the peasant best advantages.

This is surely the most ingenuous apologia ever put into the mouth of a public person. Henry, professing to envy the wretched slave who sleeps in Elysium, has invaded France in order that he may acquire a second crown which is to secure him yet more firmly in possession of a crown already in his grasp! He sighs to think that the gross brain of the peasant little wots what watch the king keeps *to maintain the peace* and within a few hours he is to win a famous victory in a war of conquest.

But still Shakespeare maintains a perfect innocence. He is not deliberately anatomising a moral humbug or plumbing the depths of self-deception to which a successful political leader may be driven. He is presenting in all simplicity a political hero—the things that a political hero, when he is Henry of Monmouth, quite inevitably does and says. Incidentally his imagination is caught and held by the very human spectacle of a man in whom physical courage and resolute will are constantly at odds with a tender conscience. Henry was determined to be not only a good sovereign but a moral paragon. He must stand well with all the world—including himself. He must be perpetually building himself up as the best of kings and the king of good fellows. Meanwhile, we cannot fail to note that, in the degree to which he loses his heroic stature, he more intimately engages the sympathy of his creator. We feel that Shakespeare is more deeply interested in the moral weakling who complains to God that he is unfairly held accountable for the lives and fortunes of his subjects than in the efficient ruler or the royal captain. There is a sense in which Henry becomes more likeable as his limitations are revealed. A king who, at the climax of an unprovoked war of aggression, contrives to see himself as God's minister watching to maintain the peace, raises a smile which has in it more charity and fellow feeling than the impersonal admiration with which we follow the political and martial excursions of his public life. Shakespeare, looking beneath the surface of his hero, exposes him not to contempt but to a more friendly understanding of his person.

The soliloquy in which Henry wistfully endeavours to come to terms with his 'hard condition' is followed by the prayer in which he makes an even more pathetic effort to come to terms with the Almighty:

> Not to-day, O Lord!
> O, not to-day, think not upon the fault
> My father made in compassing the crown!
> I Richard's body have interr'd anew,
> And on it have bestow'd more contrite tears
> Than from it issu'd forcèd drops of blood:
> Five hundred poor I have in yearly pay,
> Who twice a day their wither'd hands hold up
> Toward heaven, to pardon blood; and I have built
> Two chantries, where the sad and solemn priests
> Sing still for Richard's soul. More will I do;
> Though all that I can do is nothing worth,
> Since that my penitence comes after all,
> Imploring pardon.

It is the climax of his self-exposure. The usurpation to which he owes the crown lies heavy on his soul. His first impulse, as usual, is to deny his own responsibility: it is his father's fault for which he begs forgiveness. Secondly, he has done everything he can to mitigate the offence: he has handsomely buried the victim; he has five hundred poor men in his pay to implore heaven's pardon for the crime to which he owes his greatness; he has built two chantries where the sad and solemn priests still sing for Richard's soul. And he is penitent —so far as penitence for a fault is compatible with retaining its advantages. He has in fact done all that seems humanly possible to atone for a crime which was none of his committing and he has done all that is politically possible to carry out successfully the advice of the criminal whereby he hopes to be left in secure possession of his inheritance.

Critics great and small have found in the last Act of 'Henry V' a sad decline from the heroics of Agincourt to the King's facetious wooing of a French princess. Yet it is difficult to imagine a more fitting close to the political argument or a more consistent handling of the central character in his final appearances. A war of conquest, undertaken on the advice of a shrewd politician and with the sagacious connivance of the highest spiritual authority in the land, fittingly concludes with a friendly conclave of princes tactfully contrived by a neutral intermediary. The French King salutes his dear brother of England. The Duke of Burgundy discourses of the horrors of war and the blessings of peace. The victor is willing to be reconciled with the vanquished—provided his demands are met in full; and Henry is left to pay his addresses to a lady who is to be included in the spoils of war.

Of Henry's courtship uncivil things have been said. Attention has been concentrated on the superficial comedy of the blunt soldier who cannot mince it in love but whose heart is in the right place:

If I could win a lady at leap-frog, or by vaulting into my saddle with my armour on my neck, under the correction of bragging be it spoken, I should quickly leap into a wife. Or if I might buffet for my love, or bound my horse for her favours, I could lay on like a butcher and sit like a jack-an-apes, never off. But, before God, Kate, I cannot look greenly nor gasp out my eloquence, nor I have no cunning in protestation; only downright oaths, which I never use till urged, nor never break for urging. If thou canst love a fellow of this temper, Kate, whose face is not worth sun-burning, that never looks in his glass for love of any thing he sees there, let thine eye be thy cook.

A good leg will fall; a straight back will stoop; a black beard will turn white; a curled pate will grow bald; a fair face will wither; a full eye will wax hollow; but a good heart, Kate, is the sun and the moon; or rather the sun and not the moon; for it shines bright and never changes, but keeps his course truly. If thou would have such a one, take me; and take me, take a soldier; take a soldier, take a king.

On the face of it this is just a piece of light foolery to bring down the curtain on a tale that is told. If, however, we are interested in Shakespeare's handling of Henry's character, there is more to be said of it. We have had our little touch of Harry in the night, epitome of all that is most valiant and fortunate in English leadership. He is now to divert us by displaying in his winning of a wife just those characteristics which are most admired in the legendary Englishman. He can say no more than he means—though he talks twenty to the dozen. He can jest good-humouredly with his enemy—when his enemy is beaten. He can offer a sound heart to a fair lady—when her dowry is assured. He can be courteous, familiar and kind—when he has everything his own way. He can be grossly merry—when there is no call for solemnity or the high horse:

If ever thou be'st mine, Kate,—as I have a saving faith within me tells me thou shalt,—I get thee with scambling, and thou must therefore needs prove a good soldier-breeder; shall not thou and I, between Saint Denis and Saint George, compound a boy, half French, half English, that shall go to Constantinople and take the Turk by the beard?

He can claim and take a kiss in wholesome defiance of nice customs; but, for all his pleasant-spoken ways, he never loses grip of the real business in hand:

K. HENRY: Shall Kate be my wife?
FRENCH KING: So please you.
K. HENRY: I am content; *so the maiden cities you talk of may wait on her.*

There is, moreover, a final respect in which this farewell scene serves as a fitting conclusion to the dramatic life-story of Henry of Monmouth. His bluff but very competent wooing of Katharine, in which the word 'love' falls so easily from his lips, provokes in us

I

the reflection that in the whole course of his long career we have never been able to detect in him one spark of disinterested affection for a living soul. He is generously beloved of many, but gives nothing of himself in return. He can be all things to all men, provided he may keep his own affections. He is kind, provided it costs him little or nothing, and he is correspondingly cruel if his own interests or dignity are threatened. Falstaff, who loved him, refers searchingly to the 'cold blood he did naturally inherit of his father' and his father, who knew him best, warned his younger sons not to presume upon their brother's affection:

> Blunt not his love,
> Nor lose the great advantage of his grace
> By seeming cold or careless of his will;
> For he is gracious, if he be observed;
> He hath a tear for pity and a hand
> Open as day for melting charity:
> *Yet, notwithstanding, being incens'd, he's flint.*

No; the wooing of Katharine is not an impertinent trifle. There is an irony, not less delightful for being so amiably dispassionate, in this concluding picture of Henry of Monmouth heartily professing his love.

Shakespeare's Henry of Monmouth has confronted us with the question in its simplest terms: To what extent, if any, are Shakespeare's political characters brought to judgment? When, if ever, is a deliberate satire intended? How far is the dramatist aware of the havoc wrought among the great figures of history as his imagination ranges the highways of public life?

Henry is by some critics fervently extolled as an embodiment of heroic kingship, to which the imagination of his countrymen can turn in any age for comfort and assurance. By others he is denounced as an embodiment of everything that is coarse, common and insincere in political leadership. Are we, they ask, to take for our national hero a man who engages in a war of conquest from the lowest motives; who throws the moral responsibility for his crimes on Holy Church; who blames his victims in advance for the sufferings which he wantonly inflicts; who, in discarding the companions of his youth or executing his political opponents or threatening to sack a city or

giving orders that every soldier shall cut his prisoners' throats, strikes
an attitude of conscious rectitude? Did not the dramatist rather mean
to show us of what poor stuff the great worthies of history are made?

The answer must be that Shakespeare as little intended to present
as to demolish a hero. He found this man in the chronicles and,
bringing him on to the stage, gives him precisely the qualities proper
to his fame. There is neither censure nor commendation. The spectators may take Shakespeare's Henry as they please and they have so
taken him for three hundred years. According to your mood or disposition he is the happy warrior who stands with his band of
brothers at Agincourt, whose little touch of Harry in the night casts
the magic of irresistible leadership over his tattered ranks, whose
feats of arms are a national inheritance and whose voice is that of a
country called on by divine providence to blow its own trumpet to
the confusion of lesser breeds. Or he is a man who exhibits with a
disarming simplicity just those limitations of mind and heart which
enable their fortunate possessor to command the respect of his contemporaries and the applause of posterity. Shakespeare knew what
sort of man succeeds in public life and in Henry he presents us with
just that sort of man.

The qualities in Henry which have caused him to be accepted as a
national paragon need no advertisement. The negative approach is
less widely appreciated. For every thousand hearts that have thrilled
to the words and gestures of warlike Harry before Harfleur or on
the field of Agincourt barely ten or a dozen are familiar with Hazlitt's savage indictment. How Hazlitt hated this most admired of
English monarchs and how good were his reasons! 'Henry,' Hazlitt
writes, 'because he did not know how to govern his own kingdom,
determined to make war upon his neighbours. Because his own title
to the crown was doubtful, he laid claim to that of France. Because he
did not know how to exercise the enormous power which had just
dropped into his hands to any one good purpose, he immediately
undertook to do all the mischief he could. . . . Henry declares his
resolution, when France is his, to bend it to his awe or break it all to
pieces—a resolution, worthy of a conqueror, to destroy all he cannot
enslave; and, what adds to the joke, he lays all the blame of the consequences of his ambition on those who will not submit tamely to

his tyranny.' Cooling down a little, Hazlitt continues: 'He was a hero—that is, he was ready to sacrifice his own life for the pleasure of destroying thousands of other lives. . . . How do we like him? We like him in the play. There he is a very amiable monster, a very splendid pageant. As we like to gaze at a panther or a young lion in their cages in the Tower and catch a pleasing horror from their glistening eyes, their velvet paws and dreadless roar, so we take a very romantic, heroic, patriotic and poetical delight in the boasts and feats of our younger Harry as they appear on the stage and are confined to lines of ten syllables.'

Much dislike and not a little contempt—oddly blended with a reluctant admiration—have pursued this splendid figure down the years. The poets are almost unanimous. For Yeats, Henry of Monmouth was the vessel of clay which Shakespeare had to make as a companion piece to Richard of Bordeaux, his vessel of porcelain: 'He has the gross vices, the coarse nerves, of one who is to rule among violent people. . . . He is as remorseless and undistinguished as some natural force. . . . Shakespeare watched Henry V, not indeed as he watched the greater souls in the visionary procession, but cheerfully, as one watches some handsome spirited horse, and he spoke his tale, as he spoke all tales, with tragic irony.' John Masefield, among still-living poets, has stigmatised Henry as 'the one commonplace man in the eight historical plays. . . . He has the knack of life that fits human beings for whatever is animal in human affairs.'

Critics of the negative school usually extend their dislike of Henry to the play itself. Hazlitt found it second-rate. Sir Edmund Chambers writes to-day: 'With the exception of a few unconsidered words that fall from the mouth of a woman of no reputation, there is nothing that is intimate, nothing that touches the depths.'

Equally among the critics who admire or dislike Shakespeare's Henry are many who assume that their admiration or dislike was shared by the author. Those who love the lovely bully naturally have no doubt that Shakespeare was writing in praise from a full heart. Naturally, too, those who find in Henry a king of shreds and patches like to think that Shakespeare intended a satire. But oddly enough, there are also critics of the negative school who, though they themselves feel a whole-hearted contempt for Henry, yet maintain that he was Shakespeare's darling. Shakespeare, they seem to say, loved England so well that he was taken in by his own apotheosis of an English king.

Be it noted that all critics alike, however much they may differ in their estimate of Henry, discuss his behaviour and feel the impact of his personality as though he were a real person and not a character in a play. This disposes, once for all, of the question whether Shakespeare intended a panegyric or a satire. Shakespeare's concern as a dramatist was to present a man and he has here presented him to such good purpose that we dislike or admire him, quarrel about him, take one view of him to-day and another view of him to-morrow, praise his virtues or deplore his weaknesses, find him here mean or there magnificent, as we should do in the case of any man in real life who claimed to be our leader or representative in war or peace. The mere fact that different people take different views of Henry, or that the same people can be so divided in their opinions about him according to the mood or moment of their approach, is the best possible proof of Shakespeare's complete neutrality.

V

CAIUS MARCIUS CORIOLANUS

SHAKESPEARE in 'Coriolanus' takes for his theme a recurrent political problem of all times and places. A representative group of Roman patricians, whose attitudes and dispositions are embodied at a maximum in a heroically proud member of their class, is confronted with a representative group of Roman plebeians, whose grievances call for a limitation of the rights conferred by birth and privilege upon their rulers. Politics are a predominating interest in scene after scene of the play. It is true that Shakespeare's imagination, as always, is concentrated rather upon the individual men and women who play their parts in a public contention than upon the social implications of their behaviour, but in this particular tragedy the individual men and women are passionately concerned with their rights and wrongs as citizens in a community. The ultimate climax of the tragedy is a conflict between personal pride and family affection rather than a conflict between the principles of aristocratic and popular government. But the virtues and vices of the principal characters are all related to their place and function in the commonwealth; their actions and passions are almost wholly governed by their conceptions of what is due to them or expected of them as belonging to an estate of the nation.

'Coriolanus', being the most exclusively political play by Shakespeare, has naturally raised in its most acute form the question whether and, if so, to what extent the author's personal political sympathies are engaged. Careful critics and casual audiences alike, feeling the immediate impact of the play, have, according to their considered opinions or momentary prejudice, variously regarded it as an impartial presentation of the secular struggle between the few and the many, a whole-hearted indictment of democracy, or an ardent profession of faith in the aristocratic principle. Much eloquent and persuasive comment has been written in the conviction that Shakespeare definitely reveals himself as temperamentally hostile to the mutable, rank-scented many. The view has also its champions that Shakespeare, in his portrait of Coriolanus and of the ruin that overtakes him, is rebuking the insolence of caste and exposing the stupidity and selfishness of a typical autocrat. Such speculations are better left for consideration at a later stage. It will be easier—it may even be unnecessary—to discuss Shakespeare's political intentions when we have watched the drama unfold itself episode by episode to its conclusion.

The origin and merits of the political dispute which determines the action of the play are clearly stated in the opening scene. The grievances of the people, the quality of mind and temper in which they are approached alike by the patricians and the plebeians, the attitude of Marcius himself, the watchful sagacity of the popular leaders are in turn disclosed. Shakespeare states at once the principal themes of his composition, each to be further developed in its appropriate setting, and he states them with a careful precision which calls for an equally careful precision in their analysis.

It is to be noted that these citizens of Rome, who enter with clubs, staves and other weapons, have good and sufficient reason for mutiny. They are resolved to 'die rather than famish'. Caius Marcius is their enemy-in-chief, a 'very dog to the commonalty'. First Citizen, who is the most violently inclined of them all, calls God to witness that he speaks 'in hunger for bread, not in thirst for revenge', and his indictment is well-founded:

We are accounted poor citizens, the patricians good. What authority surfeits on would relieve us: if they would yield us but the superfluity, while it were wholesome, we might guess they relieved us humanely; but they think we are too dear: the leanness that afflicts us, the object of our misery, is as an inventory to particularise their abundance; our sufferance is a gain to them.

Second Citizen pleads for Marcius with a magnanimity which is very creditable in a hungry man, but First Citizen answers him shrewdly:

SEC. CITIZEN: Consider you what services he has done for his country?

FIRST CITIZEN: Very well; and could be content to give him good report for 't, but that he pays himself with being proud.

SEC. CITIZEN: Nay, but speak not maliciously.

FIRST CITIZEN: I say unto you, what he hath done famously, he did it to that end: though soft-conscienced men can be content to say it was for his country, he did it to please his mother, and to be partly proud; which he is, even to the altitude of his virtue.

SEC. CITIZEN: What he cannot help in his nature, you account a vice in him. You must in no way say he is covetous.

FIRST CITIZEN: If I must not, I need not be barren of accusations; he hath faults, with surplus, to tire in repetition.

Menenius Agrippa now comes upon the stage. He is a patrician, but 'one that hath always loved the people'. With him the citizens are ready to discuss matters in good faith. They have no quarrel with a noble Roman who has a decent regard for their interests:

> MENENIUS: Why, masters, my good friends, mine honest neighbours,
>   Will you undo yourselves?
> FIRST CITIZEN: We cannot, sir; we are undone already.
> MENENIUS: I tell you, friends, most charitable care
>   Have the patricians of you. For your wants,
>   Your suffering in this dearth, you may as well
>   Strike at the heaven with your staves as lift them
>   Against the Roman state, whose course will on
>   The way it takes, cracking ten thousand curbs
>   Of more strong link asunder than can ever
>   Appear in your impediment. For the dearth,
>   The gods, not the patricians, make it, and
>   Your knees to them, not arms, must help. Alack!
>   You are transported by calamity
>   Thither where more attends you; and you slander
>   The helms o' the state, who care for you like fathers,
>   When you curse them as enemies.

FIRST CITIZEN: Care for us! True, indeed! They ne'er cared for us yet: suffer us to famish, and their store-houses crammed with grain; make edicts for usury, to support usurers; repeal daily any wholesome act established against the rich, and provide more piercing statutes daily to chain up and restrain the poor. If the wars eat us not up, they will; and there's all the love they bear us.

Menenius retorts with his celebrated fable of the belly and its members. This passage, apart from its quality as a lively specimen of dramatic dialogue, helps indirectly to establish Shakespeare's general attitude to the citizens of Rome. First Citizen is ready to hear the fable, though he honestly warns Menenius: 'You must not think to

fob off our disgrace with a tale'. He is intrigued by the story and
alert to seize its drift. The genial, conversable style of the senator is
contrasted with the more serious, emotional approach of the man of
the people who, though his fancy is caught by the narrative and
though he contributes picturesque touches of his own, presses inexorably for a conclusion. Menenius is entirely at ease with these
people and they with him:

MENENIUS: There was a time when all the body's members
              Rebell'd against the belly, thus accused it:
              That only like a gulf it did remain
              I' the midst o' the body, idle and inactive,
              Still cupboarding the viand, never bearing
              Like labour with the rest, where the other instruments
              Did see and hear, devise, instruct, walk, feel,
              And, mutually participate, did minister
              Unto the appetite and affection common
              Of the whole body. The belly answer'd,—
FIRST CITIZEN: Well, sir, what answer made the belly?
MENENIUS: Sir, I shall tell you. With a kind of smile,
              Which ne'er came from the lungs, but even thus—
              For, look you, I may make the belly smile
              As well as speak—it tauntingly replied
              To the discontented members, the mutinous parts
              That envied his receipt; even so most fitly
              As you malign our senators for that
              They are not such as you—
FIRST CITIZEN: Your belly's answer? What!
              The kingly-crownèd head, the vigilant eye,
              The counsellor heart, the arm our soldier,
              Our steed the leg, the tongue our trumpeter,
              With other muniments and petty helps
              In this our fabric, if that they—
MENENIUS: What then?
              'Fore me, this fellow speaks! What then? what then?
FIRST CITIZEN: Should by the cormorant belly be restrain'd
              Who is the sink o' the body,—
MENENIUS: Well, what then?
FIRST CITIZEN: The former agents, if they did complain,
              What could the belly answer?

MENENIUS: I will tell you;
              If you'll bestow a small, of what you have little,
              Patience awhile, you'll hear the belly's answer.
FIRST CITIZEN: You're long about it.
MENENIUS: Note me this, good friend;
              Your most grave belly was deliberate,
              Not rash like his accusers.

There is good-natured chaff on both sides. The senator twits the
citizen with his eloquence ('Fore me, this fellow speaks!) the citizen
comments gruffly on the senator's prolixity (You're long about it).
There is no bad blood between them and, on the popular side, a
readiness to consider the other fellow's point of view. For when the
belly at last replies:

              'True is it, my incorporate friends,' quoth he,
              'That I receive the general food at first,
              Which you do live upon: and fit it is,
              Because I am the store-house and the shop
              Of the whole body: but, if you do remember,
              I send it through the rivers of your blood,
              Even to the court, the heart, to the seat o' the brain;
              And, through the cranks and offices of man,
              The strongest nerves and small inferior veins
              From me receive that natural competency
              Whereby they live.'—

First Citizen handsomely concedes: '*It was an answer.*'
    There is another point to be noted. Menenius is popular. The
citizens like him for his good humour and his honesty. But Shakespeare insists from the outset that he has no understanding of the
people's grievances, no real respect for their rights or opinions, no
grasp of the social issues involved. Menenius maintains to the last his
attitude of familiarity, man to man, with the citizens, but concludes
with the monstrous assertion that all good derives from the nobility
and that none can come of the commons:

    MENENIUS: Touching the weal o' the common, you shall find
              No public benefit which you receive

But it proceeds or comes from them to you
And no way from yourselves. What do you think,
You, the great toe of this assembly?
FIRST CITIZEN: I the great toe! why the great toe?
MENENIUS: For that, being one o' the lowest, basest, poorest,
Of this most wise rebellion, thou go'st foremost:
Thou rascal, thou art worst in blood to run,
Lead'st first to win some vantage.
But make you ready your stiff bats and clubs:
Rome and her rats are at the point of battle.
The one side must have bale.

Menenius is Shakespeare's portrait of an average member of the privileged class in any community, the speaking likeness of an English squire removed to a Roman setting. He can talk to the people as one man to another because he is entirely assured of his position. For him it is an axiom that his class is supreme in the nation by a benevolent and wholly natural dispensation of providence. He is disposed to regard these citizens with an affectionate tolerance, provided they know their place and are content to ascribe their misfortunes to heaven and not to the government of which he is a member.

That is how Shakespeare sees the good-natured aristocrat, who can be tolerant because it never occurs to him to question his own status or that of the masses. But we are now to behold an aristocrat for whom the masses have no status at all, who has a blind contempt for the common man and is impatient of any claim to consideration or fair dealing put forward by persons not of his own class.

Caius Marcius comes upon the scene as Menenius concludes his fable. Shakespeare presents his hero at once in all his superbity. He returns the greeting of Menenius with a single word and turns at once upon the citizens:

MENENIUS: Hail, noble Marcius!
MARCIUS: Thanks. What's the matter, you dissentious rogues,
That, rubbing the poor itch of your opinion,
Make yourself scabs?
FIRST CITIZEN: We have ever your good word.

MARCIUS: He that will give good words to thee will flatter
    Beneath abhorring. What would you have, you curs,
    That like nor peace nor war? the one affrights you,
    The other makes you proud. He that trusts to you,
    Where he should find you lions, finds you hares;
    Where foxes, geese.
        He that depends
    Upon your favours swims with fins of lead
    And hews down oaks with rushes. Hang ye! Trust ye?
    With every minute you do change a mind,
    And call him noble that was now your hate,
    Him vile that was your garland. What's the matter,
    That in these several places of the city
    You cry against the noble senate, who,
    Under the gods, keep you in awe, which else
    Would feed on one another? What's their seeking?
MENENIUS: For corn at their own rates; whereof they say,
    The city is well stored.

Marcius is not prepared to argue the matter. The question, for him, is not whether the demand of the citizens is just or their contention well-founded. For him it is an outrage that these men should presume to have any opinion at all and his only remedy for their grievances is a general massacre:

      Hang 'em! They say!
  They'll sit by the fire, and presume to know
  What's done i' the Capitol; who's like to rise,
  Who thrives, and who declines; side factions, and give out
  Conjectural marriages; making parties strong,
  And feebling such as stand not in their liking
  Below their cobbled shoes. They say there's grain enough!
  Would the nobility lay aside their ruth,
  And let me use my sword, I'd make a quarry
  With thousands of these quarter'd slaves, as high
  As I could pick my lance.

Menenius asks Marcius what has happened on the other side of the city, where the main body of the rebels has met the representatives of the senate. Marcius tells his story in a fashion that stresses in every line his indifference to the people's hardships and his indignation that any concessions should be accorded them. The senate, it seems, have decided to allow them representatives to defend their interests. This, in his view, is that thin end of the wedge which is the eternal bugbear of privilege:

MARCIUS: They said they were an-hungry; sigh'd forth proverbs;
    That hunger broke stone walls; that dogs must eat;
    That meat was made for mouths; that the gods sent not
    Corn for the rich men only; with these shreds
    They vented their complainings; which being answer'd,
    And a petition granted them, a strange one,—
    To break the heart of generosity,
    And make bold power look pale,—they threw their caps
    As they would hang them on the horns o' the moon,
    Shouting their emulation.
MENENIUS: What is granted them?
MARCIUS: Five tribunes to defend their vulgar wisdoms,
    Of their own choice: one's Junius Brutus,
    Sicinius Velutus, and I know not—'Sdeath!
    The rabble should have first unroof'd the city,
    Ere so prevail'd with me; it will in time
    Win upon power, and throw forth greater themes
    For insurrection's arguing.

'This is strange,' says Menenius, who as a good conservative does not take kindly to reform. But his response is neither contemptuous nor hostile.

Shakespeare, in this opening scene, clearly indicates the reasons on which Caius Marcius bases his contempt for the people of Rome. They have no liking for war and they fall short of his own high standard of valour. Then, too, they are fickle and not to be trusted. A born soldier, who is never so happy as on the field of battle, may perhaps be excused for feeling that he is a braver and better man than persons of a less martial disposition. The accusation that the citizens of Rome are uncertain in their allegiance comes less appropriately from a Roman general who, under the influence of private passion, is shortly to lead a hostile army against his countrymen.

Shakespeare, while according to Marcius the palm for valour, is careful to indicate that his hero's bravery is inspired by family feeling and love of fame rather than any desire to serve the commonwealth. First Citizen has shrewdly affirmed that 'what he did famously, he did it to that end; though soft-conscienced men can be content to say it was for his country, he did it to please his mother or to be partly proud'; and, lest we should take this to be a partisan conclusion, Shakespeare, towards the end of the scene, drives the point firmly home in a speech delivered by Marcius himself when he learns that the Volsces are in arms under Tullus Aufidius. First he exclaims that, if he were not Caius Marcius, he would wish to be Aufidius. Next he declares that, if Aufidius were on *his* side in the war, he would go over to the enemy for the sheer pleasure of fighting so excellent a soldier:

> MARCIUS: They have a leader,
> Tullus Aufidius, that will put you to 't.
> I sin in envying his nobility,
> And were I any thing but what I am,
> I'd wish me only he.
> COMINIUS: You have fought together.
> MARCIUS: Were half to half the world by the ears, and he
> Upon my party, I'd revolt, to make
> Only my wars with him: he is a lion
> That I am proud to hunt.

That the Volsces are preparing to attack his native land is meat and drink to Marcius. Here is not only a heaven-sent opportunity to increase his glory, but a chance to get even with the rabble of Rome:

> MESSENGER: Where's Caius Marcius?
> MARCIUS: Here: what's the matter?
> MESSENGER: The news is, sir, the Volsces are in arms.
> MARCIUS: I am glad on 't: then we shall ha' means to vent
> Our musty superfluity;

and he leaves the stage with a final fling at the citizens.

This opening scene concludes with a dialogue between Sicinius and Brutus, the newly-elected tribunes of the people. Shakespeare's presentation of these two men completes his statement of the major theme of the tragedy. No two characters in Shakespeare have been more severely handled by the critics. Since Dr. Johnson referred to

their 'plebeian malignity and tribunitian insolence', they have been
repeatedly held up to obloquy as a brace of intriguing, mean-
spirited rascals whose base manœuvres precipitate the tragedy and
utterly discredit the popular cause. On that issue let us again reserve
judgment till we have carefully examined their purposes and proceedings. For better or worse, these tribunes are Shakespeare's
counterfeit presentment of two labour leaders. They are the natural
products of a class war in the commonwealth. They use their wits to
defend the interests of the popular party and to remove from power
a declared enemy of the people. They have neither the wish, training
nor ability to disguise the quality or intention of their activities. In
working for their party they do not claim to be working disinter-
estedly for the nation. In resorting to the lawful and customary
tricks of the political trade they neglect the noble postures and impressive mimicries adopted by persons with a longer experience of
public life and of the deportment which public life requires. Whether
their conduct be better or worse than that of their political opponents
will appear in due course. Meanwhile it is worth noting that Shakespeare, in introducing them to the audience, draws special attention
to the quality which will be found throughout the play to distinguish
them from their rivals. They are discussing the appointment of
Marcius to be second-in-command, under Cominius, of the Roman
forces. They comment on his pride, on his contempt for the people
and for themselves. Then comes the important passage:

SICINIUS: I do wonder
            His insolence can brook to be commanded
            Under Cominius.
    BRUTUS: Fame, at the which he aims,
            In whom already he's well graced, cannot
            Better be held nor more attain'd than by
            A place below the first; for what miscarries
            Shall be the general's fault, though he perform
            To the utmost of a man; and giddy censure
            Will then cry out of Marcius 'O, if he
            Had borne the business!'
SICINIUS: Besides, if things go well,
            Opinion, that so sticks on Marcius, shall
            Of his demerits rob Cominius.

BRUTUS: Come:

> Half all Cominius' honours are to Marcius,
> Though Marcius earn'd them not, and all his faults
> To Marcius shall be honours, though indeed
> In aught he merit not.

It is not, admittedly, a generous diagnosis. It suggests that Marcius, in agreeing to serve under Cominius, is displaying a political sagacity which as a matter of fact is foreign to his nature. But, essentially, the tribunes are right and they are giving proof of precisely that 'realism' and precisely that suspicion of their political rulers which are characteristic of popular leaders in all times and places. Tribunes of the people have notoriously little respect for professions of altruism and of stainless regard for the public welfare uttered by their social superiors. Marcius did not accept the post of second-in-command with the deliberate design of advancing himself at the expense of his commander. But, in accepting a subordinate position, he certainly expected that, whatever happened, his own reputation would not be diminished by the arrangement. These tribunes are not concerned with the *motives* of Marcius in the particular case, but with the dangers inherent in his character. They are diagnosing not the man but the situation, and in their reading of the situation they are, as the event will show, entirely right. They regard themselves as watch-dogs of the people, and Shakespeare, in this opening scene, is at some pains to show that they are well-qualified for their office and that they intend to be alert and vigilant in its exercise.

We have noted a passing reference in this opening scene to the influence exercised over Caius Marcius by his mother. First Citizen's declaration that his brave deeds are inspired by filial affection rather than zeal for the republic is the first casual statement of what is to become in due course the most significant theme of the tragedy. This dutiful strain in the character of Marcius is the common talk of Rome and we await with interest the first appearance of a lady who is evidently to be held responsible in part for her son's character and achievements.

The intimacy of the bond between them can only be fully appreciated as the drama unfolds, but her disposition and the nature of her

influence are firmly indicated in a short preliminary scene. Volumnia
and Virgilia, having set them down on two low stools to sew, are
discussing their absent hero, who has gone to the war. The Roman
mother chides the Roman wife:

I pray you, daughter, sing; or express yourself in a more comfortable
sort; if my son were my husband, I would freelier rejoice in that absence
wherein he won honour than in the embracements of his bed where he
would show most love.

Volumnia thinks first of her son's glory; Virgilia thinks first of her
husband's peril:

VOLUMNIA: To a cruel war I sent him; from whence he returned, his
brows bound round with oak. I tell thee, daughter, I sprang not more in
joy at first hearing he was a man-child than now in first seeing he had
proved himself a man.

VIRGILIA: But had he died in the business, madam; how then?

VOLUMNIA: Then his good report should have been my son; I therein
would have found issue. Hear me profess sincerely: had I a dozen sons,
each in my love alike, and none less dear than thine and my good Marcius,
I had rather had eleven die nobly for their country than one voluptuously
surfeit out of action.

Volumnia then pictures her son in battle and, in doing so, shows us
from whom he derives his contempt of the people. She sees him
rallying his troops:

> Come on, you cowards! you were got in fear,
> Though you were born in Rome.

It is the very accent of Marcius, who rarely addresses his soldiers
without insulting them. Virgilia is of a very different quality. She has
none of Volumnia's delight in butchery:

VOLUMNIA: His bloody brow
                With his mail'd hand then wiping, forth he goes,
                Like to a harvest-man that's task'd to mow
                Or all or lose his hire.
VIRGILIA: His bloody brow! O Jupiter, no blood!
VOLUMNIA: Away, you fool! it more becomes a man
                Than gilt his trophy: the breasts of Hecuba,

When she did suckle Hector, look'd not lovelier
Than Hector's forehead when it spit forth blood
At Grecian swords, contemning.

A visitor is announced. Valeria has come to persuade them to lay aside their stitchery and come visiting. Virgilia begs to be excused. She has no heart for company while her husband is at the wars. Valeria chaffs her good-naturedly. Volumnia is impatient and dictatorial. But Virgilia is not to be moved. Shakespeare, to complete this family picture, prompts Valeria to inquire after Virgilia's little son. Volumnia interrupts:

He had rather see the swords, and hear a drum, than look upon his schoolmaster.

Whereupon these Roman matrons unite in their praises of this promising young warrior:

VALERIA: O' my word, the father's son: I'll swear 'tis a very pretty boy. O' my troth, I looked upon him o' Wednesday half an hour together: he has such a confirmed countenance. I saw him run after a gilded butterfly; and when he caught it, he let it go again; and after it again; and over and over he comes, and up again; catches it again; or whether his fall enraged him, or how 'twas, he did so set his teeth and tear it: O, I warrant, how he mammocked it!
VOLUMNIA: One on's father's moods.
VALERIA: Indeed, la, 'tis a noble child.

Virgilia does not share these transports. 'A crack, madam'—which is her gentle way of saying that her son is a heartless young ruffian but that he will perhaps grow out of it.

The remainder of the first Act—seven lively scenes packed with incidents of war—shows Marcius in his proper element. We see him first before Corioli. The Romans are beaten back from the walls. Marcius rallies them, leads them to the gates of the city, gets himself shut in alone with his enemies, fights his way out, captures the town, hurries off to the field where Cominius is still hard-pressed, meets Tullus Aufidius in single combat and, after victory, is crowned with oak-leaves, receiving the name of Coriolanus.

What precisely are the qualities exhibited by Marcius amid the noise and clamour of these martial episodes?

First there is his sheer delight in the exercise of his profession. This, for him, is a Roman holiday. He emerges from Corioli dripping with blood, but eager for more blows:

> My work hath yet not warm'd me: fare you well:
> The blood I drop is rather physical
> Than dangerous to me: to Aufidius thus
> I will appear, and fight.

Meeting with Cominius on the battlefield he exclaims:

> O! let me clip ye
> In arms as sound as when I woo'd, in heart
> As merry as when our nuptial day was done,
> And tapers burn'd to bedward!

Another trait, repeatedly emphasised, is his disdain of the spoils of war. He is contemptuous of any Roman who wastes time in plundering the city:

> See here these movers that do prize their hours
> At a crack'd drachma! Cushions, leaden spoons,
> Irons of a doit, doublets that hangmen would
> Bury with those that wore them, these base slaves,
> Ere yet the fight be done, pack up.

When Cominius offers him a tenth of the captured treasure, he refuses to accept 'a bribe to pay his sword' and insists on taking his common share with the soldiers.

He is equally disdainful of praise:

> Pray now, no more: my mother,
> Who has a charter to extol her blood,
> When she does praise me grieves me. I have done
> As you have done; that's what I can; induced
> As you have been; that's for my country.

Saluted with a flourish of trumpets, he exclaims that it is a profanation for the instruments of war to be flatterers. He deprecates these 'acclamations hyperbolical', begs that his 'little' should not be 'dieted in praises sauced with lies' and, when the soldiers salute him, abruptly announces: 'I will go wash'.

Lastly, for a passing instant, Marcius grows human. Note the passage well, for we shall never find him again so likeable—likeable in the gesture described, in his sudden weariness and in his call for a cup of wine:

> MARCIUS: The gods begin to mock me. I, that now
> Refused most princely gifts, am bound to beg
> Of my lord general.
> COMINIUS: Take it; 'tis yours. What is't?
> MARCIUS: I sometime lay here in Corioli
> At a poor man's house; he used me kindly:
> He cried to me; I saw him prisoner;
> But then Aufidius was within my view,
> And wrath o'erwhelm'd my pity: I request you
> To give my poor host freedom.
> COMINIUS: O, well begg'd!
> Were he the butcher of my son, he should
> Be free as is the wind. Deliver him, Titus.
> LARTIUS: Marcius, his name?
> MARCIUS: By Jupiter! forgot.
> I am weary; yea, my memory is tired.
> Have we no wine here?

There is, however, another side to the picture. Even in these scenes of war, where Marcius shows most to advantage, Shakespeare inexorably points to the qualities that make him intolerable in peace. In the first assault on Corioli his men are beaten back to their trenches. Recall, for a moment, Henry of Monmouth, rallying his soldiers at Harfleur: 'Once more unto the breach, dear friends, once more.' Now listen to Marcius:

> Boils and plagues
> Plaster you o'er, that you may be abhorr'd
> Further than seen and one infect another
> Against the wind a mile! You souls of geese,
> That bear the shapes of men.

The chidden Romans chase the Volscians back to their walls. Marcius enters the city, calling on his men to follow him through the gate. They hesitate:

FIRST SOLDIER: Fool-hardiness; not I.
SECOND SOLDIER: Nor I.
(MARCIUS *is shut in.*)
FIRST SOLDIER: See, they have shut him in.
ALL: To the pot, I warrant him.

Is it surprising that these soldiers should not be too eager to follow a man who abuses them and whose impetuosity they distrust? Note, too, that Shakespeare explicitly contrasts the quality of leadership displayed by Marcius with that of his commander-in-chief. The men following Cominius are also forced to retire before the enemy. 'Boils and plagues,' shouted Marcius. But hear Cominius:

> Breathe you, my friends: well fought; we are come off
> Like Romans, neither foolish in our stands,
> Nor cowardly in retire.

Even the qualities in Marcius that claim our admiration in these battle scenes are inherent in his defects. Shakespeare leaves in our minds an impression—to be developed later—that his contempt of praise is rooted less in modesty than in pride. What he has done seems to him so little in comparison with what he feels to be really commensurate with his prowess. And does not the admiration of these little men diminish rather than increase his stature? Are they really big enough to praise him?

Another point that Shakespeare makes in favour of Marcius at this point will turn against him even more decisively as the play continues. The victor of Corioli appeals to the patriotism of his soldiers. Let those Romans follow him, he exclaims, who love their country dearer than themselves; and we have heard him protest that what he has done was done for Rome. This, however, is the man who will shortly be marching against his country with fire and sword. That his protestations are sincere in their time and place may be allowed. Shakespeare is presenting not a hypocrite but a man, neither the first nor the last of his kind, who sincerely mistakes his love of personal glory and the impetus of his personal pride for devotion to the public service.

Meanwhile Rome is waiting for news. Menenius and his friends, 'o' the right-hand file', hoping for victory, intend to make good use of it. Marcius shall be consul. The tribunes, Brutus and Sicinius, are getting ready to face a troublesome situation. For Rome they desire success in arms, but they fear what it may mean for the liberties of the people. If Marcius be elected consul by a popular vote cast in the moment of his triumph, the concessions so recently won from the senate will be worthless. Meanwhile they must patiently endure the gibes of Menenius. War has a way of making things difficult for the popular front.

Menenius is out to enjoy himself. His friend Marcius is at the wars and likely to bring home fresh honours. He will be absolute with these fellows, but without malice. He has little taste for their company and feels himself fully entitled to say so:

I am known to be a humorous patrician, and one that loves a cup of hot wine with not a drop of allaying Tiber in't; said to be something imperfect in favouring the first complaint; hasty and tinder-like upon too trivial motion; one that converses more with the buttock of the night than with the forehead of the morning. What I think I utter, and spend my malice in my breath. Meeting two such wealsmen as you are—I cannot call you Lycurguses—if the drink you give me touch my palate adversely, I make a crookèd face at it.

When the tribunes tax Marcius with pride, Menenius has his answer:

MENENIUS: You talk of pride: O that you could turn your eyes toward the napes of your necks, and make but an interior survey of your good selves! O that you could!
BRUTUS: What then, sir?
MENENIUS: Why, then you should discover a brace of unmeriting, proud, violent, testy magistrates, alias fools, as any in Rome.

The long and short of it is that he does not like their faces; they are ambitious for poor knaves' caps and legs; they will spend a whole morning settling a trivial dispute between an orange-wife and a fosset-seller; Marcius is worth all their predecessors since Deucalion. Brutus and Sicinius take all this in good part: 'Come, sir, come, we know you well enough . . . a perfecter giber for the table than a necessary bencher in the Capitol.'

The political crisis feared by the tribunes quickly comes to a head. News is brought that Marcius is at hand. Menenius promises to make his very house reel. Volumnia rejoices that her son has two more wounds, one in the shoulder and one in the left arm, 'to show the people when he shall stand for his place.' Twenty-seven is his score and every gash an enemy's grave. Marcius enters. The trumpets sound. A herald proclaims his new title. Cominius in the Capitol re-counts his noble deeds: 'From face to foot he was a thing of blood.' The senators acclaim him consul. It only remains for him to obtain the voices of the people.

Brutus and Sicinius see well how things are going:

> All tongues speak of him, and the bleared sights
> Are spectacled to see him: your prattling nurse
> Into a rapture lets her baby cry
> While she chats him: the kitchen malkin pins
> Her richest lockram 'bout her reechy neck,
> Clambering the walls to eye him: stalls, bulks, windows,
> Are smother'd up, leads fill'd, and ridges hors'd
> With variable complexions, all agreeing
> In earnestness to see him: seld-shown flamens
> Do press among the popular throngs, and puff
> To win a vulgar station: our veil'd dames
> Commit the war of white and damask in
> Their nicely-gawded cheeks to the wanton spoil
> Of Phoebus' burning kisses.

These tribunes—as is not unusual with leaders of the people—have little confidence in those for whom they are determined to secure a better world. They know that they cannot hope to stand against the tide of gratitude and admiration which is carrying their enemy to power. Taking a longer view, however, they are not discouraged. Marcius, they foresee, 'cannot temperately transport his honours' and the commoners will soon have good reason to remember their 'ancient malice'—especially if they be seasonably prompted:

> We must suggest the people in what hatred
> He still hath held them; that to's power he would
> Have made them mules, silenced their pleaders, and
> Dispropertied their freedoms; holding them,
> In human action and capacity,

> Of no more soul nor fitness for the world
> Than camels in the war, who have their provand
> Only for bearing burdens.

They are convinced that Marcius would rather forgo the consulship than owe it to the suffrages of the popular party:

> I heard him swear,
> Were he to stand for consul, never would he
> Appear i' the market-place nor on him put
> The napless vesture of humility;
> Nor, showing, as the manner is, his wounds
> To the people, beg their stinking breaths.

> O! he would miss it rather
> Than carry it but by the suit o' the gentry to him
> And the desire of the nobles.

Their tactics in handling this very difficult situation are masterly. To denounce them as mean and contemptible is to forget that 'Coriolanus' is a political play and to display a remarkable ignorance of the conduct of public affairs during a popular election. They do not *oppose* the nomination of Marcius as consul, but suggest, not unreasonably, that, if he desires to be the first magistrate of Rome, he should show less contempt for her citizens:

> FIRST SENATOR: Masters o' the people,
> We do request your kindest ears, and, after,
> Your loving motion toward the common body,
> To yield what passes here.
> SICINIUS: We are convented
> Upon a pleasing treaty, and have hearts
> Inclinable to honour and advance
> The theme of our assembly.
> BRUTUS: Which the rather
> We shall be blest to do, if he remember
> A kinder value of the people than
> He hath hereto priz'd them at.
> MENENIUS: That's off, that's off;
> I would you rather had been silent. Please you
> To hear Cominius speak?

BRUTUS: Most willingly;
         But yet my caution was more pertinent
         Than the rebuke you gave it.

Marcius plays straight into their hands. When the senate announces that he is their choice for consul, and that it only remains for him to speak to the people, he coolly asks that the constitution should be amended so that he may be spared the indignity of having to ask for their votes in the traditional manner:

         I do beseech you,
   Let me o'erleap that custom, for I cannot
   Put on the gown, stand naked and entreat them,
   For my wounds' sake, to give their suffrage: please you
   That I may pass this doing.

The tribunes naturally insist that the laws of the country should be respected and Menenius urges Marcius to conform with usage as his predecessors have done before him and allow the citizens to play their part in the commonwealth. Marcius retorts that in his view such a part might well be taken from the people.

Here it may be observed, in parenthesis, that, while Marcius insists continually on his hereditary privileges and regards as an act of rebellion any attempt on the part of the plebeians to challenge the established order, he is prepared to over-ride any tradition that runs counter to his disposition, When, at last, he stands for election in the forum he is provoked into uttering a sentiment utterly destructive of any system of law based on precedent:

         Custom calls me to't:
   What custom wills, in all things should we do't,
   The dust on antique time would lie unswept,
   And mountainous error be too highly heap'd
   For truth to o'er-peer.

This is a strange observation to fall from the lips of a conservative nobleman, but it is entirely in character. The contempt of Marcius for the people is rooted neither in concern for his country, which he betrays, nor in allegiance to an ordered system of government, which he is prepared to reject in any particular if it does not happen to

please him. He dislikes having to seek the suffrage of the commons.
Let the suffrage be abolished. His election is opposed later on by the
tribunes. Let the tribunes be removed.

Meanwhile the citizens of Rome, for whose voices Marcius has a
contempt so absolute that it is as much as Menenius can do to bring
him to the forum, are awaiting the candidate and discussing his
chances:

> FIRST CITIZEN: If he do require our voices, we ought not to deny him.
> SECOND CITIZEN: We may, sir, if we will.
> THIRD CITIZEN: We have power in ourselves to do it, but it is a power
> that we have no power to do; for if he show us his wounds, and tell us his
> deeds, we are to put our tongues into those wounds and speak for them;
> so, if he tell us his noble deeds, we must also tell him our noble acceptance
> of them. Ingratitude is monstrous, and for the multitude to be ingrateful
> were to make a monster of the multitude.

Third Citizen caps this very reasonable presentation of the case with
an equally fair conclusion: 'I say, if he would incline to the people,
there was never a worthier man.'

Marcius, when he at last consents to stand for his election in due
and proper form, openly derides the men whose favour he requires.
From their consul-elect they expect an assurance of goodwill and
some show of care for their interests. That candidates for high office
in the state should upon their appointment profess a friendly concern for the people and show respect for their constituents is not
unusual even in communities where the forms of popular government do not extend beyond reciprocal courtesies at election time.
Marcius denies the citizens of Rome even the common amenities of
public life. The people are disconcerted at being received with
mockery but, displaying an admirable indulgence under extreme
provocation, they promise him their voices against their better
judgment. If there be any lack of sense or breeding in this scene, it
does not come from the people.

> MARCIUS: You know the cause, sir, of my standing here.
> FIRST CITIZEN: We do, sir; tell us what hath brought you to't.
> MARCIUS: Mine own desert.
> SECOND CITIZEN: Your own desert!

MARCIUS: Ay, not mine own desire.

FIRST CITIZEN: How! not your own desire?

MARCIUS: No, sir, 'twas never my desire yet to trouble the poor with begging.

FIRST CITIZEN: You must think, if we give you any thing, we hope to gain by you.

MARCIUS: Well then, I pray, your price o' the consulship?

FIRST CITIZEN: The price is, to ask it kindly.

MARCIUS: Kindly! Sir, I pray, let me ha't; I have wounds to show you, which shall be yours in private. Your good voice, sir; what say you?

SECOND CITIZEN: You shall ha't, worthy sir.

MARCIUS: A match, sir. There's in all two worthy voices begged. I have your alms: adieu.

FIRST CITIZEN: But this is something odd.

SECOND CITIZEN: An 'twere to give again,—but 'tis no matter.

(Exeunt the two Citizens.)
(Enter two other Citizens.)

MARCIUS: Pray you now, if it may stand with the tune of your voices that I may be consul, I have here the customary gown.

THIRD CITIZEN: You have deserved nobly of your country, and you have not deserved nobly.

MARCIUS: Your enigma?

THIRD CITIZEN: You have been a scourge to her enemies, you have been a rod to her friends; you have not indeed loved the common people.

MARCIUS: You should account me the more virtuous that I have not been common in my love. I will, sir, flatter my sworn brother, the people, to earn a dearer estimation of them; 'tis a condition they account gentle and since the wisdom of their choice is rather to have my hat than my heart, I will practise the insinuating nod and be off to them most counterfeitly; that is, sir, I will counterfeit the bewitchment of some popular man, and give it bountifully to the desirers. Therefore, beseech you, I may be consul.

FOURTH CITIZEN: We hope to find you our friend, and therefore give you our voices heartily.

MARCIUS: Here come more voices.

(Enter three other Citizens.)
Your voices: for your voices I have fought;
Watch'd for your voices; for your voices bear
Of wounds two dozen odd; battles thrice six

I have seen and heard of; for your voices have
Done many things, some less, some more: your voices:
Indeed, I would be consul.

FIFTH CITIZEN: He has done nobly, and cannot go without any honest man's voice.

SIXTH CITIZEN: Therefore let him be consul: the gods give him joy, and make him good friend to the people!

ALL CITIZENS: Amen, amen. God save thee, noble consul!

The forbearance of these simple men is lost on Marcius. He leaves the forum for the senate-house to claim and to enjoy the consulship, and the tribunes are left to face a situation which spells ruin for the popular cause. They find the citizens puzzled and apprehensive:

SICINIUS: He has it now, and by his looks methinks
'Tis warm at's heart.
BRUTUS: With a proud heart he wore his humble weeds.
Will you dismiss the people?
(*Re-enter Citizens.*)
SICINIUS: How now, my masters! have you chose this man?
FIRST CITIZEN: He has our voices, sir.
BRUTUS: We pray the gods he may deserve your loves.
SECOND CITIZEN: Amen, sir: to my poor unworthy notice,
He mock'd us when he begg'd our voices.
THIRD CITIZEN: Certainly,
He flouted us downright.
FIRST CITIZEN: No, 'tis his kind of speech: he did not mock us.
SECOND CITIZEN: Not one amongst us, save yourself, but says
He used us scornfully: he should have show'd us
His marks of merit, wounds received for's country.
SICINIUS: Why, so he did, I am sure.
CITIZENS: No, no; no man saw 'em.
THIRD CITIZEN: He said he had wounds, which he could show in private;
And with his hat, thus waving it in scorn,
'I would be consul,' says he: 'aged custom,
But by your voices, will not so permit me;
Your voices therefore.' When we granted that,
Here was, 'I thank you for your voices: thank you;
Your most sweet voices: now you have left your voices,
I have no further with you.' Was not this mockery?

For the tribunes only one course of action is politically possible. The election is not yet confirmed. If they are not once and for all to accept their defeat, they must advise the citizens to reconsider their promises to vote for Marcius. There is no fault to be found with their conduct of the situation. It is good, sound electioneering and it is a happy politician who has nothing worse upon his conscience:

> BRUTUS: You should have said
> That as his worthy deeds did claim no less
> Than what he stood for, so his gracious nature
> Would think upon you for your voices and
> Translate his malice towards you into love,
> Standing your friendly lord.
> SICINIUS: Thus to have said,
> As you were fore-advis'd, had touch'd his spirit
> And tried his inclination; from him pluck'd
> Either his gracious promise, which you might,
> As cause had call'd you up, have held him to;
> Or else it would have gall'd his surly nature,
> Which easily endures not article
> Tying him to aught; so, putting him to rage,
> You should have ta'en the advantage of his choler,
> And pass'd him unelected.
>
> BRUTUS: Get you hence instantly, and tell those friends
> They have chose a consul that will from them take
> Their liberties; make them of no more voice
> Than dogs that are as often beat for barking
> As therefore kept to do so.
> SICINIUS: Let them assemble;
> And, on a safer judgement, all revoke
> Your ignorant election: enforce his pride,
> And his old hate unto you; besides, forget not
> With what contempt he wore the humble weed,
> How in his suit he scorn'd you; but your loves,
> Thinking upon his services, took from you
> The apprehension of his present portance.

The tribunes, in urging the people to revoke the election, counsel them to attribute their mistake to the advice of their leaders:

Say, you chose him
More after our commandment than as guided
By your own true affections; and that your minds,
Pre-occupied with rather what you must do
Than what you should, made you against the grain
To voice him consul: lay the fault on us.

This last piece of advice from the tribunes to the citizens has frequently been denounced. Some critics go so far as to interpret it as a false and cowardly attempt by a brace of mean-spirited rogues to stand well with both sides. Admittedly it is dishonest. But do political leaders in the heat of an election always tell the truth? There is assuredly no question of double-dealing. The tribunes merely wish to provide the citizens with a reasonable excuse for revoking their choice. They also want the senators to feel that the rejection of Marcius is a spontaneous and representative act of the people. Is this manœuvre so uncommonly disgraceful? They are men in a desperate situation and they are honestly convinced that, if they allow the election to be confirmed, the inevitable popular reaction against Marcius will be all the more disastrous when it comes. Their motives —and they are good motives as far as they go—are plainly stated:

> BRUTUS: This mutiny were better put in hazard
> Than stay, past doubt, for greater:
> If, as his nature is, he fall in rage
> With their refusal, both observe and answer
> The vantage of his anger.
> SICINIUS: To the Capitol, come:
> We will be there before the stream o' the people;
> And this shall seem, as partly 'tis, their own,
> Which we have goaded onward.

These, then, are the tactics of the popular front. Now let us sample the proceedings of the politicians 'o' the right-hand file'.

Brutus and Sicinius, intercepting Marcius and the senators on their way to the forum, announce that the temper of the citizens has changed. Marcius shrewdly charges the tribunes with having effected this transformation. 'Have you not set them on?' he demands, and Cominius adds: 'You are like to do such business.' Brutus retorts: 'Not unlike, each way, to better yours.' The tribunes do not, in fact, deny their responsibility, but frankly set out to prove that they are more than a match for their opponents. Marcius now has his cue:

> It is a purposed thing, and grows by plot,
> To curb the will of the nobility:
> Suffer't, and live with such as cannot rule
> Nor ever will be ruled.

> For the mutable, rank-scented many, let them
> Regard me as I do not flatter, and
> Therein behold themselves: I say again,
> In soothing them we nourish 'gainst our senate
> The cockle of rebellion, insolence, sedition,
> Which we ourselves have plough'd for, sow'd and scatter'd,
> By mingling them with us, the honour'd number.

So, too, has Brutus:

> You speak o' the people,
> As if you were a god to punish, not
> A man of their infirmity.

Marcius develops his case for privilege. The plebeians have no right to be fed because they are less ready to fight than the nobility. The patricians, if they make concessions to a majority, will be regarded as yielding from fear what they refused to yield of their own free-will and pleasure; more than one authority in the state spells confusion. The arguments are familiar and the conclusion plain:

> They choose their magistrate,
> And such a one as he, who puts his 'shall',
> His popular 'shall', against a graver bench
> Than ever frown'd in Greece. By Jove himself!
> It makes the consuls base: and my soul aches
> To know, when two authorities are up,
> Neither supreme, how soon confusion
> May enter 'twixt the gap of both and take
> The one by the other.

> How shall this bisson multitude digest
> The senate's courtesy? Let deeds express
> What's like to be their words: 'We did request it;
> We are the greater poll, and in true fear
> They gave us our demands.'

> What should the people do with these bald tribunes?
> On whom depending, their obedience fails
> To the greater bench: in a rebellion,
> When what's not meet, but what must be, was law,
> Then were they chosen: in a better hour,
> Let what is meet be said it must be meet,
> And throw their power i' the dust.

This, declares Brutus, is 'manifest treason'. It is more than that. It is a notable affirmation that promises made by a gentleman to his inferiors need not be kept except under compulsion. Sicinius moves to arrest Marcius, who, with a riot in prospect, is now in his element: *Hence, old goat! Hence, rotten thing! or I shall shake thy bones out of thy garments.* The citizens come swarming. Menenius vainly tries to pacify both parties. Sicinius warns the people that they are at point to lose their liberties. Marcius draws his sword and undertakes to beat them on fair ground, forty to one.

Menenius hustles him from the scene:

> Pray you, be gone:
> I'll try whether my old wit be in request
> With those that have but little: this must be patch'd
> With cloth of any colour;

and is left to face the crowd, which is now, not unnaturally, incensed. His sympathies are divided. Of the citizens he exclaims: 'I would they were in Tiber'; and of Marcius: 'What the vengeance, could he not speak 'em fair?' He argues shrewdly with the tribunes:

> SICINIUS: He's a disease that must be cut away.
> MENENIUS: O! he's a limb that has but a disease;
> Mortal, to cut it off; to cure it, easy.
> What has he done to Rome that's worthy death?
> Killing our enemies, the blood he hath lost—
> Which, I dare vouch, is more than that he hath
> By many an ounce,—he dropp'd it for his country;
> And what is left, to lose it by his country,
> Were to us all, that do't and suffer it,
> A brand to the end o' the world.

Menenius pleads to such good purpose that the people are for the

moment pacified. Neither the citizens nor their leaders are unwilling
to hear reason:

MENENIUS: Consider this: he has been bred i' the wars
Since he could draw a sword, and is ill school'd
In bolted language; meal and bran together
He throws without distinction. Give me leave;
I'll go to him, and undertake to bring him
Where he shall answer, by a lawful form,
In peace, to his utmost peril.

FIRST SENATOR: Noble tribunes,
It is the humane way: the other course
Will prove too bloody, and the end of it
Unknown to the beginning.

SICINIUS: Noble Menenius,
Be you then as the people's officer.
Masters, lay down your weapons.

Menenius having promised to bring Marcius to the forum, the
stage is set for what is politically, perhaps, the most significant scene
of the tragedy. It takes place at the house of Marcius, where the
senators have met to consider the situation. The wiser ones deplore
the conduct of Marcius. They blame him, be it noted, not for his
attitude towards the people, but for showing his hand too soon. They
are set on persuading him to dissemble his hostility until he is firmly
in power and able to indulge it effectively. Marcius refuses this
advice. He can only wonder why Volumnia, who taught him to despise the people, should side with the senators who urge him to speak
the people fair:

I muse my mother
Does not approve me further, who was wont
To call them woollen vassals, things created
To buy and sell with groats, to show bare heads
In congregations, to yawn, be still and wonder,
When one but of my ordinance stood up
To speak of peace or war.

Volumnia states her position with an engaging cynicism:

MARCIUS: Why did you wish me milder? would you have me
False to my nature? Rather say I play
The man I am.

K

VOLUMNIA: O, sir, sir, sir,
                I would have had you put your power well on,
                Before you had worn it out.
    MARCIUS: Let go.
VOLUMNIA: You might have been enough the man you are,
                With striving less to be so: lesser had been
                The thwartings of your dispositions, if
                You had not show'd them how you were dispos'd,
                Ere they lack'd power to cross you.

Menenius takes precisely the same view:

    MENENIUS: Come, come, you've been too rough, something too
                rough;
                You must return and mend it.
FIRST SENATOR: There's no remedy;
                Unless, by not so doing, our good city
                Cleave in the midst, and perish.
    VOLUMNIA: Pray, be counsell'd:
                I have a heart as little apt as yours,
                But yet a brain that leads my use of anger
                To better vantage.
    MENENIUS: Well said, noble woman!
                Before he should thus stoop to the herd, but that
                The violent fit o' the time craves it as physic
                For the whole state, I'd put mine armour on,
                Which I can scarcely bear.

Still Marcius will not consent. Volumnia argues that honour and
policy must grow together. If all's fair in war, why not in peace? It is
often honour in a general to dissemble. These may or may not be
good political arguments. But if Brutus and Sicinius, for being artful
in policy, are to be denounced as rascals, what of Volumnia?
When Marcius asks her what she is driving at and why, she answers
unblushingly:

                Because that now it lies you on to speak
                To the people, not by your own instruction,
                Nor by the matter which your heart prompts you,
                But with such words that are but rooted in
                Your tongue.

> Now, this no more dishonours you at all
> Than to take in a town with gentle words,
> Which else would put you to your fortune and
> The hazard of much blood.
> I would dissemble with my nature where
> My fortunes and my friends at stake required
> I should do so in honour.

The concluding word is worth noting. It can at least be said for the tribunes that in laying *their* little plans they made no claim to be answering the call of honour.

'*Noble* lady,' exclaims Menenius. He goes on to point out that all may yet be well, if only Marcius will utter a few conciliatory words:

> This but done,
> Even as she speaks, why, their hearts were yours;
> For they have pardons, being ask'd, as free
> As words to little purpose.

In plain terms, the natural generosity of the citizens guarantees in advance the success of his noble friend's hypocrisy.

At this point we should admire Marcius for refusing to play the part assigned to him if his reluctance were prompted by a sincere dislike of the shifts to which a gentleman is reduced who must seem to gratify the people before he is permitted to please himself. We should like to think that his recoil was due to the natural repugnance of a politically honest magistrate to a bit of sharp practice urged upon him by the party caucus. But this is not so. Marcius thinks only of his personal dignity:

> Must I go show them my unbarbèd sconce?
> Must I with base tongue give my noble heart
> A lie that it must bear?

There is no hint anywhere of a protest against the political dishonesty of the course to which he is invited. He realises only that he, Caius Marcius Coriolanus, is required to be civil to the electors. He makes this point at some length and with the usual references to his prowess as a soldier.

Volumnia loses patience. She has argued and pleaded in vain. Now she applies the whip. Marcius is his mother's boy—that, indeed, is his tragedy; and in this scene, where she lashes him into submission, there is a foreshadowing of the greater scene when, at the climax of the play, she will use her terrible authority over her son to save Rome and drive him to his death. In a passage of surpassing dramatic irony, this mother, who has taught her son to be proud, now twits him with his insolence:

> VOLUMNIA: At thy choice, then:
> To beg of thee, it is my more dishonour
> Than thou of them. Come all to ruin; let
> Thy mother rather feel thy pride than fear
> Thy dangerous stoutness, for I mock at death
> With as big heart as thou. Do as thou list;
> Thy valiantness was mine, thou suckd'st it from me,
> But owe thy pride thyself.
> MARCIUS: Pray, be content:
> Mother, I am going to the market-place;
> Chide me no more. I'll mountebank their loves,
> Cog their hearts from them, and come home belov'd
> Of all the trades in Rome.

The scene concludes:

> COMINIUS: Away! the tribunes do attend you: arm yourself
> To answer mildly; for they are prepar'd
> With accusations, as I hear, more strong
> Than are upon you yet.
> MENENIUS: The word is 'mildly'.
> MARCIUS: Pray you, let us go:
> Let them accuse me by invention, I
> Will answer in mine honour.
> MENENIUS: Ay, but mildly.
> MARCIUS: Well, mildly be it then. Mildly!

And so, once again, to the forum. We have seen the patricians laying their plans to over-reach the plebeians. Shakespeare, striking a perfect balance between the parties, now shows the plebeians, or rather their leaders, laying their plans to outwit the patricians. Sicinius is giving his last instructions to the ædiles:

> Assemble presently the people hither;
> And when they hear me say 'It shall be so,

> I' the right and strength o' the commons,' be it either
> For death, for fine, or banishment, then let them,
> If I say fine, cry 'Fine'; if death, cry 'Death',
> Insisting on the old prerogative
> And power i' the truth o' the cause.

Brutus knows exactly how to handle Marcius:

> Put him to choler straight: he hath been us'd
> Ever to conquer, and to have his worth
> Of contradiction: being once chafed, he cannot
> Be rein'd again to temperance; then he speaks
> What's in his heart; and that is there which looks
> With us to break his neck.

Marcius now enters with the senators. Menenius is still urging him to be calm. Marcius agrees to abide by the decision of the people, but the tribunes, taking charge of the proceedings, lose no time in putting their agreed plan of action into effect. A single speech from Sicinius is enough:

> We charge you, that you have contriv'd to take
> From Rome all season'd office, and to wind
> Yourself into a power tyrannical;
> For which you are a traitor to the people.

Marcius hears only the one word 'traitor'—as Sicinius meant he should. He flies instantly into a passion. Menenius urges him to be temperate:' Is this the promise that you made your mother?' he asks, but all in vain. Marcius henceforth is blind and deaf:

> Let them pronounce the steep Tarpeian death,
> Vagabond exile, flaying, pent to linger
> But with a grain a day, I would not buy
> Their mercy at the price of one fair word.

Sicinius, in a speech which is not without dignity and in which every charge is well-founded, pronounces upon Marcius sentence of banishment. Marcius deserves death, but Rome must not slay her soldier. It must be admitted, even by those who dislike these tribunes, that their conduct throughout this scene is exemplary in its moderation. There is, moreover, one brief interchange which should not

be overlooked. Sicinius has declared that the offences of Marcius—
beating your officers, opposing laws with strokes—are capital. His colleague intervenes:

> BRUTUS: But since he hath
>   Serv'd well for Rome,—
> MARCIUS: What! do *you* prate of service?
> BRUTUS: I talk of that, that know it.
> MARCIUS: You?

These tribunes claim that they, too, serve the state. To Marcius this
is such absolute nonsense that he can hardly believe his ears.

Nothing now remains but for Marcius to accept his banishment.
He does so with a *tu quoque*, appropriate to his simple nature, and in
the conviction, no less appropriate, that Rome will soon have reason
to regret his absence:

> You common cry of curs! whose breath I hate
> As reek o' the rotten fens, whose loves I prize
> As the dead carcasses of unburied men
> That do corrupt my air, *I* banish *you*.
>
>   Despising,
> For you, the city, thus I turn my back:
> There is a world elsewhere.

When precisely did Marcius decide to take service with the
enemies of Rome? He drops no hint of his purpose in bidding farewell to his family and friends. He takes his leave of them all in the
high Roman fashion, chiding his mother for disregarding her own
precepts in taking the event too much to heart:

> Come, leave your tears: a brief farewell: the beast
> With many heads butts me away. Nay, mother,
> Where is your ancient courage?
>
>   You were us'd to load me
> With precepts that would make invincible
> The heart that coin'd them.

He is tender with his friend, Menenius, and with Cominius, his old
commander; affectionate with his wife; lovingly dutiful towards his
mother. These patricians are at their best among themselves:

> Come, my sweet wife, my dearest mother, and
> My friends of noble touch, when I am forth,
> Bid me farewell, and smile. I pray you, come.
> While I remain above the ground, you shall
> Hear from me still; and never of me aught
> But what is like me formerly.

There is no suggestion here of the renegade. To those who have followed him so far and realised how shallow is the love of country which he has in his pride so frequently professed, the step he is about to take will seem already to be inevitable. But Marcius does not yet know himself as we have learned to know him. He leaves Rome in a mood almost of resignation. Like to a lonely dragon to his fen he goes into exile with the thought: 'I shall be loved when I am lacked.'

Volumnia, who is shortly to plead with her son for Rome, is for the moment the more deeply incensed:

> Now the red pestilence strike all trades in Rome,
> And occupations perish!

Her love of country, which springs to attention when her family traditions are threatened, does not include the citizens of Rome. Upon the tribunes, whom she meets after seeing her son to the gates of the city, her anger is let loose without restraint:

> I would my son
> Were in Arabia, and thy tribe before him,
> His good sword in his hand.

This is a bad quarter of an hour for Brutus and Sicinius. They are relentless in their pursuit of Marcius as long as he remains upon the scene. But once the danger is removed, it is not their policy to carry to extremes their quarrel with the senators:

> Now we have shown our power,
> Let us seem humbler after it is done
> Than when it was a-doing.

In this propitiatory mood they find themselves set upon by a furious woman in the public streets. Volumnia declares that 'anger's her meat', rebukes Virgilia for her 'faint puling' and is not too careful of her epithets. Menenius, as usual, urges peace, but is left, as usual, shaking his wise old head over a situation that is altogether beyond him. The tribunes do not on the whole come so badly out of it. There is a note of sincere regret in the little speech of Sicinius:

> I would he had continued to his country
> As he began, and not unknit himself
> The noble knot he made.

That Sicinius had himself provoked Marcius to unknit his noble knot does not detract from the sincerity of the tribune's regret. He cannot, after all, be held responsible for Marcius being what he was. Sicinius and Brutus had merely helped him to show his colours.

Something has happened to Marcius when we meet him again. Shakespeare, having prepared us for his desertion to the enemy much earlier in the play, now uses his favourite trick—he will use it again to even better purpose when we come to the climax of the tragedy—of springing upon us a dramatic surprise which is, in fact, a necessary sequel of all that has gone before. We are taken unawares and held in suspense while we watch what is, in effect, a foregone conclusion. Note the superb sleight of hand with which he suffers Marcius to show us the most amiable side of his disposition at the very moment when he is about to league himself with the enemies of Rome to lay her in ashes. The dramatist exhibits in his hero at this critical moment all the most engaging qualities of the aristocrat, who, within the closed circle of his family and friends, is considerate, courteous, affectionate—soothing to his wife, devoted to his mother, loving with the companions of his choice; facing misfortune with a brave heart. Even his pride is touched with a noble fortitude, in which all rancour is for the moment stilled. By this means the shock of his next appearance as a man dedicated to an implacable vengeance is a veritable *coup de théâtre*.

The shock, when it comes, is the more tremendous in that Shakespeare's Marcius entertains a design which goes far beyond anything in Plutarch. The historical Marcius had no intention of burning Rome. His quarrel was with the popular party and his plan was to ally himself with the nobility of Antium in order to recover for himself and his friends their old ascendency in the Roman republic. Plutarch describes a situation in which a national contest between

Romans and Volscians is complicated by a social contest in both
cities between patricians and plebeians. The historical Marcius re-
sorted, in fact, to the not uncommon political device of seeking support for his party among foreigners of his own class and persuasion.
Here, in little, between two city states, was foreshadowed the
mightiest argument of these present times, when war between
nations is intricated with war between two principles of government; a vertical struggle between sovereign states being crossed at
all points by a horizontal struggle between classes in an international
community. The Marcius of Plutarch, in the terms of peace which
he offered Rome, contemplated a union of two cities in a single
commonwealth, to be ruled by the aristocracy of both. It was his intention to 'increase the malice and dissension between the nobility
and the commonalty'; and one of his devices, not infrequently
imitated by the industrial and financial leaders of modern Europe,
was to make war on the Roman people, but to spare the property
of the Roman senators. 'He was very careful', says Plutarch, 'to keep
the noblemen's lands and goods safe from harm and burning, but
spoiled all the whole country besides.'

Shakespeare totally rejects this aspect of the contention. The
climax of his tragedy is to be a conflict in Marcius between a pride
dedicated to vengeance and a natural affection responding to a call of
the blood. At the supreme moment he diverts our interest from the
feud between patricians and plebeians and concentrates on the
personal issue. Marcius is to be shown, not as an exiled nobleman
who hopes with foreign assistance to compass a return to power in
his native city, but as a man possessed with the fixed idea of wreaking
a complete and sanguinary vengeance upon the entire community
of Rome.

An interesting study might be made of the scenes which Shakespeare preferred to leave unwritten. For everything that takes place
on his stage we have to imagine a hundred things that take place behind the scenes. His men and women, unlike the carefully constructed characters of the common stage, do not exhaust themselves
in public. They come before us filled with actions past and leave
us primed for action to come. Shakespeare, at this point of his
tragedy, might have shown how Marcius, who has just taken a

loving farewell of his friends at the city gates, first formed his resolution to burn Rome. He might have lifted his curtain upon Marcius brooding in exile, laid bare the bitterness of his thwarted expectation that the senators would somehow arrange for his recall, shown the monstrous growth in him of a determination to be revenged not only on the people he despised but on the friends who had failed him. But Shakespeare avoids the explanatory or intermediary incident. He proceeds, as we have said, by surprise, concealing rather than obtruding the means used in its preparation.

Marcius thus appears before the house of Aufidius with his decision taken, abruptly revealing the quality of his dreadful enterprise in a soliloquy upon the fragility of alliances between states and cities. Simple men may fight for things which seem permanent and dear, but the great ones know better:

> O world, thy slippery turns! Friends now fast sworn,
> Whose double bosoms seem to wear one heart,
> Whose hours, whose bed, whose meal and exercise,
> Are still together, who twin, as 'twere, in love
> Unseparable, shall within this hour,
> On a dissension of a doit, break out
> To bitterest enmity: so, fellest foes,
> Whose passions and whose plots have broke their sleep
> To take the one the other, by some chance,
> Some trick not worth an egg, shall grow dear friends
> And interjoin their issues.

Marcius served Rome, as long as he could count himself one of her masters. He will now serve Antium, if he can come to terms with Aufidius:

> My birthplace hate I, and my love's upon
> This enemy town. I'll enter: if he slay me,
> He does fair justice; if he give me way,
> I'll do his country service.

Marcius is not less Marcius for having come to the house of his enemy in mean apparel, muffled and in disguise. He beats the servants who try to turn him away and his appeal to Aufidius is far from being that of a suppliant. He speaks, first and last, as one gentleman

to another, confident of the outcome though he may seem reckless
in his address:

> My name is Caius Marcius, who hath done
> To thee particularly, and to all the Volsces,
> Great hurt and mischief.
>
>   Now this extremity
> Hath brought me to thy hearth; not out of hope,
> Mistake me not, to save my life, for if
> I had fear'd death, of all the men i' the world
> I would have 'voided thee; but in mere spite,
> To be full quit of those my banishers,
> Stand I before thee here. Then if thou hast
> A heart of wreck in thee, that will revenge
> Thine own particular wrongs and stop those maims
> Of shame seen through thy country, speed thee straight,
> And make my misery serve thy turn: so use it
> That my revengeful services may prove
> As benefits to thee, for I will fight
> Against my canker'd country with the spleen
> Of all the under fiends.

Accept this offer, he concludes, or here is my throat:

> Which not to cut would show thee but a fool,
> Since I have ever follow'd thee with hate,
> Drawn tuns of blood out of thy country's breast,
> And cannot live but to thy shame, unless
> It be to do thee service.

What sort of man is Tullus Aufidius to whom this agreeable
dilemma is presented? Shakespeare has made him just the man for his
purpose—as proud and as valiant as Marcius himself, as besotted with
his prowess as a warrior, as ready to change his allegiance if his
personal dignity is affronted. When Corioli was taken by the
Romans, and he was assured that the town would be delivered back
to him 'in good condition', he exclaimed:

>   Condition!
> I would I were a Roman; for I cannot,
> Being a Volsce, be that I am. Condition!

> What good condition can a treaty find
> I' the part that is at mercy?

and in the bitterness of defeat he swore that nothing should stand
between him and the destruction of his rival:

> My valour's poison'd
> With only suffering stain by him; for him
> Shall fly out of itself: nor sleep nor sanctuary,
> Being naked, sick, nor fane nor Capitol,
> The prayers of priests, nor times of sacrifice,
> Embarquements all of fury, shall lift up
> Their rotten privilege and custom 'gainst
> My hate to Marcius: where I find him, were it
> At home, upon my brother's guard, even there,
> Against the hospitable canon, would I
> Wash my fierce hand in 's heart.

This outbreak of Aufidius in the first Act may prompt in the
simple spectator a fearful expectation that he will take Marcius at his
word and slay him instantly. But no man was more likely than
Aufidius to receive with delight the advances of a hated enemy so
obviously at his mercy. Generosity in such a case feeds the very pride
in which the ancient malice was rooted. Such a man is as likely to comfort his enemy when defenceless as to cut his throat in the church as
soon as he shows signs of recovery. Each gesture, apparently so different in kind, is rooted in the same principle. In both cases there is a
cordial gratification of the sense of power.

Aufidius accordingly receives Marcius with rapture. This is even
better than washing his fierce hand in the heart of his rival:

> Let me twine
> Mine arms about that body, where against
> My grainèd ash an hundred times hath broke,
> And scarr'd the moon with splinters: here I clip
> The anvil of my sword, and do contest
> As hotly and as nobly with thy love
> As ever in ambitious strength I did
> Contend against thy valour. Know thou first,
> I loved the maid I married; never man
> Sigh'd truer breath; but that I see thee here,

Thou noble thing! more dances my rapt heart
Than when I first my wedded mistress saw
Bestride my threshold.

Aufidius offers Marcius half his commission. They will march
together against Rome.

The scene concludes with some shrewd commentary by some servants on this unexpected alliance. It should seem odd to those who
find in this play evidence of Shakespeare's contempt for the people
that he goes out of his way, in scene after scene, to show us plain
citizens and soldiers speaking more wisely than their magistrates and
generals of current events and policies. We have heard two officers
in Rome, laying cushions in the Capitol as they discuss the character
of Marcius. Said First Officer: 'To seem to affect the malice and displeasure of the people is as bad as that which he dislikes, to flatter
them for their love.' The retainers of Aufidius at Antium are
equally shrewd in taking the measure of their masters. Third Serving-
man describes the reception of Marcius by the nobility of Antium
with a wit grown caustic in observation of the great:

Why, he is so made on here within, as if he were son and heir to Mars;
set at upper end o' the table; no question asked him by any of the senators,
but they stand bald before him: our general himself makes a mistress of
him; sanctifies himself with 's hand and turns up the white o' the eye to
his discourse. But the bottom of the news is, our general is cut i' the middle,
and but one half of what he was yesterday; for the other has half by the
entreaty and grant of the whole table.

These are lively, level-headed fellows. 'Peace', says First Serving-
man, 'makes men hate one another.' 'Reason', replies Third Serving-
man, 'because they need one another less in peace than in war'—
which is perhaps the profoundest observation on a political subject
made in the play. It can hardly be maintained that such interludes
are merely intended to mark time between the high-and-mighty
doings of the great. They have the effect, not presumably accidental,
of exposing to the light of common sense the inordinate pretensions
of Marcius and of those who live under the spell of his achievements.

The Romans, meanwhile, are ignorant of the pact between
Marcius and their secular enemy. The tribunes can for the moment

congratulate themselves on their seasonable audacity in procuring his banishment and on their policy of appeasement in dealing with the senators:

> We hear not of him, neither need we fear him;
> His remedies are tame i' the present peace
> And quietness o' the people, which before
> Were in wild hurry. Here do we make his friends
> Blush that the world goes well, who rather had,
> Though they themselves did suffer by 't, behold
> Dissentious numbers pestering streets, than see
> Our tradesmen singing in their shops and going
> About their functions friendly.

Menenius, up to a point, agrees:

> All's well; and might have been much better, if
> He could have temporis'd.

Rome is at peace within and without and the tribunes can only wish regretfully that Marcius had loved the people well enough to share these blessings. With Menenius they discuss the situation without rancour or apology:

> SICINIUS: This is a happier and more comely time
> Than when these fellows ran about the streets,
> Crying confusion.
> BRUTUS: Caius Marcius was
> A worthy officer i' the war; but insolent,
> O'ercome with pride, ambitious past all thinking,
> Self-loving,—
> SICINIUS: And affecting one sole throne,
> Without assistance.
> MENENIUS: I think not so.
> SICINIUS: We should by this, to all our lamentation,
> If he had gone forth consul, found it so.
> BRUTUS: The gods have well prevented it, and Rome
> Sits safe and still without him.

Then comes the fatal news, chapter by chapter. The Volsces are in arms. The tribunes refuse at first to believe it; it is a rumour set on foot by the patricians:

> Raised only, that the weaker sort may wish
> Good Marcius home again.

The Volsces are a warlike, aggressive people, but leaders on the left often find it difficult to believe in the unregenerate militarism of their neighbours:

> BRUTUS: It cannot be
> The Volsces dare break with us.
> MENENIUS: Cannot be!
> We have a record that very well it can,
> And three examples of the like have been,
> Within my age.

One messenger succeeds another. The news that Marcius is coming with Aufidius to revenge himself on Rome seems yet more incredible. His friends are equally staggered with his enemies. But the report is quickly confirmed. The unfortunate tribunes then find themselves in the classic position of a labour government facing a war for which they are unprepared, an opposition which is able very plausibly to hold them entirely responsible for the situation and an electorate which turns right about and disowns their policy. 'O! you have made good work!' exclaims Cominius. 'Good work,' echoes Menenius, 'you and your apron-men.' The citizens recall that, in banishing Marcius, they were in two minds: 'That we did, we did for the best; and though we willingly consented to his banishment, yet it was against our will.' This is a bad moment for Brutus and Sicinius. Nevertheless they put a good face upon it; they even venture a thrust at their enemies which is not altogether wide of the mark:

> Go, masters, get you home; be not dismay'd:
> These are a side that would be glad to have
> This true which they so seem to fear.

It is to be noted that in this vivid presentation of a political situation with which modern statesmen are not unfamiliar, no word of criticism is passed by the patricians on the conduct of Marcius. 'Who is't can blame him?' demands Cominius. 'If he could burn us all into one coal, we have deserved it,' says Menenius:

> If he were putting to my house the brand
> That should consume it, I have not the face
> To say, 'Beseech you, cease.'

That Marcius should be bringing up an army to burn Rome is, in fact, regarded by his friends as the perfectly natural gesture of an angry nobleman. Cominius, in a later scene, describes how he begged Marcius in vain to spare the city. He relates how first he urged that it was royal to pardon when mercy was least expected and how he then reminded Marcius that there were people of his own party in Rome who should be dear to him. Marcius replied that he could not trouble himself with distinguishing one Roman from another. Cominius took it for granted that Marcius had every right to avenge himself on the Roman people but expected to excite the compassion of Marcius for his family and friends. Menenius, urged by Cominius and the tribunes to plead in person with Marcius, seems equally unaware of the enormity of the situation. He merely thinks it hard lines that the nobility of Rome should have to suffer for the sins of the Roman people:

> COMINIUS: I offer'd to awaken his regard
> For's private friends: his answer to me was,
> He could not stay to pick them in a pile
> Of noisome musty chaff: he said 'twas folly,
> For one poor grain or two, to leave unburnt
> And still to nose the offence.
>
> MENENIUS: For one poor grain or two!
> I am one of those; his mother, wife, his child,
> And this brave fellow too, we are the grains:
> You are the musty chaff; and you are smelt
> Above the moon: we must be burnt for you.

So much emphasis has been laid on Shakespeare's anti-democratic bias that these speeches are worth noting. The patricians, faced with invasion, still think mainly of themselves. Only the tribunes plead for Rome, urging the senators to forget their feud and think of the common peril:

> SICINIUS: Nay, pray, be patient: if you refuse your aid
> In this so never-needed help, yet do not
> Upbraid's with our distress.
>
> MENENIUS: What should I do?
> BRUTUS: Only make trial what your love can do
> For Rome, towards Marcius.

MENENIUS: Well, and say that Marcius
           Return me, as Cominius is return'd,
           Unheard; what then?
           But as a discontented friend, grief-shot
           With his unkindness? say't be so?
SICINIUS: Yet your good will
           Must have that thanks from Rome, after the measure
           As you intended well.

Menenius consents to undertake the mission. Marcius was his friend, had called him 'father'. He finds it difficult to believe that his hero can be so utterly relentless as Cominius reports. His engaging resilience and disarming trust in human nature keep the upper hand despite all his prejudices of blood and station. He sets off on his forlorn errand in a hopeful spirit—almost with zest:

           I think he'll hear me. Yet, to bite his lip,
           And hum at good Cominius, much unhearts me.
           He was not taken well; he had not din'd:
           The veins unfill'd, our blood is cold, and then
           We pout upon the morning, are unapt
           To give or to forgive; but when we have stuff'd
           These pipes and these conveyances of our blood
           With wine and feeding, we have suppler souls
           Than in our priest-like fasts: therefore I'll watch him
           Till he be dieted to my request,
           And then I'll set upon him.

That Shakespeare had a soft corner in his heart for Menenius is never so strongly felt as in the handling of his mission to the Volscian camp. Challenged by the sentries, he commends them for their vigilance, states his business and, when they refuse to let him pass, ingenuously affirms that Marcius is his friend:

           I tell thee, fellow,
           Thy general is my lover: I have been
           The book of his good acts, whence men have read
           His fame unparallel'd, haply amplified;
           For I have ever glorified my friends,
           Of whom he's chief, with all the size that verity

> Would without lapsing suffer: nay, sometimes,
> Like to a bowl upon a subtle ground,
> I have tumbled past the throw.

He asks whether the general has dined, for 'I would not speak with him till after dinner.' The sentry bids him return to Rome and prepare for execution. At this point Marcius enters and Menenius confidently calls on the sentry to witness how he shall be received: 'Behold now, and swoon for what's to come upon thee.' His appeal to Marcius is brief and of trustful simplicity. The reply is crushingly final:

MENENIUS: O my son, my son! thou art preparing fire for us; look thee, here's water to quench it. I was hardly moved to come to thee; but being assured none but myself could move thee, I have been blown out of your gates with sighs; and conjure thee to pardon Rome, and thy petitionary countrymen. The good gods assuage thy wrath, and turn the dregs of it upon this varlet here,—this, who, like a block, hath denied my access to thee.

> MARCIUS: Away!
> MENENIUS: How! away!
> MARCIUS: Wife, mother, child, I know not. My affairs
> Are servanted to others.
>
>   Therefore, be gone.
> Mine ears against your suits are stronger than
> Your gates against my force.
>
>   Another word, Menenius,
> I will not hear thee speak.

A brief epilogue to this scene is poignantly diverting. Marcius betrays what it has cost him to dismiss his old friend; he armours himself in his pride and calls on Aufidius to witness this crowning proof of his loyalty; the sentries mock Menenius, but his spirit is unbroken and he shares with Marcius their reluctant admiration:

> MARCIUS: This man, Aufidius,
> Was my beloved in Rome: yet thou behold'st!
> AUFIDIUS: You keep a constant temper.
>   (*Exeunt* CORIOLANUS *and* AUFIDIUS.)
> FIRST GUARD: Now, sir, is your name Menenius?

SECOND GUARD: 'Tis a spell, you see, of much power: you know the way home again.

FIRST GUARD: Do you hear how we are shent for keeping your greatness back?

SECOND GUARD: What cause, do you think, I have to swoon?

MENENIUS: I neither care for the world nor your general. . . . He that hath will to die by himself fears it not from another: let your general do his worst. For you, be that you are, long; and your misery increase with your age! I say to you, as I was said to, Away! (*Exit.*)

FIRST GUARD: A noble fellow, I warrant him.

SECOND GUARD: The worthy fellow is our general: he's the rock, the oak not to be wind-shaken.

Marcius pictures his friend as leaving the Volscian camp utterly prostrated:

> This last old man,
> Whom with a crack'd heart I have sent to Rome,
> Loved me above the measure of a father;
> Nay, godded me, indeed.

Menenius, however, though out of countenance, is by no means overthrown. There is no sign of a cracked heart. He receives his dismissal with dignity, more than holds his own with the sentries and, on his return to Rome, describes his reception by Marcius with a zest in which reprobation and admiration are divertingly mingled:

> The tartness of his face sours ripe grapes: when he walks, he moves like an engine, and the ground shrinks before his treading: he is able to pierce a corselet with his eye; talks like a knell, and his hum is a battery. He sits in his state, as a thing made for Alexander. What he bids be done is finished with his bidding. He wants nothing of a god but eternity and a heaven to throne in.

'There is no more mercy in him than milk in a male tiger', he concludes and, turning upon Sicinius, maintains to the last that the tribunes are to blame. Marcius he regards as a divine scourge upon the city for its ingratitude:

> No, in such a case the gods will not be good unto us. When we banished him, we respected not them; and, he returning to break our necks, they respect not us.

The contrast here presented between Marcius, outwardly insolent but inwardly shaken, and Menenius, outwardly discomposed but inwardly invincible, is a typical example of the covert dramatic irony in which Shakespeare excels all other dramatists.

The scene in which Marcius is persuaded to spare Rome by the arguments and entreaties of his mother, like so many of Shakespeare's most famous scenes, owes much of its effectiveness to the fact that it combines a superficial simplicity with psychological implications not immediately apparent to an inattentive spectator. A Roman matron pleads with her son for Rome. Mother, wife and child confront son, husband and father, who is 'tearing his country's bowels out'; they can pray neither for his victory, which means the destruction of Rome, nor his defeat, which entails his ruin. Volumnia argues well and her success might well seem to be the triumph of an advocate with a good brief competently handled. Is Marcius to destroy his noble reputation? Is his name to be forever abhorred as that of a man who laid in ashes the city of his birth? Is it honourable for a noble man always to remember his wrongs? Is it wise to persist in war when peace can be made with fair advantage to both sides? Is it human for a man to spurn all natural ties?

Such an appeal, with its effect on Marcius, suffices in itself to hold the full attention of an audience whose interest in the argument has been skilfully stimulated in the immediately preceding episodes. We have been led to expect that nothing can affect the attitude of Marcius short of a faultless presentation of an overwhelming case on the opposite side, or an appeal to the profoundest emotions of which he is capable. We are braced to witness a dramatic conflict between two characters equally wilful and resolute. Nor are we disappointed. The scene between Marcius and his mother constitutes an absorbing climax to the drama in which we are immersed, regarded simply as an argument on which depends the fate of Rome and of all the persons concerned.

But Shakespeare, in this justly admired scene, has done more than present an effective situation in which dramatic suspense is superficially exploited to the fullest possible extent. He has again performed that miracle, which is his own peculiar secret, of surprising us with an event which was in fact ordained. Shakespeare might well have said of all his tragedies: In my end is my beginning. He moves to a point determined from the outset by the inexorable play of character and circumstance, and yet contrives to make every step towards his conclusion seem like the adventure of a free spirit. He thus reproduces with fidelity the ultimate paradox of life itself, namely a constant opposition of free-will with necessity.

The scene between Volumnia and Marcius is a crowning example of this sublime double-dealing which lies at the root of Shakespeare's dramatic method. He stimulates our suspense as the crisis approaches, but he has prepared us long ago to accept the result. He has even provided us in advance with a preliminary study or model for this conclusive episode. Marcius, prior to his banishment, refused to temporise with the citizens and stubbornly rejected the arguments of his friends. He was finally whipped into submission by his mother. The extent to which Volumnia dominates his life and conduct has been emphasised from the rise of the curtain. The manner in which she overcomes his resistance in the earlier scene is as significant as the achievement itself. She argues with him and pleads with him in vain. Finally she simply *scolds* him into compliance with her wishes—an angry mother reducing her child to obedience by an exhibition of offended impatience, partly sincere and partly assumed. Marcius, in that earlier scene, unconvinced by her arguments, yielded at once to her displeasure.

This is precisely what happens again in their final encounter. Marcius, if you examine the scene attentively, does not succumb to his mother's arguments but, again, to the rough edge of her tongue. In both scenes she appeals in vain to his reason and good sense. Then, giving him up as hopeless, she makes as though she would leave him to his own devices, with the result that he immediately collapses. This is a fundamental trait in the character of our hero. He is essentially the splendid oaf who has never come to maturity. His vanity in the field, his insolence to persons outside his own particular set, his intolerance of anything outside his special code of honour are more characteristic of an adolescent than a grown man. It is this, in fact, that makes his conduct, which would be intolerable in a responsible adult, so far acceptable as to qualify him for the part of a tragic hero.

Marcius intimates in advance that, if he is to be shaken, it will not be by the force of reason or any social principle. He arms himself for the encounter, not against love of country or any sense of civic responsibility, but against the natural affection that binds him to his wife, mother and son:

> My wife comes foremost; then the honour'd mould
> Wherein this trunk was fram'd, and in her hand
> The grandchild to her blood. But out, affection!
> All bond and privilege of nature, break!
> Let it be virtuous to be obstinate.

Here it is necessary to consider for a moment a character so far wilfully neglected. The wife of Marcius plays a very secondary part in the tragedy. She has so far uttered just over twenty lines. To Marcius when he returns in triumph from the wars, she says just nothing at all and she is not present when Volumnia persuades her son into making a last attempt to placate the citizens. Her character and presence are nevertheless felt throughout the play and she lives immortal in that famous greeting of Marcius in the second Act:

> My gracious silence, hail!
> Wouldst thou have laugh'd had I come coffin'd home,
> That weep'st to see me triumph? Ah, my dear,
> Such eyes the widows in Corioli wear,
> And mothers that lack sons.

Was there ever presented a true marriage of opposites in so brief a compass? Marcius, at sight of his gentle, self-effacing wife, is moved to the only phrase in all his many speeches where true feeling prompts that sheer felicity of utterance which springs from the heart. Virgilia at that instant takes her place beside Cordelia with her 'Nothing, my lord.' She lives in a lovely seclusion, with thoughts too deep to be readily expressed and feelings at the same time too delicate and too assured to be relieved by any first word that springs to the lips. In the presence of this gracious silence the voluble greetings of Volumnia sound froward and fulsome. But note how Marcius, having revealed in two words how dear to him is the serene self-effacement of Virgilia, rallies her with a clumsy gaiety which shows how deep is the difference between them. Who but Marcius at such a moment would remind Virgilia, who hated bloodshed, of the husbands and sons he had slaughtered at Corioli? It is oddly touching —this unconsciously comical approach towards a woman tenderly loved and sensitively appreciated for the very qualities which he so unwittingly offends.

That Virgilia loves Marcius is emphasised in the short domestic interlude early in the play which accounts for sixteen of her twenty odd lines. She trembles for his safety and will stay indoors till his return. But a dove will peck the raven when her beloved is hurt or threatened. Shakespeare, in one of those carelessly subtle touches of character which so often puzzle his commentators, makes this gentle creature, who shrinks from Volumnia's perpetual gossip of broken heads and bloody noses, turn so fiercely on Sicinius when her husband is banished that more than one editor has inferred a mistake in the text and transferred the line to her mother-in-law.

How dearly Marcius loves Virgilia, and how passionate the bond between them, is not fully exposed till the scene is reached in which she comes with Volumnia to plead with him for Rome. She takes no part in the argument. Her presence is argument enough—'*those doves' eyes which can make gods forsworn.*' Marcius is shaken to the soul at the mere sight of her:

> I melt, and am not
> Of stronger earth than others.

> Best of my flesh,
> Forgive my tyranny; but do not say
> For that, 'Forgive our Romans.' O, a kiss
> Long as my exile, sweet as my revenge!
> Now, by the jealous queen of heaven, that kiss
> I carried from thee, dear; and my true lip
> Hath virgin'd it e'er since.

But it is Volumnia who carries the full weight of the scene. To behold her kneeling at his feet outrages his every instinct:

> My mother bows,
> As if Olympus to a molehill should
> In supplication nod:

> You gods! I prate,[1]
> And the most noble mother of the world
> Leave unsaluted.
>
> What is this?
> Your knees to me? to your corrected son?
> Then let the pebbles on the hungry beach
> Fillip the stars.

The matriarch is stressed in every line. 'Thou art my warrior, I holp to frame thee,' Volumnia reminds him. 'I kneel before thee and *unproperly* show duty.' She presents Valeria, a noble lady, loved and esteemed by Marcius. Here, too, is his boy, with an 'aspect of intercession which great Nature cries, "Deny not" ':

> VOLUMNIA: This is a poor epitome of yours,
> Which by the interpretation of full time
> May show like all yourself.
> MARCIUS: The god of soldiers,
> With the consent of supreme Jove, inform
> Thy thoughts with nobleness; that thou mayst prove
> To shame invulnerable, and stick i' the wars
> Like a great sea-mark, standing every flaw,
> And saving those that eye thee!
> VOLUMNIA: Your knee, sirrah.
> MARCIUS: That's my brave boy!
> VOLUMNIA: Even he, your wife, this lady, and myself,
> Are suitors to you.

The tableau is set for the argument. Marcius has steeled himself in advance:

> I'll never
> Be such a gosling to obey instinct, but stand
> As if a man were author of himself
> And knew no other kin;—

and, on the top of this, he warns his mother that he is not to be moved with anything she may have to say:

---

[1] He is 'prating' of his love for Virgilia. The word is characteristic. It betrays an unconscious contempt of the one touch in his life of a beauty that disarms his pride.

> Do not bid me
> Dismiss my soldiers, or capitulate
> Again with Rome's mechanics; tell me not
> Wherein I seem unnatural: desire not
> To allay my rages and revenges with
> Your colder reasons.

But Volumnia is not to be put off:

> Yet we will ask;
> That, if you fail in our request, the blame
> May hang upon your hardness.

Volumnia's 'colder reasons' are well-urged, but the heart of the contention lies elsewhere. This is not, in essentials, a conflict of class prejudice with civic patriotism, though Volumnia is free enough with references to her country. It is a conflict of personal pride with a sense of what is due from Marcius to 'great Nature'. Driven by pride, he has defied both instinct and reason. To reason he remains deaf to the end, but instinct carries the day:

> VOLUMNIA: Thou shalt no sooner
> March to assault thy country than to tread—
> Trust to't, thou shalt not—on thy mother's womb,
> That brought thee to this world.
> VIRGILIA: Ay, and mine,
> That brought you forth this boy, to keep your name
> Living to time.
>
> VOLUMNIA: There's no man in the world
> More bound to's mother; yet here he lets me prate
> Like one i' the stocks. Thou hast never in thy life
> Show'd thy dear mother any courtesy,
> When she, poor hen! fond of no second brood,
> Has cluck'd thee to the wars and safely home,
> Loaden with honour.

Marcius rises in a vain effort to escape:

> Not of a woman's tenderness to be,
> Requires nor child nor woman's face to see.
> I have sat too long.

His will breaks at last, but only when Volumnia, having reasoned with him in vain, accuses him of unfilial neglect and loses her temper, as we imagine must have frequently happened in her encounters with Marcius in childhood. 'Come, let us go,' she exclaims:

> This fellow had a Volscian to his mother.
>
> I am hush'd until our city be afire,
> And then I'll speak a little.

It is her last word, and it suffices. *After holding her by the hand, silent*— Shakespeare's stage directions are rare and this one is tremendous— he speaks:

> O mother, mother!
> What have you done? Behold! the heavens do ope,
> The gods look down, and this unnatural scene
> They laugh at. O my mother, mother! O!
> You have won a happy victory to Rome;
> But, for your son, believe it, O! believe it,
> Most dangerously you have with him prevail'd,
> If not most mortal to him.

Proud Marcius in submission assumes the full stature of a tragic hero. Shakespeare, having anatomised his pride and folly with superb detachment, allows him, in the act that determines his fall, a glory without stint. He is for the instant transfigured by his act of mercy. There is great dignity in his address to Aufidius at the end of the scene:

> MARCIUS: Now, good Aufidius,
>   Were you in my stead, would you have heard
>   A mother less? or granted less, Aufidius?
> AUFIDIUS: I was moved withal.
> MARCIUS: I dare be sworn you were:
>   And, sir, it is no little thing to make
>   Mine eyes to sweat compassion. But, good sir,
>   What peace you'll make, advise me: for my part,
>   I'll not to Rome, I'll back with you; and pray you,
>   Stand to me in my cause.

Hitherto he has carried his business with a high hand in despite alike of his friends and enemies. But now he seeks advice; he prays that he may not stand alone. Yet he knows—during this brief instant when his pride is in abeyance—that, by the very act in which he has achieved nobility, he is doomed. His mother, in prevailing, has been 'most mortal to him'. There can be no place for him henceforth, either in Antium or Rome.

What Marcius feels instinctively the spectator knows from the evidence. Shakespeare, to heighten the effect of his hero's capitulation, has already indicated that Aufidius is waiting for just this opportunity to compass the ruin of his confederate. Aufidius, uncontrollably gratified that his enemy should have come defenceless to his hearth, gave to Marcius one half of his commission. Scarcely was the alliance sealed, however, when we find the Volscian complaining to his lieutenant that Marcius, whether as friend or foe, is still preeminent:

LIEUTENANT: I do not know what witchcraft's in him, but
Your soldiers use him as the grace 'fore meat,
Their talk at table, and their thanks at end;
And you are darken'd in this action, sir,
Even by your own.
AUFIDIUS: I cannot help it now,
Unless, by using means, I lame the foot
Of our design. He bears himself more proudlier,
Even to my person, than I thought he would
When first I did embrace him; yet his nature
In that's no changeling; and I must excuse
What cannot be amended.

Aufidius goes on to prophesy that, when it comes to a final reckoning, Marcius will be ruined by those very qualities in which he towers above his fellows. He cannot 'carry his honours even'; he has the pride which ever taints the happy man, and a defect of judgment which makes it impossible for him to dispose wisely of his chances; he cannot move 'from the casque to the cushion', but must forever be 'commanding peace' with the 'same austerity and garb as he controlled the war.' It is a shrewd and bitter analysis which, nevertheless, grudgingly concludes: 'He has a merit to choke it in the utterance.'

We are aware, then, of Aufidius intently watching the scene of intercession and waiting to take advantage of any compassion which

Marcius may show to Rome. His aside, as the scene closes, points to a catastrophe now inevitable:

> I am glad thou hast set thy mercy and thy honour
> At difference in thee: out of that I'll work
> Myself a former fortune.

The scene in which Marcius is goaded to his death by Aufidius reproduces in a different key the scene in which he was formerly goaded by Sicinius into exile. The echoes are deliberate. Aufidius even uses the same word as the tribune to precipitate in Marcius the loss of self-control which destroys him. Marcius has had his supreme moment. Shakespeare now brings him ruthlessly back to normal. He is again the man who cannot refrain from taking the lead—even in the house of a stranger. Aufidius, who could not endure a rival, has had to tolerate a master:

> He came unto my hearth;
> Presented to my knife his throat: I took him;
> Made him joint-servant with me; gave him way
> In all his own desires; nay, let him choose
> Out of my files, his projects to accomplish,
> My best and freshest men; serv'd his designments
> In mine own person; holp to reap the fame
> Which he did end all his; and took some pride
> To do myself this wrong: till, at the last,
> I seem'd his follower, not partner.

But let Marcius speak for himself, facing the senators and commoners of Antium:

> You are to know
> That prosperously I have attempted and
> With bloody passage led your wars even to
> The gates of Rome. Our spoils we have brought home
> Do more than counterpoise a full third part
> The charges of the action. We have made peace
> With no less honour to the Antiates,
> Than shame to the Romans; and we here deliver,
> Subscribed by the consuls and patricians,
> Together with the seal o' the senate, what
> We have compounded on.

All that he claims is true, but his cool assumption of authority to make war or peace as the humour seizes him is less staggering than the way in which he takes it for granted that the lords of Antium must needs approve his action.

Marcius, rising above his pride at the supreme moment of the tragedy, had realised that his decision to spare Rome might have mortal consequences. Shakespeare allowed him that flash of insight. But Marcius was not the man to be permanently changed by experience. He shows, in this final scene, his familiar incapacity to measure or even to consider the effect of his conduct on other men and in this he runs true to type. The contrast between his behaviour in Antium and the mood in which he yielded to his mother is one of those inconsistencies which throw into high relief the fundamental coherence and veracity of Shakespeare's portrayal of human character.

Aufidius knows his man. For this proud, hot-tempered Roman one word will suffice and, as we have noted, it is the same word which was used by Sicinius on a previous occasion. Marcius hands his treaty to the senators:

> AUFIDIUS: Read it not, noble lords;
> But tell the *traitor*, in the high'st degree
> He hath abus'd your powers.
> MARCIUS: Traitor! how now?
> AUFIDIUS: Ay, traitor, Marcius!

Aufidius then states the case:

> You lords and heads o' the state, perfidiously
> He has betray'd your business, and given up,
> For certain drops of salt, your city Rome,
> I say 'your city', to his wife and mother;
> Breaking his oath and resolution like
> A twist of rotten silk, never admitting
> Counsel o' the war, but at his nurse's tears
> He whin'd and roared away your victory,
> That pages blush'd at him, and men of heart
> Look'd wondering each at other.
> MARCIUS: Hear'st thou, Mars?
> AUFIDIUS: Name not the god, thou boy of tears!

Marcius is now his old rampaging self:

> Cut me to pieces, Volsces; men and lads,
> Stain all your edges on me. Boy! false hound!
> If you have writ your annals true, 'tis there,
> That, like an eagle in a dove-cote, I
> Flutter'd your Volscians in Corioli:
> Alone I did it. Boy!
>
> O, that I had him,
> With six Aufidiuses, or more, his tribe,
> To use my lawful sword!

There is little beauty, save that of an inexorable process, in the death of this tragic hero. Not for him the flights of angels that sing Hamlet to his rest; the royal simplicity of 'pray you, undo this button' that attends the passing of Lear; the proud verse in which Othello declaims his heartbreaking epitaph; the silver tongue that mourned for Antony and found nothing left remarkable beneath the visiting moon; not even the poor garland with which Titinius crowned dead Cassius or the sedate tribute paid to Brutus by his enemy. Marcius has but a few perfunctory words from the man who struck him down and the cold judgment of Second Lord:

> His own impatience
> Takes from Aufidius a great part of blame.
> Let's make the best of it.

Yet how appropriate and how inevitable is the note on which Shakespeare closes his play. For one brief moment it rose to the tragic level. Marcius, forgoing the revenge to which his pride and self-will had incited him, was seen for an instant above himself. We beheld in that huge creature the fulfilment of a destiny which reached its climax when the proud man whom no social consciousness could tame and no patriotic principle confine, who had sworn to plough and harrow Italy, who would 'never be such a gosling to obey instinct', but would stand 'as if a man were author of himself and knew no other kin', capitulated to great Nature and suffered his mother most dangerously to prevail. What, after that, could happen but a blundering of our simple giant to destruction? There could be no exquisite poetry or solemn music to put this fractious and stubborn child to sleep. He died calling for six Aufidiuses on which to use his lawful sword. But one Aufidius was enough to compass his death and to cry as childishly as his victim: 'Yet he shall have a noble memory.'

The reticence of that stark conclusion is in keeping with the mood sustained throughout the tragedy. There is not in this great play a line of great poetry. There is consummate felicity of phrase and tireless nobility of utterance, thought and feeling lightly fitted or flowing as freely as the hearts and minds of the speakers. There is often a touch of the hyperbolical, but the cause is not in the verse but in the emotion behind it. The lines, where they are fulsome or exaggerated, betray an inordinate passion or a disordered intelligence. To accuse them of turgidity is like reproving for its swell of canvas a great ship carrying full sail before the wind.

We have been less concerned with the quality of 'Coriolanus' as a masterpiece of poetic tragedy than with its political significance. A great deal has been written concerning its pride of place among the greater plays of Shakespeare. Critics have often wondered why a play so often proclaimed to be one of the noblest of his achievements has never been really popular with the English public. Many reasons could and have been given. There is perhaps an aesthetic reason: the English love pictures but have no taste or discrimination in statues, and 'Coriolanus' has all the qualities of the finest statuary. It has the boldness and simplicity of a classic monument. It commands respect for its weight and substance, for the impression it gives of being determined in its form by the material of which it is wrought, for an ascetism which rejects all superfluous ornament. It is a composition without light or shade. It stands, as it were, in the public square. We can walk all round it, admire its proportions, acknowledge the mastery of the hand that gave it shape, see it completely for what it is without any tremulous reaching out of the spirit to something that lies beyond. It is, in a word, a work of art which is affirmative, self-explicit, harmonious and entirely consistent. It is the only English tragedy that provokes a comparison with Corneille and, for that reason, it is the most popular of Shakespeare's plays in France as it is the least popular in England. It is for the same reason a remarkable and unique achievement—a play in which Shakespeare, with the infallible response of a great artist to his material, abstained from using gifts in which he was richer than all his tribe, but which were inappropriate to his design. We feel at times as though he had said: 'I will write this Roman play in the Roman fashion; there shall be no music, no colour, no speculation, no imagery, no by-paths, no prolongations from sound into silence, no whisper of anything beyond, not a tint or a sigh or a touch of the magic that poets use. This play of mine shall march to its conclusion like the Roman legions on a broad highway.'

The result is a play that has been finely praised, but little loved. Swinburne's ecstatic judgment: 'A loftier or more perfect piece of work was never done in all the world than this tragedy of Coriolanus,' rings out like a trumpet above an orchestra of muted strings. Of the modern critics Hudson, Bradley and Middleton Murry are the most acutely sensitive to its appeal as a tragic masterpiece. For Hudson it represents Shakespeare's 'highest maturity of thought and power.' Bradley places it, a little reluctantly, beside 'Lear', 'Macbeth' and 'Othello'. Middleton Murry celebrates its 'economy, its swiftness, its solidity, its astonishing clarity and poignancy of language' and describes it as a 'magnificent example of creative control'. Most commentators, however, have tended to judge the play for its political rather than its aesthetic significance. 'It illustrates', says Coleridge, 'the wonderfully philosophic impartiality of Shakespeare's politics.' Hazlitt writes: 'Anyone who studies it may save himself the trouble of reading Burke's 'Reflections' or Paine's 'Rights of Man' or the debates in both Houses of Parliament since the French Revolution or our own. The arguments for and against aristocracy or democracy, on the privileges of the few and the claims of the many, on liberty and slavery, power and the abuse of it, peace and war, are very ably handled, with the spirit of a poet and the acuteness of a philosopher.'

We are here confronted with the paradox which lies in wait for all who study with attention the political plays of Shakespeare. 'Coriolanus', as we have seen, is more exclusively concerned with politics than any other play he ever wrote. The politics are nevertheless in the last analysis incidental. Shakespeare is intent on persons, not on public affairs. His interest, when he writes of Coriolanus, as when he writes of Brutus or Henry or Richard, is in a human character who happens also to be a politician. There are more politics to be found in his plays than in those of any other dramatic writer. We invariably find, however, that his theme, as it takes shape and moves to a climax, is not essentially a political problem but the adventure of a human spirit. We discover, in fact, that Shakespeare, who wrote more genuinely political plays than any other dramatist before or since, is only indirectly concerned with the political principles and ideas in which they abound. Hazlitt refers to the arguments in 'Coriolanus' for and against aristocracy and democracy. There are no such arguments. There are only aristocrats and democrats. He refers to power and the abuse of it. There is no discussion of this problem. There is only a proud man who assumes the right to despise persons of a lesser breed. And, when the climax of the play is reached, we find that Shakespeare is presenting a conflict, not between private inclination and public duty, not between the merits of peace and war, not between party-feeling and patriotism, not between the privileges of the few and the claims of the many—not in fact between any of the political opposites mentioned by Hazlitt—but between the stubborn self-regarding pride of Caius Marcius Coriolanus and the promptings of great Nature which make it impossible for him to disregard a mother's intercession. If, as Hazlitt suggests, we were to read 'Coriolanus' as a substitute for Burke's 'Reflections' or Paine's 'Rights of Man' we should expect the climax of the play to be a grand confrontation of the aristocratic and popular parties; we should look for a statement of the principles at issue on both sides and a dramatic conflict between qualified representatives of those principles who knew what they were fighting for and loved what they knew. But Shakespeare gives us instead Menenius and First Citizen; a fable of the belly and its members from an old gentleman more conversable with the buttock of the night than with the forehead of the morning; some typical knavery on the part of a group of senators and a brace of tribunes; a few simple, good-natured men in the street who are disconcerted by a government which tries to obtain their support by equivocation and moved to a not unreasonable indignation against it by the leaders of the opposition. Here are politics but they appear

L

as men walking. 'Coriolanus' is not the dramatisation of a political thesis. It is not a play in which the supreme conflict is one of political principle.

Still less is it a play in which Shakespeare took sides in a political controversy. The warning of Coleridge, who found in it a supreme example of the impartiality of Shakespeare's politics, deserves more attention than it has received. Too many critics have preferred to follow Hazlitt who wrote: 'Shakespeare himself seems to have had a leaning to the arbitrary side of the question, perhaps from some feeling of contempt for his own origin, and to have spared no occasion of baiting the rabble.'

The significance of 'Coriolanus' as a play in which Shakespeare is supposed to have revealed a political bias in favour of aristocracy and to have expressed contempt for the people raises the whole question of his attitude to politics in general and to the politics of his own generation in particular. The time has now come to deal more directly with this question, adducing such further evidence as may be necessary to form a conclusion.

CONCLUSION

SHAKESPEARE was born a citizen of the New Monarchy. He belonged to a generation of Englishmen who lived contentedly under the jurisdiction of Star Chamber and the Queen's commissioners. The agents of the Privy Council were ubiquitous and their authority unquestioned. Her Majesty's Government determined at discretion with whom her subjects were in a state of war or peace, what they should read or hear, how they should worship God, how and with whom they should trade. The man who in a Yorkshire tavern or from a pulpit in Devon uttered lewd words—which was the Privy Council's official description of any criticism of the established order —did so at his own risk and peril. Nothing escaped the Queen's Majesty, whose writ ran to good purpose in every hamlet and shire. A subject accepted his place; his only alternative was to be a master-less man or a vagabond. Each was content to abide by Her Majesty's pleasure, to the loss of his goods, dignities, liberties or even his head. And if you should be condemned to a traitor's death, you thanked God and blessed the sovereign.

We should expect a dramatic author of plays, with no consuming interest in public life, to reflect the fundamental social convictions of his generation. Chief among these convictions was a strong belief that anything was better than infirmity in the Government or disorder in the community. Nearly a century had passed since England had emerged from the Anarchy of the Roses, but men still lived in dread of civil strife and in a passionate determination to maintain and in-crease the unity of the realm. This state of mind inevitably found expression in the theatre at a period when actors might with justice claim to be brief and abstract chronicles of the time. When Shake-speare began to write his political plays, the citizens of London were already applauding dramatic histories which depicted the awful con-sequences of the 'Contention of the Two Famous Houses of York and Lancaster', or were following with anxious solicitude the devious progress of their forebears through the 'Troublesome Raigne of John, King of England'. They savoured upon the stage the calamities from which by God's grace and the Tudor system of government they had successfully emerged, and nourished a growing pride in themselves as a united people.

Shakespeare, as the only 'Johanes factotum or shakescene' of his company, found himself committed to providing it with this form of popular entertainment along with the rest. Political plays were in demand and their subjects already determined. There was no escaping Richard of Bordeaux, in whose person the sanctity of kings had found its traditional martyr, or Richard of Gloucester, in whose legend of the wicked uncle, closing a chapter in English history blotted with faction and stained with the tragical ends of princes, was good pleasure and sound policy to believe. There was no evading the dark theme of states divided, which Shakespeare's Bolingbroke declared to have been the whole argument of his troubled reign; which Mark Antony announced over the dead body of Caesar; which recurs in prophecy or fulfilment in so many famous scenes and speeches of the Elizabethan stage. Still less was it possible to ignore the fair sequel of Tudor supremacy. When Shakespeare permitted his one wise Greek to speak in 'Troilus and Cressida', he had no choice but to allow him the wisdom of his age. Ulysses, praising the unity and married calm of states, speaks the only language which would have been recognised as that of a statesman in the sixteenth century:

> O! when degree is shaked,
> Which is the ladder to all high designs,
> The enterprise is sick. How could communities,
> Degrees in schools and brotherhoods in cities,
> Peaceful commerce from dividable shores,
> The primogenitive and due of birth,
> Prerogative of age, crowns, sceptres, laurels,
> But by degree, stand in authentic place?
> Take but degree away, untune that string,
> And, hark, what discord follows!
>
> Then everything includes itself in power,
> Power into will, will into appetite;
> And appetite, an universal wolf,
> So doubly seconded with will and power,
> Must make perforce an universal prey,
> And last eat up himself.

> The providence that's in a watchful state
> Knows almost every grain of Plutus' gold,
> Finds bottom in the uncomprehensive deeps,
> Keeps place with thought, and almost, like the gods,
> Does thoughts unveil in their dumb cradles.
> There is a mystery—with whom relation
> Durst never meddle—in the soul of state,
> Which hath an operation more divine
> Than breath or pen can give expressure to.

These are sentiments appropriate to an Elizabethan councillor. Shakespeare, presenting a political sage, naturally attributes to him opinions in conformity with the accepted ideology of his time. It does not necessarily follow that Shakespeare was himself a political disciple, still less a political partisan. As a dramatist he was interested in politics only in so far as they afforded him an opportunity of identifying himself with human characters undergoing the tugs and stresses of public life, moved by ambition, challenging or recoiling from their responsibilities, driven by social prejudice or passion, reaching for power or wry from its exercise. There is no reason to suppose that he felt either more or less interest in what passes for politics in the narrow sense than in any other form of human activity. Certainly there is no conclusive evidence in his plays of any political bias. Indeed, his presentation of public persons and incidents has often a kind of innocence which can with difficulty, or not at all, be distinguished from deliberate irony.

Famous critics have nevertheless found in Shakespeare's political plays strong evidence that he had a hatred of the people, contempt for their ignorance and inconstancy, abhorrence of their brutality, no sympathy with their grievances; that he was, in fact, a 'very dog to the commonalty'. Hazlitt's observation on 'Coriolanus', 'Shakespeare himself seems to have had a leaning to the arbitrary side of the question,' has become a favourite text with commentators. But Hazlitt, who suspected that Shakespeare in 'Coriolanus' was baiting the plebeians, had no doubt whatever that he was very effectively baiting a patrician. No one trounces the haughty Roman more soundly than Hazlitt or holds the scales more evenly between right and left. 'Coriolanus', writes Hazlitt, 'complains of the fickleness of the people:

yet the instant he cannot gratify his pride and obstinacy at their expense, he turns his arms against his country. . . . He rates the people as if he were a god to punish and not a man of their infirmity. He scoffs at one of their tribunes for maintaining their rights and franchises: "Mark you his absolute *shall?*" not marking his own absolute *will* to take everything from them, his impatience of the slightest opposition to his own pretensions being in proportion to their arrogance and absurdity.' Hazlitt's total reaction to the play is, in fact, not essentially different from that of Coleridge who found in 'Coriolanus' an illustration of the 'wonderfully philosophic impartiality of Shakespeare's politics.'

The assumption that Shakespeare was by conviction and temperament 'o' the right-hand file' reached a climax in Georg Brandes. Brandes discovers Shakespeare's contempt of the people in the unlikeliest places—even in the sonnets. But let him, in a paragraph that sums up the whole business, speak for himself. He writes of 'Coriolanus':

'This much, at any rate, can be declared with absolute certainty, that the anti-democratic spirit and passion of the play sprang from no momentary political situation, but from Shakespeare's heart of hearts. . . . A detestation of the mob, a positive hatred of the mass as mass, can be traced in the faltering efforts of his early youth. We may see its workings in what is undoubtedly Shakespeare's description of Jack Cade's rebellion in the Second Part of 'Henry VI' and we divine it again in the conspicuous absence of any allusion to Magna Carta in 'King John'.'

The handling by Shakespeare of the mass as mass, in the two plays where it is of capital importance, has been attentively studied in these pages. In 'Julius Caesar' we saw how an assembly of citizens, individually decent, shrewd and without rancour, was transformed into a collectively brutal and senseless monster by an unscrupulous orator. The phenomenon described by modern experts as collective psychology was there shown in dramatic action. But hatred of the beast was no more evident in that scene than hatred of Antony who made the beast. That Shakespeare was inspired with an anti-democratic passion because he exhibited a mob behaving like a mob is a non-sequitur. Even though you dislike a mob, you do not necessarily dislike the people who have been turned into a mob by a bad man. To dislike the bad man would be more to the purpose. Shakespeare's treatment of the crowd that tore to pieces Cinna, the poet, for his bad verses does not, in fact, suggest hatred. It suggests, on the contrary, an amused tolerance, such as we feel for a creature which has ceased to be morally accountable. The scene is grotesque. There is something in it of the joviality which Coleridge discovered to be Shakespeare's prevailing mood in dealing with the mass as mass. 'You will observe', says Coleridge—and many excellent critics would have done well to observe it, 'the good nature with which Shakespeare seems always to make sport with the passions and follies of a mob, as with an irrational animal. He is never angry with it, but hugely content with holding up its absurdities to its face; and sometimes you may trace a tone of affectionate superiority; something like that in which a father speaks to his child.'

In 'Coriolanus' the citizens of Rome are with difficulty goaded into becoming a mob by the provocation of their leaders and the insufferable behaviour of Marcius himself. Nor does their behaviour, even as a mob, compare at all unfavourably with that of the senatorial party. There is no evidence in this play that Shakespeare hated the people unless we fall into the strange assumption that Caius Marcius Coriolanus speaks for the author. Marcius certainly hated the people and that was why he came to a bad end. To quote the speeches in which he expresses an immeasurable contempt for plebeians—and thereby reveals a conspicuous lack of judgment and humanity—as though they sprang from Shakespeare's heart of hearts is almost to deny that Shakespeare had the capacity to be a dramatist. There is, it is true, a gusto in those speeches which, to a critic who leans to the arbitrary side, is irresistibly pleasing. But there is an equal gusto in Iago's scorn of Othello's simplicity and in Richard of Gloucester's contempt of Lady Anne. Yet no one has ever sought to identify Shakespeare with Iago or with Richard.

The contention that Shakespeare hated the common people has found much comfort and support in the fact that he never loses an opportunity of reminding us that they smell. Poor suitors have strong breaths. The many are not only mutable but rank-scented. The citizens on the Capitol uttered such a deal of stinking breath that it almost choked Caesar. The laws that are to come from the mouth of Jack Cade will be 'stinking law, for his breath stinks with eating toasted cheese.' Brutus, the tribune, heard Marcius declare that he would never show his wounds to the people or 'beg their stinking breaths.' Marcius hated their breath as 'reek of the rotten fens'. The citizens who banished him threw up their 'stinking greasy caps.'

This would seem to prove not that Shakespeare hated the people, but that he had a sensitive nose. It was a nose, moreover, that was not offended only by odours of low degree. The offence of Claudius, King of Denmark, was rank; it smelled to heaven. Not all the perfumes of Arabia could wash the smell of blood from the patrician hand of Lady Macbeth. The hand of Lear smelled of mortality and he called for an ounce of civet to sweeten an imagination that reeked with the proud iniquities of man. Hamlet's last gesture over the skull of poor Yorick was to stop his nose. Shakespeare's world was as full of smells, good and bad, as Prospero's island was full of noises.

The people smell worse in 'Coriolanus' than anywhere else and it is not therefore surprising that this play has been most often called in evidence for Shakespeare's dislike of the masses. It should therefore be noted that, in writing 'Coriolanus', he went out of his way to exonerate the citizens of Rome from the worst charges brought against them by the historian from whom he adapted his material. Shakespeare deliberately amended Plutarch[1] in two important particulars, on both occasions in favour of the people and to the detriment of the right-hand file. One of his amendments, as we noted in reading the play, was to attribute to Marcius the terrible design of destroying Rome, whereas in Plutarch his plan was more in the nature of a project to secure success for the aristocratic Roman party with the help of the corresponding party in Antium. The second emendation is even more significant. The Roman citizens in Plutarch are not flouted by Marcius when he stands for the consulship. Their behaviour, as reported by the historian, has none of the somewhat bewildered generosity in the face of menace and strikingly

[1] For a detailed exposition of Shakespeare's handling of the Roman citizens in 'Coriolanus' and of his deviations from Plutarch in their favour see the excellent study by R. W. Chambers entitled 'Shakespeare's Hand in the Play of Sir Thomas More' (Cambridge, 1923).

magnanimous forbearance in the face of insult on which Shakespeare so vividly insists. Shakespeare, who follows Plutarch with
remarkable fidelity in all other respects, here departs from his
authority in order to put the conduct of the citizens in a better light.
Their behaviour in the play is more reasonable than in Plutarch,
more comprehensible, more calculated to secure the sympathy of the
spectator, while the behaviour of Marcius is correspondingly less
reasonable, less comprehensible and less likely to obtain indulgence.
Whoever is bent on identifying Shakespeare with his characters, and
thereby detecting his political inclinations, would be driven to conclude, upon a careful comparison of his play with its historical
source, that he had a bias, not towards authority, but towards the
popular principle. No such bias need, however, be presumed.
Shakespeare deliberately weighted the scales against Marcius and in
favour of the people because his dramatic intention made it essential
for him to do so. He was writing the tragedy of a man whose contempt for the people was beyond all reason, whose pride offended
natural justice and fair dealing. The audience must accordingly be
made to understand that the speeches in which Marcius condemns
the people are intended to reveal the senseless arrogance of the
speaker, and not to be read as statements of political truth. Shakespeare, in his deviations from Plutarch, tried to make this plain to the
simplest spectator. He did not succeed with some of his commentators, whose own bias in favour of authority has tempted them to
receive those speeches as Shakespeare's political testament.

Mention has been made of Jack Cade and his rebellion. Cade is
often quoted in support of the contention that Shakespeare disliked
the people. Let us therefore make his closer acquaintance.

If Shakespeare passionately detested the mob—if he were inspired
by an anti-democratic passion that sprang from his heart of hearts—
here was his chance. Political moralists 'o' the right-hand file' could
find no better object of their spleen. Cade is a self-confessed impostor. He is vain, ignorant and cruel. His programme is to kill all
the lawyers, pull down the schools, open the prisons, abolish property and decapitate peers of the realm. Then, too, he is absurdly inconsistent. He is in rebellion against arbitrary government yet *his*
'mouth shall be the Parliament of England'. He is 'inspired with the

spirit of putting down kings and princes', but would nevertheless himself be king.

Now the odd thing is that Shakespeare, having brought upon the stage so suitable a figure on which to visit his alleged anti-democratic passion, presents him with no ill-feeling whatsoever. He obviously prefers Cade's company to that of my lord Clifford or the Duke of York. He gives him an engagingly frank impudence in imposture, real courage, a hearty dislike of things unpopular with men of goodwill and a patriotism which does not easily accept a bad bargain for his country. He 'vows reformation' and his programme compares very well with most of the platforms erected by reputable political parties of the left, before and since. There shall be in England seven halfpenny loaves sold for a penny: the three-hooped pot shall have seven hoops. Or, better still, there shall be no money; the realm shall be in common; all shall be apparelled in one livery that they may all agree like brothers. He would kill all the lawyers; but when have lawyers ever been popular? 'Is not this a lamentable thing, that of the skin of an innocent lamb should be made parchment' and that 'that parchment, being scribbled o'er, should undo a man?' He sends Lord Say to the block, but better men have been hanged on lighter charges. Had not this unfortunate nobleman 'given up Normandy unto Monsieur Basimecu, the dauphin of France.' To conclude all, Cade thinks it intolerable that my lord's horse 'should wear a cloak, when honester men than he go in their hose and doublets.'

All this is put with an agreeable simplicity, from which it is impossible to extort a trace of malice in the author. But we need not leave it at that. For Shakespeare has gone out of his way to give this coarse man of the people a touch of humanity which he not unseldom denies to men of better blood. Lord Say pleads eloquently for his life and Cade is moved to compassion:

(*Aside.*) I feel remorse in myself with his words; but I'll bridle it: he shall die, an it be but for pleading so well for his life. Away with him! he has a familiar under his tongue; he speaks not o' God's name. Go, take him away.

It is strange that those who find in Cade's barbarity an indication of Shakespeare's horror of the mob should neglect to find in the barbarity of Queen Margaret or of my lords Clifford and York an indication of his horror of the nobility. Admittedly Cade, with his severed heads, is a ruffian: 'Let them kiss one another, for they loved well when they were well alive. Now part them again, lest they consult about the giving up of some more towns in France.' But was Queen Margaret less a ruffian, when she mocked York with a paper crown, or the sons of York, when they stabbed Prince Edward at Tewkesbury? Some will prefer the urchin ferocity of Cade to the solemn rancour of his better-born contemporaries.

Shakespeare, moreover, has given to Cade a spice of the quality which he reserves for all the more likeable of his public persons. Cade is an impostor, but not a humbug. He has a keen eye for the absurdities of his enterprise. 'They are all in order and march towards us,' reports Dick Butcher. 'But then are we in order when we are most out of order,' declares Cade of his own rapscallions.

It should be noted, too, by those who charge Shakespeare in this episode with being a very dog to the commonalty, that there is one person in the play who has something to say on behalf of Cade and his rabble, none other than the royal saint, Henry of Winchester. Henry would come to terms with these ruffians:

> For God forbid so many simple souls
> Should perish by the sword! And I myself,
> Rather than bloody war shall cut them short,
> Will parley with Jack Cade, their general;

and when news is brought that they have slain two noble lords, Henry exclaims: 'O graceless men! they know not what they do.'

This episode of Cade's rebellion, cited as a supreme example of Shakespeare's anti-democratic spirit, turns out on examination to be an interlude graced with touches of humanity and humour for which we shall look in vain on the aristocratic fields of Towton or Tewkesbury. It leaves us with the impression that stupidity and ruthlessness in a mob are less repulsive than stupidity and ruthlessness in high places.

There remains the charge that Shakespeare wrote a play about King John and neglected to mention Magna Carta.

A brief examination of the origin, intention and quality of Shakespeare's play entitled 'The Life and Death of King John' will confirm certain conclusions already suggested. We have seen how Shakespeare, in 'Richard II', took for his subject a political theme of passionate interest to his contemporaries. We have noted that, for attending a performance of this play in circumstances which underlined its political implications, certain gentlemen laid themselves open to a charge of high treason. But no one thought of blaming the author—not even Queen Elizabeth, though she realised that in the minds of some of her subjects she was identified with the principal character.[1] Shakespeare in 1601 eluded the critics who thought to convict him of writing tendentiously and he has eluded them ever since. He took a subject bristling with political ideas of perilous consequence and he handled them with the fearless brilliance of an artist too fervently intent on his imaginative purpose to bother about any political implications which might be read into his play by interested parties. He escaped calumny, not by careful steering through the quicksands, but by making straight for the open sea. His interest was in Richard of Bordeaux, who *happened* to be a king and who *happened* to be deposed. He presented the man and the situation for what it was worth, and he was able, in this instance, to merge in the person of his hero all the political, mystical and aesthetic elements of which it was historically composed. The political elements were, of course, an important factor and they could be plausibly invoked by partisans anxious to claim him as a champion of their own persuasion. But Queen Elizabeth, who exculpated Shakespeare, was right, and the followers of Essex, who inculpated him, were wrong. Shakespeare wrote for his contemporaries a political play on a burning question without incurring rebuke from Star Chamber. That should have sufficed to establish his indifference in matters of political doctrine or prejudice for all time.[2]

---

[1] See above, p. 118.

[2] Shakespeare towards the end of his career participated in the writing of another play even more intimately concerned with the political and religious controversies of his day than 'Richard II' or 'King John'. 'The Famous History of the Life of Henry VIII', however, though an examination of its political content might well reinforce the conclusions drawn from its predecessors, is too uncertain a text to provide any sure basis of argument. Those who are tempted to find in this play

'The Life and Death of King John' is in some ways an even more instructive testimony to Shakespeare's political innocence. In 'Richard II' Shakespeare succeeded in merging both the political and the psychological implications of his theme in the human tragedy of a king deposed. He thus produced a play remarkable for its unity of design and temper. In 'King John' he failed to concentrate his material upon a central figure. The political issues were diverse and refractory; they refused to cohere. The play is accordingly little more than a succession of episodes, some of them brilliantly executed. It is for this reason of special interest for those who try to segregate Shakespeare's politics from his art. Here, if anywhere, we might hope to catch the dramatist unawares. His political themes are not assimilated to one imaginative purpose and his politics, if he had any, not being lost in the general design, might be expected to obtrude.

King John is for Catholic writers an impious king who persecuted the Church and defied the Pope: for liberal writers he is a tyrannical king who oppressed the people and was compelled by his barons to sign Magna Carta; for patriotic writers he is a feeble king who placed his crown between the hands of a papal legate and laid his kingdom open to invasion by a French prince; for ethical writers he is a wicked king who murdered his nephew. For writers of the New Monarchy, however, he was a noble king who, like Moses, had brought his people out of Egypt and shown them the promised land, which three centuries later they were to inherit under Joshua, in the person of Henry VIII. For Shakespeare's contemporaries John was not a monarch who murderously usurped the crown and was brought to his knees by noble champions of the liberties of England. He was a monarch who first dared to challenge the jurisdiction of Rome. He had a 'princely heart', says Holinshed, and could not well abide the 'pride and pretended authority of the clergy'. His crimes—if they were not merely due to 'envious report' uttered by monkish chron-

evidence concerning Shakespeare's attitude to contemporary events will do well to remember those unfortunate critics who have deduced that Shakespeare was a convinced and militant Protestant from Cranmer's celebrated prophecy of infinite blessings to be enjoyed by the realm under the wise government of Elizabeth and James—a speech which Shakespeare most certainly never wrote.

iclers—were of little consequence in a spiritual predecessor of the Tudors. As for Magna Carta, the Elizabethans had never heard of it.

King John, when Shakespeare took him for a hero, had already figured for over half a century on the English stage. A company of actors, on January 2nd, 1539, performed a play under the auspices of Archbishop Cranmer in which it might be perceived that John was as 'noble a prince as ever was in England and that he was the beginning of the putting down of the Bishop of Rome'. The play in question was presumably a composition by John Ball which is still extant. John is beatified and Stephen Langton, one of the noblest figures in English history, appears as a common poisoner—which only shows what political plays are like when they are written by men with robust political convictions.[1]

The immediate predecessor and source of Shakespeare's play—a piece entitled 'The Troublesome Raigne of King John of England'—stoutly sustains the Tudor tradition. It whole-heartedly exploits the anti-Catholic bias of Protestant England. It is true that John desires Arthur to be slain, but he dies repentant, comparing himself with a yet more famous king who sinned and was yet a man after God's own heart:

> But in the spirit I cry unto my God,
> As did the kingly prophet David cry,
> Whose hands, as mine, with murder were attaint:
> I am not he shall build the Lord a house,
> Or root these locusts from the face of earth:
> But if my dying heart deceive me not,
> From out these loins shall spring a kingly branch
> Whose armies shall reach unto the gates of Rome,
> And with his feet tread down the strumpet's pride,
> That sits upon the chair of Babylon.

We may here observe Shakespeare at work upon a political subject which lay to his hand in a definite text. He was writing from an original which throughout betrays an assured bias. He was dealing as in 'Richard II' with a topical theme and, in this case, we can see

---

[1] The full story of King John's beatification under the Tudors is brilliantly expounded by Dr. Dover Wilson in his preface to the New Cambridge Edition of Shakespeare's play.

precisely where and how he differed in handling it from an author who approached his subject from a contemporary and sectarian point of view.

To begin with, he found it humanly impossible to present King John as the noble prince of Tudor mythology. To Shakespeare, dramatist and searcher of hearts, John, as presented in the older play, was a man who wished his nephew dead but had not the courage to name the deed for which he was morally responsible; who defied the Pope, when passion and interest inclined him to do so, but whose defiance collapsed in abject submission when he needed clerical support against his secular enemies. Here was a veritable king of shreds and patches, audacious without courage, intelligent without wisdom, stubborn without strength of purpose. And the world in which he moved was as chaotic as the man himself. Here were English nobles leagued with a foreign prince to overthrow their English sovereign; a representative of Christ's vicar on earth provoking war between Christian princes; solemn treaties no sooner made than broken; coalitions for which it was impossible to find any basis in right or wrong; loyalties divided and confused.

Shakespeare could make no dramatic sense of this distempered world. He just stands back and admires the fine confusion. There was nothing in John's character to give form and significance to the play. There was nothing sufficiently vital or positive in the events of his troublesome reign to give unity or design to the record. Shakespeare, coming to grips with his principal character, falters in his design and falls into a strange mood of compassionate horror.

Finding no focus for his play in the King, Shakespeare contrives to give it at least an appearance of unity by introducing a character whose function it is to provide a point of sanity or reasonable court of appeal in a world at sixes and sevens. The result is a group of political persons and a series of political situations objectively described for what they are worth and the reaction to these types and situations of a character who, while he takes an active part in the events of the play, is also in a sense its chorus. The Bastard of Faulconbridge is a principal player, but he is also a blunt, fearless and candid critic of the scene, well aware of what all the doings are worth—including his own.

What sort of man is this Faulconbridge, who speaks in this play, if not for Shakespeare himself, at least for the minimum of sanity, honesty and humour which Shakespeare considered necessary as a point of reference? He chooses to be the bastard son of Cœur-de-Lion rather than legitimate heir to an estate of five hundred pounds a year. He will be 'lord of his presence and no land beside'. He will follow his blood and seek his fortune: 'I would not be Sir Nob in any case.' With a disarming candour he makes his profession of faith: he will take the world as he finds it, follow his fortune wherever it may lead and be no more scrupulous than other men:

> Who dares not stir by day must walk by night,
> And have is have, however men do catch:
> Near or far off, well won is still well shot,
> And I am I, howe'er I was begot.

He means to exploit the manners of the time and so earn his place in the story:

> And not alone in habit and device,
> Exterior form, outward accoutrement;
> But from the inward motion to deliver
> Sweet, sweet, sweet poison for the age's tooth:
> And though I will not practise to deceive,
> Yet, to avoid deceit, I mean to learn;
> For it shall strew the footsteps of my rising.

He is superbly honest with himself, a quality which distinguishes him from every other person in the play and makes him a touchstone for all that is false, unstable and pretentious in his surroundings.

This is the man who, having played his own very effective part in the action, is left alone upon the stage to deliver judgment: *Mad world! mad kings! mad composition!* and, if this be not the judgment of Shakespeare, it comes as near to it as any we shall find.

Consider the political scene which prompted it. King Philip of France has come upon the stage with his forces to champion Prince Arthur. The Duke of Austria is also present. Each is full of the noble cause that has brought them together 'in such a just and charitable war'. To them enters King John, claiming to be 'God's wrathful agent'. The two kings defy one another in resounding terms. Two queens contribute to the chorus. Appeals to the 'supernal judge' alternate with hearty give-and-take between the kings and some shrill bickering between the queens. The kings unite in calling the queens to order. Then each of them, in turn, begs the citizens of Angiers, under whose walls this exchange of views is taking place, to let him into the town. The citizens very sensibly suggest that the kings should first settle matters between themselves; they will admit the soldier who proves his right by force of arms. The kings retire to fight it out. Each in turn sends a herald back to the city to claim a victory. But the citizens call it a draw. The kings come again before the walls, but the citizens still refuse either of them admittance. Faulconbridge begins to perceive that their Majesties are making fools of themselves:

> By heaven, these scroyles of Angiers flout you, kings,
> And stand securely on their battlements,
> As in a theatre, whence they gape and point
> At your industrious scenes and acts of death.

He sardonically suggests that the kings should join forces, take the city by storm and afterwards resume their battle. The kings agree. They will knit their powers—

> And lay this Angiers even with the ground;
> Then after fight who shall be king of it.

The citizens naturally dislike this suggestion and propose another solution. Let the kings make peace. France has a son. England has a niece. Let son and niece be married. King Philip will secure as dowry the fiefs in France which properly belong to Prince Arthur, and King John will secure King Philip's recognition of his title to the crown of England. The match is made and the terms agreed. King Philip, who set out to establish Arthur's rights, agrees to share them with King John who is usurping them.[1]

[1] It is to be noted that Shakespeare, charged with anti-democratic bias for neglecting to mention Magna Carta, a document unknown to him either as myth or history, allows the plain citizens of Angiers to be privileged spectators of the essentially comic behaviour of two royal suitors for their favour. These citizens, moreover, speak more to the purpose than the great ones who threaten them with destruction.

Shakespeare presents these disgraceful proceedings with high solemnity. Irony is implicit in the facts and usually he allows it to remain implicit. But in this case he has his own observer present. *Mad world! mad kings! mad composition!* For all alike are ruled by 'that sly devil, that smooth-faced gentleman, tickling Commodity':

> Commodity, the bias of the world;
> The world, who of itself is peisèd well,
> Made to run even upon even ground,
> Till this advantage, this vile-drawing bias,
> This sway of motion, this Commodity,
> Makes it take head from all indifference,
> From all direction, purpose, course, intent.

Shakespeare's English histories in their political aspect are so many variations on this theme of commodity—commodity as between principle and practice, between passion and interest, between conscience and ambition. Expediency lies at the heart of public affairs, however splendid the outward show, however high the profession of faith. It cries aloud with the voice of honour, speaks in the accents of reason, even borrows the language of the heart. Or, as with Faulconbridge, it looks itself straight in the face and accepts itself without illusion. Shakespeare prefers it that way. The judgment of Faulconbridge has all the more weight in that he includes himself in the picture:

> And why rail I on this Commodity?
> But for because he hath not wooed *me* yet.
>
> Well, whiles I am a beggar, I will rail,
> And say there is no sin but to be rich;
> And being rich, my virtue then shall be
> To say there is no vice but beggary:
> Since kings break faith upon commodity,
> Gain, be my lord, for I will worship thee!

Faulconbridge is Shakespeare's catalyst, not only for the matter, but the manner of the political scene. 'Twice fifteen thousand hearts of England's breed,' declaims King John. 'Bastards and else,' slips in Faulconbridge. 'As many and as well-born bloods as those,' counters King Philip. 'Some bastards, too,' interposes Faulconbridge. He pounces on kings, lords and citizens alike when they become grandi-loquent or fulsome. He has a quick ear for the fine phrase that hides a false heart or for the fustian that exceeds the modesty of nature:

> Here's a large mouth, indeed,
> That spits forth death and mountains, rocks and seas,
> Talks as familiarly of roaring lions
> As maids of thirteen do of puppy-dogs!
> What cannoneer begot this lusty blood?
> He speaks plain cannon fire, and smoke and bounce;
> He gives the bastinado with his tongue;
> Our ears are cudgelled—not a word of his
> But buffets better than a fist of France:
> Zounds! I was never so bethumped with words
> Since I first called my brother's father 'dad'.

Mark how he strips the Dauphin of his fine feathers as he courts the Lady Blanche for her dowry:

> K. PHILIP: What say'st thou, boy? look in the lady's face.
> LEWIS: I do, my lord, and in her eyes I find
> A wonder, or a wondrous miracle,
> The shadow of myself form'd in her eyes;
> Which, being but the shadow of your son,
> Becomes a sun, and makes your son a shadow:
> I do protest, I never lov'd myself,
> Till now infixèd I beheld myself,
> Drawn in the flattering table of her eye.
> BASTARD: Drawn in the flattering table of her eye!
> Hang'd in the frowning wrinkle of her brow!
> And quarter'd in her heart! he doth espy
> Himself love's traitor: this is pity now,
> That, hang'd and drawn and quarter'd, there should be,
> In such a love, so vile a lout as he.

Among his peers the Dauphin passes for a brave and capable prince, neither more nor less tickled by commodity than the rest of them. To Faulconbridge he is no more than a lout in gold lace, whose euphuistic wooing of a fair lady is merely ridiculous.

Faulconbridge, however, is still at the beginning of his pilgrimage. He has yet to plumb the depths of that commodity which he so

sturdily professes. King Philip, who for commodity espoused
Arthur's cause and who for commodity makes peace with John,
breaks faith again at the bidding of a papal legate who, for commodity, argues that to keep a vow made with an enemy of the
Church is to be forsworn in the sight of heaven. The Dauphin who
invades England as the Church's warrior, and makes a solemn league
with the nobility of England to put down the usurper, refuses to lay
down his arms at the Church's bidding upon John making his submission to Rome, and decides to cut off the heads of his English sup-
porters when they have served his turn. King John, to whom Faulconbridge has sworn loyalty and devotion, commits a foul crime for
which he cravenly abjures responsibility. Small wonder that Shakespeare's plain dealer in commodity shrinks at last in horror from its
awful consequences:

> I am amaz'd, methinks, and lose my way
> Among the thorns and dangers of this world.
>
> The life, the right and truth of all this realm,
> Is fled to heaven; and England now is left
> To tug and scamble, and to part by th' teeth
> The unow'd interest of proud-swelling state:
> Now, for the bare-pick'd bone of majesty,
> Doth doggèd war bristle his angry crest,
> And snarleth in the gentle eyes of peace:
> Now powers from home and discontents at home
> Meet in one line; and vast confusion waits,
> As doth a raven on a sick-fall'n beast,
> The imminent decay of wrested pomp.
> Now happy he whose cloak and ceinture can
> Hold out this tempest.

Faulconbridge proves better than his word. He professes allegiance
to commodity, but his deeds are those of a brave, honest and compassionate man. He is Shakespeare's living contrast to all the other
public persons of the play, whose politic words and martial gestures
are commodity's fine cloak. Majesty is picked to the bone and holiness, speaking through a prince of the Church, whispers in the
Dauphin's ear that he has everything to gain and nothing to lose if
King John should be so foolish as to murder his nephew. The play

acquires unity only if it is viewed from this angle. Commodity is the villain; Faulconbridge is Shakespeare's device for stripping the villain of his disguise. There is, in fact, no sense in the play at all unless we regard it as the recoil of a free spirit from the tug and scamble of a political world which has fallen to the estate described by Ulysses—will into power, power into appetite.

Faulconbridge, who bluffly accepts commodity for his device, exposes commodity for all to see in its true colours and, when it comes to the point, himself behaves like a true man. He remains loyal to the King and to the cause which he has taken up. He does his best to put spirit into his royal master when things are at their worst:

> But wherefore do you droop? why look you sad?
> Be great in act, as you have been in thought;
> Let not the world see fear and sad distrust
> Govern the motion of a kingly eye.

On hearing of John's submission to the papal legate and of his readiness to parley with the Dauphin, he exclaims:

> O inglorious league!
> Shall we, upon the footing of our land,
> Send fair-play orders and make compromise,
> Insinuation, parley and base truce
> To arms invasive? shall a beardless boy,
> A cocker'd silken wanton, brave our fields,
> And flesh his spirit in a warlike soil,
> Mocking the air with colours idly spread,
> And find no check?

and when John, unable to act himself, bids him take charge—*Have thou the ordering of this present time*—he complies without expostulation. To the foreign invader and the rebellious English nobles he gives the rough edge of his tongue:

> Now hear our English king;
> For thus his royalty doth speak in me.
> He is prepared; and reason too he should:
> This apish and unmannerly approach,
> This harness'd masque and unadvisèd revel,
> This unhaired sauciness and boyish troops,

> The king doth smile at; and is well prepared
> To whip this dwarfish war, these pigmy arms,
> From out the circle of his territories.
>
> And you degenerate, you ingrate revolts,
> You bloody Neroes, ripping up the womb
> Of your dear mother England, blush for shame.

Finally, when the English lords have returned to their allegiance, it is Faulconbridge who speaks the famous epilogue:

> This England never did, nor never shall,
> Lie at the proud foot of a conqueror,
> But when it first did help to wound itself.
> Now these her princes are come home again,
> Come the three corners of the world in arms,
> And we shall shock them: nought shall make us rue,
> If England to itself do rest but true.

That Faulconbridge, who openly affects to play the ruffian, should come finally to rest in the simple faith of a loyal Englishman puts the finishing touch to Shakespeare's exposure of the pretensions to honour, godliness and high principle of the professional politicians which is the fundamental inspiration of the play. Faulconbridge, who exclaims:

> Bell, book, and candle shall not drive me back,
> When gold and silver becks me to come on—

is the one really disinterested person in this distinguished company. Contrast with him Lewis, the Dauphin, who, in bribing the English nobles to support his marauding Frenchmen with promises of spoils to come, claims God's warrant for his enterprise:

> Come, come; for thou shalt thrust thy hand as deep
> Into the purse of rich prosperity
> As Lewis himself: so, nobles, shall you all,
> That knit your sinews to the strength of mine.
>
> Look, where the holy legate comes apace,
> To give us warrant from the hand of heaven,
> And on our actions set the name of right
> With holy breath.

What, meanwhile, has become of the political tract from which Shakespeare derived his material? Here, again, we find revealed, as nowhere else, the quality of his reactions to political themes and persons. The solemn bigotry of the original is utterly transformed even in the passages where Shakespeare allows his characters to reject, with point and passion, the clerical pretensions of Rome. There is no anti-Catholic bias in the play. Shakespeare's papal legate is presented, first and last, as one among the rest of the politicians. On him, as on the kings and princes, the same cool dispassionate irony is brought to bear. If he suffers more from this treatment than the lay politicians, that is only because his moral pretensions are higher and therefore less consistent with his behaviour. Complacently he tries to use each of the royal parties in turn to secure the temporal ends of the Church and in the end is rejected by both. He is almost a comic character. His bland assumption of authority is as genially mocked by the event as the claim of Polonius to have discovered the true cause of Hamlet's madness; and when he persuades King Philip that by breaking his promise he is really keeping his word, there is more than a hint of that most wise counsellor to King Claudius who was begged to dispense more matter with less art. A lambent mischief plays about all the proceedings of these public persons. The scene in which Pandulph coolly invites the Dauphin to make peace with John after having urged him to make war has a touch of humour such as the contemplation of public life is very apt to inspire in a detached observer; and the comedy is complete when Faulconbridge, on behalf of King John, and Lewis, on behalf of King Philip, equally determined to fight one another, nevertheless agree in rejecting his authority:

> PANDULPH: The Dauphin is too wilful-opposite,
>   And will not temporise with my entreaties;
>   He flatly says he'll not lay down his arms.
> BASTARD: By all the blood that ever fury breath'd,
>   The youth says well!

The solemnity of the original in its treatment of the anti-Catholic theme is retained by Shakespeare only where it is strictly required by the historical facts. John's celebrated challenge to papal authority could not, of course, be omitted:

> What earthly name to interrogatories
> Can task the free breath of a sacred king?
>
> Tell him this tale; and from the mouth of England
> Add thus much more: that no Italian priest
> Shall tithe or toll in our dominions;
> But as we, under heaven, are supreme head,
> So under Him that great supremacy,
> Where do we reign, we will alone uphold,
> Without the assistance of a mortal hand:
> So tell the Pope.

Even in dealing with this supreme political topic of the play, however, Shakespeare is clearly concerned less with stating a religious or social doctrine than with presenting a series of situations in which the overweening pretensions of a political agent who plays with moral and human forces beyond his control are effectively exposed. The rival parties accept the legate's authority only so long as he is ready, with holy breath, to set upon their actions the name of right. Pandulph blandly assumes that he can bind or loose these princes by virtue of the spiritual powers which he misuses for material ends:

> It was my breath that blew this tempest up,
> Upon your stubborn usage of the Pope;
> But since you are a gentle convertite,
> My tongue shall hush again this storm of war.

Never was a self-constituted master of the event more swiftly disillusioned. He is Shakespeare's supreme example of the politician who, like the sorcerer's apprentice, finds himself drowning in a flood which he has started and cannot arrest. His claim to spiritual authority is accepted by Lewis when it lends an air of respectability to his temporal proceedings, as it is accepted by John when it is used in an attempt to save England from the consequences of a French invasion. It is rejected by Lewis when it is used to dissuade him from

his enterprise, as it is rejected by John when it is used to extort
English money for the papal funds:

> Your grace shall pardon me; I will not back:
> I am too high-born to be propertied,
> To be a secondary at control,
> Or useful serving-man and instrument
> To any sovereign state throughout the world.
> Your breath first kindled the dead coal of wars
> Between this chastis'd kingdom and myself,
> And brought in matter that should feed this fire;
> And now 'tis far too huge to be blown out
> With that same weak wind which enkindled it.

Shakespeare discards the sectarian thesis of the old play, giving us
instead a dramatic sequence in which he presents the discomfiture of
an eminent public person who assumes that God can be made to
serve his turn in the manipulation of human affairs. He likewise discards John as a national hero and spiritual precursor of the Tudors.
He retains only so much of the heroic king as common sense and
common humanity allows. His John has presence and dignity. He
speaks like a king. He is ready in war and apt in council. But Shakespeare was not greatly interested in him as a political character. He
was interested in the man who committed a crime which he had not
the courage to name and who was thereby struck with a moral
paralysis.[1] There is insurrection, not only in John's kingdom, but in
his soul, and it was the spiritual ruin which Shakespeare took for his
theme:

> My nobles leave me; and my state is brav'd,
> Even at my gates, with ranks of foreign powers:
> Nay, in the body of this fleshly land,
> This kingdom, this confine of blood and breath,
> Hostility and civil tumult reigns
> Between my conscience and my cousin's death.

John, in fact, retires as a public personage before the play is done,
leaving the political issues to be determined by Faulconbridge. He
dies remote from all affairs, his mind pricked with strange fancies.

[1] See above, pp. 102 (*note*), 323.

He does not even live to hear the end of the story. For him the final bulletins are but 'dead news in as dead an ear'. Shakespeare, turning for a moment from the public scene, suffers Prince Henry to grace the passing of a tormented soul with a brief elegy, in whose music sounds the infinite compassion of a poet for a most unhappy man:

> I am the cygnet to this pale faint swan,
> Who chants a doleful hymn to his own death,
> And from the organ-pipe of frailty sings
> His soul and body to their lasting rest.

Here, then, we find as plain an answer as we shall anywhere receive to the question with which we started. A citizen of the New Monarchy takes a political tract of the times. To a large extent he ignores the political issues which formed the basis and inspiration of the older play. His interest in the King as a traditional political figure is so slight that he allows him to die, in the political sense, 'off-stage'. His concern with serious political and religious issues is so small that his play depends for sense and unity upon a character whose conduct and presence serve constantly to underline the irony implicit in the conduct of political affairs. Faulconbridge is the vehicle of Shakespeare's genial contempt for the grandiloquent impostures of public life. He helps us to understand why of all Shakespeare's political characters Richard of Gloucester is the most attractive. Shakespeare liked Richard best because he was the least a humbug. Faulconbridge supplies us with the clearest evidence that the mood in which Shakespeare contemplated politics as such was one of ironic detachment. He was impartial because he was in the last resort indifferent. This explains the paradox to which reference has so frequently been made—namely that Shakespeare, who gave to the stage a gallery of political characters unequalled in any literature for their historical veracity, had no great interest in public affairs. He was interested in persons and many of them just happen to have been public persons. Though he could draw for us a masterly portrait of a successful king, a republican worthy, a great soldier or a proud nobleman, though he could present the tragical fall of princes as intimately as the not less tragical rise of pretenders to sovereignty and power, he will turn aside at the critical moment to give us some touch of nature. The public scene fades or vanishes and we find ourselves alone with a human soul in triumph or disaster. Richard of Bordeaux calls for a looking-glass. Coriolanus obeys his mother.

COMIC CHARACTERS OF SHAKESPEARE

PUBLISHERS' NOTE

The five studies contained in this section, though complete in themselves, represent only part of the much longer work JOHN PALMER had planned. They were finished shortly before his death in 1944.

INTRODUCTION

'THIS world', said Horace Walpole, 'is a comedy to those who think, a tragedy to those who feel'. The aphorism is well-worn, having served as a text for many essays on the comic, as distinguished from the tragic, approach to men and things.[1]

It is a true saying, as far as it reaches, and false for anything, which means nearly everything, that lies beyond. Therein it smacks of the period. English thinkers in the eighteenth century, with a few splendid exceptions, were tidy in their habits, almost as tidy as their French contemporaries, from whom, in despite of King George, who gloried in the name of Briton, they took their fashions in dress, deportment, philosophy and letters. It assumes that characters in a comedy, if we are to laugh at them, must be presented with detachment and that characters in a tragedy, if we are to weep for them, must be presented with sympathy. We might otherwise find the comic characters uncomfortably pathetic or the tragic characters unseasonably ridiculous. It explains why the French for generations insisted on keeping their heads in a comedy and losing their hearts in a tragedy. It explains why so many comic writers have valiantly insisted that they were satirical, unfeeling rogues, inviting us to laugh contemptuously at silly or wicked people. It explains why so many tragic writers have piously refrained from allowing their common sense to blunt their uncommon sensibility. It inspires the Bergsonian assumption that laughter is a social gesture whose evolutionary purpose is to keep men sensitive to their environment and that it is the business of comedy to correct excess, whether in the fool or the philosopher:

> La parfaite raison fuit toute extrémité
> Et veut que l'on soit sage avec sobriété.

Comedy, according to Walpole, is an act of judgment. We are to

[1] Including an essay on Comedy by the present author published years ago, in which with the staggering insolence of youth he surveyed the whole field of human laughter from a cabinet minister chasing his hat in Palace Yard to Falstaff, between the sheets, babbling of green fields.

suppose that a comic character is a personage, presented for our derision, in whom some folly of the time or vice of nature is anatomised.
We are invited to behold the activities of mortal men as they must
appear to a reasonable being sufficiently disinterested to find them
persistently amusing. We are summoned in that mood, to laugh
heartily or to smile complacently at absurdities and misfortunes
which we know to our cost to be anything but a laughing matter for
those whose interests, passions, foibles and weaknesses are engaged.

Note, however, that even the participants in a comedy or tragedy
can themselves be aware of the antithesis. Persons involved in a
comical situation often exclaim: 'If this were not so terribly funny it
would be really tragic'. Persons involved in a tragical situation exclaim just as often: 'If this were not so dreadfully serious it would be
really funny'. In these two exclamations Walpole's distinction is
partially justified. There *are* two sides, the comic and the tragic, to
almost every predicament. But Walpole's clear-cut opposition here
reaches its limit. For it presupposes that the heart is idle when the
head is active, and that the head ceases to function when the heart is
in control. It denies that a man may laugh and be sorry at the same
time, relish the humour of his own distresses, deride the fool and yet
acknowledge a companionship in his folly, smile at extravagances to
which he is himself as liable as their victim, be diverted by the
exhibition of a weakness and yet retain a lively sympathy for the
weakling, delight in the misadventures of a rascal and yet recognise
him for a kindred spirit. It ignores, in fact, the essential quality of
humane comedy, which only appears when the distinction between
heart and head is obliterated; for, in the finest and most satisfying
laughter, there is just that element of emotional sympathy which
Walpole declared to be incompatible. This element is present even
in the laughter provoked by a satirist who, in deriding the things
which he wishes to destroy, invites us to recognise that we are all
equally liable to the errors, vanities and obsessions at which he aims.
There is more fellow-feeling than detachment even in the comedies
of Molière if we look below the surface and reflect upon the source
and quality of our amusement, and when we come to the comedies
of Shakespeare the distinction simply vanishes.

Shakespeare's detachment is admittedly absolute in the sense that he never appears in his own person. His characters, once created, exist in their own right. Shakespeare is silent when Titania speaks. But this is not the detachment of a man who thinks as opposed to the sympathy of a man who feels. It implies on the contrary the complete negation of such a man. Shakespeare's detachment was from himself and not from his creatures. Almost the whole secret of his power is the facility with which he identifies himself imaginatively with all sorts and conditions of men and women. He is almost incapable of the judicial approach. In the very act of holding up a villain to reprobation or a fool to derision he enters their minds and hearts. He is entirely *objective* in that the personality of William Shakespeare avoids the stage and that the personal equation is never allowed to distort the independence and veracity of his portraiture. He is entirely *subjective* in the sense that he completely identifies himself in imagination with the ideas and sentiments portrayed. He loses himself in the thing he contemplates; suppresses himself in the act of giving life to the creatures of his fancy. The secret of his genius lies in what Keats described as his 'negative capability'. He is never Shakespeare; he is in turn Hamlet, Cressida or Caliban.

Comedy, if it implies detachment of the author from his characters and their presentation for intellectual judgment undisturbed by emotion, was consequently foreign to his whole process of creation. Where the comic writer, within the narrow limits assumed by Walpole, stands aloof to survey mankind in the light of reason, Shakespeare, presenting a fool, is the fool incarnate; and, laughing at a fool, laughs at something which he requires us to recognise as flesh of our flesh and bone of our bone. Shakespeare, in fact, never wrote a comedy within the commonly accepted sense of the term or put on the stage a comic character for the critical diversion of an audience assumed to be celestially immune from the normal infirmities of human nature. Once or twice, during that strange period in his creative progress when his infinite charity of mind was in eclipse, he resolutely tried his hand at this kind of spectacle. The result was a play like 'Troilus and Cressida' or 'Measure for Measure', in which

M

he deliberately struck the Olympian attitude, taking his stand for a
moment with the wise gods who 'laugh at us while we strut to our
confusion'. But how soon was the satirical mood abandoned! Shakespeare set out in derision, but nature was too strong for him. He
begins in a mood of artificial detachment, but cannot sustain it.
Almost at once he is caught up in the perplexities and distresses of his
victims. Cressida, while he remembers to be a satirist, is presented as
one of the 'daughters of the game', to be numbered among the
'sluttish spoils of opportunity'. Troilus is a poor fool who dotes upon
a false mistress. But at the mere contemplation of these unhappy
lovers, exchanging frail vows while Sir Pandarus holds the door,
Shakespeare relents. Cressida is startled by the same lark, herald of
the morn, that sang so out of tune in the ears of Juliet and she loses
Troilus to as sad a strain as Shakespeare ever wrote:

> Injurious time now with a robber's haste
> Crams his rich thievery up, he knows not how:
> As many farewells as be stars in heaven,
> With distinct breath and consign'd kisses to them,
> He fumbles up into a loose adieu,
> And scants us with a single famish'd kiss,
> Distasted with the salt of broken tears.

Who, after that, can read 'Troilus and Cressida' in the mood of
comic detachment? Even more startling is the collapse of Shakespeare, the comic censor, in 'Measure for Measure'. The play is
colder and more deliberate in its cynicism than 'Troilus and Cressida',
and there is less fellowship in this play than in any other of his writing. Its good providence is an 'old fantastical duke of dark corners'
and its heroine a lady whose self-centred virtue chills us to the
marrow. The rest form such a group as were never before or since
assembled on the author's stage; among them one Claudio, who
esteems his own life more highly than his sister's chastity. But
beside Shakespeare the heartless comedian stood Shakespeare the
poet, to whom no human heart was a stranger, and at the supreme
moment, when the satirist was putting his finishing touch of obloquy
upon his wretched victim, the poet suddenly took charge and the

man who has been exposed to our derision breaks into a cry that makes him one with ourselves:

> Ay, but to die, and go we know not where;
> To lie in cold obstruction and to rot;
> This sensible warm motion to become
> A kneaded clod;
>
> To be imprison'd in the viewless winds,
> And blown with restless violence round about
> The pendent world;
>
>   'tis too horrible!
> The weariest and most loathèd worldly life
> That age, ache, penury and imprisonment
> Can lay on nature is a paradise
> To what we fear of death.

The sentiment is not heroic, but there can be no pretence that Shakespeare is here making that critical gesture of the spirit which is commonly expected of the comic dramatist.

If Shakespeare, at a time when, for some reason as yet unfathomed, he was casting himself for the part of Thersites in a distracted world, was unable to sustain the mood of comic detachment, it is not surprising that in the comedies which reflect his more natural genius he was quite incapable of bringing his fellow men to judgment. His comic characters are not so much persons at whom we are invited to laugh as persons who please us to the point of laughter only in so far as we are able and ready to identify ourselves with their moods and perceptions. Comedy which springs from the strain of cruelty which many find to be inseparable from laughter, which excludes all sympathy with the victim, is to Shakespeare so uncongenial that, even when he takes for his subject a stock figure of fun, he tends to humanise it to such a degree that actors and critics are often tempted to exaggerate the element of pathos in his achievement. Shylock, the Jew, presented in the grotesque framework of a plot intended to throw into relief the least engaging qualities of his race, becomes the almost tragic representative of a persecuted minority. This comic character turns suddenly upon his audience: *If you prick us, do we not bleed?* That is a question which no comic character has any right to ask. There are moments when Shakespeare deals with Shylock as Molière dealt with Harpagon. Indeed, the scene in which the Jew alternately rejoices to hear of Antonio's misfortunes and rages to hear of Jessica and his lost ducats is the most Molièresque scene he ever wrote. But Shakespeare could not keep to this level. The Jew, even in this comic display of greed and passion for revenge, reflexively stimulated so that he may exhibit them at a maximum, grows too terrible for comedy: *I would my daughter were dead at my foot, and the jewels in her ear! Would she were hearsed at my foot, and the ducats in her coffin!* And he grows at the same time too human in his torment: *Hath not a Jew eyes? hath not a Jew hands, organs, dimensions, senses, affections, passions?*

Shakespeare's refusal to draw any clear distinction between a comic character, at whom a wholly reasonable person may laugh, and a tragic character, with whom a normally sensitive person must feel in sympathy, was not the deliberate decision of an artist consciously pursuing a method, but the natural expression of his imaginative reaction to human nature. For him the dichotomy did not exist. This explains the fact, so disconcerting to his French critics and to the pre-romantic commentators, that some of his most notable comic characters turn up at the most unexpected moments and in the most unlikely places. Juliet's nurse springs to life in a tragedy. Polonius treads in the footsteps of a ghost from the grave. The Alsatia in which Falstaff flourishes as a Lord of Misrule is just one province in a land where an English king dies of a broken heart and an English prince self-consciously prepares to assume his inheritance. The partitions are thin which divide comedy and tragedy in Shakespeare's world. Polonius in the tragedy of 'Hamlet' is more recognisably a comic character than Orsino in the comedy of 'Twelfth Night' or Jaques in the comedy of 'As You Like It'.

Who, then, *are* the comic characters and when *are* they truly comic? In what does the comic element consist?

No general or precise answer can be given to a question which ignores the essential quality of Shakespeare's imaginative process. All we can do is to take, as we find them, characters which all the world agrees to be amusing and to inquire into the source of our peculiar pleasure. We shall expect in advance to discover that the secret of Shakespeare's comedy lies in the quality of his imaginative reaction to life itself. We shall find ourselves watching, in an infinite variety of moods and forms, that constant interplay of thought and feeling, detachment and sympathy, ridicule and affection, serene judgment and passionate self-identification which lies at the heart of his genius.

There is a recurrent device in the comedies of Shakespeare which offers a preliminary clue to the labyrinth into which we are about to venture. When Malvolio reads a famous letter writ in the sweet Roman hand, and so falls into the pit of absurdity digged for him by his adversaries, the contrivers of his disgrace are behind a hedge in Olivia's garden watching his every gesture and heartlessly enjoying the performance. When Benedick and Beatrice are caught in the snare laid for them by Don Pedro and his friends, the architects of their discomfiture are there to take pleasure in the mischief. When the King of Navarre and his backsliding companions are exhibited as false to their academic vows, there is a progressive company of eavesdroppers, each of them prompt to enjoy the decline and fall of his recreant predecessor. When Titania is enamoured of an ass, there is Oberon to triumph in her delusion, and when a quartet of young lovers is plagued in A Wood near Athens, there is Puck to delight in their follies. Shakespeare, in making fun of his characters, usually contrives that there shall be someone present on the stage to hold a watching brief for the comic muse. The spectator thus perceives not only the victim but the unsympathetic witnesses by whom the victim is derided. He is invited to realise that there are two parties to the jest and to divide his sympathies. There are occasions, too, when even the contrivers of the mischief cease to be entirely merciless. Even Puck has his moments of sympathy:

> Cupid is a knavish lad
> Thus to make poor females mad.

Oberon frankly relents in the prosecution of his trick upon the fairy queen: *Her dotage now I do begin to pity;* and Sir Toby feels a twinge of compunction when the jest against Malvolio has been carried to extremes: *I would we were well rid of this knavery*.

Satirical comments by onlookers upon the stage provoke the on-lookers in front to react in favour of the persons who are made ridiculous. The dramatist says in effect: 'Here, as in life, is someone who is made to look foolish and here, too, are people quick to flout them and proudly immune from their distresses; but you, who see the comedy as a whole, might just as easily find yourself on one side of the hedge as the other'.

Sympathy, then, and not satire, is the inspiration of Shakespeare's comedy. The appeal of his comic characters, even as we laugh at them, is to the touch of nature which makes the whole world kin. A delicate balance is constantly sustained in the persons of the play between the folly which makes them laughable and the simplicity which makes them lovable, between the frailties or faults which lay them open to rebuke and a common humanity with ourselves which calls for charity and secures for them an immediate understanding. The balance varies from scene to scene and from play to play. Each comedy shows the essential geniality of Shakespeare's comic ap-proach in a different mood, and the mood is so nicely determined that each of the characters, to be seen without distortion, must appear in its own environment. Malvolio would be as out of place in the Forest of Arden as Bully Bottom in Olivia's garden or as Rosa-lind in A Wood near Athens. Each of these comic characters is but one figure in a composition where every touch has reference to the work as a whole; and to study any one of them apart from its context would be like looking at a single figure taken from a picture by Michael Angelo or Botticelli consigned as an illustration of 'detail' to an artist's portfolio. The melancholy Jaques is an effectively comic philosopher as the co-mate and brother-in-exile of the banished Duke. Orsino is an exquisitely comic man of sentiment as suitor to Olivia. Benedick is a vivaciously comic misogynist as the pre-destined husband of Beatrice. Remove them from a setting whose colour, form and rhythm—the very air they breathe—are all nicely calculated to delineate and illumine their absurdity and the spell is broken.

Shakespeare himself once made the mistake of removing one of his comic characters from his natural surroundings; and the victim of this experiment, though of all his creatures the most robust and self-sufficient, nearly died of his translation. Sir John Falstaff, at home in Eastcheap and on Shrewsbury Field, moving as freely in low life as in high policy, well nigh perished in the bourgeois confines of Windsor Park. His great figure could only be truly seen against the violent background of civil war, the full-blooded mischief of highway robbery and the swaggering humours of the tavern. There is nothing perceptibly wrong with Falstaff in his misadventures with the merry wives. There is no decline in his eloquence, no abatement of relish, no change even of the means whereby he is inspired to show his essential quality—for Falstaff is never more himself than when he rises irrepressibly above the ignominies designed for him by the lilliputians. Yet the critics find him at Windsor diminished to a shadow of his former self. They feel that something rather terrible has happened to Falstaff and they are right. He is living out of his time and place. He has become an awful example in a homily of good life. His environment forces us to acknowledge that he is not respectable. It is as though Tom Jones had strayed into a novel by Jane Austen.

Shakespeare committed this act of comic misprision in deference to a royal request that he should show Falstaff in love. He could not go quite so far as that and it was a miracle that he should have gone as far as he did without killing his man outright. Let us take this warning to heart and insist on viewing these comic characters of Shakespeare under the lights and shadows that play upon them in the gardens and palaces, the fields and taverns, the streets and chambers, where they meet and move for our pleasure.

I

BEROWNE

Love's Labour's Lost

THE greatest comic dramatist since Aristophanes—assuming that Shakespeare is ineligible to compete—sprang into fame with a genial satire upon the metaphysical exquisites of the blue *salon* of the Marquise de Rambouillet. Molière, when he came to Paris in 1658, impudently challenged the established arbiters of literary taste with a comedy as devastating in its effect upon the fashionable wits and poets of the day as the little child's remark upon the Emperor's new clothes in Andersen's fairy tale. *Les Précieuses Ridicules,* by a young dramatist who had recently arrived from the provinces, destroyed in a gale of laughter a literary and social sect which no one until that moment had ventured to find ridiculous.

By a happy coincidence Shakespeare, at an almost identical point in his career, came upon the London stage with a 'Pleasant Conceited Comedy Called Love's Labour's Lost', in which the exquisites of his own time and country were brought to book. It is instructive to compare the spirit in which these two men of genius approached a very similar enterprise. Their subject was the same; they had a like intention, which was to be amusing at the expense of the verbal and sentimental affectations of the period; their audience in both cases was a select company of persons passionately addicted to the follies at which they were invited to laugh. These follies, moreover, had a superficial resemblance.

Here, then, is a unique opportunity of observing two great comedians at work upon the same theme, writing under much the same conditions, basing their comic appeal on the same conflict of broad humanity with social artifice, of common sense with intellectual extravagance, of truth to nature with the distortions of fancy. Everything seems to be prompting them to the same conclusions and consequences. The result is, nevertheless, a contrast at all points

349

between the two achievements and a revelation of essential qualities that divide their authors in everything but their firm grasp of the abiding realities of the human spirit.

The first point of contrast lies in the fact that Molière, in mocking the exquisites of the blue *salon*, was deriding a coterie whose standards of taste and whose approach to literature and life were quite definitely alien and pernicious. There could be no comedy in France such as Molière was determined to write, till the *alcovistes*, not born of a father and mother but secreted by the alcove as an oyster secretes the pearl, ceased to plot their way on the Map of the Tender Passion towards the City of Sensitive Esteem, through forty leagues of Friendly Sentiment, to the Hamlet of Gallant Addresses, where a mistress was expected tenderly to entertain her lover without enjoyment and substantially to enjoy her husband with aversion.[1] Molière was always much more than a satirist, but he was often provoked by his enemies into announcing that satire was what he intended and, in the preface to *Les Précieuses Ridicules*, he explicitly declared that 'the correction of social absurdity must at all times be the matter of true comedy'. In writing his first pugnacious comedy he deliberately challenged and destroyed something for which he felt an actively wholesome contempt. These exquisites were not only corrupters of taste and manners; they were veritable misleaders of youth, setting up false standards of sentiment and behaviour in whose presence common sense and good feeling were almost ashamed to show their honest faces. Molière, moved to a genuine derision, was determined to put out of court and countenance absurdities which were naturally antipathetic to his genius.

Very different was the mood and purpose of Shakespeare in his 'pleasant conceited comedy'. Admittedly he set out to make fun of the sophisticated and metaphysical wits of London. But he was ridiculing absurdities which, on occasion, he was quite happy to share with his contemporaries and he amused his audience with a display of virtuosity in an art of which he was himself a notable practitioner. There is nothing destructive or contemptuous in his

[1] For Molière's Battle with the Exquisites see Chapter VIII of the present author's *Molière*.

handling of these pedantical lords and subtle ladies. Their sentimental encounters, in which phrases and fancies run extravagantly wild for our pleasure, are mocked with an indulgence that implies affection rather than reprobation. Who, after all, was Shakespeare to castigate man or woman for exuberance in 'conceit', extravagance in the manipulation of words, profligacy in the pursuit of a fair image, prodigality in the expense of imagination? How could Shakespeare, who was one day to present on his stage Benedick and Beatrice, allow himself to suggest that Berowne and Rosaline were too silly for words? Admittedly he invites us to laugh at their antics. Berowne is often exquisitely ludicrous. But all this is chaff rather than satire, provoking us to laugh companionably at a fool with whom his author is ready to change shoes at any moment.

The difference of mood in which Molière and Shakespeare undertake their strange adventure—*l'étrange entreprise de faire rire les honnêtes gens*—strikingly reveals the temperamental abyss that lies between the French and the English comedian. It is also to be noted that, despite many striking similarities, there is a very real difference between the objects of their mirth. The French exquisites of the seventeenth century carried to excess a tradition which had lost its vitality. They had played with words till the words had lost their meaning. They had refined upon their sentiments till there was no real feeling left. 'These people', wrote La Bruyère, wise after the event, 'left to the commonalty the art of speaking intelligibly. One thing, expressed with no great clarity, led to another even more obscure, which was in turn improved upon by the delivery of riddling redes which were always greeted with prolonged applause. From an exaggeration of what they described as delicacy of feeling and refinement of expression, they finally reached the point of being entirely ambiguous and of failing to understand even one another'. The extravagant conceits of the Euphuists of Elizabethan England, though equally complicated, were not anaemic. They were rather the result of an abnormally high blood pressure. For the French exquisites words were like coins worn thin with too much jingling. For the Elizabethans every word came fresh from the die. They loved the glitter and music of their chime. Shakespeare, introducing

Armado in 'Love's Labour's Lost'—the figure of fun in whom the
English Euphuists were mocked—uses this very simile:

> A man in all the world's new fashion planted,
>   That hath a *mint* of phrases in his brain:
> One who the music of his own vain tongue
>   Doth ravish like enchanting harmony.

and Berowne, making ready to welcome the Euphuist, declares:

> Armado is a most illustrious wight,
> A man of fire-new words, fashion's own knight.

Armado, 'child of fancy', is brought into the play to 'relate in high-
born words', things which will certainly exceed the modesty of
nature; and we are invited to share the pleasure which the King of
Navarre means to take in his performances:

> How you delight, my lords, I know not I,
> But I protest I love to hear him lie,
> And I will use him for my minstrelsy.

This game, we perceive, is to be played with the bright counters
of a speech whose unexplored resources were as exciting a challenge
to the poets of Elizabethan England as were the shores of the Spanish
Main to her gentlemen adventurers.

The difference between Molière, setting out to correct social
absurdity, and Shakespeare, promising his audience rare sport
among the Euphuists, is incarnate in the principal person of the play.
Berowne is the first of a long line of characters in whom Shakespeare,
to the extent in which he mocks the victims of his comedy, renders
them only the more attractive.

Shakespeare will so easily lose the satirical purpose with which he
started, and so often provoke us to wonder whether he is ridiculing
excess in his characters or sharing their intoxication, that it is well to
get the main design of the play clearly cut in our minds before
allowing outsiders to be absorbed in its details. The King of Navarre
induces a group of noble lords to go with him into intellectual re-
treat. They will for the space of three years forswear the company of

women, eat only one meal a day, fast a day in every week and sleep for not more than three hours in the night. They hope by this discipline to attain a knowledge of things 'hid and barred from common sense' which is 'study's god-like recompense'. Unfortunately for these prospective monks of the new learning the King of Navarre is obliged to receive an embassy from the King of France which comes to discuss matters of state. The embassy is led by an accomplished and beautiful princess attended by her ladies. The King of Navarre will not admit them into his house but he cannot refuse to parley with them beyond the gates. So, in the words of the Victorian Euphuist, Walter Pater, we have 'on one side, a fair palace: on the other the tents of the Princess of France; ... in the midst, a wide space of smooth grass. The same personages are combined over and over again into a series of gallant scenes'. The princes, of course, fall in love with the ladies and each tries to conceal his treason:

> For oaths are straws, men's faiths are wafer-cakes
> And hold-fast is the only dog, my duck;—

as was to be said one day by that fiercest of all the Euphuists, Ancient Pistol.

The princes woo the princesses in disguise, with intricate tributes in verse and pyrotechnical displays of ingenious wit and pretty sentiment. Finally there is a general recantation. Artifice is abandoned and nature carries the day.

Berowne has a very special place in this playful satirical design. Along with the rest he is mocked by his author and is a target for the ladies. But he fully appreciates the comedy of his predicament. He speaks for nature, though caught in the toils of artifice; and, at the end, delivers the moral of the piece in which he has, in effect, played the part of Chorus on his author's behalf. It is as though Shakespeare had said: 'Here, if you like, is a satire; but, if you insist on laughing at these fantastical persons, please remember that we are all painted with the same brush and note that, if this fellow Berowne, with whom I am obviously on excellent terms, has my permission to moralise the spectacle, that is only because he has been well content to play the fool for your diversion'.

Let us now follow Berowne more closely through the peripatetics of his adventure.

The King of Navarre announces his plan:

> Therefore brave conquerors—for so you are,
> That war against your own affections
> And the huge army of the world's desires—
> Our late edict shall strongly stand in force,
> Navarre shall be the wonder of the world,
> Our court shall be a little academe,
> Still and contemplative in living art.

Berowne declares that he is ready to study with the King for three years but protests against the conditions:

> O, these are barren tasks, too hard to keep,
> Not to see ladies, study, fast, not sleep.

He would prefer swearing to a better purpose:

> Come on then—I will swear to study so,
> To know the thing I am forbid to know:
> As thus—to study where I well may dine[1]
>   When I to feast expressly am forbid,
> Or study where to meet some mistress fine
>   When mistresses from common sense are hid.

He nevertheless signs the articles and is the first to perform a brilliant euphuistic exercise on the theme of the comedy, in which, while showing himself to be a master of the game, he stoutly maintains that it is a sport contrary to nature. There is little profit in poring upon books or naming the stars:

> Why, all delights are vain, but that most vain
> Which, with pain purchased, doth inherit pain—
> As painfully to pore upon a book,
>   To seek the light of truth, while truth the while

---

[1] Compare the declaration in which Molière's Sosie cuts the knot of his metaphysical perplexities:

> Le véritable Amphitryon
> Est l'Amphitryon où l'on dîne.

Doth falsely blind the eyesight of his look:
  Light, seeking light, doth light of light beguile:
So ere you find where light in darkness lies,
Your light grows dark by losing of your eyes.

Study is like the heaven's glorious sun,
  That will not be deep-searched with saucy looks:
Small have continual plodders ever won,
  Save base authority from others' books.
These earthly godfathers of heaven's lights,
  That give a name to every fixèd star,
Have no more profit of their shining nights,
  Than those that walk and wot not what they are. . . .
Too much to know, is to know nought but fame:
And every godfather can give a name.

Light, seeking light, doth light of light beguile. Dr. Johnson said: 'The whole sense of this jingling declamation is only this—that a man by too close study may read himself blind, which might have been told with less obscurity in fewer words'. He was evidently not amused.[1] But the Euphuists who attended the play in 1597, 'as presented before Her Highness this last Christmas', found the words neither too many nor obscure. Words, for Johnson and his contemporaries, had lost their magic. They were not things to play with, but things to be rounded up and impounded in a dictionary. They must be definite, precise and serviceable. For the Elizabethans, however, they might still be used as spells and incantations. The jingling declamation in which Johnson found but a single meaning evoked in Shakespeare's auditors a manifold delight. For them there were overtones in the jingle. They saw Johnson's plain sense of the matter, namely that a man may read himself blind. But they caught also the suggestion that a man in seeking more knowledge may

[1] The whirligig of time brings in his revenges. Coleridge ridiculing the poetic diction of Johnson himself was fond of quoting the following couplet from 'The Vanity of Human Wishes':
      Let observation with extensive view
      Survey mankind from China to Peru;
which is as much as to say: Let observation with extensive observation observe mankind extensively.

grow less in wisdom. They found in this line a light that sparkled and changed—light of the eyes, light in the printed word, light of the intelligence and a light beyond even that—a light divine that may be lost in following its earthly reflection.

Berowne goes into the adventure with no illusions as to the sequel:

> I'll lay my head to any goodman's hat,
> These oaths and laws will prove an idle scorn.

He is first of the noble lords to fall from grace and there is no more pleasant conceited speech in this pleasant conceited comedy than that in which he announces his predicament:

> And I—
> Forsooth in love, I that have been love's whip!
> A very beadle to a humorous sigh,
> A critic, nay, a night-watch constable,
> A domineering pedant o'er the boy,
> Than whom no mortal so magnificent—
> This whimpled, whining, purblind, wayward boy,
> This Signior Junior, giant-dwarf, Dan Cupid,
> Regent of love-rhymes, lord of folded arms,
> Th'anointed sovereign of sighs and groans,
> Liege of all loiterers and malcontents,
> Dread Prince of Plackets, King of Codpieces,
> Sole imperator and great general
> Of trotting paritors—O my little heart!
> And I to be a corporal of his field,
> And wear his colours like a tumbler's hoop.

So much for the general. What follows is more particular:

> Nay, to be perjured, which is worst of all;
> And among three to love the worst of all—
> A whitely wanton with a velvet brow,
> With two pitch-balls stuck in her face for eyes,
> Ay and, by heaven, one that will do the deed,
> Though Argus were her eunuch and her guard!
> And I to sigh for her, to watch for her,
> To pray for her, go to: it is a plague
> That Cupid will impose for my neglect
> Of his almighty dreadful little might. . . .

Well, I will love, write, sigh, pray, sue, and groan—
Some men must love my lady, and some Joan.

Longaville, Dumaine and the King wear their folly with a difference. They have not Berowne's capacity to appreciate their own
absurdity. There is an exquisite gradation in their successive exposure. First comes Berowne inditing a sonnet, but before he can make
an end, the King approaches and he too carries a script. Berowne
climbs into a tree and overlooks his companions as one after another
they reveal their discomfiture and hide in turn from the next
arrival:

Like a demigod here sit I in the sky,
And wretched fools' secrets heedfully o'er-eye.

Securely aloft, he overhears how 'love may vary wit'. He observes
how each offender pretends to innocence and denounces his predecessor, till at last he descends to chide all three:

You found his mote; the king your mote did see;
But I a beam do find in each of three. . . .
O, what a scene of fool'ry have I seen,
Of sighs, of groans, of sorrow, and of teen.

Finally he is himself unmasked and shares in the general disgrace.

Berowne, however, is the first of the irrepressibles who in the
Elysian Fields acknowledge Falstaff for their leader. He snatches a
victory for nature from the defeat of pretension:

Sweet lords, sweet lovers, O let us embrace!
As true we are as flesh and blood can be—
The sea will ebb and flow, heaven show his face;
Young blood doth not obey an old decree:
We cannot cross the cause why we were born;
Therefore of all hands must we be forsworn.

And now he is ready to break into his great speech in praise of fair
women:

From women's eyes this doctrine I derive—
They are the ground, the books, the academes,
From whence doth spring the true Promethean fire.

> A lover's eyes will gaze an eagle blind;
> A lover's ear will hear the lowest sound,
> When the suspicious head of theft is stopped;
> Love's feeling is more soft and sensible
> Than are the tender horns of cockled snails;
> Love's tongue proves dainty Bacchus gross in taste.
> For valour, is not Love a Hercules,
> Still climbing trees in the Hesperides?
> Subtle as Sphinx, as sweet and musical
> As bright Apollo's lute, strung with his hair;
> And, when Love speaks, the voice of all the gods
> Make heaven drowsy with the harmony;

and so he advances to his practical conclusion:

> Then fools you were these women to forswear;
> Or, keeping what is sworn, you will prove fools.
> For wisdom's sake, a word, that all men love;
> Or for love's sake, a word that loves all men;
> Or for men's sake, the authors of these women;
> Or women's sake, by whom we men are men;
> Let us once loose our oaths, to find ourselves,
> Or else we lose ourselves to keep our oaths.

The sport, however, is not yet concluded. These sophisticated gentlemen have so far acknowledged the laws of nature as to forswear their unnatural enterprise, but they have still to win the ladies, and they set about it, not in the downright way of simple courtship, but with strange pastimes—masked as Russians, with a conned speech for 'a holy parcel of the fairest dames', with music and the King's petition that his Princess will 'vouchsafe some motion to it', with a splitting of jests and metaphors in which they are pitifully mocked and routed:

> The tongues of mocking wenches are as keen
>   As is the razor's edge invisible,
> Cutting a smaller hair than may be seen:
>   Above the sense of sense.

The remainder of the comedy turns less upon a quartet of lovers irretrievably forsworn as on the conduct of the ladies they are pledged to overcome. Who, then, are these ladies and what is their part in the play?

The Princess of France has been unfairly neglected. Shakespeare has not yet at his command the gifts which he will shortly bestow on his comic heroines—the music of Viola, the voluble precision of Rosalind, the glitter of Beatrice, the eloquence of Portia. But the Princess of France already bears the stamp royal. She has just that commingling of good sense and lively imagination, of quick feeling and clear thinking, of instinctive reserve and an equally instinctive candour, which distinguishes all Shakespeare's happy women who give away their hearts without losing their heads. She is the first flower upon a branch that was to bear blossoms of a deeper colour and a headier scent, all different and yet so unmistakably from the same stem; and there is a freshness in this first budding of an immortal type which has its special charm. Her first sedate challenge to the King, not without a hint of mischief, confronts him neatly with his own preposterous dilemma:

> I hear your grace hath sworn out house-keeping:
> 'Tis deadly sin to keep that oath, my lord,
> And sin to break it.

Her comment on the recreant lovers flies straight to the target:

> None are so surely caught, when they are catched,
> As wit turned fool. Folly, in wisdom hatched,
> Hath wisdom's warrant, and the help of school,
> And wit's own grace to grace a learned fool;

and at the last, upon news of her father's death, she announces her departure with an exquisite grave courtesy:

> I thank you, gracious lords,
> For all your fair endeavours, and entreat,
> Out of a new-sad soul, that you vouchsafe
> In your rich wisdom to excuse, or hide,
> The liberal opposition of our spirits,
> If over-boldly we have borne ourselves
> In the converse of breath—your gentleness

> Was guilty of it. Farewell, worthy lord:
> A heavy heart bears not a nimble tongue.

She puts the King and his fellow suitors in their place firmly but with the same courtesy:

> We have received your letters, full of love;
> Your favours, the ambassadors of love;
> And in our maiden council rated them
> At courtship, pleasant jest, and courtesy,
> As bombast and as lining to the time:
> But more devout than this in our respects
> Have we not been, and therefore met your loves
> In their own fashion, like a merriment.

Her final verdict tempers justice with mercy. She is willing to surrender but only upon fair terms and proofs of honour:

> KING: Now, at the latest minute of the hour,
> Grant us your loves.

> PRINCESS: A time methinks too short
> To make a world-without-end bargain in:
> No no, my lord, your grace is perjured much,
> Full of dear guiltiness; and therefore this—
> If for my love (as there is no such cause)
> You will do aught, this shall you do for me:
> Your oath I will not trust, but go with speed
> To some forlorn and naked hermitage,
> Remote from all the pleasures of the world;
> There stay until the twelve celestial signs
> Have brought about the annual reckoning.
> If this austere insociable life
> Change not your offer made in heat of blood,
> If frosts and fasts, hard lodging and thin weeds,
> Nip not the gaudy blossoms of your love,
> But that it bear this trial, and last love:
> Then, at the expiration of the year,
> Come challenge me, challenge by these deserts,
> And by this virgin palm now kissing thine,
> I will be thine.

Shakespeare took more care to provide this early comedy with an appropriate and finished conclusion than he showed in some of his later works. The Princess of France maintains to the last the serenity and poise which contrast so effectively with the wayward and extravagant behaviour of her royal suitor. Zestfully offering 'There's no such sport as sport by sport o'erthrown', she never loses her hold upon reality in pursuit of its shadow. She is adorably serious. The King, embarking upon his fantastic adventure, grandly exclaims:

> Let fame, that all hunt after in their lives,
> Live registred upon our brazen tombs.

The Princess, when she chides herself for seeking to shed the poor deer's blood in order to show her skill, discards this last infirmity of noble minds:

> And, out of question, so it is sometimes:
> Glory grows guilty of detested crimes,
> When for fame's sake, for praise, an outward part,
> We bend to that the working of the heart.

Rosaline, the first of Shakespeare's dark ladies, is second only to the Princess of France in securing pride of place for the women of the play. She is whole-hearted in her affection and generous in her praise:

> Berowne, they call him—but a merrier man,
> Within the limit of becoming mirth,
> I never spent an hour's talk withal.
> His eye begets occasion for his wit,
> For every object that the one doth catch
> The other turns to a mirth-moving jest,
> Which his fair tongue—conceit's expositor—
> Delivers in such apt and gracious words,
> That aged ears play truant at his tales,
> And younger hearings are quite ravishèd,
> So sweet and voluble is his discourse.

But she is of the Shakespearean sisterhood who, though won, must still be wooed:

> How I would make him fawn, and beg, and seek,
> And wait the season, and observe the times,

> And spend his prodigal wits in bootless rhymes,
> And shape his service wholly to my hests,
> And make him proud to make me proud, that jests!

She plagues her lover with an inverted tenderness and in the knowledge that he is a man who prizes spirit in a woman and looks for no easy victory. He must do penance with the rest and prove his claim to be wise and faithful. Her sentence is well delivered:

> The world's large tongue
> Proclaims you for a man replete with mocks,
> Full of comparisons and wounding flouts;
> Which you on all estates will execute
> That lie within the mercy of your wit. . . .
> To weed this wormwood from your fructful brain,
> And therewithal to win me, if you please—
> Without the which I am not to be won—
> You shall this twelvemonth term from day to day
> Visit the speechless sick, and still converse
> With groaning wretches; and your task shall be,
> With all the fierce endeavour of your wit,
> To enforce the painèd impotent to smile;

and she concludes in wisdom:

> A jest's prosperity lies in the ear
> Of him that hears it, never in the tongue
> Of him that makes it.

Berowne defends himself as well as he may—and not so badly either. It may be true, as Rosaline affirms, that 'better wits have worn plain statute caps', but—

> your beauty, ladies,
> Hath much deformed us, fashioning our humours
> Even to the opposèd end of our intents.

Let these damsels therefore bear some part of the blame for what 'in us hath seemed ridiculous':

> As love is full of unbefitting strains,
> All wanton as a child, skipping and vain,

Formed by the eye, and therefore, like the eye
Full of strange shapes, of habits and of forms,
Varying in subjects as the eye doth roll
To every varied object in his glance.

Therefore, ladies,
Our love being yours, the error that love makes
Is likewise yours: we to ourselves prove false,
By being once false for ever to be true
To those that make us both—fair ladies, you.
And even that falsehood, in itself a sin,
Thus purifies itself and turns to grace.

But Berowne has the grace to know that he is beaten and the humour to appreciate his discomfiture:

Thus pour the stars down plagues for perjury.
Can any face of brass hold longer out?
Here stand I, lady—dart thy skill at me,
Bruise me with scorn, confound me with a flout,
Thrust thy sharp wit quite through my ignorance,
Cut me to pieces with thy keen conceit.

His final repentance is devout and his promise of amendment made without reserve:

Taffeta phrases, silken terms precise,
Three-piled hyperboles, spruce affectation,
Figures pedantical—these summer-flies
Have blown me full of maggot ostentation.
I do forswear them, and I here protest,
By this white glove (how white the hand, God knows!)
Henceforth my wooing mind shall be expressed
In russet yeas and honest kersey noes.

Thus, in this pleasant conceited comedy, simple nature and good sense prevail over subtle sentiment and false conceit. All follies are redeemed and none is left in the stocks. In the conduct of plot and character the author keeps his wonted mean between sympathy and satire. It is yet more significant that in the Euphuistic embroideries of his theme Shakespeare shows the same tendency to identify himself

with the object of his derision. He means to mock these fine gentlemen for their preciosity, but, when he comes to write their verses,
we are often in doubt whether to admire their skill or smile at their
perversity. We begin to laugh and are caught by a melody. We
come to scoff and remain to pray that the music may continue.
Berowne, of whom it is said that every word is a jest and every jest
but a word, suddenly slips a line into his sonnet:

> Those thoughts to me were oaks, to thee like osiers bowed;

and we feel that Shakespeare, lost in the object of his mirth, has given
him something for which no poet need crave indulgence. The
King's sonnet, precious enough in all conscience, admirably sustains
the conceit on which it is founded and, though we may be jolted
into mockery as we ride along, it lands us at last in a crystal coach
upon the broad highway of the muses:

> So sweet a kiss the golden sun gives not
>   To those fresh morning drops upon the rose,
> As thy eye-beams, when their fresh rays have smote
>   The night of dew that on my cheek down flows:
> Nor shines the silver moon one half so bright
>   Through the transparent bosom of the deep,
> As doth thy face through tears of mine give light:
>   Thou shin'st in every tear that I do weep,
> No drop but as a coach doth carry thee:
>   So ridest thou triumphing in my woe.
> Do but behold the tears that swell in me,
>   And they thy glory through my grief will show:
> But do not love thyself—then thou wilt keep
> My tears for glasses, and still make me weep.

If this be parody it is such that only a poet, indulgently smiling at a
brother's extravagance, could write. It is written in sport, but might
have fallen from the sheaf inscribed to Mr. W. H. Shakespeare is
smiling at his own excess, standing aside as it were, from the solemn
achievement of his younger muse, presenting it for our merriment.
The pure comedian, flouting absurdity, would have written for his
poetasters effusions that were wholly ridiculous. Molière, satirising a

precious marquis, indites for him an impromptu whose pretentious
inanity is heightened by the absurd comments of his admirers:

> Oh, oh, je n'y prenais pas garde:
> Tandis que, sans songer à mal, je vous regarde,
> Votre œil en tapinois me dérobe mon cœur.
> Au voleur, au voleur, au voleur, au voleur!

Congreve composes for Mr. Brisk after the same fashion:

> For as the sun shines every day,
> So, of our coachman I may say,
> He shows his drunken fiery face,
> Just as the sun does, more or less.
> And when at night his labour's done,
> Then too, like heaven's charioteer the sun,
> Into the dairy he descends,
> And there his whipping and his driving ends;
> There he's secure from danger and from bilk,
> His fare is paid him, and he sits in milk.

There is no fellow-feeling in Molière for Mascarille or in Congreve
for Mr. Brisk, as they spout and posture to their coteries of half-wits.
The mood, intention and result are entirely different. Shakespeare
can laugh at his Euphuists and love them, too.

Nor does Shakespeare's sympathy so generously extended to the
finer wits of his comedy stop short at grosser manifestations of the
literary fashion at which he aims. His wits 'have been at a great feast
of languages and stolen the scraps' and upon such as 'have lived long
on the alms-basket of words' he can be downright satirical:

> This fellow pecks up wit, as pigeons pease,
> And utters it again when God doth please.

> A' can carve too, and lisp: why, this is he
> That kissed his hand away in courtesy.
> This is the ape of form, monsieur the nice,
> That when he plays at tables chides the dice
> In honourable terms; nay, he can sing
> A mean most meanly, and, in ushering,
> Mend him who can. The ladies call him sweet.
> The stairs as he treads on them kiss his feet.

But how he delights in Holofernes, the schoolmaster, speaking by the book; Sir Nathaniel, the priest, adoring a text; Don Armado, the fantastical knight, composing a letter; Costard, the clown, who must needs be in the fashion, too! What zest he imparts to the display of their talents! They have all drunk of the cup of Dionysus, and Shakespeare, sharing their intoxication, comprehends their contempt for any dullard to whom the Pierian spring supplies no headier draught than plain mineral water:

> Sir, he hath never fed of the dainties that are
>   bred in a book.
> He hath not eat paper, as it were; he hath not
>   drunk ink:
> His intellect is not replenished, he is only an
>   animal, only sensible in the duller parts:

Holofernes blesses God for his gift and Shakespeare enjoys it with him even as he parodies its exercise:

This is a gift that I have, simple, simple; a foolish extravagant spirit, full of forms, figures, shapes, objects, ideas, apprehensions, motions, revolutions. These are begot in the ventricle of memory, nourished in the womb of pia mater, and delivered upon the mellowing of occasion. . . . But the gift is good in those in whom it is acute, and I am thankful for it.

These fantastical fellows have their own standard of excellence and Shakespeare enjoys their company. Listen to Sir Nathaniel, the curate, and Holofernes, the schoolmaster, discussing the qualities of good conversation and the merits of Don Armado:

SIR NATHANIEL: I praise God for you, sir. Your reasons at dinner have been sharp and sententious; pleasant without scurrility, witty without affection, audacious without impudency, learned without opinion, and strange without heresy. . . I did converse this quondam day with a companion of the king's, who is entitled, nominated, or called Don Adriano de Armado.

HOLOFERNES: Novi hominem tanquam te. His humour is lofty, his discourse peremptory: his tongue filed, his eye ambitious, his gait majestical, and his general behaviour vain, ridiculous, and thrasonical. . . . He is too picked, too spruce, too affected, too odd as it were, too peregrinate as I may call it.

SIR NATHANIEL: A most singular and choice epithet. (*Draws out his table-book.*)

HOLOFERNES: He draweth out the thread of his verbosity finer than the staple of his argument. I abhor such fanatical phantasimes, such insociable and point-devise companions, such rackers of orthography.

Holofernes is undeniably a figure of fun, but Shakespeare identifies himself with his folly as completely as with the more delicate absurdity of Berowne, and in his boundless geniality suffers the pedant to rebuke with simple dignity the fine gentlemen who bait him when he brings on the Nine Worthies for their entertainment: *This is not generous, not gentle, not humble.*

Don Armado is admittedly a caricature, but he is no empty husk. To him also Shakespeare gives of his best and our mockery stands abashed when suddenly he, too, is touched with his author's magic and pleads for Hector: 'The sweet war-man is dead and rotten; sweet chucks, beat not the bones of the buried.'[1] Nor is he easily put down. Flouted by the lords and 'infamonized among potentates' he retains our respect even in confessing that he has no shirt and he retires with dignity:

For mine own part, I breathe free breath: I have seen the day of wrong through the little hole of discretion, and I will right myself like a soldier.

In his courtship of Jaquenetta he calls to mind, for all his absurdity, the wooing of Audrey by the melancholy wise man who was shortly to epitomise the seven ages of man and shows himself the more likeable fellow of the two. For Armado is in love—so deep in love that he is struck as speechless in the presence of his monosyllabic mistress as he is voluble in her absence:

ARMADA: Maid.
JAQUENETTA: Man.
ARMADO: I will visit thee at the lodge.
JAQUENETTA: That's hereby.

[1] Shakespeare, in the flush of his young genius, could not foresee that he would one day commit the very impiety which Don Armado here denounces. There is an odd thrill in these lines for those who have seen their author astray and beating the bones of the buried in 'Troilus and Cressida'.

ARMADO: I know where it is situate.
JAQUENETTA: Lord, how wise you are!
ARMADO: I will tell thee wonders.
JAQUENETTA: With that face?
ARMADO: I love thee.
JAQUENETTA: So I heard you say.
ARMADO: And so farewell.
JAQUENETTA: Fair weather after you!

And his devotion is put to a proof that brings him quite literally to earth:

> I am a votary; I have vowed to Jaquenetta
> To hold the plough for her sweet love three year.

Even in a ludicrous misemployment of words and fancies Shakespeare is seldom remote from his own felicity. 'Arts-man', says Armado, taking Holofernes by the elbow, 'perambulate. We will be singled from the barbarians'. He continues: 'It is the King's most sweet pleasure and affection to congratulate the princess at her pavilion in the posteriors of this day, which the rude multitude call the afternoon'. Holofernes snaps at this preposterous image: 'The posterior of the day, most generous Sir, is liable, congruent and measurable for the afternoon: the word is well called, chose—sweet and apt'. Mere foolery but nearly twenty years later Shakespeare's Menenius was to describe himself as more conversible 'with the buttock of the night than the forehead of the morning'. Or take the scene in which the King's gentlemen cap one another in finding similitudes for the peaked face of Holofernes—the head of a bodkin . . . a death's face in a ring . . . the face of an old Roman coin . . . the carved-bone face on a flask . . . the pummel of Caesar's falchion. It is a catalogue that beckons us forward to a certain tavern in Eastcheap where Sir John Falstaff will grow breathless with base comparisons: you starveling, you elf-skin, you dried neat's tongue . . . you tailor's yard, you sheath, you bow-case, you vile standing tuck!' Then, too, we come upon Armado and Moth seated beneath the trees in the Park of Navarre. 'Warble, child, make passionate my sense of hearing', prays Armado. 'Come, warble, come,' urges the

melancholy Jaques in the Forest of Arden. The mood is consonate
and the place contiguous.

Costard, the clown, is allowed a touch of nature which brings
him to life and endears him to the spectator:

COSTARD: 'I Pompey am, Pompey surnamed the Big'—
DUMAINE: The Great.
COSTARD: It is 'great,' sir.—'Pompey surnamed the Great,
    That oft in field with targe and shield did make my foe to
    sweat,
    And travelling along this coast I here am come by chance,
    And lay my arms before the legs of this sweet lass of France.'
    (*Casts down shield and sword.*)
    If your ladyship would say, 'Thanks Pompey,' I had done.
PRINCESS: Great thanks, Great Pompey.
COSTARD: 'Tis not so much worth; but I hope I was perfect. I made a
    little fault in 'Great'.

And Sir Nathaniel, the curate, driven from the scene by the
mockery of the fine gentlemen who have not their author's embrac-
ing love for a simpleton, is accorded a testimonial which puts him,
too, among those who are forever redeemed by the love of their
creator:

COSTARD: There, an't shall please you, a foolish mild man—an honest
man, look you, and soon dashed. He is a marvellous good neighbour,
faith, and a very good bowler: but for Alisander, alas you see how 'tis—a
little o'erparted.

Molière, satirising a literary fashion in his *Les Précieuses Ridicules*,
presented a group of exquisites which were not only true to the
period but true of all the exquisites who ever lived. His characters
were from life and there was not a phrase or gesture in his comedy
which could not be matched from the conversation and behaviour of
his originals. So long as complicated fashion is liable to corrupt
natural simplicity his play will remain amusing and intelligible. He
successfully avoided, in fact, the faults which he was denouncing,
refraining from a preciosity which might have tempted him to
multiply his local and personal allusions and would in time have

rendered much of his comedy incomprehensible to posterity. Shakespeare's 'Love's Labour's Lost', though in essentials it is broader in humanity than Molière's play, has, on the contrary, become in places difficult and here and there forever meaningless even to the scholar. The reason, again, is to be sought in the fact that Shakespeare, less intent than Molière on the 'correction of social absurdity', is absorbed into the game from which Molière held aloof in a more critical frame of mind. Molière looked on at the follies which he denounced. Shakespeare romps whole-heartedly with his fools. His play is more in the nature of a family diversion in which intimate private jests are exchanged for the fun of the thing. To many of these witticisms we have lost the clue. They remain embedded in his play, to use the vivid metaphor of Dr. Dover Wilson, as 'persistent flies in its amber'. There is 'a crowd of ephemeral references and allusions which, undissolved, irritate as specks of grit irritate the eye'. Dr. Johnson, discussing these blemishes, charged the author with sacrificing permanent interest to personal satire. Shakespeare, he argues, in presenting Holofernes, was so bent on ridiculing the local schoolmaster that his portrait has little value for those who are unacquainted with the original. 'It is of the nature of personal invectives', Johnson writes, 'to be soon unintelligible: and the author that gratifies private malice, *animam in vulnere ponit,* destroys the future efficacy of his own writings and sacrifices the esteem of succeeding time to the laughter of a day.' Very trenchant and very true; but wholly irrelevant. There is no private malice in the presentation of Holofernes or Moth or Armado. There is not even a sustained criticism of their extravagance. If Shakespeare in this comedy sacrificed the esteem of succeeding time to the laughter of a day, it was not owing to any malice, private or general, but to a warm interest in his characters, and boundless pleasure in their oddities of mind.

It is possible by study and the exercise of imagination to recover something of that laughter of a day which for the casual reader is irretrievably lost.[1] But we are seeking here confirmation that in the

[1] Dr. Dover Wilson has recovered all but ninety per cent. of it. 'Love's Labour's Lost' has an irresistible charm and attraction for the best critics. Pater devotes to it one of his finest 'Appreciations'; Granville Barker one of his notable 'Prefaces' and

topicalities of the play as in its general design Shakespeare, so far from gratifying any private malice, was presenting a picture of contemporary manners to an audience which was more than ready to take everything in good part—that he was offering it, in fact, not a personal invective but, in the words of the title-page, a pleasant conceited comedy. Whether, in point of fact—as seems not at all unlikely—we may identify Holofernes with John Florio, Moth with Thomas Nashe, the little Academe of the King of Navarre with the group of Copernicans and black magicians whose poet was George Chapman, there can be no doubt whatever that 'Love's Labour's Lost', as played before the Queen in 1597, was a topical piece packed with open and covert allusions to a piece of social history in which many members of the distinguished audience had, in fact, themselves participated. His theme, moreover, was not only topical but dangerous. Shakespeare in the comic vein contrived in 'Love's Labour's Lost' to do precisely what he did more seriously, and just as successfully, in 'Richard II' and 'King John', namely to write a play bristling with perilous implications and to escape either censure or calumny because he wrote it with an entire absence of prejudice, putting a natural emphasis upon its broadly human as opposed to its narrowly social, political or sectarian aspects, exhibiting a tolerance that embraced every man in his humour, passions, affections, foibles and infirmities.[1] It was an almost unique achievement. His contemporaries seldom meddled with subjects of public or social interest without paying the penalty. Jonson, Nashe, Kyd, Chapman—all experienced the untender mercies of Star Chamber. To write a topical play under Elizabeth or James was to ask for trouble and in most cases to get it promptly and in full measure. But Shakespeare was never molested. He wandered freely in a world in which neither the Queen who was quite prepared to hang a man for witnessing a play with treason in it, nor the King who put Jonson in prison

Dr. Dover Wilson, in collaboration with Quiller-Couch, an 'Introduction' which is as sensitive to its enduring magic as it is erudite and ingenious in the elucidation of its fugitive allusions.

[1] See the present author's *Political Characters of Shakespeare*, published in 1945.

for a play which made fun of the Scots, ever challenged his conduct
or authority.

To those who are unfamiliar with the social background to
'Love's Labour's Lost' it must seem impossible that it should contain
anything perilous to life or liberty. The play is, nevertheless, charged
with brimstone:

> Black is the badge of hell,
> The hue of dungeons and the School of Night.

The King of Navarre is here treading on dangerous ground and
Berowne with his enigmatic praise of black ladies and commendation of ebony as a wood divine is inviting disaster. In the spring of
1593 the Queen's Privy Council were taking a sinister interest in a
small society which counted among its initiates Chapman, Kyd and
Marlowe, among the dramatists, and no less a person than Sir
Walter Raleigh among the nobility. These men studied the stars;
they were proficient in the art of numbers and were even suspected
of raising the devil. A warrant was issued for Marlowe's arrest, but
he was killed in a brawl before he could be brought to trial. Kyd
was put to the torture. Raleigh, already in disgrace, was later examined by a special commission appointed to investigate his 'heresies'.
Into the thick of all this comes Shakespeare, smiling, with a pleasant
conceited comedy in his hand; and the comedy is presented to the
Queen at Christmas. In it he presents a little academe of seclusive
gentlemen who also study the stars and swear to sleep for only three
hours in twenty-four. The play abounds in cryptic allusions to
numbers and chapmen's tongues. Berowne sings the praises of sable
beauty. But Shakespeare seems not to be in the least aware of his
peril. He makes fun of these fantastical gentlemen, but it is all done
in pure kindness of heart. His references to certain poets, head-over-
heels implicated in some very dangerous proceedings, are not in the
least censorious. He seems to be neither of one side nor the other. He
promises a satire on the wicked and a castigation of fools; but the
wicked prove on acquaintance to be excellent company and the
fools are merely diverting. Was there ever a more striking example
of charity in genius covering a multitude of sins any one of which
was a hanging matter in the eyes of authority?

And so we revert to Berowne himself, who of all the characters in this strangely enchanting medley of wit and poetry most fully expresses its mood and purpose. For Shakespeare in Berowne is smiling not merely at follies with which after the fashion of his comic genius he puts himself for the time being in imaginative sympathy, but at folly to which he was himself as a poet peculiarly liable in his own person. There is in all that Berowne utters what Pater has described as 'a delicate raillery by Shakespeare himself at his own chosen manner . . . He has at times some of its extravagance or caricature also, but the shades of expression by which he passes from this to the "golden cadence" of Shakespeare's own most characteristic verse, are so fine that it is sometimes difficult to trace them . . . . That gloss of dainty language is a second nature with him: even at its best he is not without a certain artifice: the trick of playing on words never deserts him; and Shakespeare, in whose own genius there is an element of this very quality, shows us in this graceful, and, as it seems, studied, portrait, his enjoyment of it'.

Pater was concerned more with the literary than with the dramatic significance of Berowne. He sees in Berowne 'a reflex of Shakespeare himself, when he has just become able to stand aside from and estimate the first period of his poetry'. He is fascinated by that 'foppery' of language which 'satisfies a real instinct in our minds—the fancy so many of us have for an exquisite and curious skill in the use of words'. This, however, is but one aspect of the matter. Berowne is the first of Shakespeare's characters in which the essential quality of his comic genius becomes apparent. He is the first fine product of that imaginative process whereby Shakespeare identifies himself with the object of his mirth, thus combining in a single gesture of the spirit, detachment with sympathy, serene judgment with congenial understanding, the objectivity of a creating mind with an entire subjection of the imagination to the thing created.

To conclude all, the cuckoo sings:

> When daisies pied, and violets blue,
>   And lady-smocks all silver-white:
> And cuckoo-buds of yellow hue,
>   Do paint the meadows with delight:

> The cuckoo then, on every tree,
> Mocks married men; for thus sings he,
> Cuckoo. . . .
> Cuckoo, cuckoo: O word of fear,
> Unpleasing to a married ear.
>
> When shepherds pipe on oaten straws,
> And merry larks are ploughmen's clocks:
> When turtles tread and rooks and daws,
> And maidens bleach their summer smocks:
> The cuckoo then, on every tree,
> Mocks married men; for thus sings he,
> Cuckoo. . . .
> Cuckoo, cuckoo: O word of fear,
> Unpleasing to a married ear.

And the owl sings, too:

> When icicles hang by the wall,
> And Dick the shepherd blows his nail:
> And Tom bears logs into the hall,
> And milk comes frozen home in pail:
> When blood is nipped, and ways be foul,
> Then nightly sings the staring owl,
> To-whit to-who. . . .
> A merry note,
> While greasy Joan doth keel the pot.
>
> When all aloud the wind doth blow,
> And coughing drowns the parson's saw:
> And birds sit brooding in the snow,
> And Marian's nose looks red and raw:
> When roasted crabs hiss in the bowl,
> Then nightly sings the staring owl,
> To-whit to-who. . . .
> A merry note,
> While greasy Joan doth keel the pot.

Shakespeare withdraws from his little academe and destroys by example all that he has seemed to encourage by precept in his pleasant conceited comedy. The exquisites whom he was too kind to destroy as Molière destroyed those of a later day, fade away like bright figures in a tapestry as suddenly a window is thrown open upon a meadow in Warwickshire and in place of a gay and pretty masque of quaint lords and sweet ladies, Dick the shepherd blows his nail and greasy Joan doth keel the pot.

The author's script, enigmatic to the last, concludes with a sentence attributed to none of the characters: *The words of Mercury are harsh after the songs of Apollo*. Is there here a hint of the secret we are after? One would like to imagine that this Delphic line, printed large in the quarto, was a comment written on Shakespeare's MS by a friendly critic who had been struck by that peculiar quality of indulgence which distinguishes the comedies of Shakespeare from all others of his time.

These are the songs of Apollo, after which all other words come harsh upon the ear.

II

TOUCHSTONE

As You Like It

AMONG the dramatic styles enumerated by Polonius in announcing the players at Elsinore was the pastoral-comical. It was coming well into fashion at the beginning of the seventeenth century and Shakespeare was bound sooner or later to handle it. Pastoral-comical is not of course confined to the theatre. It satisfies the craving of civilised people in all ages to assume a simplicity which is, in effect, only a further step in sophistication. My lady of fashion fancies herself as a Dresden shepherdess; the raffish young gentleman sees himself piping on an oaten straw. Poets, painters and composers, great and small, have ministered down the ages to this affectation, which has been responsible for more bad verse, insipid pictures and commonplace music than has sprung from any other reputable source on Parnassus.

Shakespeare, writing his first draft of 'As You Like It' in 1593, could hardly forbear to remember that in Christopher Marlowe England had just lost an author who had made a very notable contribution to the sylvan muse:

> Dead shepherd, now I find thy saw of might,
> Who ever loved that loved not at first sight?

Spenser had published 'The Shepherd's Calendar' and Sidney his 'Arcadia'. Plays, poems and novels, in which the deceitful amenities of court and city life were contrasted with the simple pleasures of the countryside, were in high demand. The fashion had come from Italy and it had come to stay. There was as yet no Hazlitt to deplore its anaemic graces. Hazlitt described 'Arcadia', which in 1590 had started upon a triumphant career which was to carry it far and wide over Europe, as 'one of the greatest monuments of the abuse of intellectual power'. But by that time the pastoral-comical had flourished for over two centuries. Fletcher had sentimentalised it in

'The Faithful Shepherdess'; Ben Jonson had weighted it with his
learning; in numerous masques Molière had collaborated with Corneille to give it liveliness and gravity; Inigo Jones had devised suitable
costumes and appropriate settings for its nymphs, shepherds and
divinities; Milton had converted it from pastoral-comical to pastoral-
ethical in his 'Comus'; English cavaliers and French exquisites had
flattered or flouted their mistresses in rustical odes, sonnets and
impromptus; Marie Antoinette had postured as a dairymaid at
Trianon, and Rousseau had written a political treatise in which it was
assumed that man might solve all his social problems by making a
fresh start from the state of nature.

Pastoral-comical, returning to the age of innocence, harks back to
the mythology of the antique world. Its devotees are as conscientiously erudite as they are resolutely simple-minded. The shepherd
courts his mistress in an eclogue and is passionate by the book. The
nymph, in her daydreaming, quotes Ovid or, taking up her lute,
extemporises a madrigal:

> Love in my bosom like a bee
>   doth suck his sweet:
> Now with his wings he plays with me,
>   now with his feet.
> Within mine eyes he makes his nest,
> His bed amidst my tender breast,
> My kisses are his daily feast;
> And yet he robs me of my rest. . . .

and keeps it up for as many stanzas as you please.

All the divinities in the Graeco-Roman calendar must be invoked
to picture her:

The blush that gloried Luna when she kist the shepherd on the hills of
Latmos was not tainted with such a pleasant dye as the vermilion flour-
isht on the silver hue of [her] countenance; her eyes were like those lamps
that make the wealthy covert of the heavens more gorgeous, sparkling
favour and disdain; courteous and yet coy, as if in them Venus had placed
all her amorets, and Diana all her chastity. The trammels of her hair,
folded in a caul of gold, so surpassed the burnisht glister of the metal as
the sun doth the meanest star in brightness: the tresses that fold in the

brows of Apollo were not half so rich to the sight; for in her hairs it seemed love had laid herself in ambush, to entrap the proudest eye that durst gaze upon their excellence.

The sylvan scene is set with an artifice that matches a wooing of swains who, if their mistresses cannot be moved in the mother tongue, are ever ready to try the effect of a Latin tag or a French sonnet:

The ground where they sat was diapred with Flora's riches, as if she meant to wrap Tellus in the glory of her vestments: round about in the form of an amphitheatre were most curiously planted pine trees, interseamed with lemons and citrons, which with the thickness of their boughs so shadowed the place that Phoebus could not pry into the secret of that arbour; so united were the tops with so thick a closure that Venus might there in her jollity have dallied unseen with her dearest paramour. Fast by, to make the place more gorgeous, was there a Fount so crystalline and clear that it seemed Diana with her Dryads and Hemadryads had that spring as the secret of all their bathings.

The pleasures of a simple life are recommended with an artful duplicity:

Envy stirs not us, we covet not to climb, our desires mount not above our degrees nor our thoughts above our fortunes. Care cannot harbour in our cottages, nor do our homely couches know broken slumbers; as we exceed not in diet, so we have enough to satisfy; and, Mistress, I have so much Latin, *Satis est quod sufficit.*

Their love-gifts are apples and chestnuts and it would stain the honour of a shepherdess to set the end of passion upon pelf. But they are well read in the satyrical Roman rogue: *quarenda pecunia primum, post nummos virtus.* Crowns have crosses when mirth is in cottages; but your shepherd, though he be dying for love, is not inaccessible to argument and knows that a maid who is beautiful, virtuous *and wealthy* has three deep persuasions to make love frolic. The nymph, though she shroud her pains in the cinders of modesty, protects her face from the sun with a chaplet of roses and is not unaware of the fetching picture she makes in a petticoat of scarlet covered with a green mantle. They would hoodwink you into

believing that, taking bag and bottle to the field, where they have
such cates as country state may allow, sauced with sweet content and
engaging prattle, they have learned to forswear courtly junkets; but
we begin to have some doubt about the sincerity of this rustic conversion when we find the lady taking good care to provide herself
with a kirtle so fine that she seems some heavenly nymph harboured
in country attire or when the gentleman comes in apparelled all in
tawny to signify that he is forsaken, on his head a garland of willow
and on his sheephook two sonnets as labels of his loves and fortunes.

The learnèd reader will by now have realised that he is in the forest
of Arden—not yet Shakespeare's Arden but the Arden of Thomas
Lodge, whose 'Golden Legacie', attributed to Euphues and fetched
from the Canaries, was brought to London in 1590 and published
with a dedication to the Lord Chamberlain of her Majesty's household.

Lodge's tale of Rosalynde is a pretty piece of work, perhaps the
most instructively typical of its kind in the English language. It is
worth reading for itself and it has an interest for the historian who
seeks acquaintance with the social and literary taste of the period.
For those who have tried so often and so unsuccessfully to come upon
Shakespeare in the act of diverting to his purpose a unique and
original source its value is inestimable. No older play has been found
to stand between the author of 'As You Like It' and the original
fount of his inspiration. Shakespeare's comedy comes straight out of
the novella of Thomas Lodge—theme, characters and incidents.
The cribbing is everywhere manifest. Yet though everything is
taken, nothing remains the same. The likenesses everywhere serve
only to display the difference. In no play of Shakespeare are his
native wood-notes more freshly heard. There is dew on every shoot.
In no play is the language so apt, lucid and free. The dramatist finds
his material sophisticated, mannered, artfully ingenuous, studied in
playfulness, affected in sentiment. This he transmutes into something
which conveys an impression of unfettered simplicity. Light and
shade in this comedy ripple to the movement of forest leaves in the
wind. It is as voluble as a bird in April, as happy as a summer day is
long. Here, as the mood takes them, men fleet the time carelessly as

in the golden world or under the shade of melancholy boughs lose
and neglect the creeping hours of time. Shakespeare, imparting a
genuine innocence to a style that merely affects it, plays the same
trick with the characters and incidents. The wicked brother in
Lodge's tale, the usurping Duke, the loves of Rosader (Orlando)
and Rosalynde, the reformation of Saladyne (Oliver) and his wooing
of Aliena (Celia) are treated with all the solemnity and particularity
that befits a pastoral tale of knights and ladies. Shakespeare changes
none of the incidents; some of the smallest details crop up unexpectedly in a phrase or turn of the action. But as with the style, so
with the matter. The transmutation is complete. The quarrel between the brothers, which in Lodge is a desperate sustained feud, full
of sound and fury, is presented in Shakespeare's comedy as a boyish
squabble, to be taken just as seriously as the plot requires and no
more:

OLIVER: Know you where you are, sir?

ORLANDO: O, sir, very well: here in your orchard.

OLIVER: Know you before whom, sir?

ORLANDO: Ay, better than him I am before knows me; I know you are
my eldest brother, and in the gentle condition of blood you should so
know me: the courtesy of nations allows you my better, in that you are
the first-born, but the same tradition takes not away my blood, were
there twenty brothers betwixt us: I have as much of my father in me as
you, albeit I confess your coming before me is nearer to his reverence.

OLIVER: What, boy!

ORLANDO: Come, come, elder brother, you are too young in this.

OLIVER: Wilt thou lay hands on me, villain?

ORLANDO: I am no villain: I am the youngest son of Sir Rowland de
Boys, he was my father, and he is thrice a villain that says such a father
begot villains.

Lodge expends as much time on the bad brother's conversion as
on the adventures of Rosalynde. Shakespeare takes the bad brother
for his plot but never takes him seriously as a person and throws him
into Celia's arms at the end of the story with a nonchalance which,
among other odd consequences, entails the presence of a lioness in
the heart of Warwickshire. Lodge winds up his romantic pastoral
with a battle in which the banished duke lays on 'such loade upon

his enemies that he showed how highly he did estimate of a crown'. The usurper is slain and the reader invited to reflect that 'such as neglect their father's precepts incur much prejudice'. Shakespeare winds up his comedy with a graceful litany that pleasantly mocks its own formality:

> PHEBE: Good shepherd, tell this youth what 'tis to love.
> SILVIUS: It is to be all made of sighs and tears,
>   And so am I for Phebe.
> PHEBE: And I for Ganymede.
> ORLANDO: And I for Rosalind.
> ROSALIND: And I for no woman.
>
> SILVIUS: It is to be all made of fantasy,
>   All made of passion, and all made of wishes,
>   All adoration, duty and observance,
>   All humbleness, all patience, and impatience,
>   All purity, all trial, all observance;
>   And so am I for Phebe.
> PHEBE: And so am I for Ganymede.
> ORLANDO: And so am I for Rosalind.
> ROSALIND: And so am I for no woman.

But Shakespeare's 'translation' of the 'Golden Legacie' into his own sweet style is only half the miracle. For he uses here his old trick— the trick played in 'Love's Labour's Lost'—of throwing himself heart and soul into a convention and at the same time of subjecting it to the searching eye of the comic muse.[1] How dulcetly lovelorn is his quartet of amorists! Shakespeare plays the game to perfection. But, suddenly: 'Pray you, no more of this,' exclaims Rosalind, ''tis like the howling of Irish wolves against the moon.' It is a final fling of mother nature against pastoral-comical in which the author merrily libels his own performance. Shakespeare creates his illusion of a golden world, imposing on our imagination with an imperious felicity; but, once we are securely naturalised within its borders, we become aware that beside us, forever whispering, is an ironic spirit which, knowing what it loves, can smile indulgently on what it knows. Shakespeare leads us into the forest of Arden in all good

[1] See above, p. 25.

faith. This is a place where civilised men seek release from themselves in a return to nature. How delightful! Yet, at the same time, how preposterous! For human nature in the forest of Arden is still human nature—the same there as anywhere else and no-one can escape it.

Shakespeare makes not the slightest effort to rusticate us among the shepherds with set descriptions of fields, fountains, arbours and glades or return us to an antique world with constant allusions to the classical mythos. We are not impelled to be conscientiously agrestic. We just slip away, as with a countryman returning home, to meet a fool i' the forest, to find Orlando under a tree like a dropped acorn or the melancholy Jaques lying beside the brook that brawls along this wood. It is a forest that grows easily about us, and truant songs, tuned to the sweet bird's throat, make us free of simple faring in all its seasons:

> And this our life, exempt from public haunt,
> Finds tongues in trees, books in the running brooks,
> Sermons in stones and good in everything.

The winter wind bites and blows to the tune of 'Hey-ho the holly'; a lover and his lass pass over the green cornfields in springtime. It is all done so happily that Shakespeare, himself in a holiday mood, is tempted to applaud his own felicity:

> Happy is your grace
> That can translate the stubbornness of fortune
> Into so quiet and so sweet a style.

The spell is immediate for those who are content to accept from Shakespeare no more than the freedom of this sylvan city, who go with Rosalind and Celia to liberty and not to banishment, who venture forth with Orlando and old Adam to light upon some settled low content, who make one of the charmed circle who listen while the sententious, melancholy Jaques moralises the spectacle of a weeping deer or descants upon the seven ages of man. In the words of 'Q', he who knows this Arden 'has looked into the heart of England and heard the birds sing in the green midmost of a moated island'. But other and finer pleasures are in store. Shakespeare, entering into Arden, yields his fancy to its enchantment, but does not therefore leave behind him his mother wit or sense of proportion. He takes with him as large a charter as the wind to blow on whom he pleases. His genial irony plays about each character in turn, his fellowship with these happy outlaws being all the more complete for his ability to see them in the light of nature. There is no desire or intention to bring them to judgment. Each abounds in his own grace or folly, his absolute quality emerging from his encounters and relationships with all the rest.

In most of Shakespeare's comedies there is a character who stands, as it were, at the centre. To get a clear view of the composition as a whole we must take up our position as near as possible beside him.

In 'Love's Labour's Lost' we found our point of reference for the comic values of the play in Berowne. In 'A Midsummer Night's Dream' it may be said concerning Bottom that 'if he come not, the play is marred'. For 'As You Like It' the author has named his own Touchstone. It is as though Shakespeare, setting out for Arden, where so many excellent poets have lost themselves in affected sentiment, mislaid their common sense in refining upon their sensibility and, in their self-conscious pursuit of nature, found themselves grasping a pale misfeatured shadow, had determined in advance to take with him a guide who should keep him in the path of sanity. Touchstone puts all things and every person in the play, including himself, to the comic test. Entering Arden with Touchstone you cannot go astray or mistake the wood for the trees.

It is his function to 'speak wisely what wise men do foolishly' and he loses no time about it. We are to accept him at once as no respecter of false persons:

TOUCHSTONE: Mistress, you must come away to your father.
CELIA: Were you made the messenger?
TOUCHSTONE: No, by mine honour, but I was bid to come for you.
ROSALIND: Where learned you that oath, fool?
TOUCHSTONE: Of a certain knight, that swore by his honour they were good pancakes, and swore by his honour the mustard was naught: now I'll stand to it, the pancakes were naught and the mustard was good, and yet was not the knight forsworn.

CELIA: How prove you that, in the great heap of your knowledge?

ROSALIND: Ay, marry, now unmuzzle your wisdom.

TOUCHSTONE: Stand you both forth now: stroke your chins, and swear by your beards that I am a knave.

CELIA: By our beards (if we had them) thou art.

TOUCHSTONE: By my knavery (if I had it) then I were: but if you swear by that that is not, you are not forsworn:

We are next to observe that this Touchstone has a lively sense of the fitness of things. Le Beau enters to tell the ladies of much good sport —how Charles, the wrestler, has broken the ribs of three proper young men, of excellent growth and presence:

TOUCHSTONE: But what is the sport, monsieur, that the ladies have lost?

LE BEAU: Why, this that I speak of.

TOUCHSTONE: Thus men may grow wiser every day. It is the first time that ever I heard breaking of ribs was sport for ladies.

We are to esteem him also as a loyal servant who, without any illusions as to the sequel, is ready at a word to 'go along o'er the wide world' with his mistress. This is no merely incidental touch. That Touchstone should set out in sturdy devotion, with an agreeably romantic expectation, is a fact essential to our appreciation of his quality. *His* part in the comedy is to shed the light of reality and common sense upon its fanciful figures and diversions. To play such a part he must be either a true cynic or one that affects his cynicism to mask a fundamentally genial spirit. Now a true cynic would be out of place in the forest of Arden. So Touchstone must be a thoroughly good fellow at heart. His brain may be as dry as the remainder biscuit after a voyage but he must be essentially a genial spirit. His acidity must be no more than skin-deep. He will see things as they are but without malice. He will have a keen flair for absurdity in people and things—not least for his own infirmities. He will, moreover, bring all things to the test of action, and the climax of *his* comedy will be to marry a slut so that he may embrace in reality the simple life which for his companions is no more than a holiday affectation.

How characteristic is his entry into the pastoral pleasaunce:

ROSALIND: O Jupiter! How weary are my spirits!

TOUCHSTONE: I care not for my spirits, if my legs were not weary.

ROSALIND: Well, this is the forest of Arden.

TOUCHSTONE: Ay, now am I in Arden, the more fool I. When I was at home, I was in a better place, but travellers must be content.

This is wholesome correction and it comes most aptly between a touching scene in which Adam displays 'the constant service of the antique world', and our first encounter with Silvius and Corin—a young man and an old in solemn talk. Note, too, how he pricks the bladder of sentiment, not by rejecting its appeal, but by claiming a share in its manifestations. The love of Silvius for Phebe and of Rosalind for Orlando prompts him to declare: 'We that are true lovers run into strange capers; but as all is mortal in nature, so is all nature in love mortal in folly'; and he is driven to remember—nor do we doubt the fidelity of the reminiscence—his own love for Jane Smile and the kissing of her batler and the cow's dugs that her pretty chopt hands had milked. All Touchstone is in that little speech—his quaint pretension to philosophy and a capacity for romance, rooted in nature but aware of its own excess. Jane Smile's hands were pretty but the eye of the realist could not avoid noticing that they were chopt.

Touchstone, coming to terms with the simple life, cannot forget that he has been, and remains, a courtier. He cannot refrain from airing his graces and indulging his gentility. But there is no conceit nor any hint of unkindness in his teasing of a country bumpkin. It is a fault in him to show off in this way and he knows it for one:

It is meat and drink to me to see a clown. By my troth, we that have good wits have much to answer for; we shall be flouting; we cannot hold.

But even his flouting has about it a quality which distinguishes him from all the rest. Touchstone, 'above all things', is *interested* in people and places and ways of life. He must get to the bottom of a subject and take its measure. Of Corin he asks, as much in an honest desire to know as in a spirit of mockery: 'Hast any philosophy in thee, shepherd?' And when Corin expounds—

No more, but that I know the more one sickens, the worse at ease he is; and that he that wants money, means and content is without three good friends; that the property of rain is to wet and fire to burn; that good pasture makes fat sheep; and that a great cause of the night is lack of the sun—

Touchstone's rejoinder ('Such a one is a natural philosopher') is a shrewd companionable comment and no sneer. He must, as he confesses, be flouting. He takes an impish pleasure in maintaining that Corin, never having been at court or seen good manners, is damned; but Corin takes it all—as Touchstone intends it—in good part and serenely states his simple faith in the knowledge that, though it may be amiably mocked, it will nevertheless be respected:

Sir, I am a true labourer. I earn that I eat, get that I wear, owe no man hate, envy no man's happiness, glad of other men's good, content with my harm; and the greatest of my pride is to see my ewes graze and my lambs suck.

The whole thing is an epitome of Shakespeare's management of the pastoral theme. He presents the simple life with a most convincing innocence, but Touchstone is there to relate it justly to the scheme of things entire:

CORIN: And how like you this shepherd's life, Master Touchstone?
TOUCHSTONE: Truly, shepherd, in respect of itself, it is a good life; but in respect that it is a shepherd's life, it is naught. In respect that it is solitary, I like it very well; but in respect that it is private, it is a very vile life. Now in respect it is in the fields, it pleaseth me well; but in respect it is not in the court, it is tedious. As it is a spare life, look you, it fits my humour well; but as there is no more plenty in it, it goes much against my stomach.

Even the incomparable Rosalind, whose tide of wit and flush of love set her above any need of correction by the comic spirit, must be brought to the test if only to show how triumphantly she survives it. Orlando's rhymes are redeemed by the sincerity of his passion. But some of them have more feet than the verses will bear and the feet are lame. Indeed they are very tedious homilies of love, and all this she merrily declares. And Touchstone must also have his say. It is he who, on his author's behalf, must intimate very clearly that poetasters of the pastoral school are more deserving of mockery than imitation:

ROSALIND: 'From the east to western Ind,
No jewel is like Rosalind.
Her worth being mounted on the wind,
Through all the world bears Rosalind.
All the pictures fairest lined
Are but black to Rosalind.
Let no face be kept in mind
But the fair of Rosalind.'

TOUCHSTONE: I'll rhyme you so eight years together, dinners, and suppers, and sleeping-hours excepted: it is the right butter-women's rank to market.

ROSALIND: Out, fool!

TOUCHSTONE: For a taste. . . .
If a hart do lack a hind,
Let him seek out Rosalind:
If the cat will after kind,
So be sure will Rosalind:
Wintered garments must be lined,
So must slender Rosalind.
They that reap must sheaf and bind,
Then to cart with Rosalind.
Sweetest nut hath sourest rind,
Such a nut is Rosalind.
He that sweetest rose will find,
Must find love's prick and Rosalind.

This is the very false gallop of verses. Why do you infect yourself with them?

ROSALIND: Peace, you dull fool! I found them on a tree.

TOUCHSTONE: Truly, the tree yields bad fruit.

Orlando's poem is itself a parody. Touchstone's is a parody twice over. Again he plays for us the author's trick. The pastoral exercise is pleasant in itself but still more pleasant for being so easily mocked.

Touchstone's place in the comedy is ridiculed as much by what he may do as by what his author carefully disallows. It is true that he makes antic hay of Orlando's verses and is reminded of Jane Smile on seeing his mistress in love, but he is not permitted to intrude into the courtship of Rosalind and Orlando. Rosalind stands in no need of correction save by her own true heart and wholesome intelligence.

She is her own touchstone and carries her own comedy in person. There is never any danger of our losing this child of nature in affectation or masquerade. Her first thought on hearing of Orlando in the forest is 'Alas the day, what shall I do with my doublet and hose?' Every word declares the impatient vivacity of a woman alive from head to heel. She must have an answer in one word to nine impetuous questions:

What did he when thou saw'st him? What said he? How looked he? Wherein went he? What makes he here? Did he ask for me? Where remains he? How parted he with thee? and when shalt thou see him again?

She cannot let Celia tell her tale but must interrupt her at every word:

ROSALIND: But doth he know that I am in this forest and in man's apparel? Looks he as freshly as he did the day he wrestled?

CELIA: It is as easy to count atomies as to resolve the propositions of a lover: but take a taste of my finding him, and relish it with good observance. I found him under a tree, like a dropped acorn.

ROSALIND: It may well be called Jove's tree, when it drops forth such fruit.

CELIA: Give me audience, good madam.

ROSALIND: Proceed.

CELIA: There lay he, stretched along, like a wounded knight.

ROSALIND: Though it be pity to see such a sight, it well becomes the ground.

CELIA: Cry 'holla' to thy tongue, I prithee; it curvets unseasonably. He was furnished like a hunter.

ROSALIND: O ominous! he comes to kill my heart.

CELIA: I would sing my song without a burthen—thou bring'st me out of tune.

ROSALIND: Do you not know I am a woman? when I think, I must speak. Sweet, say on.

Apparelled like a man and using her disguise to be securely wooed in proxy, she has no doublet and hose in her disposition and, caught by her own counterfeiting, swoons at the sight of a bloody napkin. Each new touch that reveals her is comedy distilled and carries its own commentary. So possessed is Rosalind by the comic spirit that, though she cannot endure her lover to be absent for two hours, she must recurrently mock at love with her mind as she yields to it unreservedly with her heart:

ROSALIND: Love is merely a madness, and I tell you deserves as well a dark house and a whip as madmen do: and the reason why they are not so punished and cured is, that the lunacy is so ordinary that the whippers are in love too.

ROSALIND: Am I not your Rosalind?
ORLANDO: I take some joy to say you are, because I would be talking of her.
ROSALIND: Well, in her person, I say I will not have you.
ORLANDO: Then in mine own person, I die.
ROSALIND: No, faith, die by attorney: the poor world is almost six thousand years old, and in all this time there was not any man died in his own person, videlicet, in a love-cause: Troilus had his brains dashed out with a Grecian club, yet he did what he could to die before, and he is one of the patterns of love: Leander, he would have lived many a fair year, though Hero had turned nun, if it had not been for a hot midsummer night; for, good youth, he went but forth to wash him in the Hellespont and being taken with the cramp was drowned, and the foolish chroniclers of that age found it was 'Hero of Sestos'. But these are all lies. Men have died from time to time, and worms have eaten them, but not for love.

No need here for Touchstone to keep the comedy sane and true; he would be out of place and could only spoil its perfection.

This applies also to the Duke with his co-mates and brothers in exile. Touchstone has expressed his own view of Arden and its amenities: when I was at home, I was in a better place. But Shakespeare, having translated the stubbornness of fortune into so quiet and so sweet a style, is not going to spoil the effect with flouting. The Duke, so far as he is corrected, corrects himself. We are never really deceived by his pastoral affectation, because he never wholly yields to it himself. It is always quite obvious that, for all his praise of life in the wilderness, he is making the best of a bad business. Old custom hath made this life more sweet than that of painted pomp; but adversity is a toad, even though it may wear a precious jewel in his head. This Duke, we realise, would normally prefer to find his books in the library than to look for them in the running brooks, and go to a well-appointed chapel for his sermons than to seek them in stones. He is quick to remember the benefits of civilisation:

> ORLANDO: I thought that all things had been savage here,
> And therefore put I on the countenance
> Of stern commandment. But whate'er you are
> That in this desert inaccessible,
> Under the shade of melancholy boughs,
> Lose and neglect the creeping hours of time;
> If ever you have looked on better days;
> If ever been where bells have knolled to church;
> If ever sat at any good man's feast;
> If ever from your eyelids wiped a tear,
> And know what 'tis to pity and be pitied,
> Let gentleness my strong enforcement be:
> In the which hope I blush, and hide my sword,
>
> DUKE: True is it that we have seen better days,
> And have with holy bell been knolled to church,
> And sat at good men's feasts, and wiped our eyes
> Of drops that sacred pity hath engendred:
> And therefore sit you down in gentleness,
> And take upon command what help we have
> That to your wanting may be ministred.

A minute later he lets the cat out of the bag with a vengeance—

> Thou seest we are not all alone unhappy:
> This wide and universal theatre
> Presents more woeful pageants than the scene
> Wherein we play in.—

and at the last he embraces his return to the comforts of city life with a most ingenuous alacrity:

> First, in this forest, let us do those ends
> That here were well begun and well begot:
> And after, every of this happy number,
> That have endured shrewd days and nights with us,
> Shall share the good of our returnèd fortune,
> According to the measure of their states.

The mellifluous Duke himself thus artlessly reveals the true quality of his rustication. Shakespeare accordingly refrains from contriving a meeting between him and Touchstone till the play is drawing to an end and even then the encounter is managed with considerable tact. Touchstone, in fact, simply ignores the happy exile and treats him instantly as a person of quality, adopting at once his courtliest manner and falling naturally back into his profession as a jester whose business it is to exercise his wit on behalf of the company:

TOUCHSTONE: Salutation and greeting to you all!

JAQUES: Good my lord, bid him welcome: this is the motley-minded gentleman that I have so often met in the forest: he hath been a courtier, he swears.

TOUCHSTONE: If any man doubt that, let him put me to my purgation. I have trod a measure—I have flattered a lady—I have been politic with my friend, smooth with mine enemy—I have undone three tailors—I have had four quarrels, and like to have fought one.

JAQUES: And how was that ta'en up?

TOUCHSTONE: Faith, we met, and found the quarrel was upon the seventh cause.

JAQUES: How seventh cause? Good my lord, like this fellow.

DUKE: I like him very well.

TOUCHSTONE: God 'ild you, sir, I desire you of the like; I press in here, sir, amongst the rest of the country copulatives, to swear and to forswear, according as marriage binds and blood breaks. . . . A poor virgin, sir, an ill-favoured thing, sir, but mine own—a poor humour of mine, sir, to take that that no man else will: rich honesty dwells like a miser, sir, in a poor house, as your pearl in your foul oyster.

DUKE: By my faith, he is very swift and sententious.

Whereupon he breaks into his brilliant analysis of the seven causes of quarrel between gentlemen, a virtuoso performance which concludes with the most celebrated of his quiddities: 'Your If is the only peace-maker: much virtue in If.'

The supreme test for Touchstone is his encounter with Jaques. But it is well, before we examine an incident which will determine our outlook on the entire comedy, to become more intimately acquainted with the man himself. Shakespeare affords us an opportunity in the episode of Touchstone's courting of Audrey. Here we behold the man who has no illusions concerning nature frankly responding to her call. The others merely trifle with her; Touchstone sees, hears and obeys:

As the ox hath his bow, sir, the horse his curb, and the falcon her bells, so man hath his desires; and as pigeons bill, so wedlock would be nibbling.

He has found rich honesty, dwelling like a miser in a poor house, 'as your pearl in your foul oyster', and, having found it, has the courage of his convictions and will not let it go. His wooing of Audrey is at the same time a burlesque and a true reflection in nature of the three romantic courtships among which it intrudes. There is conscious irony in his claim to be pressing in 'among the rest of the country copulatives, to swear and to forswear, according as marriage binds and blood breaks', for none knows better than Touchstone himself that he alone is paying a genuine tribute to the ancient gods of the forest. His surrender to the great god, Pan, is the more complete, and certainly the more entirely comic, for his being clearly aware of what he is doing. He is still the courtier and he must still be flouting—even at the 'poor virgin, sir, an ill-favoured thing, sir, but mine own'. He will go so far as to suggest that 'not being well-married, it will be a good excuse hereafter to leave my wife'. But all these floutings are superficial. Touchstone's comedy, in fact, shows all the rest of the comedy in reverse. His wooing of Audrey is irony in action. Orlando, Rosalind, Silvius, Phebe and the rest affect their pastoral simplicity but remain entirely civilised. Touchstone affects his urbanity but is at heart a truly natural philosopher. None knows better than he what he is doing, for it is of the essence of his character to see himself as he sees everyone else in the play in detachment:

A man may, if he were of a fearful heart, stagger in this attempt; for here we have no temple but the wood, no assembly but horn-beasts. But what though? Courage!

He begins his courtship with a double pun and a sidelong mockery of the whole pastoral outfit:

I am here with thee and thy goats, as the most capricious poet, honest Ovid, was among the Goths—

but his deeds in plain English speak louder than the word-play in
Latin.

Now that we begin to know our Touchstone we can have no
doubt of what really happened upon his first encounter with Jaques.
It is Jaques himself who describes the meeting:

> A fool, a fool! I met a fool i' th' forest,
> A motley fool—a miserable world!—
> As I do live by food, I met a fool,
> Who laid him down and basked him in the sun,
> And railed on Lady Fortune in good terms,
> In good set terms, and yet a motley fool.
> 'Good morrow, fool,' quoth I: 'No, sir,' quoth he,
> 'Call me not fool till heaven hath sent me fortune.'
> And then he drew a dial from his poke,
> And looking on it with lack-lustre eye,
> Says very wisely, 'It is ten o'clock:
> Thus we may see', quoth he, 'how the world wags:
> 'Tis but an hour ago since it was nine,
> And after one hour more 'twill be eleven,
> And so from hour to hour, we ripe, and ripe,
> And then from hour to hour, we rot, and rot—
> And thereby hangs a tale.' . . . When I did hear
> The motley fool thus moral on the time,
> My lungs began to crow like chanticleer,
> That fools should be so deep-contemplative;
> And I did laugh, sans intermission,
> An hour by his dial. . . . O noble fool!
> O worthy fool! Motley's the only wear.

Jaques relates how he has been amusing himself with a fool, but
Touchstone, we perceive, has been amusing himself—and more to
the purpose—with a philosopher. While Jaques was laughing at the
fool, the fool was taking his measure and pulling his leg. Here
Touchstone saw at once was a fashionable cynic, venting a shallow
disappointment with men and things in well-turned homilies upon
the way of the world. Playing up to his man the fool rails on Lady
Fortune in good set terms. The philosopher is hooked and the fool

lands his fish with a solemn descant upon the passage of time. Jaques, completely taken in, marvels that a fool should be so *deep-contemplative*.

We would give a good deal to have been present at this meeting, but Shakespeare decided otherwise and for a very good reason. If we had actually *seen* Jaques so obviously mocked, crowing like chanticleer but missing the whole point of the jest, we could never for a moment have regarded him as anything else but a figure of fun. But by merely *reporting* the incident Shakespeare leaves us to draw our own conclusions. He is not unwilling that Jaques should up to a point impose on his audience and be for the purposes of the play accepted at his own valuation. This melancholy gentleman was a popular stage character and none knew better than Shakespeare that a dash of sentimental cynicism goes down very well in a light comedy. Jaques is to be its purveyor and he must not therefore be too plainly exposed as a counterfeit philosopher who does not even know when the laugh is against him. Again our dramatist means to have it both ways. He will entertain us on the lower level with Jaques as a moralist and let those who like him thus be taken in if they will. But those who look a little deeper shall also have their fun.

Shakespeare so artfully plays this double game that it is quite possible to enjoy the comedy without allowing ourselves to become aware that the melancholy Jaques is, first to last, a purely comic character. Some critics have even gone so far as to compare him with Hamlet and most actors deliver his speech on the seven ages of man to a hushed audience as though it were a deep epitome of human experience. Shakespeare in fact has his little joke with the audience. Let those with a taste for Sir Oracle enjoy him as such. Observe how skilfully the dramatist builds him up. Our first reputed glimpse of him charms equally the eye and ear:

> FIRST LORD: Today my Lord of Amiens and myself
> Did steal behind him as he lay along
> Under an oak, whose antique root peeps out
> Upon the brook that brawls along this wood,
> To the which place a poor sequestred stag,
> That from the hunter's aim had ta'en a hurt,

> Did come to languish; and, indeed, my lord,
> The wretched animal heaved forth such groans,
> That their discharge did stretch his leathern coat
> Almost to bursting, and the big round tears
> Coursed one another down his innocent nose
> In piteous chase: and thus the hairy fool,
> Much markèd of the melancholy Jaques,
> Stood on th' extremest verge of the swift brook,
> Augmenting it with tears.
>
> DUKE: But what said Jaques?
> Did he not moralize this spectacle?
>
> FIRST LORD: O, yes, into a thousand similes.
> First, for his weeping in the needless stream;
> 'Poor deer,' quoth he, 'thou mak'st a testament
> As worldlings do, giving thy sum of more
> To that which had too much': then, being there alone,
> Left and abandoned of his velvet friends;
> ''Tis right,' quoth he, 'thus misery doth part
> The flux of company': anon a careless herd,
> Full of the pasture, jumps along by him
> And never stays to greet him; 'Ay,' quoth Jaques,
> 'Sweep on, you fat and greasy citizens!
> 'Tis just the fashion; wherefore do you look
> Upon that poor and broken bankrupt there?'

Note, however, that the spell is laid by First Lord and not by the subject of his tale. Not a word which Jaques is reported as saying shows real feeling or felicity. Antique root, sequestered stag, innocent nose, hairy foot, velvet friends, careless herd—it is an entrancing picture and Jaques gets credit for being included, though all he actually contributes is the moralising. His first actual appearance in the play is managed with equal cunning. There it is Amiens, singing of winter and rough weather, who lays the spell. Jaques again has all the advantage of being attractively presented. But his first words reveal him to the alert spectator as a misanthropist for whom all occasions are but opportunities to display an affected misanthropy. What is music to him?—*I can suck melancholy out of a song as a weasel sucks eggs.*

The craft with which Shakespeare builds him up is only equalled by the pertinacity with which he puts him down. Jaques comes off badly in his encounters with every person in the play. He is never happy unless he is showing off his melancholy to good advantage and he trails after each character in turn rather like a bore determined at all costs to corner his victim. Professing to love solitude, nothing but sheer rudeness can stay his eloquence or drive him away:

JAQUES: Will you sit down with me? and we two will rail against our mistress the world, and all our misery.

ORLANDO: I will chide no breather in the world but myself, against whom I know most faults.

JAQUES: The worst fault you have is to be in love.

ORLANDO: 'Tis a fault I will not change for your best virtue. I am weary of you.

JAQUES: By my troth, I was seeking for a fool when I found you.

ORLANDO: He is drowned in the brook—look but in, and you shall see him.

JAQUES: There I shall see mine own figure.

ORLANDO: Which I take to be either a fool or a cipher.

JAQUES: I'll tarry no longer with you. Farewell, good Signior Love.

ORLANDO: I am glad of your departure: adieu, good Monsieur Melancholy.

JAQUES: I prithee, pretty youth, let me be better acquainted with thee.

ROSALIND: They say you are a melancholy fellow.

JAQUES: I am so: I do love it better than laughing.

ROSALIND: Those that are in extremity of either are abominable fellows, and betray themselves to every modern censure worse than drunkards.

JAQUES: Why, 'tis good to be sad and say nothing.

ROSALIND: Why, then, 'tis good to be a post.

Note the sly comedy of that deliciously inappropriate observation—'Why, 'tis good to be sad *and say nothing*.' Jaques is the most loquacious person in the comedy. Rather than say nothing he will address a herd of deer and in the encounter with Rosalind he justifies his melancholy in a veritable spate of words:

I have neither the scholar's melancholy, which is emulation; nor the musician's, which is fantastical; nor the courtier's, which is proud;

nor the soldier's, which is ambitious; nor the lawyer's, which is politic; nor the lady's, which is nice; nor the lover's, which is all these: but it is a melancholy of mine own, compounded of many simples, extracted from many objects, and indeed the sundry contemplation of my travels, in which my often rumination wraps me in a most humorous sadness.

But Rosalind is not impressed:

And your experience makes you sad: I had rather a fool to make me merry than experience to make me sad—

and she dismisses him in a broadside which comes as near to downright chiding as it is her nature to come:

Farewell, Monsieur Traveller: look you lisp and wear strange suits; disable all the benefits of your own country; be out of love with your nativity, and almost chide God for making you that countenance you are; or I will scarce think you have swam in a gondola.

The unkindest cut of all comes, however, strangely enough, from the Duke. The Duke is the only person in the play who expresses a liking for Jaques. 'He hath been all this day to look for you,' says Amiens. 'And I', says Jaques, 'have been all this day to avoid him'. The Duke evidently enjoys a good argument. 'I love to cope him in these sullen fits, for then he's full of matter', declares his Grace. Jaques—and this is another sly stroke of comedy at his expense—is less fond of the Duke's company. Why? Because the Duke, if you please, *talks too much*. 'He is too disputable for my company', says Jaques. 'I think of as many matters as he, but I give heaven thanks and make no boast of them.' There is no-one like your much talker to resent loquacity in another.

Yet it is the Duke who, without any real provocation, suddenly rounds on his crony and pulls him to tatters:

JAQUES: Invest me in my motley; give me leave
              To speak my mind, and I will through and through
              Cleanse the foul body of th'infected world,
              If they will patiently receive my medicine.
DUKE: Fie on thee! I can tell what thou wouldst do.
JAQUES: What, for a counter, would I do but good?

DUKE: Most mischievous foul sin, in chiding sin:
For thou thyself hast been a libertine,
As sensual as the brutish sting itself,
And all th'embossèd sores and headed evils,
That thou with licence of free foot hast caught,
Wouldst thou disgorge into the general world.

This is an astonishing outburst and not quite in character. It looks as though Shakespeare himself had for a moment lost his equanimity and that his heavenly patience with all sorts and conditions of men was ruffled. Nor is this to be wondered at. The fellow who on the score of his own small unfounded grievances against the world rails against all mankind would be least congenial to our author. Be this as it may, the clue is not to be missed. Jaques is here denounced by the one man in the play who takes any real pleasure in his company.

These reactions of Orlando, Rosalind and the Duke, however, are but confirmations of the test applied by Shakespeare in the encounters of Jaques with Touchstone. The relations between the pair are unobtrusively maintained throughout the play. When Jaques, in search of someone from whom to suck melancholy as a weasel sucks eggs, follows Touchstone and Audrey through the forest and overhears their conference, Touchstone, though Jaques has laughed sans intermission an hour by his dial, does not even remember his name—or affects not to remember it. 'Good-even, good Master What-ye-call 't' is his greeting. Touchstone, in fact, is as indifferent in his dealings with Jaques as Jaques is eager to improve the acquaintance. For Jaques, Touchstone is a collector's piece—*un objet d'art et de vertu*. He introduces him to the Duke with a 'Good my lord, give him welcome: this is the motley-minded gentleman that I have so often met in the forest; he hath been a courtier, he swears'. Touchstone plays up to Jaques in their last as in their first encounter. He gives the Duke, as we have noted, a taste of his quality. Jaques plays the part of a delighted *compère*, showing off the paces of the fool like a circus master, prompting him to perform worthily before company and not to let his sponsor down. '*Good my lord, like this fellow. . . . Is not this a rare fellow, my lord? He's as good at anything and yet a fool.*' And the cream of the jest is that Jaques casting himself for the part of exhibitor is really the exhibitionist. Touchstone is only too willing to give the Duke a run for his money but pays not the slightest attention to Monsieur Melancholy.

But what of the seven ages of man? They too serve the double purpose. The speech is good hearing. It holds the stage and lingers in the memory. It is the most successful example of sententious commonplace declamation in English literature. At the same time it exposes the speaker for what he is and puts a final touch to his character. It is a good summary of life lived on the average. It has no depth, not a touch of magic, no suggestion of anything beyond its narrow limits; and it is coloured throughout by the bilious disposition of the orator. The infant mewls, the schoolboy whines, the lover sighs, the soldier swears, the judge proses, the pantaloon shrinks and the old man loses his teeth. Nor is there any indication anywhere that anyone has truly striven, aspired, suffered, meditated or seen beyond the end of his nose.

'As You Like It' has been the least fortunate in its critics of all the plays of Shakespeare. It has often been injudiciously praised—or scandalously dispraised—for its obvious merits to the neglect of its finer qualities. Shakespeare in this play brought off two achievements on two different lines of appreciation. The first was to present his native Arden, to show us true love running happily to a foregone conclusion (no easy matter), to convey in his own sweet idiom the pastoral pleasures of woodland and sheep-cote, to moralise agreeably on the changes of fortune and the simple life—in a word to give us a sample of the pastoral-comical stripped of its more elaborate affectations. This part of his task he performed so well that it has been praised with eloquence and propriety by many critics who are content to look no further.

Shakespeare's second achievement has been obscured by the success of his first. The charming, life-like, conversible comic figures of the story have been too easily accepted at their own valuation. The gentle irony that plays about them and their relationships, the constant reference of character, conduct and environment to the test of nature, the poise maintained in every scene between permitted romance and prohibitive reality—these often tend to be partly misconceived or wholly ignored.

The case of Jaques is exemplary. No character in the play is more consistently put down but he nevertheless imposes upon actors and spectators alike. 'The prince of philosophic idlers; his only passion is thought', exclaimed the great Hazlitt of a person whose 'philosophy' betrayed him into an ecstasy of admiration of a fool's parody—

> And thus from hour to hour we ripe, and ripe,
> And then from hour to hour we rot, and rot—

and whose 'thought' never once emerges above the commonplace.

But Jaques was almost bound to impose on the romantics. The melancholy man of the Renaissance, a figure of fun at the beginning of the seventeenth, was a serious literary incubus at the beginning of the nineteenth century. The romantic critics saw Jaques through a mist of sorrowful Werthers, itinerant Childe Harolds and mysterious Manfreds. They were making ready for an orgy that culminated in the neo-gothic masterpieces of Victor Hugo and the rosicrucian imbecilities of Lord Lytton. They could no more think of smiling at Jaques than a devout Anglican would think of laughing in church. 'Son œil est encore vif et beau; mais sa bouche est une tombe où le sourire est enseveli . . . Au fond de ses récriminations contre le genre humain, je vois toujours briller l'amour du vrai et la haine du mal, comme les étoiles derrière les nuages sombres.' The author is George Sand who in the nineteenth century adapted Shakespeare's play to the taste of her own time and country. Jaques becomes the active and ubiquitous hero of the comedy. Fascinated by Monsieur Melancholy she has little or no time to spare for heavenly Rosalind. Jaques must show himself at court as well as in the forest, masterly in action as well as profound in speculation, and in the end be redeemed for happiness when Celia swears that she loves him by the roses of spring, the virginity of lilies, by youth, by faith and by honour.

The play is worth reading. It shows what may happen to an Arden without Touchstone for a guide, counsellor and friend.

III

SHYLOCK

The Merchant of Venice

THE political career of Thomas Devereux, Earl of Essex, frequently impinges upon the dramatic career of Mr. William Shakespeare. In 1593 this proud, capricious, brilliant and foolish nobleman was stimulating the Queen's commissioners to suppress the 'School of Night'. This affair elicited from Shakespeare the first of his notable comedies, 'Love's Labour's Lost'.[1] Eight years later, in 1601, the friends of Essex conspired to stage a revival of 'Richard II', the first of Shakespeare's great tetralogy of histories, which resulted in at least one member of the audience being hanged.[2] Meanwhile, in June 1594, Essex was actively concerned in the persecution of one, Roderigo Lopez, a Jew of Portuguese descent, physician to the Queen, wrongfully accused of plotting to poison Her Majesty for reasons that have ceased to have any great interest for posterity. Essex, who manufactured the evidence, also presided at the trial, an arrangement which greatly simplified the procedure. The unfortunate Jew was hanged, drawn and quartered at Tyburn in the presence of an excited crowd who marvelled that he should dare, in his last moments, to utter the name of Jesus.

The trial and death of Roderigo Lopez was the second *cause célèbre* in a twelvemonth which had for Shakespeare a personal and professional interest. Marlowe and Kyd had been involved in the scandal which led to the suppression of the 'School of Night'. The death of Lopez came yet nearer home. It is not unlikely that Shakespeare was personally acquainted with the man. Lopez, a member of the College of Physicians, was the medical attendant of many notable persons, including the Earl of Leicester, patron of the Company of 'servants and players' in which Shakespeare was a 'sharer'. It is not

[1] See above, p. 24.
[2] See the present author's *Political Characters of Shakespeare*, pp. 119, 120.

improbable that Shakespeare witnessed the butchery at Tyburn. Quite certainly he heard the case discussed in the taverns of London, where the lamentable theme of Jewry's place in a Christian commonwealth must have been frequently debated among the free spirits of the time. It is not suggested that Shakespeare, in portraying Shylock, had any political or social intentions. 'The Merchant of Venice' is not a transcript from contemporary life, still less a political morality. It is essentially a fairy-tale or, more precisely, a combination of two fairy-tales. Whether Burbage, in playing Shylock, trimmed his beard to the cut of Lopez or whether the spectators who witnessed the trial of Shylock before the Duke of Venice were prompted to remember the trial of Lopez before the Earl of Essex, is neither here nor there. Gratiano when he declares in his speech to Shylock:

> Thy currish spirit
> Governed a wolf, who hanged for human slaughter,
> Even from the gallows did his fell soul fleet,
> And whilst thou layest in thy unhallowed dam,
> Infused itself in thee

may or may not have been punning on the name Lopez (Lopez= Lupus=Wolf). It is a point for the scholars and we may feel with Horatio when invited by Hamlet to trace the noble dust of Alexander, till he find it stopping a bung-hole, that ' 'twere to consider too curiously, to consider so'. What really matters is the effect on Shakespeare's imagination of this particular fragment of personal experience. He was the likelier, if he had known a Jew with more than one fair daughter (Lopez had three), to find a place for Jessica in his play and to insist, if he had witnessed the savage spectacle at Tyburn, that a Jew, if you prick him, will most certainly bleed. Nor was he likely to forget the indignant mirth of a Christian mob execrating a Jew who in his last agony presumed to call upon Jesus Christ.[1]

[1] That Shakespeare had Lopez in mind when he set out to portray Shylock is incidentally confirmed by the lines that slip into the mouths of Bassanio and Portia at Belmont. Lopez, prior to his prosecution by the Crown, made some damaging admissions concerning the plot of which he was accused, but pleaded at his trial that he had much belied himself in his confession *to save himself from racking*. The use

The Elizabethan theatre reflected the life and mind of the nation and, when Shakespeare sat down to write 'The Merchant of Venice' in 1594, anti-semitism was in fashion. Marlowe had exploited it four years previously with all the resources of his poetic genius and there seemed little more to do or say. Barabbas, the Jew of Malta, embodied in his wicked person all the qualities which a persecuting majority commonly attributed to its victims. For four years Marlowe's Jew had held the stage and, during the excitement aroused by the trial of Lopez, between May and December, 1594, his play was twenty times revived. Barabbas was greedy as a pike, cruel as a cat and artful as a wilderness of monkeys. He was sinister and yet ridiculous, impressive in the intensity of his passion and grotesque in the versatility of his performance. He was robbed of one fortune by the State, but remained master of another. He contrived that two Christian suitors for the hand of his daughter should kill one another; and, when his daughter became a Christian, he killed her, too. He strangled a monk and poisoned a whole nunnery. He betrayed the Christian to the Turk and the Turk to the Christian. Finally he fell into a cauldron which he had artfully contrived for his principal benefactor and was boiled alive.

Such was the play about a Jew which held the London stage when Shakespeare was asked to supply his company with another. Charles

of torture to obtain evidence was a legally respectable institution under Elizabeth; but we need not necessarily conclude that normally decent people regarded it as morally defensible or even a sensible practice. It has always been the habit of English citizens individually to question or condemn proceedings and institutions which for some strange reasons they tolerate or even applaud collectively. Shakespeare's personal views on men and things rarely disturb or colour his imaginative presentation of a character or a situation; but they may be occasionally inferred from a casual epithet or metaphor. There is no reason why Shakespeare, when Bassanio is professing his love for Portia, should suddenly think of the rack. The metaphor just occurs to him because it stood for something freshly present in his mind:

BASSANIO: Let me choose!
For as I am, I live upon the rack.
PORTIA: Upon the rack, Bassanio! Then confess
What treason there is mingled with your love.

Ay, but I fear you speak upon the rack
Where men enforcèd do speak anything.

Lamb, gazing with aversion upon Barabbas, finds him 'a mere monster brought in with a large painted nose to please the rabble ... just such an exhibition as a century or two earlier might have been played before the Londoners by Royal Command when a general pillage and massacre of the Hebrews had been resolved on in the cabinet'. Lamb wrote in the comfortable conviction that such exhibitions had ceased for ever to have any relation to practical politics.

Officially there were no Jews in Shakespeare's England. Edward I had driven them all out in 1290. But there was nevertheless a Jewish question, actual as well as legendary, and, in appreciating 'The Merchant of Venice', we shall do well to remember that Marlowe's Barabbas still held the stage when Shakespeare created Shylock. The fashion was fixed and Shakespeare must seem to follow it. It did not matter how absurd or improbable the plot of his play might be, because the public was ready to believe anything about a Jew. Any horrible mischief which a Jew might contrive would be credited and any device by which the Jew might be foiled of his purpose, however childish or improbable, would be commended.

Then why not use that old story of Gernutus, the Jew of Venice, who in merry jest had induced a Christian merchant to sign a bond for a pound of his flesh and who, in cruel earnest, had claimed the forfeiture? This same Gernutus had for some time been a popular figure. There were shortly to be ballads about him, sung to the tune of 'Black and Yellow':

> In Venice town not long ago
> A cruel Jew did dwell,
> Which livèd all on usury,
> As Italian writers tell.
>
> His heart doth think on many a wile
> How to deceive the poor;
> His mouth is almost full of muck,
> Yet still he gapes for more.

Nearer to the purpose were the merry tales of Ser Giovanni Fiorentino, one of those Italian books that sold in Elizabethan England like hot cakes, so that Schoolmaster Ascham was moved to warn his pupils: 'These be the enchantementes of Circes, brought out of Italie to marre men's manners in England.' Ser Giovanni had the whole story almost ready for the theatre: a Venetian youth who had won the lady of Belmonte, a merchant who supplied the youth with money borrowed from a Jew, the pound of flesh, the notorious quibble whereby the merchant was rescued in court by the lady, in disguise, even the mystification about a ring which she received from her bridegroom as a reward for saving his friend. All the dry bones of Shakespeare's play, except for the caskets, were waiting here for the man who could make them live upon the stage.

Nor was it necessary for Shakespeare to look very far for his caskets. They had been lying about for centuries—genuine antiques, bequests from the Greek monk of St. Saba in Syria which, after appearing in places of less repute, had turned up in the *Gesta Romanorum,* a collection of tales so popular with the Elizabethans that no less than six editions of an English translation were published between 1577 and 1601.

It is doubtful whether Shakespeare was even put to the trouble of combining the story of the pound of flesh with that of the caskets. For in 1579, fifteen years before he wrote 'The Merchant of Venice', the actor and dramatic author, Stephen Gosson, leaving the stage for the pulpit, published a 'pleasant invective against poets, pipers, players, jesters and such like caterpillars of the commonwealth', in which he trounced the abuses of the theatre and referred incidentally to two plays showing at the Bull Tavern. One of these plays, entitled 'The Jew', he describes as 'representing the greediness of worldly chusers and the bloody minds of usurers'. From this it must presumably be inferred that a play had been produced either in 1579 or before that date, in which the casket theme (the greediness of worldly chusers) and the story of the pound of flesh (the bloody minds of usurers) had already been woven into a single piece. Thus it seems hardly possible to avoid the conclusion that Shakespeare, in writing 'The Merchant of Venice', was working from an old play in which every essential feature of his double plot already figured.[1]

[1] Another exasperating example of the way in which the critic who hopes to surprise Shakespeare at work finds the ground removed from under his feet. How

There is no means of assessing the merits of the old play from which Shakespeare very probably derived his comedy. But these fashionable Jew plays were probably all very much alike. Dekker wrote one which has been lost. The illiterate Henslowe alludes in his diary to a 'Venesyon Comoedy' produced in August 1594. Another English Jew play of the period, 'Der Jud von Venedig', has survived in a German text. An English company, strolling on the Continent, performed it before a German audience at Halle in 1611. As in Shakespeare's comedy, a second Daniel comes to judgment. If this, or something like it, was the sort of play which Shakespeare had at his disposal when he wrote 'The Merchant of Venice', we can only marvel at the transformation. For this German manuscript is a bawdy, vulgar and brutal piece of work. The essential features of Shakespeare's plot are there, but the result is what might be expected of an attempt by anyone but Shakespeare to present a fairy-tale in the 'Blue Bird' tradition as a contribution to the secular pastime of baiting the Jew.

There is, of course, another side to the picture. The execution of Lopez, while it gratified the Jew-baiters, seems to have provoked indignation and even a searching of hearts among the more reasonable and sensitive citizens of London. Elizabeth, who believed that Lopez was innocent, at first refused to sign his death warrant. She yielded to popular clamour, stimulated by Essex and his friends, but against her better judgment. The feeling inspired by the execution of Lopez in civilised spectators was much the same as that of the pale, fair Briton observed by Heine at Drury Lane who, at the end of the fourth act of Shakespeare's play, several times exclaimed with tears in her eyes: *The poor man is wronged.* In 1596, two years after the

interesting to study in detail the way in which the story of the caskets is dovetailed into the story of the bond as related by Ser Giovanni, if we could be sure that Shakespeare had really done the work! The dramatist rejects passages in the story of the bond which would be ineffective on the stage and replaces them with material from another source. We admire the craft with which the one theme is grafted upon the other and the sure sense of the theatre which prompted the acceptance or rejection of this or that particular feature. All this would provide valuable indications concerning Shakespeare's method and workmanship. But what if all this preliminary work had already been done before Shakespeare put his quill to paper?

production of 'The Merchant of Venice', a book was published in London entitled 'The Orator', a translation from the French of a collection of model speeches or declamations on subjects of historical or contemporary interest. Moral and legal problems were handled in speeches put into the mouths of advocates arguing for or against a particular case. Among the declamations was one which shows that even in Shakespeare's time opinions were divided on the Jewish question. It is a speech such as Shylock might have made in appealing against the sentence of the Venetian Court. The Jew, very ably and convincingly, puts his judges in the wrong, both on moral and legal grounds. What right have these Christians to deny him his pound of flesh? Do they not themselves condemn their debtors to worse for-feits, 'binding all the body into a most loathsome prison or into an intolerable slavery'? Did not the Romans regard it as 'lawful for debt to imprison, beat and afflict with torments the free citizens'? Debtors who fail to keep their contracts must abide the conse-quences. It is lawful to kill a soldier, if he should come to the wars an hour late, or to hang a thief, though he steal never so little. Is it then so great a matter to take a pound of flesh from one who by breaking his promise has endangered his creditor's solvency and reputation, which to a man of business is more precious than life itself?

The Jew here turns the tables on the Christian and, under the cover of a shrewd defence, carries the war to the enemy. The inclusion of such a homily in a book translated and published in 1596 is convincing proof that Shakespeare, in presenting Shylock to the public in 1594, was not writing for an audience incapable of appreciating the more humane aspects of his comedy.[1]

---

[1] The legend of the pound of flesh is not, in fact, either by origin or in some of its post-mediæval developments, directed against the Jews. There is no Jew in the earliest European version of the tale as narrated by Herbert, the troubadour, in 1223; and in what is perhaps the most amusing version of all, which purports to be an incident in the life of Pope Sixtus V as narrated by Leti, his fanciful biographer, the tables are turned with a vengeance. For in this account it is the Christian who claims a pound of flesh from the Jew (a situation which some may regard as pos-sibly more agreeable to the facts of history); and the good Pope, with magnificent impartiality, condemns both parties to death: the Christian, for entering into a contract with intent to murder the Jew, and the Jew, for signing a bond which virtually involved him in the crime of suicide.

These, then, are the circumstances in which Shakespeare's comedy stands as a piece of contemporary literature: a topical interest in Jews which had led to the production of several Jew plays on the stage, one of which very possibly combined the story of the pound of flesh with that of the caskets; some lively discussion in the London taverns of the rights and wrongs of a distinguished member of that unhappy race, executed at Tyburn; an audience which expected a stage Jew to be presented as a comical and merciless villain; a possible tendency on the part of more judicious spectators to deplore the barbarity of a public act recently committed and to regard the stage Jew of the period as an inhuman travesty.

Shakespeare, having regard to these circumstances, contrived to write a play in which what the contemporary public wanted to meet a topical occasion was with superb felicity combined with what posterity has accepted on its merits as one of his major achievements as a comic dramatist. Here was the 'mere monster brought in with a large painted nose to please the rabble', claiming his pound of flesh; there were the traditional caskets and here was the lady whose locks hung on her temples like a golden fleece—two fantastical stories, one of them wickedly grotesque and the other prettily fanciful, which had somehow to be brought into harmony with one another and to be presented as humanly credible within the limits of a play. Was ever a more formidable challenge presented to a poet, called on to create a mood and to suggest an environment in which these quaint figures and incidents might be accepted, or to a dramatist, called on to create the characters in which we might believe as beings of a like nature with ourselves? Portia, first to last, is as legendary a figure as Shylock. But these legendary figures behave, within their limits, as recognisable creatures of flesh and blood. Humanity comes creeping, or even breaking, into the composition. The people of the play, within a magic circle drawn by the poet, successfully assert their reality.

Shakespeare has so brilliantly succeeded in this part of his task that the veracity of his characters relative to the play—which is just sufficient to carry his design—has been accepted as absolute. Critics and editors insist on viewing every character and incident in the broad light of common day. Bassanio, legendary Jason of the old story, is removed from the play and, because Shakespeare has made him sufficiently real for his purpose, is discussed as though he were a person whom we should hesitate to invite to dinner. He is charged with being a spendthrift and a gold-digger. He sponges on his best friend and marries for money. Antonio, for all his fine speeches and impressive deportment, is a spineless nonentity; Jessica a heartless minx who robs her father. Each character, removed from its context, is submitted to everyday tests of moral worth and social decorum. Shakespeare, in giving to these people just enough reality to make them humanly credible for the purpose of his story, has succeeded to such good purpose that they are brought to judgment as human beings true for all time or in any place.[1]

The severity of the investigations made from time to time into the conduct of these legendary figures, in the course of which they are submitted to all the tests that common decency and common sense would apply to the ordinary affairs of life, is amusingly illustrated by the observations passed upon the character and proceedings of Bassanio by Sir Arthur Quiller-Couch.[2] Take, for example, Bassanio's request that his friend, Antonio, should finance the expedition to Belmont:

> 'Tis not unknown to you, Antonio,
> How much I have disabled mine estate,
> By something showing a more swelling port
> Than my faint means would grant continuance;

That, says 'Q', is a mighty fine way of saying that you have chosen to live beyond your income. Then, 'Q' continues, there is some 'windy nonsense about shooting a second arrow after a lost one':

[1] Witness the celebrated outburst of Heine: 'Antonio is a poor-spirited creature, with the heart of a worm, whose flesh is really worth nothing else but to bait fish withal. . . . Bassanio is a downright fortune-hunter; he borrows money to show a more swelling port with and to capture a rich heiress. As for Lorenzo, he is an accomplice in a most infamous burglary and under Prussian law he would have been condemned to fifteen years in the penitentiary. The other noble Venetians, who appear in the scene as the comrades of Antonio, do not seem to hate money very much and for their poor friend, when he is in ill-luck, they have nothing but words.'

[2] In his admirable preface to 'The Merchant of Venice'; New Cambridge Edition.

> In my school-days, when I had lost one shaft,
> I shot his fellow of the self-same flight
> The self-same way, with more advisèd watch,
> To find the other forth, and by adventuring both,
> I oft found both: I urge this childhood proof,
> Because what follows is pure innocence. . . .
> I owe you much, and, like a wilful youth,
> That which I owe is lost—but if you please
> To shoot another arrow that self way
> Which you did shoot the first, I do not doubt,
> As I will watch the aim, or to find both,
> Or bring your latter hazard back again,
> And thankfully rest debtor for the first.

Following this 'windy nonsense' comes a speech which 'Q' describes as 'bad workmanship and dishonouring to Bassanio':

> In Belmont is a lady richly left,
> And she is fair, and, fairer than that word,
> Of wondrous virtues—sometimes from her eyes
> I did receive fair speechless messages. . . .
> Her name is Portia, nothing undervalued
> To Cato's daughter, Brutus' Portia—
> Nor is the wide world ignorant of her worth,
> For the four winds blow in from every coast
> Renownèd suitors, and her sunny locks
> Hang on her temples like a golden fleece,
> Which makes her seat of Belmont Colchos' strand,
> And many Jasons come in quest of her. . . .
> O my Antonio, had I but the means
> To hold a rival place with one of them,
> I have a mind presages me such thrift,
> That I should questionless be fortunate.

Why, demands 'Q', should Bassanio build anything on Portia's speechless messages and why should he 'questionless be fortunate', since he knows perfectly well, but does not tell his friend, that all will depend on his choosing the right one of three caskets—a two-to-one chance that Antonio will ever see his money?

These are very pertinent questions if we insist on applying to Bassanio's conduct everyday tests of logic and morality. But we have to consider not whether Bassanio is or is not a suitable young man to be received by a wise father as an eligible suitor for his favourite daughter, but what Shakespeare is doing for his audience. The dramatist has to get this preposterous story of Antonio's bond to the Jew smoothly and effectively under way. This is a play in which impossible things are to happen and they must appear to happen as naturally as possible. Bassanio inevitably takes a mighty fine way of saying that he has lived beyond his income, since we are to enter a world in which the illusion necessary to carry a romantic plot can only be sustained by persons with a mighty fine way of saying most things. Bassanio's little anecdote about the arrows, seriously considered, may be 'windy nonsense', but nothing could be more conducive to the mood in which we are invited to follow his adventures. It may be singularly inappropriate for a young spendthrift to use so childish an argument in seeking to persuade a long-headed man of business to invest his money. But the argument is entirely appropriate to the major purpose of the scene. Antonio is *not* essentially a long-headed man of business or the play could never have been written. The anecdote of the two arrows establishes at once the atmosphere of a play in which the values of the market-place, the processes of the law and the questing of a young man after beauty and fortune are to be ingredients in a tall story—one of the tallest stories ever put upon the stage. Bassanio's reversion to his 'schooldays' is from this point of view a stroke of genius. It sets the tone for all that is to follow, which, again to quote Bassanio, is 'pure innocence'. The same pure innocence informs the speech which 'Q' pronounces to be 'bad workmanship and dishonouring to Bassanio'. It is not bad but consummate workmanship. Consider, for example, that reference to Jason which announces at once the legendary quality of Bassanio's adventure. Nor is there any question of dishonour. Bassanio in effect invites his friend to take a two-to-one risk in helping him to win a lady who, as he surmises, has found him not unpleasing. He is not presenting Antonio with a commercial proposition, but with a sporting chance, and Shakespeare intends his audience to accept all this, with more to follow, as we accept the premises of any tall story in which we can be persuaded to believe for our pleasure if we allow the author to suggest or to dictate the mood in which we look and listen.

Parenthetically it may be observed that Shylock never comes within sight or hearing of Belmont. Shakespeare had two equally preposterous stories to tell in his play. Each has its own setting and atmosphere, in which each is credibly presented. Each would destroy the other if they came together and nothing could be more adroit than the way in which the author, in combining the two plots, keeps them moving upon different planes of illusion and yet contrives to make each serve the purpose of the other by contrast. Belmont with its opulent leisure, its merry conversation, its princely adventurers after love and fortune, echoing with 'those dulcet sounds in break of day that creep into the dreaming bridegroom's ear', where young Jason, if he lose, may make 'a swan-like end, fading in music', presents a world in which it is as impossible to imagine Shylock as to imagine the Prince of Morocco, with his shadowed livery of the burnished sun, coming within a mile of that sober house of Israel from which all sounds of shallow foppery are permanently shut. Yet we are persuaded to believe in them both, and the more devoutly for their difference. Each of them is contrived to create its own illusion. And how each of them grips the simple spectator! We follow the choice of the caskets—though we most assuredly know the result—as breathlessly as we follow the turns and twists of the trial. Shakespeare has in each case created conditions in which we suspend all disbelief and are content to hear a story twenty times over without losing interest in the event. He induces in his audience an imaginative suspense in which we identify ourselves with the persons of the tale as distinguished from the cruder suspense of merely wondering what is going to happen next.

Shakespeare's triumph is most marked where probability is most severely strained. The play comes to a climax in the trial scene. Here everything—the laws expounded, the procedure followed, the conduct of the parties, the deportment of all concerned—is, by all normal standards of human conduct, utterly fantastic. This scene, however, has been so carefully prepared, and the mood of the audience is so exactly attuned to receive it, that the case in dispute has been hotly and minutely debated by accomplished lawyers as though it were a serious contribution to the common law of nations. It makes nonsense of every known principle of jurisprudence. It is nevertheless received without misgiving as an authentic leaf from the judicial records of the State of Venice and has become a text for learned Counsel seriously debating the legal issues. Advocates on the one side contend that Shylock was defrauded of his rights by a quibble which no court of law could in decency accept; that Portia, in demanding that a pound of flesh should be cut from Antonio, without shedding a drop of Christian blood, was ignoring an essential principle in the law of contract, since the right to perform a certain act, in this case the cutting of a pound of flesh, confers a right to the necessary incidents of the act, in this case the shedding of blood; that Portia's insistence upon Shylock's cutting exactly a pound, neither more nor less, was legally absurd, since anyone who in law has the right to take a certain amount of anything certainly has the right to take less; that a court which had allowed the legal validity of Shylock's bond could not possibly convict him of a criminal offence for presenting it.

Advocates bringing to bear an equally impressive weight of legal opinion have argued as cogently on the other side. To the plea that, if flesh be removed, blood is implied, it is gravely argued by Portia's advocates that bargains of this nature are to be strictly interpreted and in doubtful points against the party in whose power it lay to make the points of the agreement more explicit; that the sentence in equity is good, though its judicial premises may be irregular; that Portia's victory over Shylock dramatically presents a necessary historic process in the evolution of jurisprudence whereby rigid forms of law inherited from antiquity are brought into harmony with more enlightened conceptions of legal right.[1]

[1] Needless to say these more serious observations are for the most part contributed by German writers.

But nothing quite equals the discovery of a Mr. John T. Doyle, published in 1886, that the procedure followed by the Venetian Court reproduces the essential

If Shakespeare, in handling the secondary characters and legal incidents of his play, achieved so strong an illusion of reality that they have been discussed for generations and are still discussed to-day as though he were presenting a transcript from the social life of Venice in the sixteenth century, his delineation of Shylock has had results even more remarkable. He set out to write a comedy about a stage Jew involved in a grotesque story about a pound of flesh. But Shylock, to satisfy his author, must seem to act as a recognisably human being would behave in the given circumstances and Shakespeare has *humanised* him to such good purpose that this comic Jew has become, for many brilliant and sensitive critics, a moving, almost a tragic, figure. Some even go so far as to exclaim of Shylock in his anguish: O what a noble mind is here o'erthrown!

How exactly has this come about? Why and when, if ever, does Shylock cease to be a comic character? Going to Shakespeare's text for an answer to these questions we shall perhaps find a clue not only to the nature of Shakespeare's achievement but to the process by which it is attained.

There is a school of critics which, in reaction from those who discuss Shakespeare's characters as though they were real live persons created without reference to the plays in which they are required to perform certain acts, tend to insist that everything they say or do is determined by some necessity of the plot or technical requirement of the stage. These commentators are often able to show that, where a poet or a psychologist applauds what appears to be a stroke of unfettered genius, the dramatist is merely getting on with what Hamlet called some 'necessary question of the play'. They demonstrate that this soliloquy or that speech, this sequence or that incident, is determined by the mechanics of the Elizabethan stage, by the gifts or limitations of the available actors, by the accepted conventions of the contemporary drama. Then, too, there is always the mere business of keeping the plot in action and putting the characters through such

features of legal practice used in the courts of Nicaragua, with whose Spanish traditions Shakespeare is of course presumed to have been acquainted. For a summary of these legal controversies the reader is referred to twenty pages of notes in the Furness Variorum Edition of the play.

paces as are necessary to that end. A predetermined story has to be told. There is no free-will in the mimic world of the theatre. All we can hope to see is the puppets dallying. Why, for example, should we break our heads over the problem of Hamlet's procrastination? If Hamlet had killed Claudius immediately the play would have come to an end at the close of the first act. Why should we go about to find any special significance in the arrival of Fortinbras when at long last Hamlet lies dead upon the stage? Fortinbras had to enter at that particular moment or there would have been no-one to carry off the bodies, which, in the absence of a curtain, could neither be left merely lying about nor allowed to come alive again and walk off. Maurice Baring has amusingly parodied this approach to Shakespeare, the playwright, in one of his 'Diminutive Dramas', in which Shakespeare, at a rehearsal of 'Macbeth', is sent away to write an extra speech for Burbage, who urges that more effective use should be made of the announcement that the queen is dead. Shakespeare, to Burbage's consternation, obliges with 'To-morrow and to-morrow and to-morrow', which accordingly ceases to be a significant stroke of the poet's genius and may be dismissed as a merely technical concession to the vanity of his leading man.

There is everything to be said in favour of keeping constantly in mind such technical necessities. But to conclude that they limited Shakespeare's creative activity or impaired what was absolute in his characterisation is equivalent to maintaining that the quality and scope of Beethoven's music was determined by the fact that in composing a symphony he accepted limitations of form which required him to state, develop and repeat his subjects in conformity with an approved system of key relationships; or that Bach, in composing 'The Art of Fugue', had, in obedience to technical necessity, no choice but to write precisely the notes which posterity, somewhat tardily, decided to rescue from oblivion as conveying a profound utterance of the human spirit.

There is no better example of interplay between technical craft and creative imagination than the way in which the character of Shylock, apparently predetermined by the necessities of the story in which he figures and by the expectations of the audience to which he was presented, assumes the dimensions and habit of a character which exists freely and in its own right. Admittedly his behaviour in the play is settled in advance. But Shakespeare immediately identifies himself with the sort of person who must inevitably behave in that particular way. Shylock, setting forth upon the stage, is at once a man with hands, organs, dimensions, senses, affections, passions, and the plot to which he must conform soon appears to be no more than an opportunity for bringing him to life. The plot determined the kind of character which Shakespeare created; but the character, once created, determines everything he says or does. It is the paradox of great art that limitations arising from the nature of a given subject, the quality of the materials used and the restrictions imposed by necessary conventions merely serve to concentrate the activity of a free spirit on the business in hand. The artist with little or nothing to express complains of the discipline imposed upon him by the laws of his craft, wastes his energy in quarrelling with his tools or devotes more attention to the invention of a new technique than to the exploitation and development of an inherited tradition. Not so the man of genius. Shakespeare, taking Shylock's merry bond for a theme and accepting all the restrictions of the Elizabethan theatre, expressed himself as freely and profoundly as Beethoven when he unlocked his heart and disclosed the entire length, breadth and depth of his genius, in thirty-three variations on a merry waltz by Diabelli.

Shakespeare in presenting Shylock has so artfully combined the necessities of his plot with the revelation of a character that it is difficult, almost impossible, to say of any single incident or speech which of the two purposes is better served. The man lives in every word that he utters. He has a distinct language of his own and every syllable denotes his quality. His first words are of ducats; his introductory conversation with Bassanio might be cross-headed: Any usurer to any client: *Three thousand . . . ducats . . . For three months . . . Antonio shall become bound . . . Antonio is a good man . . . Yet his means are in supposition . . . The man is notwithstanding sufficient . . . Three thousand ducats—I think I may take his bond.* There is nothing here that seems to serve any other purpose than to present the comic Jew and to get the story under way. But the man is already alive. We shall know him again as soon as he opens his lips—a man whose words are stubborn in his mouth, in whose speech there is no ease or warmth or levity, who hammers out his phrases and can find no way of varying them once they are uttered. *Three thousand ducats . . . Antonio bound.* It is the utterance of a man whose mind is concentrated, obsessed, focused upon a narrow range of fixed ideas. Shylock had the trick of compulsive repetition characteristic of the man in whom imagination, such as it is, forever sits on brood. It is the speech of one who is incapable of humour, whose words will always precisely fit his meaning, in whom no play or flight of fancy is possible:

Ships are but boards, sailors but men. There be land-rats and water-rats, land-thieves and water-thieves—I mean pirates. And then there is the peril of waters, winds and rocks.

Such is the eloquence of Shylock. So literal is his habit of mind that he must interrupt his recitation of the bleak hazards of trade to explain that by water-thieves, a phrase which strikes him as possibly too picturesque to be exactly understood, he means pirates. Contrast with this plain, surly, intensive style of utterance the warm, easy flow of the Venetian gentleman, Salerio, speaking to the same theme:

> My wind, cooling my broth,
> Would blow me to an ague when I thought
> What harm a wind too great might do at sea.
> I should not see the sandy hour-glass run
> But I should think of shallows and of flats,
> And see my wealthy Andrew docked in sand,
> Vailing her high-top lower than her ribs
> To kiss her burial. . . . Should I go to church
> And see the holy edifice of stone,
> And not bethink me straight of dangerous rocks,
> Which touching but my gentle vessel's side
> Would scatter all her spices on the stream,
> Enrobe the roaring waters with my silks,
> And, in a word, but even now worth this,
> And now worth nothing?

Here, then, is Shylock revealed at his first appearance in every phrase that he utters as a certain kind of man and, what is equally to the purpose, as a totally different kind of man from his Christian adversaries. His tricks of speech already project a character, unmistakeably alive, which will be recognisably true to itself in all that follows. They will recur throughout the play till they culminate in those stubborn, reiterated appeals to his bond of a man possessed by a single thought expressed in a phrase that has become almost an incantation.

Meanwhile Shakespeare must come immediately to grips with his story of the comic Jew and the pound of flesh. He grasps the nettle firmly in an aside wherein Shylock discloses his intention and the motives behind it:

> How like a fawning publican he looks!
> I hate him for he is a Christian:
> But more for that in low simplicity
> He lends out money gratis, and brings down
> The rate of usance here with us in Venice. . . .
> If I can catch him once upon the hip,
> I will feed fat the ancient grudge I bear him. . . .
> He hates our sacred nation, and he rails,
> Even there where merchants most do congregate,
> On me, my bargains, and my well-won thrift,
> Which he calls interest. . . . Cursèd be my tribe,
> If I forgive him!

There is no hint in this speech, and there has been as yet no suggestion in the play, that Shylock has any human justification for his monstrous project. For the moment Shakespeare is satisfied with presenting his comic Jew in all the stark, ugly simplicity of the legend with which his audience was familiar. Shylock detests Antonio because he is a Christian; because he lends out money gratis and brings down the rate of usance; because he 'hates the Jews and dislikes their way of doing business'. Shylock, in this first exhibition of his malice, is a comic figure and so he remains in the passages that follow: debating of his present store; delivering the traditional patter of the moneylender about the difficulty of making up the sum required; justifying his practice of usury by citing the trick played by Jacob on Laban over the parti-coloured lambs.

Then comes the first intimation that Shakespeare, having undertaken to supply his audience with a comic Jew committed to a barbarous enterprise, not only intends to make his conduct psychologically credible but has already realised in imagination what it
means to wear the star of David:

SHYLOCK: Signior Antonio, many a time and oft
               In the Rialto you have rated me
               About my moneys and my usances:
               Still have I borne it with a patient shrug,
               For suff'rance is the badge of all our tribe.
               You call me misbeliever, cut-throat dog,
               And spet upon my Jewish gaberdine,
               And all for use of that which is mine own. . . .
               Well then, it now appears you need my help:
               Go to then, you come to me, and you say,
               'Shylock, we would have moneys'—you say so!
               You that did void your rheum upon my beard,
               And foot me as you spurn a stranger cur
               Over your threshold—moneys is your suit.
               What should I say to you? Should I not say
               'Hath a dog money? is it possible
               A cur can lend three thousand ducats?' or
               Shall I bend low, and in a bondman's key,
               With bated breath, and whisp'ring humbleness,
               Say this:

               'Fair sir, you spet on me on Wednesday last—
               You spurned me such a day—another time
               You called me dog: and for these courtesies
               I'll lend you thus much moneys'?

That is perhaps the most remarkable speech in the play. It suggests
for the first time on any stage that the Jew has a case. The Jew, moreover, puts that case with a deadly logic, sharpened by persecution to
the finest edge, and with a passion which no amount of suff'rance
can conceal. It reveals a mind so intensely concentrated upon itself,
so constricted in its operation, that it can only express itself in
repetitions of a rhythmic, almost hypnotic, quality. *You have rated me*

about my moneys . . . Shylock, we would have moneys . . . moneys is
your suit. . . . You call me misbeliever, cut-throat dog. . . . Hath a dog
money? . . . You called me dog and, for these courtesies, I'll lend you thus
much moneys. And spet upon my Jewish gaberdine. . . . You that did void
your rheum upon my beard. . . . Fair sir, you spet on me on Wednesday
last.

Neither in logic nor in passion can Shylock be assailed and the
Christians do not even attempt a rejoinder. Antonio, in fact, calls
down upon himself the doom that awaits one side or the other in any
conflict that passes the bounds of reason:

> I am as like to call thee so again,
> To spet on thee again, to spurn thee too.
> If thou wilt lend this money, lend it not
> As to thy friends—for when did friendship take
> A breed for barren metal of his friend?—
> But lend it rather to thine enemy,
> Who, if he break, thou mayst with better face
> Exact the penalty.

And so we come to the business of the bond. It is a difficult
moment. But note how quickly and easily it is handled. The passages
that precede it may be likened to the patter of a conjurer who dis-
tracts the attention of his audience as he prepares to play his master-
trick. Shylock's speech and Antonio's reply have fixed our attention
on the fundamental issue of the play as between Christian and Jew
and, before we have recovered our emotional balance sufficiently to
realise what is happening, hey presto! the thing is done:

SHYLOCK: Why, look you, how you storm!
            I would be friends with you, and have your love,
            Forget the shames that you have stained me with,
            Supply your present wants, and take no doit
            Of usance for my moneys, and you'll not hear me:
            This is kind I offer.
ANTONIO: This were kindness.
SHYLOCK: This kindness will I show.
            Go with me to a notary, seal me there
            Your single bond, and, in a merry sport,

> If you repay me not on such a day,
> In such a place, such sum or sums as are
> Expressed in the condition, let the forfeit
> Be nominated for an equal pound
> Of your fair flesh, to be cut off and taken
> In what part of your body pleaseth me.
>
> ANTONIO: Content, in faith—I'll seal to such a bond,
> And say there is much kindness in the Jew.

It is done, too, in a fashion which in no way detracts from the reality of the characters or their relationship. Shylock, in forwarding the plot, is still revealing himself as the kind of man who will later come into court with his knife and scales. There is nothing more sinister-comic in the whole literature of hypocrisy than the two speeches to Antonio. *This is kind I offer. . . . And in a merry sport.* Shylock kind! Shylock merry! Why, even as he makes his proposal, the secret passion that moves him is strong enough to penetrate and subdue his victim who is, as it were, hypnotised into adopting Shylock's own characteristic trick of repetition. 'This were kindness', says Antonio; 'there is much kindness in the Jew.'

The ease with which Antonio is trapped into the bond with Shylock is a good example of the way in which Shakespeare turns to advantage the limitations imposed upon him by his material. Antonio is predestined to sign a contract which will put his life at the mercy of a mortal enemy whom he has every reason to distrust. That is a tall order. Shakespeare does not evade the difficulty, but uses it to serve perhaps the most striking purpose of his play, which is to contrast the narrow, alert and suspicious character of the Jew, member of a persecuted race, with the free, careless and confident disposition of the Christian sure of his place in the sun. It is a contrast maintained in every scene of the play. Shylock in word and deed is typical, intense and precise; the Christians are impulsive, sentimental and wayward. Shylock trusts in his bond; the Christians trust to luck—whether it be Bassanio staking love and fortune on the choice of a casket or Antonio gambling on the ships which fail to come home. Shylock tells us of his 'bargains' and his 'well-won thrift', but riches fall from a window on to the head of Lorenzo. The character-

istic qualities on either side are respectively those of the oppressed
and the oppressor. If in Shylock we stand appalled by the warping of
mind and spirit which oppression inflicts on those who suffer it, we
are not less repelled by the infatuated assumption of Antonio and his
friends that to them all is permitted in the best of possible worlds.
The point is constantly emphasised in the minutest particulars of
dialogue and incident. When Shylock, justifying his bargains, cites
the case of Jacob and the parti-coloured lambs:

> This was a way to thrive, and he was blest :
> And *thrift* is blessing if men steal it not;

Antonio rejoins:

> This was a venture, sir, that Jacob served for—
> A thing not in his power to bring to pass,
> But swayed and fashioned by the hand of heaven.

Here, incidentally but in a nutshell, the careful husbandry of the Jew
is contrasted with the careless genial improvidence of the Christian.
Such touches of character, constantly repeated, not only prepare us
for Antonio's easy acceptance of the bond but dispose us to swallow
the whole preposterous story as entirely natural to the persons con-
ceived.

From the sealing of the merry bond we pass to the story of Jessica.
No incident in the play has so richly contributed to the transformation of Shylock, the comic Jew, into a lamentable victim of Christian
bigotry and licence. This metamorphosis reached its literary climax
in Heine:

I heard a voice with a ripple of tears that were never wept by eyes. It
was a sob that could come only from a breast that held in it all the martyr-
dom which, for eighteen centuries, had been borne by a whole tortured
people. It was the death-rattle of a soul, sinking down dead tired at
heaven's gates. And I seemed to know the voice, and I felt I had heard it
long ago when in utter despair it moaned out, then as now, 'Jessica, my
girl'.

On the stage it attained its theatrical climax, for those who remember
it, when Henry Irving returning by the light of a lantern knocked on

the door of an empty house. Where, now, is your monster with a large painted nose? This is a patriarch of Israel, wronged in his most sacred affections. Small wonder if, after this, the afflicted Jew grows blind to the quality of Christian mercy.

Alas for those who, seeking to find Shakespeare in one part only of his design, lose or pervert the whole! There is as little warrant for the voice that moaned in Heine's ear as for the Irving interpolation which made of that tragic figure beating on the door a sublime and pathetic incident to wring your hearts.

What are the facts?

Shylock, bidding farewell to his daughter, is more truly comic than at any point of the story so far reached:

> I am bid forth to supper, Jessica.
> There are my keys. But wherefore should I go?
> I am not bid for love—they flatter me.
> But yet I'll go in hate, to feed upon
> The prodigal Christian. Jessica, my girl,
> Look to my house. I am right loath to go—
> There is some ill a-brewing towards my rest,
> For I did dream of money-bags to-night.

This, then, is the voice, the death-rattle of a soul sinking down dead tired at heaven's gates. *Jessica, my girl, look to my house.* Heine, in underlining the pathos, has missed the essential quality of the scene. Shakespeare did not write '*Jessica, my girl*', but '*Jessica, my girl, look to my house*', and 'house' is the operative word. In claiming for Shylock the heartbroken misery of a loving father bereft of his child the man of sentiment loses the essential genius of the dramatist who created him. It is the house which stands at the core of Shylock's being; Jessica is no more than the daughter of the house:

> Do as I bid you. shut doors after you:
> Fast bind, fast find.

Not only the doors but the windows must be shut:

> Lock up my doors, and when you hear the drum
> And the vile squealing of the wry-neck'd fife,
> Clamber not you up to the casements then,

> Nor thrust your head into the public street
> To gaze on Christian fools with varnished faces:
> But stop my house's ears, I mean my casements,
> Let not the sound of shallow fopp'ry enter
> My sober house.[1]

Shylock, speaking of his house, is moved almost to poetry. The house is for him a living thing—*Stop my house's ears;* and the word once used, since it stands for one of the few things on which his mind is passionately centred, must be repeated—'*Let not the sound of shallow fopp'ry enter my sober house.*' And that word will be heard again:

> Nay, take my life and all, pardon not that.
> You take my house, when you do take the prop
> That doth sustain my house.

Shylock's farewell to Jessica, which established him for Heine as a tragic figure, leaves him still comic in the play that Shakespeare wrote. Shakespeare has done no more in this scene—but how much it is—than humanise the stage qualities of the comic Jew. Every stroke aims at our sense of comedy. 'Thou shalt not gormandise, as thou hast done with me', he tells Lancelot who is quitting him to serve Bassanio, and, in bidding farewell to this 'huge feeder', he exhibits a malevolence which, like all fixed ideas in a living creature, is at the same time ludicrous and terrible:

> Drones hive not with me.
> Therefore I part with him, and part with him
> To one that I would have him help to waste
> His borrowed purse.[2]

Is Shylock, mourning his daughter's flight, any less comic than

[1] Note in this speech a delicious characteristic parenthesis. Having been betrayed into what for his precision is a flight of fancy, he instinctively corrects himself: 'Stop my house's ears, *I mean my casements*'. We have surprised him once before in this same revealing trick of speech when, after talking of water-rats and water-thieves, he felt it necessary to add: 'I mean pirates.'

[2] Let anyone who is disposed to over-sentimentalise Shylock's relations with his daughter ponder his sly warning: *Perhaps I will return immediately.* Distrusting her obedience he cautions her that he may be back sooner than she expects.

Shylock bidding his daughter to shut his doors and windows? A careful study of the scene with Salerio and Tubal provokes conclusions profoundly disconcerting to the heirs of the romantic tradition. It is supremely comic in itself and Shakespeare deliberately contrived in advance that the comic element should prevail over its emotional implications. Far from intending us to sympathise with an afflicted father, he has emphasised before the event that Shylock's affection is abnormally possessive and, in depicting the Jew's reaction to her flight, he subordinates even this self-centred affection to the fury of a man of property upon whose well-won thrift an unspeakable outrage has been committed. *My own flesh and blood to rebel. . . . I say, my daughter is my own flesh and blood.* This chimes perfectly with 'Jessica, my girl, look to my house'. His daughter, his own flesh and blood, has abandoned his house and 'she is damned for it'. She has made off, too, with his jewels and his ducats. There was no need for Shakespeare to introduce this incident at all. It detracts from the pleasure which his audience is clearly intended to take in the sweet infidel who holds a candle to her shames and it encourages romantics and realists alike to take a very poor view of Bassanio's friend, Lorenzo. Heine, as we have seen, would have given Lorenzo fifteen years in the penitentiary. But Shakespeare had other fish to fry. Jessica gilds herself with Shylock's ducats so that Shylock may reveal himself more effectively as an essentially comic character:

SHYLOCK: How now, Tubal! what news from Genoa? hast thou found my daughter?

TUBAL: I often came where I did hear of her, but cannot find her.

SHYLOCK: Why there, there, there, there—a diamond gone, cost me two thousand ducats in Frankfort—the curse never fell upon our nation till now, I never felt it till now—two thousand ducats in that, and other precious, precious jewels. I would my daughter were dead at my foot, and the jewels in her ear! would she were hearsed at my foot, and the ducats in her coffin! No news of them? Why, so—and I know not what's spent in the search: why, thou loss upon loss! the thief gone with so much and so much to find the thief, and no satisfaction, no revenge, nor no ill luck stirring, but what lights o' my shoulders, no sighs but o' my breathing, no tears but o' my shedding. (*he weeps*)

That is admittedly a rather terrible scene. But it is undeniably comic, the victim growing more ludicrous as he becomes more poignantly enslaved to his obsession; and the passage that follows in which Shylock alternately rages at the thought of Jessica squandering his ducats and rejoices to hear of Antonio's losses at sea, brings the comedy to a climax. Shylock's responses to Tubal are like the jerking reflexes of a marionette. They give him just that appearance of a human automaton which is one of the most characteristic effects of pure comedy:

TUBAL: Yes, other men have ill luck too. Antonio, as I heard in Genoa—
SHYLOCK: What, what, what? ill luck, ill luck?
TUBAL: —hath an argosy cast away, coming from Tripolis.
SHYLOCK: I thank God, I thank God! Is it true? is it true?
TUBAL: I spoke with some of the sailors that escaped the wrack.
SHYLOCK: I thank thee, good Tubal, good news, good news: ha, ha! Where? In Genoa?
TUBAL: Your daughter spent in Genoa, as I heard, one night, fourscore ducats.
SHYLOCK: Thou stick'st a dagger in me. I shall never see my gold again —fourscore ducats at a sitting! fourscore ducats!
TUBAL: There came divers of Antonio's creditors in my company to Venice, that swear he cannot choose but break.
SHYLOCK: I am very glad of it, I'll plague him. I'll torture him, I am glad of it.
TUBAL: One of them showed me a ring that he had of your daughter for a monkey.
SHYLOCK: Out upon her! thou torturest me, Tubal—it was my turquoise—I had it of Leah when I was a bachelor: I would not have given it for a wilderness of monkeys.
TUBAL: But Antonio is certainly undone.
SHYLOCK: Nay, that's true, that's very true. Go, Tubal, fee me an officer, bespeak him a fortnight before. I will have the heart of him if he forfeit, for were he out of Venice I can make what merchandise I will.[1]

The conclusion is worth noting. Shylock has lost his daughter. He has been wounded to the quick of his personal feeling and racial

[1]As suggested above, this particular passage comes nearer in spirit and treatment to the comedy of Molière than any other scene in Shakespeare. (See Introduction, p. xii).

pride. But Shakespeare still insists on the point from which he started. The Jew hates Antonio because he lends out money gratis and brings down the rate of usance. He will have the heart of Antonio, for 'were he out of Venice I can make what merchandise I will'.

Nevertheless it is this scene from which the romantic tradition of Shylock is mainly derived. For it contains the great speech, so often read and quoted with too little regard for its context, which has misled so many critics into praising Shakespeare as a champion of tolerance and humanity where they might more pertinently have admired his genius as a dramatist and his imaginative intimacy with all sorts and conditions of men:

SHYLOCK: Hath not a Jew eyes? Hath not a Jew hands, organs, dimensions, senses, affections, passions? fed with the same food, hurt with the same weapons, subject to the same diseases, healed by the same means, warmed and cooled by the same winter and summer, as a Christian is? If you prick us, do we not bleed? if you tickle us, do we not laugh? if you poison us, do we not die?

That sounds like a plea for charity. Taken in its context, however, it is something less, and at the same time something more. Shylock's theme is not charity but revenge. He will have Antonio's flesh, if only to bait fish withal:

He hath disgraced me and hindred me half a million, laughed at my losses, mocked at my gains, scorned my nation, thwarted my bargains, cooled my friends, heated mine enemies—and what's his reason? I am a Jew.

and he concludes:

If a Jew wrong a Christian, what is his humility? Revenge. If a Christian wrong a Jew, what should his sufferance be by Christian example? Why, revenge. The villainy you teach me, I will execute, and it shall go hard but I will better the instruction.

Thus, what is commonly received as Shylock's plea for tolerance is in reality his justification of an inhuman purpose. That does not, however, lessen, but rather increase its significance. The most dreadful consequence of injustice is that it degrades not only the oppressor but the oppressed. Shakespeare is concerned to present only the human truth of a situation which he has accepted for the purpose of his play. Shylock, since his motives must be more humanly comprehensible, is presented as a natural product of Christian intolerance; but he does not thereby cease to be a comic character or become an advocate of the humaner virtues. There is something grotesque even in his pleading. *If you tickle us, do we not laugh?* Shakespeare was not here concerned—he never is concerned—with pleading a case in morality. He was presenting Shylock as Shylock lived in his imagination and, in so doing, he showed us how a dramatist, intent only upon his vision, incidentally achieves a moral effect wider in scope and more profound in its implications than a dramatist who consciously devotes himself to an ethical purpose. The comically distorted image of Shylock the Jew is in effect a more telling indictment of Christian oppression, though Shakespeare was not primarily concerned with that aspect of the matter, than the fictitiously sentimentalised presentment of the character created for modern playgoers by Edmund Kean and his successors. Many fine plays have been written by dramatists which expressly indict man's inhumanity to man, but no work of art created with an express political or moral intention is in the last resort so effective, even in the attainment of its purpose, as a work of art which achieves excellence in the form and spirit proper to itself. Critics and actors who, to enhance Shakespeare's hypothetical message, do their best to make Shylock humanly impressive and invite our commiseration for the ruins of a noble nature are likely to discover in the end that they have not only spoiled a comedy but defeated their own object and impaired the moral effect of the play.

There is one other point to be noted in Shakespeare's handling of Jessica. It is often insinuated by commentators who are determined to elevate the issue between Shylock and Antonio, that the Jew was goaded into claiming his pound of flesh by the abduction of his daughter. Here, again, Shakespeare has, in the biblical sense, prevented them. Shakespeare uses the Jessica incident to make Shylock's behaviour in court more acceptable to the audience. We must have seen for ourselves some reason for the Jew's hatred of Antonio made real and visible in dramatic form. Having witnessed the flight of

Jessica and Shylock's reaction to it, we shall be more likely to believe in the inexorable dog who sharpens the knife on his sole. But Shakespeare having used the incident to make the Jew's conduct in court seem less improbable suddenly realises that, in so doing, he may have left us with an impression that Shylock was moved to extremity by paternal anguish, and, as though he foresaw the use to be made of this episode by a romantic posterity, he slips in an explicit repudiation of any such interpretation. When the news of Antonio's arrest reaches Belmont and is discussed with Portia, Jessica assures Bassanio:

> When I was with him, I have heard him swear
> To Tubal and to Chus, his countrymen,
> That he would rather have Antonio's flesh
> Than twenty times the value of the sum
> That he did owe him.[1]

Shakespeare here goes out of his way to inform us expressly that Shylock had made up his mind to kill Antonio long before Jessica's flight with Lorenzo—that he had, in fact, been in the habit of delivering at home speeches of the kind which he was shortly to repeat in the court-house:

> If every ducat in six thousand ducats
> Were in six parts and every part a ducat,
> I would not draw them, I would have my bond!

'Shylock no miser' declared Coleridge in a lecture on Shakespeare delivered on February 6th 1812 to a 'numerous and genteel audience'. He was maintaining that Shakespeare 'drew from the eternal of our nature' and that the miser being but a 'transitory character', peculiar to a certain type of society, could find no place in his imagination. Coleridge would probably have agreed to the obverse of his proposition, namely, that Shakespeare, in depicting a 'transitory character', almost inevitably gave to it a permanent reality. 'Shylock no miser' is a true bill in the sense that he is a man of many parts and qualities. Shakespeare did not, like Jonson, see men as humours walking. He presents us not with character parts or stage types, but with complete

[1] This speech of Jessica's incidentally helps us to understand why she had so little compunction about leaving her father's house.

and often unaccountable human beings. 'Shylock no miser' is true in
the general sense that he is more than a personification of avarice.
'Shylock no miser' is equally true in the more particular sense that,
though he dreams of money-bags and wishes his daughter hearsed at
his foot with the ducats in her coffin and hates Antonio for bringing
down the rate of usance, he would not for any number of ducats
forgo his revenge on the merchant and refuses thrice the sum due to
him in open court. Shakespeare nevertheless never allows us to lose
sight of the fact that the most *abiding* element in his character is hatred
of extravagance. He may not love money for its own sake, but it
stands for the cardinal virtues in his calendar of sober thrift and
respect for material values. That he should be cheated of his hard-
won bargains by the easy-handed gentlemen of Venice touches him
to the quick. It destroys the very foundations on which he bases his
conduct and assesses his own personal worth. Jessica's behaviour is
an outrage. That she should make away with his ducats is bad
enough. That she should have bartered her turquoise ring—and her
mother's ring at that—for a monkey makes sacrilegious nonsense of
the thrift that in Jacob was blest by the God of Israel.[1]

Shylock makes only one other appearance before his case is heard
and Shakespeare takes this occasion to remind us once again of his
principal grievance against Antonio. The Jew meets him in custody:

> Gaoler, look to him. Tell me not of mercy.
> This is the fool that lent out money gratis.

There is no reference here to a lost child or even to his sacred nation;
and the essentially comic quality of the Jew's mind and utterance,
with its compulsive repetitions, is admirably sustained. The word
'bond' occurs six times:

---

[1] 'Shylock no miser' inevitably calls to mind Harpagon in Molière's 'L'Avare'.
Molière in his characterisation runs more truly to type than Shakespeare. But the
comic characters of Molière, though they embody more systematically some master
passion of the play, are far from being stage figures with generic labels attached to
them. Molière, like Shakespeare, gets his finest comedy from a conflict of inconsistencies. Shylock, preferring a pound of carrion flesh to thrice three thousand
ducats—one passion driving out another—,recalls Harpagon who in his desire to
cut a figure in the eyes of Mariane, organises a banquet.

I'll have my *bond,* speak not against my *bond,*
I have sworn an oath that I will have my *bond*:
Thou call'dst me dog before thou hadst a cause,
But since I am a dog beware my fangs.

I'll have my *bond*—I will not hear thee speak.
I'll have my *bond*, and therefore speak no more.
I'll not be made a soft and dull-eyed fool,
To shake the head, relent, and sigh, and yield
To Christian intercessors . . .Follow not—
I'll have no speaking, I will have my *bond*.

Shakespeare is now ready—and his audience, too—for the confrontation in court by which his comedy will stand or fall. His task was to get the maximum dramatic effect out of an intrinsically improbable situation. So well did he succeed that the scene is theatrically one of the most effective ever put upon the stage. It is, at the same time, a scene which, owing to the skill with which the playwright solved his technical problems and brought his characters imaginatively to life as dramatic persons, has moral implications which exceed the author's immediate purpose. Critics tend to ignore the technical achievement and make too much of the implications, finding here a noble plea for Christian charity or there an exposure of Christian barbarity. The court scene is frequently read or produced as though its prime purpose and title to fame were Portia's very adequate but by no means outstanding discourse upon the quality of mercy, whereas, in fact, that speech is merely one of many in which Shakespeare exploits the dramatic possibilities of the situation.[1]

Shylock, in this scene, achieves his discomfiture by the very qualities which distinguish him most conspicuously as a comic character. He digs with his own hands the pit into which we know that he will most assuredly fall and supplies his enemies with the very weapons by which he is defeated. From the moment in which he enters the court, he stands inexorably upon the letter of the law.

---

[1] The dramatic significance of this speech lies in its inconsistency with the behaviour of the Christians who applaud it. From this point of view it may be regarded as a striking example of the way in which Shakespeare's habit of presenting things as they are constantly reveals the irony of character and circumstance.

The Duke, when the case is opened, entreats him to glance an eye of pity on the losses of Antonio. But Shylock has sworn to have his bond. The Duke asks how he can hope for mercy if he renders none. But Shylock has no need of mercy; Antonio's flesh is dearly bought, 'tis his and he will have it. Portia, finding the bond correct, declares that the Jew must be merciful. But Shylock admits no such compulsion; and, when Portia, echoing the Duke, urges that men should be merciful as they hope for mercy, he exclaims: 'My deeds upon my head, I crave the law.' When Portia begs him to take the money and to forgo the pound of flesh, he charges her by the law to proceed to judgment; he stays upon his bond. The flesh must be cut from the merchant's breast—nearest his heart. So says the bond—those are the very words. Portia asks for a surgeon. But Shylock can find no mention of a surgeon. Is it so nominated in the bond?

Thus, speech by speech, Shakespeare prepares for the moment when Shylock's own insistence upon the letter of the law will be turned against him and when his repudiation of charity will bring its own retribution. Portia's speech on the question of mercy is dramatically merely an item in the comic process.

Note, too, how Shylock increases his own discomfiture—again it is the comic process—by accepting Portia in advance as a worthy representative of the law by which he stands. Portia has been scolded by some critics for keeping the wretched Antonio and his friends on tenterhooks. Surely it was most unkind to bring the poor merchant to the point of baring his breast for the knife when she had it in her power at any moment to shatter the whole case against him.[1] Shakespeare, by lending verisimilitude to this impossible scene, has again betrayed his commentators into applying to it the standards of normal behaviour. He sees to it, as a craftsman, that the scene shall be played for all it is worth and that Shylock shall in every particular

---

[1] Mr. M. J. Landa in a searching study of the Shylock myth is provoked into a notable outburst on the inhuman conduct of Portia in the trial scene: 'She plays cat and mouse . . . hypocrite to boot.' All this, and much more, equally unanswerable, just shows what happens when we allow ourselves to be misled by Shakespeare's theatrical skill into praising or blaming his characters for conduct which, however true and appropriate in its setting, fails to conform with our standard notions of a good companion.

turn the tables on Shylock. The Jew is self-entrapped not only into supplying the Christian advocate with a plausible justification for strictly rendering the letter of the law against him but into finding for his enemies the very words with which they taunt him in his overthrow. *Most rightful judge! Most learned judge! A Daniel come to judgment!* Portia, proceeding to extremes against Antonio, earns these praises from Shylock in order that they may in poetic justice be used against him. Her behaviour throughout the scene is conditioned by the part which Shakespeare requires her to play in achieving the comic catastrophe.

Shylock is never more Shylock than when he bears the full burden of this incredible scene. He has the same tricks of speech, the same obsessions, the same compulsive habits of thought and expression. The clear stubborn logic of his mind still enables him to confound his enemies by justifying his own practice from Christian example. He has rated Christian hypocrisy—*How like a fawning publican he looks!* He has declared that the Jew, equally with the Christian, knows how to revenge a wrong and can even better the instruction. He now turns in court on the men who counsel mercy and try to argue him out of his rights with the same unanswerable logic:

> You have among you many a purchased slave,
> Which, like your asses and your dogs and mules,
> You use in abject and in slavish parts,
> Because you bought them—shall I say to you,
> Let them be free, marry them to your heirs?
> Why sweat they under burthens? Let their beds
> Be made as soft as yours, and let their palates
> Be seasoned with such viands? You will answer,
> 'The slaves are ours.' So do I answer you—
> The pound of flesh, which I demand of him,
> Is dearly bought, *'tis mine,* and I will have it.

On his own ground, which he claims to share with his persecutors, Shylock is impregnable. He knows, none better, that Christian society is *not* based on the mercy for which the Duke and Portia so ingenuously plead. He asks no more than that the Christians shall apply to his case the principles whereby their own affections and affairs are ruled. A man may do what he will with his own. Antonio's flesh is his, legally acquired and dearly bought, and, if he likes to use it to bait fish withal, that is entirely his affair:

> You'll ask me why I rather choose to have
> A weight of carrion flesh than to receive
> Three thousand ducats: I'll not answer that!
> But say it is my humour, is it answered?
> What if my house be troubled with a rat,
> And I be pleased to give ten thousand ducats
> To have it baned? what, are you answered yet?

He has successfully contrived a situation which enables him to do for once what they are in the habit of doing every day of their lives and he means to make good use of it:

> Some men there are love not a gaping pig,
> Some that are mad if they behold a cat,
> And others when the bag-pipe sings i' th' nose
> Cannot contain their urine: for affection,
> Master of passion, sways it to the mood
> Of what it likes or loathes. Now, for your answer:
> As there is no firm reason to be rendered,
> Why he cannot abide a gaping pig;
> Why he, a harmless necessary cat;
> Why he, a woollen bag-pipe; but of force
> Must yield to such inevitable shame,
> As to offend, himself being offended;
> So can I give no reason, nor I will not,
> More than a lodged hate and a certain loathing
> I bear Antonio, that I follow thus
> A losing suit against him! Are you answered?

Shylock, carrying his hatred to extremes, exposes the injustice and ferocity of the social institutions from which it springs. He appeals to the twin laws of retribution and property on which the society in which he lives is based. Nothing is further from Shakespeare's mind than to convey a lesson. But the lesson is there, product of a perfectly balanced and sensitive mind intent upon the dramatic presentation of human realities. The debated question whether Shakespeare writing

certain passages of 'The Merchant of Venice' was pleading for tolera-
tion or indicting Christian hypocrisy, exalting equity above the law
or divine mercy above human justice, does not arise. He presents a
situation in which all these issues are involved, characters in which
their effects are displayed, arguments appropriate to the necessary
incidents and persons of the comedy; and leaves it to his critics to
draw the indictment or convey the apology. His purpose was to
write a comedy and he is never more intent on this purpose than in
the scene whose moral implications have excited so much interest
among those who study the play in the light of their own ethical and
social standards. Shylock eagerly producing the bond for Portia's
inspection—the bond which is to prove his own undoing—is undeniably comic. So is Shylock examining the bond to verify that the
flesh must be cut from Antonio nearest his heart. So is Shylock looking in vain for any mention of a surgeon. So is Shylock applauding
the wisdom of the judge who is about to ruin him. So, above all, is
Shylock promptly asking for the return of his money when he
realises that his claim to Antonio's flesh will not be allowed.

And behind all this obvious comedy is the indifferent irony of the
comic spirit which, in presenting the human realities of a situation,
necessarily exposes the blindness of human beings to their own
inconsistencies: Portia, singing the praises of mercy when she is
about to insist that the Jew shall have the full rigours of justice
according to the strict letter of the law; Antonio, congratulating
himself on his magnanimity in the very act of imposing on his
enemy a sentence which deprives him of everything he values;
Christian and Jew mutually charging one another with an inhumanity which is common to both parties.

How Shylock, imagined by Shakespeare as a comic figure and
sustaining his comic character to the last, was yet able to become a
depositary of the vengeance of his race (Hazlitt), the ruins of a
great and noble nature (Hudson) and the most respectable person in
the play (Heine) is now perhaps sufficiently evident. The question
when and how, if ever, Shylock ceases to be comic answers itself as
we read the play. To the question when? the answer, if we bear in
mind that Shakespeare's comedy springs from imaginative sympathy

and not from intellectual detachment, is: never for an instant. The question how? should not therefore arise. But alas for logic and the categories! No-one can remain wholly insensible to the emotional impact of the play. The imaginative effort expended by Shakespeare in making his Jew a comprehensibly human figure has imparted to him a vitality that every now and then stifles laughter and freezes the smile on our lips. If these passages are rightly handled by the actor or accorded their just place and value by the reader, the comedy remains intact. If, on the contrary, these passages are thrown into high relief and made to stand out of their context, the comedy is destroyed. Heine maintained that Shakespeare *intended* to write a comedy but was too great a man to succeed.[1] This comes very near the truth, but what really happened was something rather more subtle and difficult to describe. Shakespeare took the comic Jew for a theme, and wrote a true comedy. But it was a comedy after his own pattern and desire —a comedy in which ridicule does not exclude compassion, in which sympathy and detachment are reconciled in the irony which is necessarily achieved by the comic spirit in a serene presentation of things as they are.

Shylock as a comic character held the stage for over a century. Then came an interval of forty years, from 1701 to 1741, when good taste imposed on English audiences a mangled version of the play by Lord Lansdowne, a nonentity whose trimmings and embellishments may be recommended to the curious as an upstanding monument to the complacency with which an eighteenth-century nobleman was able to view the achievements of a barbarian:

> The first rude sketches Shakespeare's pencil drew
> But all the shining master-strokes are new;
> This play, ye critics, shall your fury stand
> Adorn'd and rescu'd by a faultless hand.

---

[1] Heine wrote: 'Shakespeare intended perhaps, for the amusement of the 'general', to represent a tormented, fabulous creature that thirsts for blood, and of course loses his daughter and his ducats, and is ridiculed into the bargain. But the genius of the poet, the genius of humanity that reigned in him stood ever above his private will and so it happened that in Shylock, in spite of all his uncouth grimacings, the poet vindicates an unfortunate sect, which, for mysterious purposes, has been burdened by Providence with the hate of the rabble both high and low, and has reciprocated this hate—not always by love.

Shylock was still a comic character, for whom Lord Lansdowne was good enough to provide fresh occasions for mockery, notably at a banquet where the Jew drinks to his money-bags. Then, in 1741, came Macklin of whom Pope, not without good reason, indited a famous epitaph:

> Here lies the Jew
> That Shakespeare drew.

There is some evidence that it was Macklin who first suggested to an English audience that Shylock was pathetic. 'The Jew's private calamities', says Davies, who saw Macklin at Drury Lane, 'made some tender impressions on the audience'. But Macklin's Shylock was in the comic tradition and it gave birth to a whole generation of comic Shylocks who devoted their considerable talents to building up the grotesque figure denounced by Hazlitt: a 'decrepit old man, bent with age and ugly with mental deformity, with the venom in his heart congealed in the expression of his countenance, sullen, morose, gloomy, inflexible, brooding over one idea, that of his hatred, and fixed on one unalterable purpose, that of his revenge'.[1]

All these Shylocks were destroyed in a single night by Edmund Kean on January 26th, 1814. Kean converted Hazlitt and for the next hundred years Hazlitt's judgment was never seriously challenged. All the great actors conspired to perpetuate and adorn the new reading. The nobility of Macready's Shylock was in due course exceeded by the priestly dignity of Henry Irving (1879) and the aristocratic good form of Forbes Robertson.[2] The actor's triumph over the author was by the end of the nineteenth century complete.

Shakespeare has finished with Shylock when he stumbles from the court:

> I am not well. Send the deed after me
> And I will sign it.

---

[1] See Harold Child's note on the *Stage History of the Play*; New Cambridge Edition.

[2] Within living memory there have nevertheless been notable attempts to restore Shakespeare's comic character to the stage. Sir William Poel, in 1898, conveyed to a modern audience some idea how Shylock comported himself in the Elizabethan theatre, and Mr. Michael Sherbrooke in 1914 bravely insisted that Shylock, even at his most terrible, was essentially ludicrous.

P

The law which he invoked pursues him to the last, and the bond in which Antonio signed away his life is replaced by the deed in which the Jew must sign away his property. Shakespeare, who has used all his art to put Shylock credibly before our eyes in flesh and blood, now takes us back to the pleasant estate of Belmont which, with a skill that will claim your admiration if you look into it at all closely, he has kept so carefully secluded from the harsh realities of the ghetto and the market-place. We hear the music to which the ears of Shylock's house were closed. Music in Shylock's Venice is a vile squeaking of the wry-necked fife or a bag-pipe that sings i' th' nose. Music at Belmont now enters with moonlight to take entire possession:

> LORENZO: How sweet the moonlight sleeps upon this bank!
> Here will we sit, and let the sounds of music
> Creep in our ears—soft stillness and the night
> Become the touches of sweet harmony.
> Sit, Jessica. Look how the floor of heaven
> Is thick inlaid with patines of bright gold,
> There's not the smallest orb which thou behold'st
> But in his motion like an angel sings,
> Still quiring to the young-eyed cherubims;
> Such harmony is in immortal souls!
> But whilst this muddy vesture of decay
> Doth grossly close it in, we cannot hear it.
>
> The man that hath no music in himself,
> Nor is not moved with concord of sweet sounds,
> Is fit for treasons, stratagems, and spoils,
> The motions of his spirit are dull as night,
> And his affections dark as Erebus:
> Let no such man be trusted.

The little candle in Portia's hall throws its beams; so shines a good deed in a naughty world. We are back in the age of innocence when tales are told indoors by candlelight, and beyond the window, Peace ho, the moon sleeps with Endymion! Here we can believe again in the lucky caskets and are caught up in a pretty confusion of rings and posies. Antonio's ships can now come home and the story of Shylock lingers in the memory as an old, unhappy tale.

But it was a tale in which we believed—and to such good purpose that for generations its rights and wrongs, its arguments and incidents and the persons who figured in it, have been seriously debated as matters pertaining to the 'eternal of our nature'.

IV

BOTTOM

A Midsummer Night's Dream

If he come not, then the play is marred. It is Bully Bottom who, by reason of his special quality, holds firmly together the gossamer structure of that most aery fabric of a vision which is Shakespeare's 'A Midsummer Night's Dream'. It is not a quality to be easily defined. The French have a word for it. Bottom is *débrouillard*—equal to all occasions and at home wherever he may be. Nothing can disconcert or put him down or prevent him from being entirely and happily himself. He wears an ass's head as imperturbably as he bestows advice upon his rustic companions or corrects Duke Theseus for suggesting that Wall should speak out of his cue. He has been rated for conceit and pushing himself forward overmuch. But that is unjust. He engrosses the play not because he is obtrusive, but because he is ingenuously eager to meet all occasions and to throw himself into any part in life that offers. Nor does his love of life exceed his ability to cope with it. He does not unduly press either himself or his suggestions on the company but yields with good grace to the common voice.

He is, in fact, just the man for Shakespeare's purpose. There has to be someone who can be equally at home in each of the three compartments of this trinity of fantastic worlds—classical antiquity, rural Britain and the kingdom of the fairies. Duke Theseus brings home to Athens a mythological bride won with his sword, exercises patriarchal authority over men and maidens, and hunts with hounds bred out of the Spartan kind. Hippolyta, the bride aforesaid, consorted in her maiden days with Hercules and Cadmus. We are here immersed in the legends of ancient Greece—except that round the corner is a convent in which disobedient daughters may be consigned to wither on the virgin thorn. From legendary Athens we are suddenly transported to a village obviously in the heart of Tudor England, where a carpenter, a weaver, a bellows-maker, a tinker, a tailor and a joiner are met together to devise a pastime for the local squire. Finally we pass, without warning given, to a world to whose inhabitants the cowslips are tall and where elves creep into acorn-cups to hide themselves in fear from the chiding of Oberon and Titania.

How does Shakespeare contrive to pass so easily from one of these three compartments of his play to another without disturbing our sense of their mutually destructive realities? Duke Theseus is more than life size; the fairies are minute. In between, like Gulliver alterna-tively with the Brobdingnagians and the Lilliputians, is the company of Peter Quince. Each group has its own standards of size, quality, sentiment and behaviour. Yet we easily believe in all three at once. Each part confirms the illusion of the whole.

To effect this miracle Shakespeare needs a magician who is none other than Bully Bottom. For Bottom impersonates the quality which puts the poet at the centre of his creation. To Bottom, as to Shakespeare, all these beings, fairy, heroic or human, are equally congenial. Bottom has a welcome ready for all that may betide. He takes everything in his stride of simple, indomitable assurance. His readiness to play the tyrant, the lover, the lady or the lion in the most lamentable comedy and most cruel death of Pyramus and Thisbe enables him, in a wood near Athens, to hold his court as to the manner born among the 'little people', accepting without question the cosseting of Titania and ingenuously confessing to a great desire for a bottle of hay.

In no other play is Shakespeare's skill in weaving one harmonious design of several strands more notable. The three themes are con-trasted, but there is an underlying unity between them. We pass from key to key, but the keys are related and the modulations from one to another contrived with a disarming simplicity. Unity of mood and texture is established by a certain quality of innocence that runs through all. The Athens of Duke Theseus, where fathers are as gods to their children, where Hippolyta's moon is like to a silver bow new-bent in heaven, where the court rises early to observe the rite of May, takes us back to that golden world to which poets of the Renaissance so often reverted. To this primitive world belong

Hermia and Lysander who fly to the wood; Helena who 'tells on' her friend, the rival gallants who breathe love, contempt, fire and slaughter as occasion prompts, and the little, fierce maid who was a vixen when she went to school:

> Your hands than mine are quicker for a fray,
> My legs are longer though to run away.

These be nursery humours, as Corporal Nym would say. The tale of Theseus and his bouncing Amazon, of the moonstruck gallants in the wood and Titania's theft of the little changeling boy—all is silly sooth

> And dallies with the innocence of love
> Like the old age.

From a ball in the palace of Duke Theseus to a room in the cottage of Peter Quince is accordingly no such distance as it seems. For here, too, is a simplicity of the same pristine quality and it is easy going from one to the other.

To pass thence into the kingdom of Oberon is a more hazardous journey. But the mood is still pure innocence. These fairies are the simplest of creatures. They are of a world which has not yet grown up. Robin Goodfellow's idea of a jest is of the same order as Bottom's delight in roaring like a lion:

> And sometimes lurk I in a gossip's bowl,
> In very likeness of a roasted crab,
> And, when she drinks, against her lips I bob,
> And on her withered dewlap pour the ale.
> The wisest aunt, telling the saddest tale,
> Sometime for three-foot stool mistaketh me:
> Then slip I from her bum, down topples she,
> And 'tailor' cries, and falls into a cough.

Oberon and Titania make much of their jealousy, but it is jealousy for a plaything. The fairies steal honey-bags and pluck the wings from painted butterflies. Oberon slips from fairyland to play on pipes of corn or listen to the song of a mermaid. Titania is sung to sleep with a lullaby while a sentinel stands on guard to drive away spotted snakes, thorny hedgehogs, newts, spiders, blackbeetles, worms and snails. These fairies provoke the critic to excel himself in dainty epithets such as trim, pretty, elegant, graceful, comely. Their hardest labour is picking apricots and dewberries; their sport is killing a red-hipped humble-bee on the top of a thistle; their pleasure is dancing ringlets to the whistling wind or singing a roundelay by firelight through a silent house when everyone else is in bed. It is the golden age of Theseus in miniature and the commentator, grown solemn, is moved to observe that in these little lives there are no attributes of the properly natural and moral soul, nothing of reason or conscience in their felicity.

Observe how the composer of this little symphony moves from key to key.

Note for example how he prepares us in the Duke's palace to accept the amative caprices of a wood near Athens. Lysander wooing Hermia with knacks and nosegays, with trifles and gauds, has 'stolen the impression of her fantasy'. Love, which is to spring alive or vanish at the touch of a magic herb, is already half childish and three parts fanciful:

> Love looks not with the eyes, but with the mind:
> And therefore is winged Cupid painted blind.
> Nor hath Love's mind of any judgment taste:
> Wings and no eyes figure unheedy haste.
> And therefore is Love said to be a child:
> Because in choice he is so oft beguiled.

Demetrius is 'this spotted and inconstant man' before ever he falls a victim to Puck's mischief. It needs no fairy come from the grove to tell us that young lovers can be fickle and young love itself

> Momentany as a sound,
> Swift as a shadow: short as any dream;
> Brief as the lightning in the collied night,
> That, in a spleen, unfolds both heaven and earth;
> And ere a man hath power to say 'Behold!'
> The jaws of darkness do devour it up:
> So quick bright things come to confusion.

Shakespeare is singing us into the mood in which we shall accept without question the magic of Oberon and his little western flower, whose liquor—

> on sleeping eyelids laid,
> Will make or man or woman madly dote
> Upon the next live creature that it sees—

and, having sung us into the mood where Titania rounds the hairy temples of an ass with a coronet of fresh and fragrant flowers and where four human lovers are bewitched into preposterous confusions and rivalries, he sings us out again in the measured accents of Theseus:

> Lovers and madmen have such seething brains,
> Such shaping fantasies, that apprehend
> More than cool reason ever comprehends.
> The lunatic, the lover, and the poet
> Are of imagination all compact.
> One sees more devils than vast hell can hold;
> That is, the madman. The lover, all as frantic,
> Sees Helen's beauty in a brow of Egypt.
> The poet's eye, in a fine frenzy rolling,
> Doth glance from heaven to earth, from earth to heaven;
> And as imagination bodies forth
> The forms of things unknown, the poet's pen
> Turns them to shapes, and gives to airy nothing
> A local habitation and a name.

More subtle is his modulation from the dream in 'A Wood near Athens' to the illusion of broad Athenian daylight. Oberon disenchants the eyes of Titania, and Puck takes from Bottom the ass's head. Elves tread a measure till Puck hears the morning lark, and Oberon remembers Theseus. The fairies vanish to follow after the shades of night and their voices fade into a music of horns heard distantly. The Duke with his foresters comes 'in the vaward of the day' to speak of hounds with 'ears that sweep away the morning dew'. The horns which first announced the new key now establish it firmly, being blown again of set purpose to awaken the sleeping lovers, and the modulation is complete.

But Bottom still lies sleeping in the sun—no longer an ass or a queen's consort in fairyland but Nick Bottom, the weaver, who must find his way back to the city. Still half-asleep, he calls aloud for his friends and fellow-players in the interrupted rehearsal. His mind is still full of his marvellous adventure and he dwells in wonder upon his 'translation', but his thoughts turn instinctively to his companions of middle earth. And what a story he has to tell! *Spread yourselves, masters*. Again the new key is established. Bottom is himself again:

BOTTOM (*awaking*): When my cue comes, call me, and I will answer. My next is, 'Most fair Pyramus'. Heigh-ho . . . Peter Quince! Flute, the bellows-mender! Snout, the tinker! Starveling! God's my life! stol'n hence, and left me asleep! I have had a most rare vision. I have had a dream—past the wit of man to say what dream it was. Man is but an ass, if he go about to expound this dream. Methought I was—there is no man can tell what. Methought I was, and methought I had . . . but man is but a patched fool, if he will offer to say what methought I had. The eye of man hath not heard, the ear of man hath not seen, man's hand is not able to taste, his tongue to conceive, nor his heart to report, what my dream was. I will get Peter Quince to write a ballad of this dream: It shall be called Bottom's Dream; because it hath no bottom.

Just as in music the return to an old key has on the ear an effect of difference, so these lovers awakened by the horns of Theseus, and Bottom emerging from his dream, bring back with them a sense of all that has gone before to colour this repetition of themselves.

DEMETRIUS: These things seem small and undistinguishable,
               Like far-off mountains turnèd into clouds.
HERMIA: Methinks I see these things with parted eye,
               When everything seems double.
HELENA: So methinks:
               And I have found Demetrius like a jewel,
               Mine own, and not mine own.
DEMETRIUS: Are you sure
          That we are awake? It seems to me
          That yet we sleep, we dream. Do not you think
          The duke was here, and bid us follow him?
HERMIA: Yea, and my father.

Bottom, though glad enough to be back with his friends, is full to the brim with wonders, drenched in the fragrance and magic of an experience which he is bursting to share with all and sundry, but which, he knows, can never be imparted:

BOTTOM: Where are these lads? where are these hearts?
QUINCE: Bottom! O most courageous day! O most happy hour!
BOTTOM: Masters, I am to discourse wonders: but ask me not what; for if I tell you, I am not true Athenian. I will tell you every thing, right as it fell out.
QUINCE: Let us hear, sweet Bottom.
BOTTOM: Not a word of me. All that I will tell you is, that the duke hath dined.

Let us now come closer to this most lovely, gentlemanlike man and consider in some detail his part in the comedy.

We meet him first at the house of Peter Quince and, be it noted at once, Peter Quince is master of the company. It is Quince who has chosen the play, called the players together and assigned them their parts. Bottom accepts his authority and never questions his decisions. For Bottom, though prolific in advice, fancying himself in all parts, is neither envious nor pushful, but just immensely eager to get things done. Quince is obviously no leader of men. He needs counsel and support:

First, good Peter Quince, say what the play treats on: then read the names of the actors: and so grow to a point. ... Now, good Peter Quince, call forth your actors by the scroll. ... Masters, spread your-selves.

And so grow to a point. But Bottom, nudging forward his less ardent companions, is betrayed into holding up the proceedings by the very qualities which make him so helpful and necessary—sheer enthusiasm, good-fellowship, an unfailing readiness to meet all occasions and to identify himself with all sorts and conditions of men. He is set down for Pyramus, a lover that kills himself, most gallant, for love. Bottom sees himself at once in the part. It will ask some tears in the true per-forming of it and let the audience look to their eyes. He will move storms. He will condole in some measure. But his chief humour is for a tyrant. He could play Ercles rarely or a part to tear a cat in, to make all split. Note, however, that in full flight after his crowding fancies Bottom pulls himself up, not once but repeatedly. 'To the rest', he interjects, motioning Quince to proceed. 'Now name the rest of the players', he urges a moment later. But presently he is off again. He would play Thisbe, too, and speak in a monstrous little voice. Quince checks him in mid career. Bottom must play Pyramus, and Flute Thisbe. 'Proceed', says Bottom. But the lion is too much for his self-control. Lover, lady or lion—he sees himself equally well in all three. Quince begins to be put out by all this enthusiasm. He tactfully objects that Bottom is likely to play the lion only too well:

BOTTOM: Let me play the lion too. I will roar, that I will do any man's heart good to hear me. I will roar, that I will make the duke say, 'Let him roar again: let him roar again.'

QUINCE: An you should do it too terribly, you would fright the duchess and the ladies, that they would shriek: and that were enough to hang us all.

ALL: That would hang us, every mother's son.

BOTTOM: I grant you, friends, if that you should fright the ladies out of their wits, they would have no more discretion but to hang us: but I will aggravate my voice so, that I will roar you as gently as any sucking dove: I will roar you an 'twere any nightingale.

QUINCE: You can play no part but Pyramus: for Pyramus is a sweet-faced man; a proper man as one shall see in a summer's day; a most lovely, gentlemanlike man: therefore you must needs play Pyramus.

BOTTOM: Well . . . I will undertake it.

Bottom's imagination, now focused upon Pyramus, prompts him to raise the question of make-up—a matter of passionate interest to all who engage in amateur theatricals:

BOTTOM: What beard were I best to play it in?

QUINCE: Why, what you will.

BOTTOM: I will discharge it in either your straw-colour beard, your orange-tawny beard, your purple-in-grain beard, or your French-crown-colour beard, your perfect yellow.

Dr. Johnson, who is very severe on Bottom, regards this passage as a deliberate satire upon the 'prejudices and competition' of players. 'Bottom, who seems bred in a tiring-room, is for engrossing every part and would exclude his inferiors from all possibility of distinction. . . . Here, again, he discovers a true genius for the stage by his solicitude for propriety of dress and his deliberation which beard to choose among many beards, all natural.' But where is the evidence that Bottom would exclude his inferiors? And is he for engrossing every part? He certainly enjoys *the idea of himself* in any part that life or the stage may offer, but that is not at all the same thing. Shakespeare has much more in hand than a satire upon the prejudices and competition of players. He is establishing a character who is shortly to play such a part as has not yet entered into the tongue of man to conceive nor his heart to report. Bottom's interest in beards is shared by any villager who undertakes to figure in a local pageant and it is expressed in terms such as would be used quite naturally by a weaver with a professional interest in the dyes of his craft.

Peter Quince's theatrical company arrange to meet at the Duke's oak in Palace Wood. It is a marvellous convenient place for a rehearsal—this green plot shall be our stage, this hawthorn-brake our tiring-house. Here the conversation turns upon the nature of dramatic illusion, which, if Hazlitt is to be trusted, Bottom 'seems to have understood at least as well as any modern essayist'. Hazlitt, by the way, finding subtle differences between the parties to this conversation, enlarges here on what he describes as the *accidental* felicities of Shakespeare. 'It is too much to suppose all this intentional', he writes, 'but it very luckily falls out so. Nature includes all that is implied in the most subtle analytical distinctions'—an observation which is not only relevant to this present analysis of imponderables but might with propriety be inscribed upon the fly-leaf of any critical study which sets out to find reason and method in achievements attained by the more simple process of intuition.

Bottom, immersed in the most lamentable comedy of Pyramus and Thisbe, fears that his audience may mistake this mimic world for reality. He must draw a sword to kill himself, which the ladies cannot abide. He has given much thought to the matter and, being Bottom, he has a simple device to make all well:

Write me a prologue, and let the prologue seem to say—we will do no harm with our swords, and that Pyramus is not killed indeed: and, for the more better assurance, tell them that I, Pyramus, am no Pyramus, but Bottom the weaver: this will put them out of fear.

Then, too, there is still that difficulty about the lion:

BOTTOM: Masters, you ought to consider with yourselves—to bring in (God shield us!) a lion among ladies, is a most dreadful thing. For there is not a more fearful wild-fowl than your lion living; and we ought to look to 't.

SNOUT: Therefore, another prologue must tell he is not a lion.

BOTTOM: Nay: you must name his name, and half his face must be seen through the lion's neck, and he himself must speak through, saying thus, or to the same defect: 'Ladies,' or 'Fair ladies—I would wish you', or, 'I would request you', or, 'I would entreat you, not to fear, not to tremble: my life for yours. If you think I come hither as a lion, it were pity of my life. No: I am no such thing: I am a man as other men are' . . . and there indeed let him name his name, and tell them plainly he is Snug the joiner.

Finally, there is the question of how to bring moonlight into the chamber. Snout is all for plain realism. Doth the moon shine that night? Bottom, quick on the scent of any promising idea, calls for a calendar. Find out moonshine, find out moonshine! The calendar is propitious and Bottom, eagerly helpful, observes that the moon may shine in at the great casement. But Quince is no realist. Nature is all very well, but the theatre has its own properties and devices. Let someone enter with a bush of thorns and a lanthorn to present the person of Moonshine. Bottom, as quick to adopt the symbolical as the naturalistic view, not only accepts this suggestion but applies it to the solution of the problem how to bring a wall into the great chamber:

Some man or other must present wall: and let him have some plaster, or some loam, or some rough-cast about him, to signify wall; and let him hold his fingers thus . . . and through that cranny shall Pyramus and Thisbe whisper.

So ends the simple colloquy on that suspension of disbelief which philosophers have stated to be necessary to the creation of dramatic

illusion. There is perhaps something to be said for Hazlitt's contention that Bottom understood the matter as well as any man before or
since.

And so, having discoursed upon the problem of reality in art and
nature, Bottom retires into the hawthorn-brake. There he awaits a
cue for Pyramus and returns to 'the green plot which is our stage'
transformed into an ass. His companions, who have just considered
with themselves how dreadful a thing it is to bring in a lion among
ladies, are now confronted with a yet more fearful illusion and there
is here no actor with half his face seen through the ass's neck to
assure them that he is but a man as other men are. They flee, one and
all, from this fearful wild-fowl and Bottom is left 'translated' to face
his great adventure alone:

I see their knavery. This is to make an ass of me, to fright me if they
could: but I will not stir from this place, do what they can. I will walk
up and down here, and will sing that they shall hear I am not afraid.

The song which awakens the Queen of the Fairies is not unworthy:

> The ousel cock, so black of hue,
> With orange-tawny bill,
> The throstle with his note so true,
> The wren with little quill.

Bottom is neither to be flustered nor flattered. He has an unerring
sense of the fitness of things which never deserts him—a quality
which no self-centred, conceited person—as he is so unfairly charged
with being—could possibly have exhibited in such a situation. Here
is a fairy queen protesting that she loves him, voice, shape, virtue,
intelligence and all. It is a little staggering, disconcerting alike to his
modesty and good sense; but Bottom does not lose his presence of
mind:

BOTTOM: Methinks, mistress, you should have little reason for that.
And yet, to say the truth, reason and love keep little company together
now-a-days. The more the pity, that some honest neighbours will not
make them friends. Nay, I can gleek upon occasion.

TITANIA: Thou art as wise as thou art beautiful.

BOTTOM: Not so, neither: but if I had wit enough to get out of this
wood, I have enough to serve my own turn.

Titania declares that he shall stay with her whether he will or not. She is a spirit of no common rate and promises him fairies to do his pleasure. Bottom is silent but his silence is gracious. Who would interrupt such fairy talk as falls from the lips of Titania?

> Be kind and courteous to this gentleman,
> Hop in his walks and gambol in his eyes,
> Feed him with apricocks and dewberries,
> With purple grapes, green figs, and mulberries.
> The honey-bags steal from the humble-bees,
> And for night-tapers crop their waxen thighs,
> And light them at the fiery glow-worm's eyes,
> To have my love to bed and to arise,
> And pluck the wings from painted butterflies,
> To fan the moonbeams from his sleeping eyes.
> Nod to him, elves, and do him courtesies.

But these fairies who come to wait upon him must be answered. Bully Bottom, who, like his author, takes all things in nature as they come, is put upon his mettle. And how featly he rises to the occasion, with nothing but his native good-fellowship and genial acceptance of things as they are to carry him through. For each of them he has an appropriate word. He holds his court with an exquisite, royal courtesy that stoops, without pride, to claim equality with his lieges:

PEASEBLOSSOM: Hail, mortal!

COBWEB: Hail!

MOTH: Hail!

MUSTARDSEED: Hail!

BOTTOM: I cry your worships mercy, heartily; I beseech your worship's name.

COBWEB: Cobweb.

BOTTOM: I shall desire you of more acquaintance, good Master Cobweb: if I cut my finger, I shall make bold with you. Your name, honest gentleman?

PEASEBLOSSOM: Peaseblossom.

BOTTOM: I pray you, commend me to Mistress Squash, your mother, and to Master Peascod, your father. Good Master Peaseblossom, I shall desire you of more acquaintance too. Your name, I beseech you, sir?

MUSTARDSEED: Mustardseed.

BOTTOM: Good Master Mustardseed, I know your patience well. That same cowardly, giant-like, Oxbeef hath devoured many a gentleman of your house. I promise you, your kindred hath made my eyes water ere now. I desire you of more acquaintance, good Master Mustardseed.

Bottom, when next we meet him, has grown familiar with his state, but he has not therefore lost his grip upon reality. He is willy-nilly King Consort in fairyland, but nevertheless an ass, a tender ass, very hairy about the face and in need of scratching. And being an ass, he appreciates the good things of an ass's life. Good hay, sweet hay, hath no fellow. He is also, through it all, Nick Bottom, the weaver, with a reasonable ear for music, expressed in a preference for the tongs and bones, and, in the matter of provender, a handful of dried peas. This is Bottom in all his glory. Let him blaze in extenso:

BOTTOM: Where's Peaseblossom?

PEASEBLOSSOM: Ready.

BOTTOM: Scratch my head, Peaseblossom. Where's Monsieur Cobweb?

COBWEB: Ready.

BOTTOM: Monsieur Cobweb, good monsieur, get you your weapons in your hand, and kill me a red-hipped humble-bee on the top of a thistle; and, good monsieur, bring me the honey-bag. Do not fret yourself too much in the action, monsieur; and, good monsieur, have a care the honey-bag break not—I would be loath to have you overflown with a honey-bag, signior. Where's Monsieur Mustardseed?

MUSTARDSEED: Ready.

BOTTOM: Give me your neaf, Monsieur Mustardseed. Pray you, leave your curtsy, good monsieur.

MUSTARDSEED: What's your will?

BOTTOM: Nothing, good monsieur, but to help Cavalery Cobweb to scratch. I must to the barber's, monsieur, for methinks I am marvellous hairy about the face—and I am such a tender ass, if my hair do but tickle me, I must scratch.

TITANIA: What, wilt thou hear some music, my sweet love?

BOTTOM: I have a reasonable good ear in music. Let's have the tongs and the bones.

TITANIA: Or, say, sweet love, what thou desir'st to eat.

BOTTOM: Truly, a peck of provender. I could munch your good dry
oats. Methinks I have a great desire to a bottle of hay. Good hay, sweet
hay, hath no fellow.

TITANIA: I have a venturous fairy, that shall seek
          The squirrel's hoard, and fetch thee thence new nuts.

BOTTOM: I had rather have a handful or two of dried pease. But, I pray
you . . . let none of your people stir me. I have an exposition of sleep
come upon me.

TITANIA: Sleep thou, and I will wind thee in my arms.
          Fairies, be gone, and be all ways away.

Bottom, playing before Theseus, is the victim of a bad tradition.
Professional actors in presenting the lamentable comedy of Pyramus
and Thisbe, conscientiously underline every point of the farce,
embroider every absurdity and miss no opportunity for comic
business. Burlesque is only tolerable in so far as it exposes intelligently
the emptiness of a received convention, and it is effective only if
played with solemnity. Its exponents must never seem to be aware
of their absurdity:

PYRAMUS: Approach, ye Furies fell!
              O Fates, come, come,
              Cut thread and thrum,
          Quail, crush, conclude and quell!

Shakespeare abundantly supplies the nonsense. Pyramus has nothing
to do but speak with good accent and good discretion. There must
never be any doubt of the sincerity of his *passion* (Theseus' own
word). Does not Hippolyta herself declare: 'Beshrew my heart, but
I pity the man'? Bottom's famous protest to the Duke is no mere
impertinence but the forthright gesture of an artist anxious to be
well understood. Theseus, with his interruption, is spoiling the
game. He must be called to order and put right:

PYRAMUS: O wicked wall, through whom I see no bliss,
          Cursed be thy stones for thus deceiving me!
THESEUS: The wall, methinks, being sensible, should curse again.
PYRAMUS: No, in truth, sir, he should not. 'Deceiving me' is Thisby's cue:
          she is to enter now, and I am to spy her through the wall. You
          shall see, it will fall pat as I told you. . . . Yonder she comes.

This is not self-centred insolence but the disinterested enthusiasm of an interpreter. Bottom's 'She is to enter now, and I am to spy her through the wall. You shall see, it will fall pat as I told you', recalls Hamlet's more famous interpolation: 'He poisons him i' the garden for's estate; the story is extant and writ in very choice Italian. You shall see anon how the murderer gets the love of Gonzago's wife'.

It may be argued, if satire be intended in this scene, the laugh is at the expense, not of Bottom enacting the woes of Pyramus, but of the lords and ladies who condescend to find it amusing. Theseus is kindly magnanimous:

> For never anything can be amiss,
> When simpleness and duty tender it.

> Our sport shall be to take what they mistake:
> And what poor duty cannot do, noble respect
> Takes it in might, not merit.

But condescension, however amiable, is still condescension, and some will prefer the royal good-fellowship of Bottom's 'Give me your neaf, Monsieur Mustardseed', or his friendly concern that Monsieur Cobweb shall not be overflown with a honey-bag. Incidentally, the Duke's commendation of 'tongue-tied simplicity' when he is about to encounter Bottom, who was never at a loss for the right word in a situation which would certainly have reduced his heroic Grace to a state of complete incoherence, is another of those accidental felicities of which (to repeat Hazlitt) it is too much to suppose that they are intentional but which very luckily fall out so. The Duke's comments on the play as delivered fall noticeably short of Bottom's observations on the play in preparation. These gentle auditors cannot hold a candle to Bottom for courtesy or apprehension and their treatment of Moonshine is downright impertinent. Demetrius interrupts him with the stale inevitable jest about the horns he should be wearing. Theseus pointlessly objects that the man in the moon should be inside and not outside the lantern and, when they have put the poor fellow out of his part, Demetrius with a clumsy deference caps his Grace's witticism—not only the man but his thornbush and his dog should also be in the lantern.

The laugh, then, is not all on one side where it is commonly assumed to lie. Who is Demetrius to deride the antics of Pyramus, a lover in moonshine? Was he not himself but a few hours since cutting a pretty poor figure in a wood near Athens, actor in the 'fond pageant' which Puck found so delectable. Lord! what fools these mortals be! But Demetrius must be excused where generations of English actors have so sadly mistaken Pyramus and his peers. Nothing is stranger or less creditable to the English theatre than the stage history of 'A Midsummer Night's Dream'. Shakespeare was barely cold in his grave when, to set on some quantity of barren spectators to laugh, Bottom and his company had sunk to the level of the grimacing officious clowns with whom we are only too familiar. The balance of the play had been so completely destroyed that it was alluded to in 1621 by a puritan censor of public morals as 'The Comedy of Pyramus and Thisbe' and in 1661 'The Merry Conceited Humours of Bottom the Weaver' were actually published as a separate piece, which was doubtless received by the wits of Whitehall in much the same spirit as by Demetrius in Athens. The seventeenth-century producers and critics simply did not know what to make of the comedy as a whole. Pepys in 1662 spoke for his generation: 'To the King's Theatre, where we saw Midsummer Night's Dream which I had never seen before, nor shall ever again, for it is the most insipid, ridiculous play that ever I saw in my life.' Pepys found nothing to the purpose except 'some good dancing and some handsome women, which was all my pleasure'. Thirty years later Betterton was producing an operatic adaptation which concluded with a chorus of Chinamen and a dance of six monkeys. The eighteenth-century stage was held for over forty years by an operatic enormity perpetrated by Richard Leveridge. Shakespeare's play became 'The Comick Masque of Pyramus and Thisbe' which, after spawning various successors, made way for the yet more complicated perversions of Garrick and Colman. Kemble at the beginning of the nineteenth century still regarded the play as a libretto for music and spectacle, much being made of a pageant showing the victories of

Theseus. This was the production that provoked a celebrated outburst from Hazlitt: 'All that is finest in the play, was lost in the representation. The spirit was evaporated, the genius was fled; but the spectacle was fine: it was that which saved the play. Oh, ye scene-shifters, ye scene-painters, ye machinists and dressmakers, ye manufacturers of moon and stars that give no light, ye musical composers, ye men in the orchestra, fiddlers and trumpeters and players on the double drum and loud bassoon, rejoice! This is your triumph; it is not ours: and ye full-grown, well-fed, substantial, real fairies . . . we shall remember you: we shall believe no more in the existence of your fantastic tribe.'[1]

The egregious Bunn was a fit person to bring this strange, eventful history to an ignominious conclusion with a compilation presented at Drury Lane in 1883 which outraged even the blunted sensibilities of the fashionable patrons of that august establishment. The tide was on the turn and in 1840 Charles Mathews and Madame Vestris brought back Shakespeare, or a piece of him, to the stage at Covent Garden.

But Bottom had suffered too severely from his many translations easily to recover his comic identity. Phelps produced the play at Sadler's Wells in 1853 and Bottom is reported to have been one of his best parts. The critics, however, give us no idea how he played it. They are more interested in recording that in this production gas was used for the first time in any theatre, that an effect of mist was conveyed by a seamless blue net expressly ordered from Glasgow and that the effect of movement was given by a diorama. One Shakespearean actor, the ever-to-be-lamented George Weir, has within living memory presented Bottom on the stage in a way that should have annihilated once for all the clodpole tradition of the professionally funny man which is the English theatre's legacy from three centuries of successful clowning. But Weir never found a successor even among the sons of Ben.

The stiff-necked generations which mistranslated Bottom saw so

[1] Hazlitt admired Liston in the part of Bottom, but tells us nothing about it, and it is most unlikely that this capable actor did more than present the character a little less clumsily than his predecessors.

little coherence or unity in the play that they used it for two hundred years as a quarry for fairy pantomime, burlesque, operatic miscellanies, masques and ballets. Bottom is so much the projection of Shakespeare's own imagination into this mimic world that, if we fail to identify ourselves with his immortal weaver, the comedy falls to pieces. No-one but he can sustain the triple illusion. He takes us along with him by virtue of the very quality which made it possible for Shakespeare himself to creep into the small soul of a fairy as easily as into the noble heart that cracked in the passing of Hamlet—a genius for accommodation with all things within the limits of his imaginable world. From first to last this is Bottom's dream and, if he come not, the play is marred.

But if he come in the habit with which Shakespeare invested him, the play creates for us a world in which we walk as securely as in a walled garden and, when the dream is ended, with Moonshine and Lion left to bury the dead, we may call back Hippolyta to speak the final word:

> But all the story of the night told over,
> And all their minds transfigured so together,
> More witnesseth than fancy's images,
> And grows to something of great constancy—
> But, howsoever, strange and admirable.

BEATRICE AND BENEDICK

Much Ado About Nothing

THERE is much ado in this comedy about innocent Hero slandered by her lover Claudio, led to believe by a villain, with no motive for his villainy, that she comes as no maid to her marriage. And all this, the author warns us in his title, is nothing; we are not to take seriously to heart any of that dreadful business at the altar steps but to regard the splenetic Don John as no more than a black bogey in a merry tale.

It is a Renaissance piece. A lady is wooed by proxy and married behind a veil. A diabolical lord contrives a plot which casts a shadow in sunlight. There are misunderstandings, obviously to be cleared up before the curtain falls. Beauty is shown in distress, virtue under a cloud and chivalry provoked. All this was extant and writ in choice Italian—the Italian of Matteo Bandello.

Bandello's story is just one of those agreeably silly tales from which in due course the lustier novelettes of yesterday were subsequently to be evolved. Claudio loves Hero. Don John, because he is superseded by Claudio in the good graces of his Prince, but more because he is temperamentally a bad man who hates to see other people happy, undertakes to prove her wanton. He succeeds in his design and Claudio denounces his bride in the church. Hero swoons and on the advice of a holy friar is reported dead. But the plot, as required by the laws of melodrama, is discovered by the funny man of the piece and Claudio finds his dead love surprisingly restored.

To recall these familiar incidents seems hardly necessary. But most people in thinking about 'Much Ado About Nothing' are apt to forget about Hero and Claudio. They remember it as a comedy about Beatrice and Benedick, as indeed it immediately became for the first audiences who saw it on the stage. Lord Treasurer Stanhope, paying John Heminge on May 20th, 1613, for a production of the play, actually refers to it as 'Benedicte and Betteris' and in a second folio preserved at Windsor Castle you may see to this day, in the handwriting of King Charles I, to whom it belonged, 'Benedick and Beatrice' entered on the page as a second title.

This goes to show how very destructive two live characters can be, let loose in a plot which depends for its verisimilitude on a different kind of illusion. Benedick and Beatrice run away with 'Much Ado About Nothing' as Mercutio would certainly have run away with 'Romeo and Juliet' if Shakespeare had not killed him off only just in time. Whether Shakespeare meant this to happen is impossible to say, but he certainly knew what he had done when, sitting back to survey his work, he gave it a title which should plainly indicate that his borrowed plot counted for nothing in his achievement.

This borrowed plot has been severely criticised. Let us first consider the objections.

It may be argued that the distresses of Hero accord painfully or not at all with the gaiety of Beatrice and that the sable iniquity of Don John is out of place in a comedy. But this is admittedly a composite piece—Renaissance vertù was 'Q's' description, or as Walkley puts it in 'Playhouse Pleasures', a polychromatic phantasmagoria or inn of strange meetings. The whole thing is eclectic in the extreme, depending for its success on a skilful handling of contrasted styles, moods and effects. It is the least natural of all the comedies. 'Love's Labour's Lost' is straightforward Elizabethan horseplay compared with this sophisticated amalgam of Italianate romance and light comedy. The earlier play is on the surface more mannered; but if the artifice is more apparent, that is only because Shakespeare in 1593 had not yet learned to conceal it. In the later play every word, gesture and sequence is contrived and measured to a hair. Of all Shakespeare's plays it is the one in which his skill as a dramatist may best be studied as distinguished from his genius as a poet and creator of character. Even his own most personal contribution to the comedy, the affair between Beatrice and Benedick, is a deliberate exercise in virtuosity upon a given theme—in this case borrowed from himself. It is one of his favourite themes, that of an attraction between lovers manifested in a professed hostility. Shakespeare in 'Much Ado About Nothing' relies almost entirely on his dramatic and literary craftsmanship, and the success with which he conceals this fact from the critics who receive this comedy as a spontaneous revelation of the careless, sunny side of his nature shows that this man of the theatre, apart from being Shakespeare, was as cunning a playmaker as ever deceived an audience into accepting counters for true pay.

This disposes of the two-fold complaint (1) that Don John has no right to be present in so light-hearted a piece and (2) that, being present, he should have been provided with a more adequate motive. Don John, in this formal pattern, is a dark square in a brilliant patchwork. Shakespeare picks him up as he picks up his witty lady or his holy friar—not as a human character to be presented for his own sake but as a figure that looks well in the tapestry:

> I had rather be a canker in a hedge than a rose in his grace, and it better fits my blood to be disdained of all than to fashion a carriage to rob love from any: in this, though I cannot be said to be a flattering honest man, it must not be denied but I am a plain-dealing villain.

This fantastically wilful obliquity contrasts admirably with the no less fantastical glitter of his environment—Saturn in conjunction with Mercury.

Claudio, who so easily believes Hero to be false, who so brutally exposes her to public ignominy and who for all this is rewarded with good fortune and true love is more of a stumbling-block. But it cannot be said that he is out of character. Shakespeare has carefully fitted him for the ignoble part he is required to play. He is exhibited from the first as ready to distrust himself, his friends and his lady. He agrees that Don Pedro shall woo her by proxy but believes, at a hint from Don John, that Don Pedro is playing false:

> 'Tis certain so—the prince woos for himself.
> Friendship is constant in all other things
> Save in the office and affairs of love:
> Therefore all hearts in love use their own tongues.
> Let every eye negotiate for itself,
> And trust no agent: for beauty is a witch
> Against whose charms faith melteth into blood:

> This is an accident of hourly proof,
> Which I mistrusted not. . . . Farewell, therefore, Hero.

Claudio's 'Farewell, therefore, Hero', prepares us in advance for the mistrustful levity with which he will listen to Don John affirming that Hero is 'disloyal' and that he shall 'see her chamber window entered even the night before her wedding-day'. 'May this be so?' is all he has to say when Don John has concluded his tale.

Claudio in church offends us less by his credulity than by his downright bad manners. Bad manners in a comedy of manners— that is an offence against the play itself. 'In the congregation where I should wed there will I shame her' is an idea that would never have occurred to a gentleman. And this is a comedy with gentility for a theme! There is no play of Shakespeare in which special deportment counts for so much; yet here is Claudio swearing to behave like an oaf. What is worse, Don Pedro accepts the project with alacrity. What was Shakespeare to do? There could never have been such a scene as Hero's wedding if everybody had behaved with ordinary decency. Claudio and Don Pedro are sacrificed to make a Sicilian holiday. Witness the scene in which these two gentlemen, after that business in the church and the reported death of Hero, comment on their encounter with Hero's uncle and father. *We had like to have had our two noses snapped off by two old men without teeth.* Witness their bantering of Benedick when he delivers his challenge. Witness, above all, the scene in which they acknowledge their error:

> CLAUDIO: Choose your revenge yourself,
>   Impose me to what penance your invention
>   Can lay upon my sin—yet sinned I not,
>   But in mistaking.
> DON PEDRO: By my soul nor I,
>   And yet to satisfy this good old man,
>   I would bend under any heavy weight
>   That he'll enjoin me to.

Was ever an apology more ungracious? Even in promising amends they protest that they were never to blame. Shakespeare, though, with a touch here and there, keeps these persons in character, using them callously either to forward his plot or to throw into relief the comedy of Benedick and Beatrice.[1]

Attention has already been directed to the only circumstance which enables us to regard Claudio's behaviour as *theatrically* acceptable. Shakespeare artfully insists that Don John's plot will come to nothing. It is discovered by Dogberry *before* it is put into effect and publication is obviously postponed merely in order that the scene in the church may go forward. The mood in which we watch that scene is coloured by our knowledge that the constable is just round the corner waiting to put things right. The bad men are already under arrest and Leonato, if he had been less in a hurry to get to his daughter's wedding, would have got to the bottom of the mischief before it was sprung. But like Caesar ignoring Artemidorus and brushing aside the soothsayer on his way to the Capitol, Leonato goes blindly to his Ides; the scene in which he might have been warned *immediately* preceding the catastrophe. That, in itself, is an essentially comic situation and it is brought about by a device which has since become traditional in the comedy-melodrama of all ages. Villainy is undone by a simple soul. Dogberry is a trifle of Shakespeare's fancy, created for the double purpose of exposing a plot and confusing its delivery, but he is the ancestor of a comic figure which has held the stage from William Kempe to George Weir.

Shakespeare, it goes without saying, has done something else for Claudio, but no more than what he does for everybody in his comedies:

> CLAUDIO: O my lord,
> When you went onward on this ended action,
> I looked upon her with a soldier's eye,
> That liked, but had a rougher task in hand
> Than to drive liking to the name of love:
> But now I am returned, and that war-thoughts
> Have left their places vacant: in their rooms
> Come thronging soft and delicate desires,

---

[1] Shakespeare's handling of this scene between Claudio, Don Pedro and Benedick, one of the best in the play, if we focus our attention on Benedick, is discussed below, see pp. 131

> All prompting me how fair young Hero is,
> Saying I liked her ere I went to wars.
>
> DON PEDRO: Thou wilt be like a lover presently,
> And tire the hearer with a book of words.
> If thou dost love fair Hero, cherish it,
> And I will break with her, and with her father,
> And thou shalt have her: was't not to this end
> That thou began'st to twist so fine a story?

Claudio, like Bassanio, talks like an angel.

Having added this much more to all this much ado about nothing let us now turn to what is in effect the real business of the play. This is the comedy of Beatrice and Benedick in which Shakespeare used a fashion of the time to present a situation of abiding interest. The merry war between these self-professed misogamists is a courtship in disguise. It was a game which Shakespeare was always ready to play and, being a child of the Euphuists, he played it, if not *con amore*, at least without any great loss of integrity. We have seen what use he made of the wit-combat in 'Love's Labour's Lost'. Rosaline and Berowne prefigure Beatrice and Benedick, but in the later play Shakespeare is no longer concerned with its superficial absurdities, still less with exhibiting his own skill at the game. Wit which can so easily be tiresome is in Beatrice the natural overflow of a happy nature: 'But then there was a star danced, and under that was I born.' Her perpetual skirmishing is natural high spirits expressed, like everything else in the Elizabethan theatre, in a clatter of words— the Shakespearean equivalent of the knockabout contrived to amuse less loquacious generations or of the 'thwackings' which Boileau so severely deprecated in the comedies of Molière. Now high spirits fly at anything. It is hit or miss and, if we do not ourselves share in the rough and tumble for its own sake, we are more likely to find ourselves counting the misses than applauding the hits. Admittedly Beatrice is often pert rather than subtle:

BEATRICE: I wonder that you will still be talking, Signior Benedick— nobody marks you.

BENEDICK: What, my dear Lady Disdain! Are you yet living?

BEATRICE: Is it possible Disdain should die, while she hath such meet food to feed it as Signior Benedick? Courtesy itself must convert to disdain, if you come in her presence.

BEATRICE: I had rather hear my dog bark at a crow than a man swear he loves me.

BENEDICK: God keep your ladyship still in that mind, so some gentleman or other shall 'scape a predestinate scratched face.

BEATRICE: Scratching could not make it worse, an 'twere such a face as yours were.

and something of a hoyden:

DON PEDRO: You have put him down, lady, you have put him down.

BEATRICE: So I would not he should do me, my lord, lest I should prove the mother of fools.

But all this only the more firmly places her as a character—not the fine, brilliant, exquisite and witty lady of tradition but something of a bright young handful and irrepressible romp. Shakespeare continually insists on her merry heart which keeps on the windy side of care. She was 'born to speak all mirth and no matter'; and we have her father's word for it that 'she is never sad but when she sleeps and not even sad then, for . . . she hath often dreamed of unhappiness and waked herself with laughing'. That is why our pleasure in Beatrice survives the fashion of her wit and puts her among the immortal heroines of comedy. It is a pleasure in uninhibited youth and careless simplicity. There is no sophistication either of head or heart in Beatrice. Her emotions are as forthright as her social behaviour. When Don Pedro undertakes to get this chit a husband she 'would rather have one of his father's getting', and when Don Pedro offers to marry her himself she refuses with a 'No, my lord, unless I might have another for working days—your grace is too costly to wear every day'. The chit, as a chit, is irresistible. Whatever she may say, good or bad, awakes in us the pert and nimble spirit of mirth, turns melancholy forth to funerals.

Here are two young people professing an inveterate dislike. They never meet but they jar and each is equally exuberant in misogamy. They are brought artfully together by a conspiracy of matchmakers who convince Benedick and Beatrice in turn that each is dotingly in love with the other. But the plot, though it suggests with a playful indulgence, typically Shakespearean, that love is none the worse for a spice of human vanity, does no more than crown a foregone conclusion. For they are obviously interested in one another from the first—interested to the point of obsession. Their professions of dislike are inverted declarations of love. Don Pedro announces that he will 'undertake one of Hercules' labours, which is to bring Signior Benedick and the Lady Beatrice into a mountain of affection'. But Don Pedro exaggerates. It needed no great contrivance to bring these two together.

Shakespeare's inverted courtships—Berowne and Rosaline, Rosalind and Orlando, Katherine and Petruchio—in which love is expressed in a teasing conflict of wills and wits—are but one of the many delightful consequences of the fact that women were not admitted to the Elizabethan stage. Shakespeare wrote his love scenes for an audience which knew that his heroine was a man or boy dressed up to counterfeit a woman. The modern playwright, in handling a scene of sentiment or passion, has only to put a personable young man in close proximity with a desirable young woman and leave the rest to a few stammered words and disordered gestures. Shakespeare had no such easy way out. For a comedy courtship he must contrive plenty of amusing, familiar and lively conversation. For serious occasions only great poetry could serve his turn. The adolescent passion of Juliet and the immortal longings of Cleopatra had to be conveyed without any assistance from the infectious temperament or physical charms of a leading lady. The flesh and blood required by Shakespeare for his love scenes had to be supplied in prose and verse. To exhibit any form of sexual attraction, whether grave or gay, he must fire the imagination or tickle the fancy of his audience with words. What more exhilarating challenge could there be for a dramatic author whose genius throve on the solution or material difficulties? Confront Shakespeare with a technical problem and he accepts it as an opportunity.

'Much Ado About Nothing', as already suggested, is Shakespeare's nearest approach to the comedy of manners: the wit-combat between its predestinate lovers, besides being a favourite device of the author for establishing a lively familiarity between the parties, commits him to what is, in effect, the stock situation in a type of play which Congreve brought to perfection a century later. Beatrice and Benedick bickering their way into matrimony, are quite obviously assuming for our pleasure a social attitude which we know to be at variance with their true feelings and with the destiny which awaits them at the close.

In the pure comedy of manners as practised by Congreve sentiment or passion is conveyed by means of elegant understatement or downright contradiction:

MRS. MILLAMANT: I won't be called names after I'm married; positively I won't be called names.

MIRABEL: Names!

MRS. MILLAMANT: Ay, as wife, spouse, my dear, joy, jewel, love, sweetheart, and the rest of that nauseous cant in which men and their wives are so fulsomely familiar—I shall never bear that. Good Mirabel, don't let us be familiar or fond, nor kiss before folks, like my lady Fadler and Sir Francis, nor go to Hyde Park together the first Sunday in a new chariot, to provoke eyes and whispers, and then never to be seen there together again; as if we were proud of one another the first week, and ashamed of one another ever after. Let us never visit together nor go to a play together; but let us be very strange and well-bred: let us be as strange as if we had been married a great while; and as well-bred as if we were not married at all.

Millamant and Mirabel affect to have outgrown and overcome the promptings of nature.

The real point of the joke is that man is pretending to be civilised. This is the stock situation of the comedy of manners. The elaborate ritual of society is a mask through which the natural man is comically seen to look. The comedy of Millamant is that she is about to be married as a woman, and that she talks of her marriage merely like a person in society. In the comedy of manners men and women are seen holding reality away, or letting it appear only as an unruffled thing of attitudes. Life is here made up of exquisite demeanour. Its comedy grows from the incongruity of human passion with its cool, dispassionate and studied expression. It ripples forth in ironic contemplation of people born to passion high and low, posing in the social mirror. This is the real justification of the term 'artificial comedy' as applied to the plays of Congreve. We are born naked into nature. In the comedies of Congreve we are born again into civilisation and clothes. We are no longer men; we are wits and a peruke. We are no longer women; we are ladies of the tea-table. Life is absurdly mocked as a series of pretty attitudes and sayings. Hate is absurdly mirrored in agreeably bitter scandal. Perplexity and wonder are seen distorted in the mechanical turns of a swift and complicated plot. Always the fun lies in a sharp contrast between man civilised and the genial primitive creature peeping through. Artificial comedy is our holiday from the sublime and beautiful, from the coarse and the real. It is sublimation of the trivial, turning to fine art the accidents and trappings of life. It is essential to the comedy of manners that it should be well-gowned. It is the height of the comedy of manners that its protagonists should seriously encounter trifles.[1]

The comedies of Congreve and his contemporaries are slips from an Elizabethan forest intensively cultivated in a Whitehall garden. Millamant is a graft from:

BEATRICE: Lord! I could not endure a husband with a beard on his face —I had rather lie in the woollen!
LEONATO: You may light on a husband that hath no beard.
BEATRICE: What should I do with him: dress him in my apparel and make him my waiting-gentlewoman? He that hath a beard is more than a youth; and he that hath no beard is less than a man: and he that is more than a youth is not for me, and he that is less than a man I am not for him.

LEONATO: Well, niece, I hope to see you one day fitted with a husband.
BEATRICE: Not till God make men of some other metal than earth. Would it not grieve a woman to be over-mastered with a piece of valiant dust? To make an account of her life to a clod of wayward marl? No, uncle, I'll none: Adam's sons are my brethren, and truly I hold it a sin to match in my kindred.

MILLAMANT: There is not so impudent a thing in nature as the saucy

[1] From the author's essay on Comedy, pp. 32–34.

look of an assured man, confident of success. The pedantic arrogance of a very husband has not so pragmatical an air. Ah! I'll never marry, unless I'm first made sure of my will and pleasure.

My dear liberty, shall I leave thee? My faithful solitude, my darling contemplation, must I bid you then adieu?

Compare Mirabel on Millamant with Benedick on Beatrice:

MIRABEL: Think of you? To think of a whirlwind, though 'twere in a whirlwind, were a cause of more steady contemplation; a very tranquillity of mind and mansion. A fellow that lives in a windmill has not a more whimsical dwelling than the heart of a man that is lodged in a woman. There is no point of the compass to which they cannot turn and by which they are not turned; and by one as well as another; for motion, not method, is their occupation.

BENEDICK: O, she misused me past the endurance of a block: an oak with but one green leaf on it would have answered her: my very visor began to assume life and scold with her. She told me, not thinking I had been myself, that I was the prince's jester, that I was duller than a great thaw—huddling jest upon jest with such impossible conveyance upon me, that I stood like a man at a mark, with a whole army shooting at me. She speaks poniards, and every word stabs: if her breath were as terrible as her terminations, there were no living near her, she would infect to the north star. I would not marry her, though she were endowed with all that Adam had left him before he transgressed. She would have made Hercules have turned spit, yea, and have cleft his club to make the fire, too. Come, talk not of her. You shall find her the infernal Ate in good apparel—I would to God some scholar would conjure her, for certainly, while she is here, a man may live as quiet in hell as in a sanctuary.

Congreve wrote the undiluted comedy of manners, distilling pure water from the living spring. His characters must sustain to the end their manifest pretences that they have no feeling deeper than an epigram may carry; no aspiration higher than a fine coat may express; no impulse stronger than a smile may cover; no joy more thrilling than a nod may contain; no sorrow deeper than a pretty oath may convey. Shakespeare's comedy, on the other hand, consists in elaborating these pretences in order that they may at the right moment be effectively exploded. Beatrice and Benedick, who begin by seeming least likely of any in Messina to betray a genuine emotion, must in the end uncover their hearts.

These wit-combats, whether in Shakespeare or Congreve, declare the sentiments which they affect to deny. As Witwoud puts it in 'The Way of the World': 'Raillery, madam, raillery; we have no animosity—we hit off a little wit now and then but no animosity. The falling out of wits is like the falling out of lovers—we agree in the main like treble and bass.' There is never any doubt that the raillery between Benedick and Beatrice is of this order. 'You must not, sir, mistake my niece,' says Leonato. 'There is a kind of merry war betwixt Signior Benedick and her. They never meet but there's a skirmish of wit between them.' These two are obviously treading a measure which will land them at the altar steps. Beatrice's first words are an inquiry after Benedick. He is the only man returning from the wars in whom she is interested. And Benedick is no sooner on the stage than he declares his admiration for Beatrice; for, when Claudio praises Hero as the sweetest lady that he ever looked on, Benedick retorts: 'I can see yet without spectacles, and I see no such matter: there's her cousin, an she were not possessed with a fury, exceeds her as much in beauty as the first of May doth the last of December.' 'Much Ado About Nothing' is no comedy of conversion in which disdain is by vanity transformed into affection. Our pleasure lies in waiting for the artifice of the wit-combat to be discarded as soon as nature asserts herself and the combatants are disarmed. This is the real comedy and we have it in full measure. For Benedick is ready to face all extremities for love, even to be laughed at for his pains, and when Beatrice needs a champion for Hero, this 'obstinate heretic in despite of beauty' comes to attention as her dutiful knight-at-arms.

Two devices are used to bring these declared antagonists to confession—the trick played on them by Don Pedro and his friends, whereby each is assured of the other's infatuation, and the impact upon them of Hero's calamity.

Observe how artfully Shakespeare contrives to get the maximum comic effect out of Benedick's apostasy. He loses no opportunity in the early scenes of asserting his misogyny:

DON PEDRO: I shall see thee, ere I die, look pale with love.

Q

BENEDICK: With anger, with sickness, or with hunger, my lord—not with love: prove that ever I lose more blood with love than I will get again with drinking, pick out mine eyes with a ballad-maker's pen, and hang me up at the door of a brothel-house for the sign of blind Cupid.

DON PEDRO: Well, as time shall try: 'In time the savage bull doth bear the yoke.'

BENEDICK: The savage bull may—but if ever the sensible Benedick bear it, pluck off the bull's horns and set them in my forehead. And let me be vilely painted—and in such great letters as they write, 'Here is good horse to hire,' let them signify under my sign, 'Here you may see Benedick the married man.'

BENEDICK: I do much wonder, that one man seeing how much another man is a fool when he dedicates his behaviours to love, will, after he hath laughed at such shallow follies in others, become the argument of his own scorn by falling in love. And such a man is Claudio. I have known when there was no music with him but the drum and the fife, and now had he rather hear the tabor and the pipe: I have known when he would have walked ten mile afoot, to see a good armour, and now will he lie ten nights awake carving the fashion of a new doublet: he was wont to speak plain, and to the purpose (like an honest man and a soldier) and now is he turned orthography—his words are a very fantastical banquet, just so many strange dishes. May I be so converted, and see with these eyes? I cannot tell—I think not: I will not be sworn but love may transform me to an oyster, but I'll take my oath on it, till he have made an oyster of me, he shall never make me such a fool. One woman is fair, yet I am well: another is wise, yet I am well: another virtuous, yet I am well: but till all graces be in one woman, one woman shall not come in my grace. Rich she shall be, that's certain: wise, or I'll none: virtuous, or I'll never cheapen her: fair, or I'll never look on her: mild, or come not near me: noble, or not I for an angel: of good discourse, an excellent musician, and her hair shall be of what colour it please God.

All this, though it enhances the comedy of Benedick's transformation, at the same time prepares us for the event. The gentleman protests too much. Shakespeare, moreover, gives us some warning glimpses into the kind heart which hides behind all this exaggerated self-assurance. The man who said of Claudio in love, 'Alas, poor hurt fowl, now will he creep into sedges', is clearly a man of quick feeling.

Asked by this same Claudio for his opinion of Hero he demands: 'Do you question me as an honest man should do for my simple true judgment or would you have me speak after my custom as being a professed tyrant to their sex?'—an obvious suggestion that we are to distinguish between the attitude by which he is socially distinguished and the simple sincerity which he owes to a friend. Then, again, pondering his masked encounter with Beatrice, he exclaims: 'The Prince's fool! Ha, it may be I go under that title because I am merry: yea, but so I am apt to do myself wrong. I am not so reputed—it is the base, the bitter disposition of Beatrice that puts the world into her person, and so gives me out.' Benedick here shows himself uncommonly sensitive to opinion and, what is more to the point, to the opinion of Beatrice. He is gay but would not therefore be thought malicious; he makes a brave show of independence but would not therefore be found conceited.

Don Pedro and his friends in the conduct of their plot play skilfully on their knowledge of the true man beneath the social mask, attributing to him just those faults with which he most resents to be charged. 'If she should make tender of her love,' says Don Pedro, ''tis very possible he'll scorn it—for the man, as you know, hath a contemptible[1] spirit.' And again: 'I love Benedick well and I could wish he would modestly examine himself to see how much he is unworthy so good a lady.'

The abrupt wholeheartedness with which Benedick at once embraces his fortune ('I will be horribly in love with her') is delightfully absurd and at the same time increases our respect. This is no fool, hoodwinked by an appeal to his vanity, but a man who seizes a heaven-sent occasion to be himself. He easily capitulates because he has never seriously wanted to hold out and he discloses in his surrender the very modesty denied to him by his friends:

I must not seem proud. Happy are they that hear their detractions and can put them to mending.

There is here no trace of self-infatuation: he is not in the least puffed up on hearing that Beatrice is secretly in love with him

[1] i.e. in the idiom of Shakespeare, a spirit easily contemptuous of others.

They say the lady is fair—'tis a truth, I can bear them witness: and virtuous—'tis so, I cannot reprove it: and wise, but for loving me—by my troth, it is no addition to her wit, nor no great argument of her folly.

The soliloquy in which Benedick forswears his assumed indifference and the subsequent scene in which Beatrice bids him come to dinner are a typical Shakespearean sequence. He is delightfully absurd ('Love me! Why, it must be requited. . . . If I do not take pity of her, I am a villain. If I do not love her, I am a Jew. I will go get her picture'). He is the victim of a conspiracy and the laugh is against him—as no-one knows better than himself:

I may chance have some odd quirks and remnants of wit broken on me, because I have railed so long against marriage: but doth not the appetite alter? A man loves the meat in his youth that he cannot endure in his age. Shall quips and sentences and these paper bullets of the brain awe a man from the career of his humour? No—the world must be peopled. When I said I would die a bachelor, I did not think I should live till I were married.

But his absurdity, far from exciting our derision, enlists our sympathy. This is no popinjay, but verily a good man and true. There is no better example in Shakespeare of the use of comedy to put us in full sympathy with its victims.

Beatrice, being a bird of more brilliant plumage than Benedick, suffers a yet more startling transformation:

HERO: Disdain and scorn ride sparkling in her eyes,
    Misprizing what they look on, and her wit
    Values itself so highly, that to her
    All matter else seems weak: she cannot love,
    Nor take no shape nor project of affection,
    She is so self-endeared.

            I never yet saw man,
    How wise, how noble, young, how rarely featured,
    But she would spell him backward: if fair-faced,
    She would swear the gentleman should be her sister;
    If black, why nature, drawing of an antic,

Made a foul blot: if tall, a lance ill-headed;
If low, an agate very vilely cut:
If speaking, why a vane blown with all winds;
If silent, why a block movèd with none.
So turns she every man the wrong side out,
And never gives to truth and virtue that
Which simpleness and merit purchaseth.

Thus must she hear herself painted by cousin Hero and the portrait fits the character she has so merrily assumed. But here again Shakespeare has prepared us for the change. Beatrice, like Benedick, protests too much—as we have heard. She is no genuine misogamist. Witness her reaction to the betrothal of Hero with Claudio. Her pleasure in that event looks through her merriment and there is even a touch of envy, lightly expressed but not to be mistaken:

Speak, cousin, or, if you cannot, stop his mouth with a kiss, and let not him speak neither. . . . Thus goes everyone to the world but I, and I am sun-burnt. I may sit in a corner and cry 'heigh-ho for a husband'.

The expressed motive of her scorn for Benedick—and for husbands because Benedick is already the only husband she will ever fancy—is itself a clue to her veritable disposition. It is her grievance that Benedick is forever talking. He is Signior Mountanto. He affects, as she does, high insolence towards the opposite sex:

I am loved of all ladies, only you excepted: and I would I could find in my heart that I had not a hard heart, for truly I love none.

She is provoked by an assumed hostility which affronts her own unconfessed inclination towards him and the more bitterly she rails the more plainly she declares her affection. These two, indeed, are in the same case. If Benedick is Signior Mountanto who will still be talking, Beatrice is my Lady Disdain, a harpy who speaks poniards. They attack in each other the insolent contentiousness that keeps them apart and the collapse of their hostility is inevitable when each is presented to the other as horribly in love.

The capitulation of Beatrice is nicely contrasted with that of Benedick. Benedick, overhearing Don Pedro and his friends, is at first suspicious:

I should think this a gull, but that the white-bearded fellow speaks it: knavery cannot, sure, hide himself in such reverence.

This can be no trick. The conference was sadly borne.

In his soliloquy he is argumentative and looks at the situation all round weighing the pros and cons. Above all, he cuts a comical figure and knows it. It is far otherwise with Beatrice. Her soliloquy springs straight from the heart. There is neither argument nor hesitation. She has no thought to spare for the ridicule which her conversion may inspire, nor for its seeming inconsistency:

> What fire is in mine ears? Can this be true?
>> Stand I condemned for pride and scorn so much?
> Contempt, farewell! and maiden pride, adieu!
>> No glory lives behind the back of such.
> And, Benedick, love on, I will requite thee,
>> Taming my wild heart to thy loving hand.

But Beatrice and Benedick, to be completely revealed, must not be left as the mere victims of a comic mystification. Shakespeare needed a more searching test of their quality and this is effected by the emotional impact of Claudio's infamy. There were possibilities of excellent fun with these two professed misogamists if Shakespeare had brought them to a mutual confession of love as an immediate result of the trick played on them in the orchard, but he preferred to wait until they could meet upon an issue in which their feelings were more deeply engaged. He gives us just a sample of the sport he might have had with them when Beatrice calls Benedick to dinner, and, in two symmetrical scenes, he shows us Benedick chaffed by his friends and Beatrice teased by her cousin for their altered demeanour. But he artfully postpones their confrontation until he can use the plot against Hero to reveal them as 'human at the red-ripe o' the heart'.

It is to be noted that even in the gay scenes preliminary to the confrontation Shakespeare sustains the contrast to which he pointed in the two orchard soliloquies. Benedick in his evasions is purely comic. 'Gallants, I am not as I have been'—so much is too obvious for denial. He has, so he affirms, the toothache and refuses to be further drawn, but at the end of the scene he takes Leonato aside: 'I have studied eight or nine wise words to speak to you which these hobby-horses must not hear.' As a practical man, and Benedick is extremely practical, he has decided to approach the lady's guardian in good and proper form before paying his addresses to the lady herself. Benedick, in this scene, still alive to the fact that he is comic, is nevertheless not to be browbeaten. His appearance as a spruce young gentleman in love is an act of defiance and he bears himself in this scene with a manifest bravado. His friends may laugh themselves into fits but, true to his word, he will be 'horribly in love'.

Beatrice, in the corresponding scene with Margaret and Ursula, is more deeply stirred. There is none of Signior Benedick's bravado. She is 'exceeding ill' and sighs profoundly. She can hardly restrain herself from delivering the secret that fills her heart. Does she sigh for a hawk, a horse or a husband? 'For the letter that begins them all,' she answers, confession on the tip of her tongue. And there is not a flout in her—no single word of retort to the insinuations heaped upon her, merely such feeble protests as 'What pace is this that thy tongue keeps?'

The contrast conveyed in these scenes on the light comedy level is more deeply marked when these two brilliant creatures are suddenly confronted with a situation which calls into the open their rare qualities of heart and head. Watch their behaviour while the monstrous scene of Claudio's repudiation of Hero is in progress.

Benedick is the first to see that something is wrong. His quick mind takes alarm at Claudio's first obscure preliminaries. *How now! Interjections?* He would cover the situation with a laugh till Claudio's horrid bent is plain. Then it is he who makes the first comment: *This looks not like a nuptial.* The whole man, whom we now begin to know, is in those half-dozen words—a man whose quick mind and warm feeling find expression in ironical understatement. He is the first to show concern for Hero when Claudio has left the church: *How doth the lady?* The *lady,* mark you—she who has just been described by his Prince as a 'common stale'. He is the first to recover his wits. He is so attired in wonder that he knows not what to say, but his mind gets to work at once on the evidence and he asks, turning to Beatrice: 'Were you her bedfellow last night?' He is shaken and puzzled. Yet he goes straight to the point. Hero has been denounced by Claudio, Don Pedro and Don John:

> Two of them have the very bent of honour,
> And if their wisdoms be misled in this,
> The practice of it lives in John the bastard.

Finally, when the friar has made his proposal that Hero shall be given out for dead, Benedick stoutly declares himself:

> Signior Leonato, let the friar advise you,
> And though you know my inwardness and love
> Is very much unto the prince and Claudio,
> Yet, by my honour, I will deal in this
> As secretly and justly as your soul
> Should with your body.

Beatrice, meanwhile, has no reservations of any kind. She has no need of argument or evidence, but goes straight to the point. *O, on my soul, my cousin is belied!* She says nothing at all till Hero swoons and then it is the instinctive protest of one who would not herself have been so easily overcome: *Why, how now, cousin, wherefore sink you down?* She has no room for anything but love for Hero and hot indignation for the men who have so cruelly disgraced her. She is all air and fire; her other elements she gives to baser life.

The stage is thus set for the long-promised encounter in which Benedick and Beatrice, whose comedy was born in a merry hour, must prove that for all their gallant sophistication they can show a pair of hearts as sound and simple as any in Messina. We had never thought to see Beatrice moved to tears. But here she is, crying her eyes out, with Benedick standing awkwardly beside her and, all their tricks forgotten, love is confessed in the full tide of her wrath and *his* perplexity:

BENEDICK: Lady Beatrice, have you wept all this while?
BEATRICE: Yea, and I will weep a while longer.
BENEDICK: I will not desire that.
BEATRICE: You have no reason, I do it freely.
BENEDICK: Surely I do believe your fair cousin is wronged.

BEATRICE: Ah, how much might the man deserve of me that would right her!

BENEDICK: Is there any way to show such friendship?

BEATRICE: A very even way, but no such friend.

BENEDICK: May a man do it?

BEATRICE: It is a man's office, but not yours.

BENEDICK: I do love nothing in the world so well as you—is not that strange?

BEATRICE: As strange as the thing I know not. It were as possible for me to say I loved nothing so well as you—but believe me not—and yet I lie not—I confess nothing, nor I deny nothing—I am sorry for my cousin.

They must still spar a little, but they have ceased to find quarrel in a straw. The artificial wit-combat is now a genuine conflict of character. Benedick, though he believes Hero to be wronged, is still uncertain what he should do. Claudio, after all, is his friend. But Beatrice has no patience with half-measures, and a man is but half a man who will go with her only a part of the way:

BEATRICE: Will you not eat your word?

BENEDICK: With no sauce that can be devised to it—I protest I love thee.

BEATRICE: Why then, God forgive me——

BENEDICK: What offence, sweet Beatrice?

BEATRICE: You have stayed me in a happy hour, I was about to protest I loved you.

BENEDICK: And do it with all thy heart.

BEATRICE: I love you with so much of my heart, that none is left to protest.

BENEDICK: Come, bid me do anything for thee.

BEATRICE: Kill Claudio.

BENEDICK: Ha! not for the wide world.

BEATRICE: You kill me to deny it—farewell.

That, as everyone agrees, is the *clou* of the comedy. *Kill Claudio*—all we shall ever want to know of Beatrice is in those two words, and with what fire and eloquence she justifies her commandment:

BENEDICK: Is Claudio thine enemy?

BEATRICE: Is a' not approved in the height a villain, that hath slandered, scorned, dishonoured my kinswoman? O that I were a man! What, bear

her in hand until they come to take hands, and then with public accusation, uncovered slander, unmitigated rancour—O God that I were a man!
I would eat his heart in the market-place.

BENEDICK: Hear me, Beatrice——
BEATRICE: Talk with a man out at a window—a proper saying!
BENEDICK: Nay, but, Beatrice——
BEATRICE: Sweet Hero, she is wronged, she is slandered, she is undone.
BENEDICK: Beat——
BEATRICE: Princes and counties! Surely a princely testimony, a goodly
count, Count Comfect—a sweet gallant surely. O that I were a man for
his sake! or that I had any friend would be a man for my sake! But man-
hood is melted into curtsies, valour into compliment, and men are only
turned into tongue, and trim ones too: he is now as valiant as Hercules,
that only tells a lie and swears it. I cannot be a man with wishing, therefore I will die a woman with grieving.

Benedick no longer asks to be convinced. It is enough for him that
Beatrice shall declare herself to be sincere beyond all doubt.

BENEDICK: Think you in your soul the Count Claudio hath wronged
Hero?
BEATRICE: Yea, as sure as I have a thought or a soul.
BENEDICK: Enough, I am engaged.

The scene in which Benedick delivers his challenge to Claudio,
admirable in itself, is technically the most interesting in the play.
Why must Claudio descend from one base degree to another? In
Bandello's story he was a likeable young man. In Shakespeare's play
he is insupportable. We have glanced at his behaviour in church and
his subsequent callousness in the scene with Leonato and Antonio.
Even the soft and delicate desires, all prompting him how fair young
Hero is, are not confessed till he has ascertained that she will bring
her husband a fortune:

CLAUDIO: Hath Leonato any son, my lord?
DON PEDRO: No child but Hero; she's his only heir.

Shakespeare was notoriously casual in his handling of young
sprigs. Or perhaps in his careless charity he found them just so and
troubled too little about them to administer even poetic justice. But

Claudio is an extreme case and we can only assume that his author simply uses him to make a man of Benedick. Obviously he didn't greatly care what sort of man might marry Hero so long as he made it quite clear what sort of man should marry Beatrice.

In the challenge scene, Claudio, with Don Pedro to help him, odiously makes light of the situation for which he is responsible; but that is only because Benedick must show that he is dead serious. Don Pedro, speaking of his late encounter with Leonato and Antonio, flippantly remarks: 'I doubt we should have been too young for them.' That is a cue for Benedick to rebuke his Prince with a stern, becoming dignity: 'In a false quarrel there is no true valour.' Claudio, brushing aside the death of Hero and her father's distress, calls on Benedick to use his wit for their diversion so that Benedick may answer with crushing brevity: 'It is in my scabbard. Shall I draw it?' Claudio then seeks to entice him with one of those familiar wit-combats so that Benedick may rejoin: 'I pray you choose another subject.' Claudio must try to laugh Benedick out of his new-found honesty in order to show that Benedick is now fixed and constant as the northern star:

BENEDICK: You are a villain—I jest not—I will make it good how you dare, with what you dare, and when you dare: do me right, or I will protest your cowardice: you have killed a sweet lady, and her death shall fall heavy on you.

Don Pedro tries to save the situation with allusions to Beatrice, but this is no longer Benedick the Prince's fool and he doesn't so much as flinch when Claudio lets him know of the trick played on him in the orchard:

BENEDICK: You break jests as braggarts do their blades, which God be thanked hurt not. My lord, for your many courtesies I thank you. I must discontinue your company—your brother the bastard is fled from Messina: you have among you killed a sweet and innocent lady: for my Lord Lack-beard, there, he and I shall meet, and till then peace be with him.

After that, nothing is left but to prove that my lady Hero hath been falsely accused, and to bring in Benedick, the married man. He and Beatrice must still spar their way into matrimony, for 'thou and I are too wise to woo peaceably'. And before company they must still be talking:

BENEDICK: Come, I will have thee—but by this light I take thee for pity.
BEATRICE: I would not deny you—but by this good day I yield upon great persuasion, and partly to save your life, for I was told you were in a consumption.

But these two have shown themselves true lovers and none more devoutly than Benedick:

I will live in thy heart, die in thy lap and be buried in thy eyes: and moreover, I will go with thee to thy uncle's.

I'll tell thee what, prince: a college of wit-crackers cannot flout me out of my humour. Dost thou think I care for a satire or an epigram? no, if a man will be beaten with brains, a' shall wear nothing handsome about him. In brief, since I do purpose to marry, I will think nothing to any purpose that the world can say against it—and therefore never flout at me for what I have said against it: for man is a giddy thing, and this is my conclusion.

'Much Ado About Nothing' becomes in this happy conclusion the comedy of Benedick and Beatrice—a comedy that moves from sophistication to sympathy, showing how a true heart may be worn on an embroidered sleeve. It is the play of which Hazlitt wrote: 'Perhaps that middle point of comedy was never more nicely hit in which the ludicrous blends with the tender, and our follies, turning against themselves in support of our affections, retain nothing but their humanity.'

It is also the play on which Coleridge based a famous declaration concerning Shakespeare's plots: 'The interest in the plot is always on account of the characters, not vice versa, as in almost all other writers; the plot is a canvas and no more.'

Certainly there is no play of Shakespeare in which the relation of plot to character and character to plot can be more usefully studied. There could be no better instance of a plot used to exhibit the characters (Benedick and Beatrice) in which Shakespeare was specially interested. But the converse is equally true. No play affords a better

instance of characters in which the author was not specially interested
sacrificed to the main design. The characters of Claudio, Don Pedro
and Don John are ruthlessly used—and some would say misused—to
forward the plot of Beatrice and Benedick. The two procedures are
not in fact either exclusive or contradictory. Shakespeare in all his
plays has a story to tell—his own or, more usually, taken from someone else. He has to make that story credible on the stage and his characters are created for that purpose. They cannot choose but do what
the story requires and to that extent they are determined by the plot.
For Shakespeare's characters, imagined to begin with as the sort of
people who will do what they have to do, come alive in the process.
They may come so much alive that the author sometimes finds it
difficult to control them or get them to fulfil their destiny. And
almost invariably they are sufficiently alive to convince us that they
are doing of their own will and pleasure what they were appointed
to do by predestination. Our interest in the plot, as Coleridge says,
is on account of the characters, but it does not follow that the characters are doing just as they please. Shakespeare, creating for the
stage, reflects a paradox already created in the world by Providence
—free will must be squared with necessity.

Coleridge's distinction, right as far as it goes, is thus in the last
analysis unreal. The give and take between character and plot in
Shakespeare is as fluid as between character and circumstance in real
life. Shakespeare, writing for the stage, had to present men in action.
For a dramatist it is what men *do* that matters—in other words the
plot is capital. But we are interested in what men do because they are
men and therefore apparently free to do as they please. Coleridge
quotes as a crowning proof of Shakespeare's 'interest in the plot being
always on account of the characters' an instance which really cuts
both ways. He describes Dogberry and his comrades as being forced
into the service of the plot *when any other less ingeniously absurd
watchmen and night constables would have answered the necessities of the
action.* Dogberry, in other words, is to be regarded as an instance of
Shakespeare's interest in character prompting him to create a group
of persons imagined for their own sake and endowed with qualities
not essential to the dramatic business in hand. But this is not so. The

characters of Dogberry and his comrades, however much they may seem to exist by their own right and to abound freely in their own sense, are exactly determined by the part they are called upon to play in the comedy. It is not true that any other less ingeniously absurd watchmen and night constables would have answered the necessities of the action. Dogberry has to be sharp enough to discover there is a conspiracy against Hero *before* it is executed, so that the audience may know in advance that all will come right in the end. But he must also be stupid enough to prevent his discovery from taking effect till the conspiracy has served its turn. The character of Dogberry—his prolixity, his reverence for the protocol, the facility with which he meanders from the high road of detection into the by-paths of mystification, the slow mind that wastes itself upon irrelevant details but keeps obstinately moving in the right direction, the self-centred zeal that attaches as much importance to being written down an ass as to establishing that his prisoners have verified unjust things and, to conclude, are lying knaves—corresponds exactly with the necessities of the action. Dogberry, in fact, is a supreme example of the way in which Shakespeare, creating his characters to fit a pre-determined plot, brings them so abundantly to life that they seem to exist entirely for their own sake and to be following their own devices. Dogberry had to be just that sort of man for the things he had to do. Yet here is Coleridge regarding him as created by Shakespeare for the mere fun of the thing! Shakespeare's craft as a playwright successfully conceals the fact that Dogberry was expressly designed to forward—or perhaps we should say to retard—the action of the play. Shakespeare's genius in creating character nevertheless deceived Coleridge into selecting Dogberry as a supreme example of a character who, so far as the necessities of the plot are concerned, need never have been created at all.

No better text could be found in which to study the interplay of Shakespeare's dramatic art of character and situation than this most brilliant but least profound of his major achievements. To Benedick and Beatrice, once he has decided that this is to be *their* comedy, everything is sacrificed within the limits of dramatic coherence and plausibility. Don John's conspiracy is used to warm their hearts and enliven their understanding. Claudio, sacrificed in advance to the necessities of this merely secondary plot, is put without mercy through his ignoble paces so that Beatrice may show something of the generous stuff of which my Lady Disdain is made and so that Benedick may reveal that Signior Mountanto, in despite of fortune and fashion, is prepared to defy his Prince and to challenge his friend. The distresses of Hero, though necessary to the comedy, must not, however, be allowed to cast too deep a shadow. We must therefore know in advance that Don John's machinations will come to nothing. For this purpose Dogberry is haled from an Elizabethan township to play the part of a *deus ex machina* in a Sicilian city—and this he does to such perfection that he seems to be there for no better reason than that his author has taken a sudden fancy to the man and gives him free leave to come and go as he pleases.

And somehow the whole thing hangs together; an 'inn of strange meetings' where everything, or nearly everything, is accepted as we go along, a 'polychromatic phantasmagoria' in which the colours blend into one composite picture. 'Much Ado About Nothing' is not one of the great comedies. But it is one of Shakespeare's greatest triumphs as a dramatic craftsman, showing what he can do when his genius is not half engaged and he falls back on his technical skill as a playwright.

Shakespeare, on completing this comedy, might have addressed the friend of his heart, had there been such a man, in the words addressed by Hamlet to Horatio:

> They are coming to the play; I must be idle:
> Get you a place.

PRINTED IN GREAT BRITAIN
BY ROBERT MACLEHOSE AND CO. LTD
THE UNIVERSITY PRESS, GLASGOW